Tribals Participation in Naxalite Movement

PERCEPTION, MOTIVATION AND SURVIVAL

K. Anuradha
Jagannath Dash

CONCEPT PUBLISHING COMPANY PVT. LTD.
NEW DELHI-110059

ISBN-13: 978-93-5125-231-3

First Published 2016

Published and Printed by

Since 1974

Concept Publishing Company Pvt. Ltd.
Regd. Office:
A/15-16, Commercial Block, Mohan Garden,
New Delhi-110059 (INDIA)
Phones : 25351460, 25351794,
Fax : 091-11-25357109
Email : publishing@conceptpub.com
Website: www.conceptpub.com

Editorial Office: H-13, Bali Nagar, New Delhi-110 015, India.

Cataloging in Publication Data—DK Courtesy: D.K. Agencies (P) Ltd. <docinfo@dkagencies.com>

Anuradha, K., author.
Tribals participation in Naxalite movement : perception, motivation and survival / K. Anuradha, Jagannath Dash.
pages cm
Includes bibliographical references and index.
ISBN 9789351252313

1. Tribes—Political activity—India—Odisha. 2. Naxalite movement—India—Odisha. 3. Tribes—India—Odisha—Psychology. I. Dash, Jagannatha, 1955- author. II. Title.

DS481.G3A3 2016 DDC 954.035092 23

Late Shri Biswanath Pattnaik, popularly known as "Agyan", Gandhi of Koraput, who believes in principle of Satyagraha throughout his life.

Late Shri D. Bhuvan Mohan Pattnaik, the pioneer communist revolutionary, who had high respect for Agyan, who was popularly known as Adivasi Okila (Advocate of Tribals) in Koraput region.

This book is dedicated to two most social visionaries of Koraput region, who were unique in their own approach and principles

Foreword

I have immense pleasure in going through the book entitled "Tribal Participation in Naxalite Movement: Perception, Motivation and Survival" by Dr. K. Anuradha and Dr. Jagannath Dash. It is the outcome of her doctoral research undertaken under the supervision of a renowned Professor of the Center of Advanced Study on Anthropology of Utkal University – Professor Jagannath Dash. It is the by-product of intensive fieldwork undertaken by the scholar in different situations and in interior tribal habitants of South Odisha. It is also alluring to note that the naxal respondents, underground, jailed caders and passive supporters had extended their co-operation in answering the queries when interviewed and without which this study would not have been completed. Besides, the government and non-governmental officials have also supported the cause of the study.

The present study is primarily empirical and synchronise in its orientation. It is further an analystical and descriptive study which tests as many as 12 working hypotheses for arriving at conclusive justifications and it adds to the charm of the study. The authors have very sincerely and diligently portrayed the philosophy and practice of Naxalite movement with its ideological background. The social movements with their violence, conflict, tension and unrest have been systematically brought to surface. The authors have very aptly analysed the conceptual frame, genesis, ideology, internal dynamics and socio-economic consequences of the Naxalite movements. The concept of violence along with its types have been dealt with very carefully. While discussing Naxalism and Maoism the authors have dealt with the radical communism, Communist Party of India (Marxist and Leninist) etc. in order to focus insurgency and challenges. Other related concepts such as law, feud, social tension, social movement have been critically analysed in order to comprehend the crux of the problem. Very reasonably, the sociological analysis of conflict theory of Polybius, Khaldun, Machiavelli, Bodin, Hobbe, David Hume, Adam Ferguson, Turgot, Adam Smith, Thomas Malthus etc. have been clearly dissected various aspects of conflict. Further, the complex phenomena of conflict finds discussion of the hour glass model, Edward Azars theory of protracted social conflict, WHOs definition of violence, Galtungs theory of violence and its extension, social work theories including social cognitive theory, social constructive theory, feminist social work theory, development theories including modernization theory. Human development theory, the Gandhian theory of development, Galtungs theory of structured of imperialism, war, peace, have been discussed to substantiate the aims and objectives of the study.

The economic, religious and socio-political aspects of the people in the study area have been vividly discussed in order to comprehend the land and people with their social-cultural identity along with the extent of exploitation and participation of tribal people in the Naxalite movement. The genesis of Naxalite movement has been very meticulously dealt with. The different stages of development of the movement in south Odisha with their structural implications have been very carefully earmarked. From the study it is interesting to note the tribal perception of Naxalite movement and the awareness component. Their constitution and administrative set up which are two landmarks of the naxalite movement have been diagrammatically represented. The chapter on the role of tribal women and their participation in the movement in the study area speak of ground realities. The authors remark, "Tribal women have basically entered into the movement to break the barriers of clan authority, sexual exploitation, domestic violence, hard economic exploitation and the various forms of structural violence."

While outlining the causes of tribal support the authors have critically analysed the basic causes and the gradual development of tribal participation in the movement. Based on the empirical study, a four-point risk model of tribal participation has been evolved and it explains as to why tribals are joining the risky movement. Further, the tribal mindset, sentiments and perception throw light on Naxalism issues explicitly. The surrender scenario in the process of movement has been stated clearly along with the surrender policy, eligibility criteria, incentives and grants for surrender.

It is a pertinent question as to how an ingenuous solution to the Naxalite movement is possible. There are arguments and counter-arguments concerning the solution. It may be remembered that all challenges have their responses. The peace making process shall be clearly evolved in order to restore peace in the Maoist and Naxalite affected areas. It requires a committed mind set of all concerned in order to negotiate for the purpose and ultimately in place of blood and tears there will be peace and contentment.

Besides the efforts to find out a candid solution of the Naxalite movment, morc pertinent is – "why" the simple and traditional tribals are joining it gradullay. As suggested and recommended in the book, the answer is with the development process of the government. Though in policy and planning we are excellent, at the level of implementation, we have severe failures. When such failures occurred, people feel allured to some other alternative system of administration where they can be more comfortable. Such introspective endeavours at all level systems and sit-ups perhaps may give us an appropriate solution on day, though late.

Professor K.K. Mohanti
Former Professor of Anthropology, Odisha
Education Service and Retired Director,
SC and ST Research and Training Institute,
Bhubaneswar, Odisha

Preface

The Government of India did admit that the Naxal movement has influenced more than 160 districts. Several studies and reports do portray different figures on the same theme. It has also been considered as one of the biggest internal security challenges by different ruling Governments since more than one decade. Different interpretations, versions, have sometimes brought the issues very rightly and sometimes they have been camouflaged with vested interest. The Naxal issue remained a serious concern for the government for the past five to six decades and the changing patterns have been a bone of contention for ten years. The electronic and print media have come to the forefront in highlighting the issues. Different media have their own biases and own schools of thought and writings. Academic research still lacks behind in bringing the facts to public through research.

Interestingly to note that the Naxal movement is growing its tentacles in the tribal areas which are heavily abundant with minerals. The different corporations eye the minerals and in this process the naxals movement has been a major obstacle for them. There is conflict of interests, the resource conflict, and people's conflict all these together escalate the violence by militarizing the tribal areas. The physiognomy of violence has no end and becoming more complex. The movement has witnessed many contours and setbacks, but it has been able to capture the imagination of poor, the tribal and other vulnerable sections of the Indian society. The movement grows its wings in the underdeveloped areas mostly the tribal areas such as the south Odisha, where more than 60 per cent of the population belongs to tribal and other vulnerable sections of the society.

Not only south Odisha, but also in all tribal pockets of the state are now under the grip of Naxalism. Some argue that it is a kind of terrorism, but this requires a lot of debate and discourse. One thing is very clear that the tribal region is under Naxalism, several groups and outfits are engaged in this revolution now in the name of Maoism through. People are divided in two groups, while one group is describing it as an internal security issue, and the other group as development issue. Whatever may it be, but government cannot brush the issue under the carpet. There is need to address the unmet needs of the tribal and unprivileged group. We have witnessed most violent incidents, but it has not given us any peace, recognition or reconciliation. The military forces deployed in the tribal region to deal with Naxalism are also not in peace as many incidents of suicide and self-torturing incidents are on rise. So, what are we trying to address? The Government has not been able to craft and draft concrete effective policies for the state to deal with the issue peacefully. There is a low intensity conflict going on in the state. Somewhere due to different phases and cycles the naxalites have not been also put forth their clear agenda to the government.

There have been desperate situations created by the movement by kidnapping government officials, foreign tourists, making the government to opt for some kind of negotiation. But the situation is not improving rather it is negatively deviating for violence. The peace talks in the past, the negotiation during emergency situations have not improved the condition, whereas the tribal areas are going more and more under their fold. We must remember that never before in the history the tribal region has been so much exposed to security forces or militarization that south Orissa has witnessed during the last nine years. Naxals, Maoists, naxal ideologues, security forces have destroyed the peace and harmony of this region. Many tribals are in the jail on false implications, many encounter killings and also counter killings by the naxals have occurred. There are many incidents by the Naxals attacking armed depots, police training schools; police stations have been very common. The ideology has a romantic tag too and some feel elevated to be called as Naxal or Naxal sympathizer without any concrete contribution. Some see this as a survival tactics, some though motivated doesn't know what to do and end up either with frustration or face death. Now, the movement has some occasional outbursts. With their major leaders surrendering with frustrations is paving another way for the state to be generous and come forward for a peaceful solutions, so that, the tribal region can breath in peace and ventilate their aspirations. Time will answer how the state empowers this void created by the movement.

Major material of this book is an outcome of an empirical study which aimed to study the factors of tribal participation in the movement, their causes, their backgrounds, perceptions, motivations and what are the solutions possible for the future. The content is the outcome of the personal interviews with the jailed, underground Naxals, their sympathizers, government functionaries working in south Orissa, civil society organizations and community based organizations. This book aims to bring out the tribal perspective of the movement and to present facts before the larger audience.

This research work has been presented in the book consisting of 12 chapters in total in bringing out the essential processes that are working in the tribal region with different chapters as described. Chapter-1 presents the problem of the study, area of study, the concepts, the theories used, the methods of data collection, the hypotheses, and the rapport established. Chapter-2 gives the overview of the people of the area, their culture, the geographical location, the economic condition of the tribals, their poverty situation, their distress condition and other factors. Chapter-3, the overall naxal movement, its initiation, different stages of development in India and Orissa in particular. It also gives an account of the inception in the south Orissa, the study area. Chapter-4, the motivation factors of the participation both by the active and passive members. It also shows the cycle of participation by the tribals in the study area.

Chapter-5 presents the deeper analysis of the tribal members of the Naxalite movement, their sex-wise distribution, their socio-economic condition, why do they enter the movement, their belief on the movement and their training on Naxalism. Chapter-6, opens up to the constitution making by the Naxals, on how they take members, how they recruit, their modes of finance, their modules of training, their roles assigned to members etc. Chapter-7 is dedicated for the female Naxals who are working in the movement, their life, their issues and how they assess themselves. Chapter-8 describes the gradual development of the movement in the tribal area and the human rights question. Who are the actors who influence this movement and how all these actors are inter-related with each other. Chapter-9 describes the tribal perception, their mind, their gain being in the movement etc. Chapter-10 gives an overview of the surrender scene in the state and the voices on surrender. Chapter-11 discusses the gaps in the movement from the beginning till now, the dilution of the ideology, their future strategy, the direction of the movement and the possible solutions by the Naxals with the government. Chapter-12 presents the testing of hypotheses and the findings of the study under "conclusion".

I hope the book will enable the reader to understand the naxal issue in proper perspective and real causes of ongoing conflict. Hope that different viewpoints as indicated in the book will be well taken in clearer terms.

K. Anuradha
Jagannath Dash

Acknowledgements

First of all I would like to thank the almighty who always encourage me and bestows on me the inner inspiration for doing all good works.

At the outset, I am very grateful to my guide and Supervisor Prof. Jagannath Dash for his able guidance keen supervision, constant cooperation, encouragement, support and goodwill to complete this thesis. He is open to new ideas and his support was wonderful.

I would like to thank my dear husband Bidyut Bhusan Mohanty who has always been a constant source of inspiration and backing, without whom completion of this degree would not have happened. Taking care of all my needs, supporting me at the time of crisis and stress has been beyond words and articulation.

I am also thankful to my Professors who taught me at my M.Phil., but guided me all the time and encouraged me with their advice. I specially wish to thank Dr. P.C. Mohapatra, Director, COATS, Koraput and Dr. Jagabandhu Samal from COATS and Prof. Nityananda Pradhan. My sincere thanks to Late Shri K.C. Panigrahy, Director Tribal Museum, Koraput, who's ideas were always out of the box and who enthused and encouraged me a lot to complete the research.

I am highly indebted to the respondents of the four districts, who were underground, jailed cadres and the passive supporters and who also gave me their valuable time in answering all my queries patiently without which I would have failed in my deeper study on the subject. Few of them are in jail and few were encountered, but without their support my work would not have completed.

I owe a lot to Nabakrushana Center for Development Studies for their library support, Tribal Culture Research Center Library, Library of Council of Analytical Studies, Library of Scheduled Castes and Scheduled Tribes Research Training Institute, Library of SPREAD, Koraput, Library of Center for Youth and Social Development, Library of Anthropology

Department, Utkal University for their information and diverse collection of books.

I express my sincere gratitude to Shri Dandapani Mohanty, Convenor Jan Adhikar Manch for his time, which guided me well in the field. He not only extended his help with guidance, but also helped me in understanding the south Orissa situation.

I express my sincere gratitude to the I.G. Prisons of Orissa for granting me permission to interview under trial in the Jails of the South Orissa for my fieldwork. Thanks to Sukuram Gadanga, Dusmant Kumar Padhi, Ajay Behera, Umi Jaypaul, Gopal Nayak, for their support during the typing of the book.

Finally, I extend my profound appreciation to all the people who helped during the fieldwork, during my visits to Jail, all the government and non-government officials who were a great support to me throughout the completion of my book. I would also like to express my obligation to all those who helped me in typing the data and in designing the outer cover.

K. Anuradha
Jagannath Dash

Contents

Foreword by ***Prof. K.K. Mohanti*** vii
Preface xi
Acknowledgements xv
List of Tables xviii
List of Figures xxi
List of Photographs xxii
Abbreviations xxiii

1. Introduction 1
2. People and their Culture 87
3. The Genesis of Naxalite Movement 115
4. Naxal Movement in India and Orissa in General: An Overview 158
5. Tribal Members of Naxalite Movement in Orissa 167
6. Philosophy of Naxalite Movement and its Constituted Principles of Action 197
7. Role of Tribal Women 210
8. Causes of Tribal Support 220
9. Psychology of the Tribals in the Process of Involvement 264
10. The Surrender Scenario 280
11. The Solution: Possible and Not Possible 288
12. Conclusion and Findings of the Study 313

Annexures 332
Bibliography 350
Index 362

List of Tables

1.1 Universe of the Research 75

2.1 The Administrative Profile of the Study Area 89
2.2 Sex Ratio of the Study Area 90
2.3 Geographical Area (block-wise) of the Study Area (showing blocks, number of Gram Panchayats, and literacy rate of the three districts of Universe) 92
2.4 Population Growth rate of Orissa, and Tribal Population of the Study Area 94
2.5 Distribution of ST population by Religion 99
2.6 Trends in Religious Distribution of Tribals from 1961 to 2001 100
2.7 Occupational Distribution in the Study Area 102
2.8 Drinking water facilities in Koraput and Ganjam Districts (undivided) 103
2.9 Economic Condition of Distress in the Study Area 103
2.10 Land Holding status of the respondent families 103
2.11 Quality of the Land owned by the Respondent Families 104
2.12 Housing Patterns of Respondents 104
2.13 Characteristics of Backwardness in Gajapati District 106
2.14 Characteristics of Backwardness in Koraput District 107
2.15 Characteristics of Backwardness in Rayagada District 107
2.16 Characteristics of Backwardness in Malkangiri District (though it is not counted in the 69 backward list, few indicators are highlighted) 108
2.17 Literacy Rates (in %) of undivided Ganjam and Koraput Districts 108
2.18 Literacy Rates of the Study Area 108
2.19 Tribal Literacy Rate in Orissa and India from 1961 to 2001 109
2.20 Sex-wise Literacy of Tribal Population and Total Population 110
2.21 Literacy Rate of Tribals of Study Area in 1991 and 2001 110

2.22 Opinions Regarding the Sufferings 112
2.23 Acceptance Level – The Responsible factors for tribal participation 112
2.24 Suffering and Participation—The Tribal Linkage 113

3.1 Statistics of the Naxal Affected District 128
3.2 HDI of the Study Area Districts 128
4.1 Opinion Regarding the Right Path (What do you think is it the right path to establish equity and equality in the society?) 159
4.2 Factors Motivating for Participation 162
4.3 Significant Persons or aspects behind the Motivation 163
4.4 Justification of the Motivation 163
4.5 Membership base 165
4.6 Reasons of Acceptance Level by the Non-group members 166

5.1 The Intensity of the Naxalite Movement in the Study Area 169
5.2 Tribal Members of the Naxalite Movement 170
5.3 District-wise and Section-wise Distribution of Respondents 173
5.4 Age-wise and section wise Distribution of Respondents 173
5.5 Reasons for Membership 175
5.6 The awareness of the movement with regard to tribal participation 177
5.7 Acceptance of the movement 178
5.8 The Tribal Linkage (What do they do the Tribal Communities/People) 179
5.9 Reasons behind and the Disbelief the System (Why they are against the system, why they do not believe in government machinery) 180
5.10 Sex of the respondents 186
5.11 Educational Status of the Respondents 187
5.12 Land holding status of the Families of the Respondents 187
5.13 Quality of the land owned by the respondent families 188
5.14 Housing Patterns of Respondents 188
5.15 Marital Status of the Respondents 188
5.16 Family size of the Respondents 189
5.17 Their Manifesto/Propaganda 190

6.1 Role and Responsibility of the Cadres 205
6.2 Specific Role of the Respondents/Cadres 205

7.1 Female Participation in the Movement 213
7.2 Age group of the Female Cadres 214
7.3 Marital Status of the Female Cadres 215
7.4 Educational status of Female Cadres 216
7.5 Self-Assessment by Females 217
7.6 How long women have tolerated ill-treatment 218
7.7 How many times they Addressed the issue 218
7.8 Discussion for Remedial measure 218

8.1 The Life Journey of the Activists 222
8.2 Gradual Increase of Tribal Participation 224
8.3 Main turning Points in Respondent's lives for Participation 225
8.4 Respondent's good experiences in Life 226
8.5 Respondent's worst experiences in Life 226
8.6 Respondent's Good friends 227
8.7 Whom Respondents Dislike 232
8.8 Respondents' View on Socio-economic Conditions of Tribals 233
8.9 The Reasons for Distress 233
8.10 Aim of the life of the Respondents as Aspired by their Parents 235
8.11 Is Naxalism a better alternative? 236
8.12 Respondent's Self-Assessment (both Male and Female) 237
8.13 List of people killed in the recent encounters 255

9.1 Respondents' disliking on the exploiting groups 266
9.2 The Respondents' Aspirations 273
9.3 Perceptions of Non-tribals 275
9.4 Opinion on the Naxal Path 277
9.5 Opinion on Rate of Success 278

10.1 The State-wise details of Naxals surrendered in 2009 and 2010 283

List of Figures

1.1	Hour Glass Model of Conflict	54
1.2	Approaches to Conflict	55
1.3	Transformation of Protracted Social Conflict (Azar's Adaptation)	58
1.4	The Galtungs Model of Violence	59
1.5	Extension model of Galtungs Theory of Violence	60
1.6	Theory of Structural Imperialism	66
1.7	Sample of the Study	77
4.1	The Cycle of Participation	161
6.1	Administrative set-up of CPI Maoist	201
6.2	Administrative structure in the study area of CPI Maoist	202
8.1	Application of Galtungs model of violence	241
8.2	Application of Structural Imperialism	242
8.3	Four Point Risk Model of Tribal Participation	244
8.4	Azar Model, Adaptation to Naxal Conflict (Designed upon the Present empirical study)	246
9.1	Application of violence as per the Galtungs model (Based on Empirical data)	267
9.2	Intensification of conflict in the universe of study	269
9.3	Naxalite movement—mapping of actors	270
11.1	Direction of the movement	292
11.2	Approaches to Conflict	293

List of Photographs

1. Shri Dandapani Mohanty interlocutor with other senior Members of the Party in Public Meeting 327
2. Late D. Bhuvan Mohan Pattnaik, Communist leader of 1960s in South Orissa 327
3. Late Shri Biswanath Pattnaik with his team popular as Gandhi of Koraput 328
4. Jailed in 2006 from village Gillakuta of Gajapati, for watching a film called Lal Salam, they were released in 2008 and later talking about their plight in a public meeting 328
5. Malkangiri Collector in a Praja court 329
6. Martyrs Remembrance sign by the party 329
7. The alternative voices in an open meeting 330
8. Other voices of dissent 330
9. Sahid Stamba in a village bordering Koraput and Malkangiri 331
10. BSNL tower blast by the Naxals 331

Abbreviations

ABC	Attitudes, Behaviour, Contradiction
AICCCR	All India Coordination Committee of Communist Revolutionary
AOB	Andhra Orissa Border
AP	Andhra Pradesh
BJD	Biju Janata Dal
BJP	Bharatiya Janata Party
BOJ	Bihar, Orissa, Jharkhand
CC	Central Committee
CCOMPOSA	Coordination Committee of Maoist Parties of South Asia
CMAS	Chasti Mulia Adivasi Sangha
CPI (ML) PWG	Communist Party of India (Marxist- Leninist) People's War Group
CPI ML (Liberation)	Communist Party of India Marxist-Leninist, (Liberation)
CPI (M)	Communist Party of India (Marxist)
CPI (Maoist)	Communist Party of India (Maoist)
CPI (ML) PU	Communist Party of India (Marxist-Leninist) Party Unity
CPM	Communist Party Marxist
DK	Dandakaranya
DM	District Magistrate
DPM	Daman Pratirodh Manch
EPW	Economic Political Weekly
Ghenua/ Guerrilla Vahini	A group of people with revoluntioary thinkings are operating in parts of Ganjam and Narayanpata block of Koraput District
GMI	Global Military Index
GP	Gram Panchayat
GPI	Global Peace Index

GZ	Guerrilla Zone
HAL	Hindustan Aeronautics Limited
HDI	Human Development Index
HDR	Human Development Report
HR	Human Rights
IAP	Integrated Action Plan
IFAD	International Fund for Agricultural Development
ILO	International Labour Organization
J&K	Jammu and Kashmir
KFM	Kashmir Freedom Movement
LTTE	Liberation Tigers of Tamil Ealem
MCCI	Maoist Communist Centre of India
ML	Marxists and Leninists Groups
MLA	Member of Legislative Assembly
MoU	Memorandum of Understanding
NALCO	National Aluminium Company
OBC	Other Backward Castes
OC	Other Castes
OSOC	Orissa State Organizing Committee
PESA	Panchayati Raj Extension to Scheduled Areas
PM	Peoples March
POSCO	Pohang Iron and Steel Company
PSC	Protracted Social Conflict
Public	Wherever public word is uses with reference to the field data, it indicated the responses of the passive and active supporters of the movement
PUCL	People's Union of Civil Liberty
PUDR	People's Union of Democratic Rights
PWG	People's War Group
RIM	Revolutionary International Movement
RSB	Rabi Subha Behera Group of Companies
SATP	South Asian Terrorism Portal
SC	Scheduled Castes
SCSTRTI	Scheduled Castes and Scheduled Tribes Research Training Institute
SEZ	Special Economic Zone
SOC	State Organising Committee
ST	Scheduled Tribes
USSR	Union of Soviet Socialist Republics
UPA	United Progressive Alliance

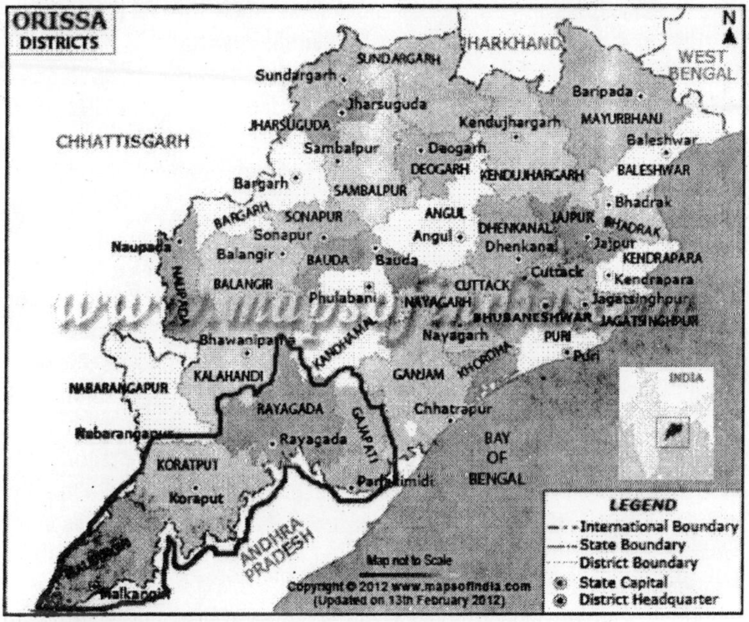

Map of Study Area

1
Introduction

> "Social movements are at once the symptoms and the instruments of progress. Ignore them and statesmanship is irrelevant; fail to use them and it is weak."
> —*Walter Lippmann*

The Problem of Study

Today our country is confining to a wide array of complex internal security problems and threats. The most significant among them is the Naxalite issue. It cannot be called as a violence or security issue because the basic character, style and approach of this phenomenon are towards addressing the socio-economic and political inequalities of our Indian Society. The vacuum which is created within the masses by our administrative and political institutions is the bent hollow space for the prevalence of the movement. The Indian governance system has created a wide gap between the rich and the poor; it is a fact that injustice and exploitation are the upward graph in our country, where the disadvantaged sections like tribals, scheduled castes, minorities and women are the most vulnerable to it. The Naxalite movement is growing due to the difference created by the system and it seeks a solution to the exploited disadvantaged population alternative system of governance, emancipating the exploited segments from the "Exploited" classes. Studies show that poorest of poor are concentrated in the States of Bihar, Jharkhand, Orissa, undivided Madhya Pradesh and Maharashtra where the Naxalite movement is showing an upward trend.[1] This is also the area where most of our disadvantaged sections mainly Tribals reside. This belt is otherwise called the heart-land of tribals, and other excluded social sections.

The Government has admitted now that its writ no longer ran in parts of more than 160 districts affected by Naxalites covering them into "Liberated" and "Semi-Liberated" zones and taking upon themselves the functions of the state administration and police. Naxalism is seen as the single largest internal security challenge ever faced by the country. Of the affected states, the movement is intense in parts of Chhattisgarh, Jharkhand, Madhya Pradesh, Maharashtra, while it is making inroads in Kerala, Karnataka, Tamil Nadu, Uttarakhand, Haryana, Punjab and J&K. It is also observed that there is a growing professionalism among the Naxal sympathizers and their growing intellectual support. While they say "we (Naxalites) know where our enemy is, but they do not know where we are". The National Common Minimum Programme of the UPA says that the Union Government does not consider the Naxal issue to be a mere law and order problem and it needs to be tackled as a Socio-Economic problem.

Ironically, this tribal heart land is gifted with water, forest and mineral wealth. This area has been under continuous exploitation for its natural wealth. In the name of national development and public purpose dams, power projects, mines and industries have come up in the areas pushing the tribals towards the borders of nowhere niche from their traditional domain. Victims of national development add another dimension to the scenario of alienations. Tribals constitute more than 40 per cent of these victims of development may be as project affected persons or as displaced persons. Begin with the colonial time, and continuing in the post-colonial era, the neo-liberal policies, all of them together by-passed the tribals, as well as the poor totally. The Forest Reservation Policies, leasing of forest land to the corporate sector for mining, forcefully evicting habitations from sanctuaries and parks by forming draconian laws, and coercive acquisition of land for development has made the Tribals resourceless, homeless, jobless, landless, socially dis-articulate and completely marginalized. So in the process of development they are excluded and thrown out to remain silent.

The tribal heart land is the most affected, and it is not surprising, therefore, the social unrest has emerged among them under the Naxalite movement. It manifests itself in defiance of the authority from simple form of demanding right to community management of forests to militancy, emancipation through barrel of gun. The state has created conditions where the tribals have resorted to take up arms, and the state commit avoid this responsibility. Half way across the globe in the Chiapas region of the Southern Mexico indigenous people declared in 1980 "we demand absolute respect from our communitarian self-determinations over our lands, over all our natural resources and over the forms of organization that we wish to give ourselves.... We are opposed to have our natural resources plundered in the name of the supposed national development.[2]

The demands of the Chiapas indigenous people in Mexico fully represent the aspiration and demands of 80 million tribals of our country as well. Way back in 1942 Mahatmaji wrote "The *Adivasis* are the original inhabitants whose material position is perhaps, no better than that of *Harijans* and who have been victims of neglect on the part of so called high classes. The *Adivasis* should have found a special place in the constructive programme"[3].

"15th August, 1947.... The Union Jack is lowered, the tri-colours spread out and reached millions. A hope is awakened, independence, freedom and a better life is expected and promised by the new rulers. A great zeal and enthusiasm envelops the country. Time passed and so does the slogans of socialism, Shastriji's 'Jai Jawan Jai Kisan' and then Indira Gandhi's 'Garibi Hatao'. After two full decades situation is the same, hope dusted and expectations turned into fictions. And on 18th March, 1967.... Revolutionaries revolt their first spark of how the poor can seize political power in semi-feudal Indian country. Peasants prepared themselves for launching their offensive against the landlords of the area. The Naxalbari owned path of revolution echoed in the country. Its vibrations created ripples in Orissa, Uttar Pradesh, Bihar, Andhra Pradesh during late 1960s. After the movement was crushed with state repression, all aimed that stringent actions will be taken for land reforms. But the situations still the same even worse. Peasants did not disappear. Tribals could not be assimilated with the mainstream populace. And the discontentment, unrest remained in a silent form all these years, waiting to get some way of hope to ventilate their agonies."

Though the movement was crushed during late 1960s and early 1970, the ideology, the aim and the aura could not be crushed. It remained within the exploited masses in various forms. And it was prominent, time and again, wherever there were injustices, resorted to violence. Today, the Naxalite movement remains a serious concern with the gradual increase in the quantum of the Naxal violence. Their hold is increasing. After the merger of Communist Party Marxist Leninist—people's war (CPIML-PW) and Maoist Communist Centre of India (MCCI), into CPI (Maoist) in September 2004, their contacts to intensify their programme has been growing.[4] As mentioned earlier, only Mahatmaji could have the moral courage during the freedom struggle to own up that the society neglected the *Adivasis.* It is not, therefore, strange to find in the party programme of Central Committee of CPI (Maoist) dated 21-9-2004: "State will ensure various forms of autonomy to all *adivasi* communities for their full-fledged development and execute special policies accordingly."[5] Why should it be left to CPI

(Maoist) or any other group to do in case our Indian state does it? The Indian state has the longest democracy in the world, the best Constitution in the world so far, where it has given equal rights to all citizens' freedom of thought, belief and expression. The British have gone, but their capital remained, their laws remained, their colonial structures remained.... Merely added was the parliamentary edifice. The British capital, was added American capital, while people continued to live in grinding poverty, the Tata's, and other big corporate filled their coffers with enormous wealth. People crying for justice were ruthlessly suppressed as it was in British Raj. The slogans of the rulers and leaders remained as mere slogans, the reality seemed different. The people are now searching, seeking something genuine, seeking real practical answers to their problems.

People are frustrated, directionless and their frustrations are seen when they are revolting against SEZs in different parts of the country, against TATA's in Kalinganagar in Orissa, against POSCO in Jagatshinghpur, against mining in Kashipur and Kalahandi. They are depressed to such an extent that, there are kegs to dry powder waiting for fire to set it. And today wherever there is injustice, there is revolution, and this Naxalite movement is seemingly increasing to threaten the establishment in all these forms. In Orissa, Undivided Koraput, Ganjam, Phulbani, Mayurbhanj, Sundargarh, Dhenkanal along with the Coastal Orissa is under the fold of this movement. The main foundation remains in the Undivided Koraput region with a contiguous patch starting from Gajapati, Rayagada, Koraput and Malkangiri districts. With the formation of CPI (Maoist) in 2004, this movement is more empowered now; the formation of Andhra-Orissa Border Special Zonal Committee which is functional in Koraput, Gajapati, Malkangiri, and parts of Rayagada district; Orissa State Committee (newly formed since 2005) active in parts of (Rayagada, Gajapati, Ganjam, undivided Phulbani) and Bihar Orissa Jharkhand Committee active in northern Orissa, the State is witnessing a qualitative as well as quantitative increase in the Naxalite movement.

Time and again this revolution movement was crushed, suppressed, but it has taken its re-birth in various near *avatars*. The rebirth of Naxalism in India in the 1990s has coincided with the second phase of national building, integrating the country with global economy. While the creamy layer of the economy easily adopted to global realities and growing at a steady 8 per cent over the years, but the other side remained silence and out of the economy where the Naxal movement operates. The contrast between the force of globalism and Naxalism in India, explains the prosperity-poverty dyad that co-exists. The reality is that both these trends are significant for national development. Equality and equity is the vision of our Constitution, a powerful document which has inspired generations yet it has failed to bring about change in millions of poor and tribals. This inability to transform the constitutional visions to the deep world of poor and tribal India was ripe for the revolutionary ideas where Naxalite movement is successfully being organized since years.

The movement has taken a position where both the major parties engaged in this have gone to a stage of conflict with lower and middle intensity. Violence occurs from both the parts and the whole of tribal area is boiling with Naxal and structural violence. Hence, Naxalism, needs to be understood as a phenomena of nation building, needing urgent palliatives essentially at the grassroots level, and this should be considered as socio-economic problem and the root causes have to be addressed. Participation understood as involving, contributing or being the members in it. As earlier stated, the tribals being the most neglected, exploited mass of our country, this study has adopted to understand the reason of their involvement, the style of the movement, the growing number in the movement, the possible ways out of the conflict and there is a mark of peace possible now to build it and keep it or at least resolve it. This study will also aim at giving a direction to focus on the long term and short term solutions of the problems to find out a peaceful strategy which can address the issue, and transform the conflict.

Area and People of Study

In India the term Naxalite refers to a variety of revolutionary struggles. Naxal movement largely depicts an expression of prevailing injustice in the society. It is described as a movement for the protection of land rights by the poor and weaker sections of the society. The Naxalites owe their nomenclature to a small village of India in West Bengal called "Naxalbari". The first clash was ignited when a share cropper was beaten by armed goons of a local landlord, when he went to plough his land with judicial orders. Tribal people in the area retaliated when the share croppers were attacked by the local goons of the landlord. This was followed by violent clash and forceful seizure of land. The struggle inspired by the Chinese Communist Party, was initially led by the Communist Party of India—Marxist-Leninist (CPI-ML) under the chairmanship of comrade Charu Mazumdar.

He was highly influenced by thoughts of Marx and Lenin with ideology of Mao Zedong theory aiming at exploitation by landlords. India has long history of peasant's uprisings since 1930. The Tebhaga Movement during 1946, which embarked on a proletariat militant struggle in North Bengal to get share of the movement. Then the Telengana Armed Struggle Movement in 1946-1951 in A.P. for land rights again. Then again in 1967 the Naxalbari Movement sparked. It was exactly 42 years ago, in May 1967, that a minor clash between a police force and a group of armed peasants took place in an obscure corner of West Bengal. Yes, one cannot deny that even after four decades of tortuous and self-divisive Odyssey, the movement that began in Naxalbari still remains a force to reckon with.

But, what is peculiar to the Naxalite movement is not its physical occupation of and administrative control over land, but its abiding appeal among the dispossessed and under-privileged rural poor in most parts of the country[6-10]. Ironically, however, if the movement is still surviving, the credit is not so much to the prescience of its leaders, as to the Indian state which, with its abysmal failures in socio-economic areas, persists in nourishing the soil for the continuation of the Naxalite movement. When the whole country's poor population is ready for agitate and they are organized, the state of Orissa which has a history of tribal movement since the early nineteenth century, and which portrays the lowest human development indicators is a fertile breeding ground for this revolutionary movement.

Development minus people's participation has always been seen as a fuel for unrest. Orissa, despite being a rich state in terms of its mines, minerals and natural resources, it has not made any real progress as far as the development of people is concerned. The Planning Commission of India has identified Orissa as having the highest overall poverty figures of any major Indian state, with around 48 per cent (17 million) of its population below poverty line. The state still has one of the highest in fect morality rates. The health care facility is in real bad shape, as it has lowest number of doctors per capita in the world. The state is poverty stricken, yet surprisingly less than 5 per cent of the populations have access to subsidized food aimed at poverty alleviation[11].

The thoughts of revolution by communist of the leftist dates back in 1950 in Orissa, where the *Bhoo-satyagraha andolana* was started under leadership of a Gandhian Sri Biswanath Pattnaik with a communist ideology. This *satyagraha* was parallel to the Telegana Armed struggle in A.P. which was initiated in Gunupur Subdivision in the then undivided Koraput District. Orissa became an independent province in 1936, and in 1948, the princely states merged with Orissa. Prior to the merger of the princely states, vast tracts of Oriya speaking areas in the undivided Koraput and Ganjam Districts were parts of the Visakhapatnam district under Madras Presidency. It was during this period that the Telugu speaking rich people, taking advantage of the innocence of the tribals living here, purchased lands and exploited them. Tribals led a miserable life and became victims of the rich landed gentry class.[12]

During 1920s tribal leaders in this Koraput region revolted both against the landed class and also against the British administration. The Tribals leaders among them who took initiative are Alluri Sitarama Raju, Tama Dora, Bangara Devi, Saheed Laxman Naik were few to name who organized Tribals to agitate against the British and their imperialism. All these agitations; the Naxalbari movement of 1967 has a strong effect on Orissa, especially on south Orissa the Koraput region. The movement became very prominent in south Orissa with communist bent of mind, and the fight continued for the land rights to the poor proletarian tribals and rural folks. The period from 1964-1970 was the peak period when the communist revolutionaries raised their voices against the landlords, organized the tribals of this region to protest (During the protest few pamphlets were circulated for proper and one such popular of communist propaganda of 1964-1966 is given here in Annexure-3)[13].

As history witnesses the south Orissa (the study area) already has a strong back drop of revolts, and Naxalbari movement with communist ideology only enriched the Tribals to organize more to amplify their voices. The movement gained momentum during late 1980s in south Orissa and strengthened its position and base in south Orissa. After the merger of MCC and PWG in 2004, and newly formed CPI (Maoist)[14], it has a strong base in predominantly 11 tribal districts, Koraput, Malkangiri, Rayagada, Gagapati, Boudha, Kandhamal, Sundargarh, Mayurbhanj, Keonjhar, Dhenkanal, Deogarh. They also have a strong support in other districts like Jajpur, Jagatsinghpur, Puri, Nayagarh, Ganjam, Sambalpur. While the above 11 districts remain a strong hold of naxals, the study area focuses on Koraput, Malkangiri, Rayagada (major part of KBK (Koraput-Bolangir-Kalahandi region) and Gajapati though it does not come under KBK region but portrays similar characteristics of those of KBK districts. The study of development processes in this study area reveals that different development projects like Dams, Industries, Factories and Mines have come up, which benefited only the fatty layer of the area, but not the poor and tribals, whose situation is same or even worse than when it was before these developmental projects.

The socio-economic indicators of the study area is the best ground for revolution, (one of the tribal respondents in Malkangiri district in the cut off area stated that dams after dams were made, Tribals were displaced, once, twice and thrice, but their houses do not have electricity, good potable water and roads. The government should know that it is due to our goodness that we did not rebel for so many years, and believed them. But that is enough, we will revolt now.) Often the population in this area is deprived of the basic amenities that are to be provided by the government. Hunger, malnourishment, death due to Cholera, starvation are the common features of these tribals. Nature has bestowed Orissa with plenty of mines and mineral resources. The south Orissa and the study area has the potential resources like Bauxite, Graphite, Granite, Marble ore etc. but wherever the resources are rich the people are poor. In all the four districts of the study area, where more than 70 per cent of population is below poverty line, to mention Koraput 78.65, Rayagada its 72.03. These districts are pioneer in having multipurpose dam projects displacing more than 40 per cent of the tribals, whose correct and accurate data is not available with the government.

Major dams like Machhkund, Upper Kolab, Indravati, Balimela, Ranigad, factories like JK Paper Mill, HAL, Mines like Utkal Alumina, Nalco, have just thrown the tribals out of the traditional cultural niche. The incomplete resettlement and rehabilitation scenario describe the plight of the people who are staying in the forest areas working to get recognition from the government since more than 30 years. They did not have any option than to run into the forest to save their lives. Those who did not run to the forest settled in the islands (known as cut off areas) and are leading miserable lives with no basic facilities. There are around 6 GPs in Malkangiri and more than 10 GPs in Koraput familiar to all as cut-off areas. In Gajapati and Rayagada districts most of the areas are inaccessible due to hilly terrain. So, in both these conditions the rural Tribals do not have any access to services and control of the resources, like land, forest and their traditional common property resources.

Wherever there are inequalities, oppression, and the governance does not reach the stake-holders, people are unhappy though they do not express. Victims of big projects, they are counted as nowhere, with lack of services, insecure in food that is the best soil for the movement to reap, start, spread and stay. The study area has all there features for the movement to grow like fire. Since, the study area is predominantly tribal dominated, so an attempt has made to bring out the socio-economic back ground of the tribals and their participation in the movement. It is that the tribals have understood the creative application of Marxist-Leninist-

Maoist thought without being literate. Why then the movement is growing only along the tribal areas and the conflict between the state and the revolutionary Naxals is on rise, what are the contradictions that is persisting which is causing so much violence. The study covered the understanding these factors, their motivations, role of tribal youth in large, which are situations that are compelling the tribals to take up arms and join the revolution. The study suggested few steps to transform the situation. This study has especially directed to know the tribal communities like Paraja, Koya, Gadaba, Bhumia, Jatapu, Kui, Kandha, Halwa, Bonda and Saura.

Review of Literature

As part of my research activity in the beginning, an extensive bibliography was prepared, which was based on view of the international scenario, the national scenario and the local scenario. The review has been done on the basis of ideology of the movement, classification of the movement, cases of the movement and their future perspective. To a great extent it was found that lot of research insight has gone into the study of the movement by sociologists and social anthropologists. This review is based on the available books, journals, from media to see the journalistic interpretation, and from the World Wide Web. The review of literature helps to develop an idea on the topic. It is interesting to note that the role of research in tribal social movements especially in Naxalite movement is not that wide and extensive as compared to other movements, due to many reasons it was still difficult to find research inputs when we specifically screen on Orissa state. And it is still more cumbersome process to find the literature in relation to the universe. So overall, it can be said that other states in India have been able to produce a number of research analysis on the Naxalite movement as compared to Orissa.

The movements have been understood here from sociological perspectives, anthropological perspectives, psycho-social perspectives, based on theories and their practical implications. Social movements are not only the concern of one discipline but its scope is widespread as its study of social structure, social processes, culture, economic structure, social changes and the inter-relationships between the all. Some of the social movements in post-independent India have their background in the colonial period, and they cannot be de linked from movements that took place in the last century, early twentieth century and in the present era. There have been many studies on social movements in India during the last four decades, but when compared to other areas their number is small. *The Indian Journal of Political Science* has published only 10 articles on movements, out of as many as 370 articles between 1965 and 1978, out of 906 doctoral dissertations in Political Science accepted by Indian universities between 1857 and 1979, only 15 dealt with movements. The situations have not changed in 1980s, 1990 and now too. During 1969, 1994-95 ICSSR sponsored 672 research projects in History, Political Science, Sociology, and Anthropology, among which only 17 were related to social movements.[15]

The political leaders and authors who used the term were concerned with the emancipation of exploited classes and the creation of a new society by changing value systems as well as institutions and/or property relationships. Paul Wilkinson gives the following working concept of "Social Movement".[16] A social movement is a deliberate collective endeavour to promote change in any direction and by any means, not excluding violence, illegality, revolution or withdrawal into 'Utopian' community. Social movements are thus clearly different from historical movements, tendencies or trends. It is important to note, however, that such tendencies and trends, and the influence of the unconscious or irrational factors in human behaviour may be of crucial importance in illuminating the problems of interpreting and explaining social movements. A social movement must support a minimum degree of organization, though this may range from a loose, informal or partial level of organization to the highly institutionalized and bureaucratized movement. Much of the literature on social movements have concerned and dealt with their history, ideology theories of movement.

The problem I have selected for research mostly confine to Naxal Movement. This is such an area of investigation that it needs prelude from so many other frontiers like socio-cultural, economic, political and psychological dimensions in order to understand and explain it in a scientific manner. In this regard the available literature is accordingly viable without mentioning of which no complete explanation would be possible. Because of its entry into vast are of socio-cultural arena, I would like to justify my review of literature very systematically in the following order:

1. Movement in human society,
2. Basic issues behind the movement such as social, political and economical,
3. Peace and violence,

4. Other forms of violence, conflict, feud, tension, unrest,
5. Ethnic movements and insurgency, and
6. Naxal movement in particular.

Movements in Human Society

Social Movements in India[17] is a collection of various movements which has moved from the interests of historians to various other fields. The social movements are not just collective mobilization for desired change but also the social processes interrelated activities, events related to ideology. Social movement characterizes protest of one kind or the other, while social movement is mainly instrumental to social change which emphasizes on conflict and contradiction. The social change brought through social movement is different from the change brought by initiation process. Social movements based on challenge, revolves uprisings, confrontation, protest opposed to request, loyalty or obedience. The change which comes out from the revolt and aggression always dismantles the traditional power structure whereas the change brought by obedience only increases the existing order. So, the social movements based on protest bring changes with conceptual problems, and other movements. The conceptual problems are outlined in terms of definition, classification, genesis, ideology, identity, organizations and leadership, internal dynamics and social consequences. The social movements are characterized by three components, viz. collective mobilization, ideology and orientation to change. Exploring the inception of social movements the theory of relative deprivation has a greater explanation as it is based on contradictions, conflicts and protest. Ideology remains as a vital part of the movement. Regarding the organization of a social movement, the aspects of recruitment, commitment and leadership, where there is formal sanctions of rewards and punishments it ceases to be a movement.

The nature of social change has three levels of a structural change—reform, transformation and revolution. The reform aims at changing the life style of the members, revolution, aims to bring sudden and total change in the society, the transformation aims to change the traditional power equations, and changing the economic and political relationships. The tribal movements always was a response to the threat to their habitat, threat to access and control of resources, the roles in the total interaction setup, searching for identity, searching the meaning of human being and nature, trying to search for more satisfactory system of control of resources. During the British the faulty land laws evoked protests, but all were aiming to free from relative deprivation. During pre and post-independence identity movements have been established by tribals, also agrarian movement with political ideology such as naxalite movement.

Social Movement in Orissa[18] shows the movement during 1936 to 1976 which majorly occurred with the four segments of society, viz. women, tribals, peasants and youth/students. This work shows that the social movements are collective in nature, what are the situations from which movements emerge and what are the theories that conceptualize the inception of these movements. This work has tried to critically examine the major trends in the movements, where the people of Orissa have raised their voice against mis-governance agrarian systems, and against the economic policy. This is an attempt to analyse the causes of unrest. This is an attempt to analyse the causes of unrest. It is described that social movement is a process whose characteristics are from history, talks of specific social and cultural forces in a society at a particular time. It brings about significant changes in social system, through collective mobilization to realize a social purpose. The work has specified the following characteristics of social movements:

- Collective mobilization of people,
- Specific goal which as a collective significance,
- Ideological interpretation of the collective goal committed workers, and
- Leadership with an organized core workers.

Social movements can be for the transformation of the economic, social and political life of a class or category of people which involved movements like peasantry, workers and women's movements. Or, it can be focused on the present problems of a class or category. Most social movements involve several classes and categories. The study of social movements follows either Marxist or non-Marxist framework for analysis. For Marxist the causes are located within the economic structure of the society non-Marxist take the contradiction of interests of the owning class and the working class which is inherent in the society. The owning or the propertied class uses the instruments of the state to exploit the working class and to control them. But the working class resist, protest organized against this. In the above the social movements among tribes indicated in five phases: (a) up to 1857, (b) from 1857 to the beginning of twentieth century, (c) tribals movements during first three decades of twentieth century, (d) period from 1920 till 1947, and (e) from 1947 till the end of 1976.

The Oriya Movement[19] by Niranjan Pattnaik (1919) is a presentation of the patriotism and after an inspiration to all young Orissa which will arouse a noble duty towards their mother land from its pages. To the outside Indian world, other than Orissan, this place is constantly affected by floods, famines has a no history almost, with full of forest, and the people very loyal to the administrators. This is a land were poverty is there in its fate. The Oriya continent has been divided in a unique way from the territory of the Indian. The British never thought of the people in this region, but they wanted to rule this part and collect taxes. For this collection purpose the British appointed non-Oriya agents who act as the agents and had a good start in this Oriya region and settled in the borders and later in the heart of it. This way a portion of south Orissa was annexed to Madras Presidency under the British, a portion on the west to the central province and other went to Bengal province. So slowly, these outsiders started imposing their culture in the region which was very much done by the government remaining behind them. The government never took any interest to understand the problems of the people and their aspirations. Gradually, the wealth of the outsiders increased with the support of the government and the people became deprived of their lands which were auctioned in cities like Calcutta. The vested interests took the primary position in extracting resources from the area. There was a distant awakening among the people of Orissa who wanted to express in their mother tongue and wanted to assert their rights through spread of literature. The natural resistance which was present among the masses also added to the awakening of the Oriyas. The Utkal Union Conference in 1903 was pioneer in expressing their own ideas. When similar movements like Andhra movement was drawing inspirations, the Oriya movement started evolving to unify the Oriya tract. The Orissa was one such region which was spread over all the three provinces under the British, no other region in India was so much distributed. Orissa had three different administrations; these factors did influence the people politically to free themselves. This book gives at length how the policies created the situations for the people which took a shape of a movement for identity.

Basic Issues Behind the Movement such as Social, Political and Economical

Many authors have given their own concepts on the issues behind the movement. Few have classified them into classes and others have categorized them into factors. *Intelligentsia as a ruling class*, Ashok Rudra, has given a clear description of the various concepts and issues behind the movement[20]. The ruling class defines as the big capitalists involved in industrial projects, big land owners, the difference, i.e. one with agriculture base and other with industrial base. It is defined class, ruling class, network among the ruling classes and the intelligentsia. The class explained as the social groups but not all social groups come under class. Class means any collection of individuals with common characteristics, interests which is economic in nature. Here the individuals are the owners of means of production. These individuals do not have any contradiction among them but have contradiction with other classes who engage with them. Ruling class do not rule directly, but help the state apparatus with some specialization, for legislature, bureaucracy, judiciary, armed forces, police and the local bodies etc. These people who run the state apparatus do belong to a particular set of origins, and by examination it is found that all these show a particular nature or character. A ruling clan, therefore, is one such service to keep the interests of the ruling class at the cost of other non-ruling classes. The policies undertaken by the state in long run, is kept well by the ruling class in their own interests. So, there is a strong nexus between the ruling classes, be it the police, contractors, any government officials or politicians. It is also said that according to Marxian social sciences, the central proposition is that the state is never neutral between different classes in the society. The state necessarily serves the interests of the certain class (or classes) at the cost of others.

The intelligentsia is the set of individuals who earn their income by selling their mental labour which comprises all white collar jobs in the organized private sector, all office workers in the State administration from top to bottom. Teachers in schools and colleges, doctors, lawyers, judges, engineers, journalists, writers, artists, skilled workers, engaged in various industries, free-lancers, professional politicians, trade union leaders etc. The professional politicians, who form important sections of the ruling class, prepare institutions which shape the politics of the state, and it is their own will to undertake things which always favour them to the other ruling classes. So, it is always the interests of the intelligentsia are in balance with the interests of the sections who own property; and always in contradiction with the labour class who generate surplus.

In sociology the decade of 1970 marked the beginning of studies on social movement. The first book by a sociologist on social movement in

India was that of T.K. Oommen published in 1972; with the title *Charisma, Stability and Change.*[21] Subsequently, examining different issues in movement was started. S.C. Malik[22] (1977) tried to clarify concepts relevant in the study of movement, in a special number of Sociological Bulletin[23] (1977), T.K. Oommen and P.N. Mukherji discussed conceptual and theoretical issues. Studies of different types of movement were reported in works of M.S.A. Rao (1978 and 1979) and A.R. Desai (1979). According to M.S.A. Rao, Movements may be classified keeping in mind different criteria, viz. consequence of a movement, super-ordinate and subordinate relationships—transformative nature of the movement, locus of a movement's, scale and spatial period; dominant issue of interest. He also observed that classification only helps to identify the main features of a movement, it does not fully explain its origin, growth dynamic and consequences. Any classification is bound to be inadequate for a movement tends to acquire new features during its course and any classification can only be relative to a particular phase in its development.

The Naxalite movement which started with peasant's protests in 1967, during the four decades it has changed its style, approach and its course. The collective actions may take several forms such as protests, agitations, *Satyagrahas*, *Hartals*, *Gheraos*, and riots. Agitations and protests are not strictly social movements, but it begins with protests and agitations and during the course of time it develops to a form of social movement. Initially, it does not require any organization/party, ideology for change, but it may have its own direction for action. When we are talking of change it is always change in economic structures and it is political in nature. The change is directed towards the state. Sometimes, resistance of the people against dominance, direction and commands of the dominant groups and the state is treated as a social movement. Resistance is certainly an expression of protest. It is direct action by large number of people who confront authority termed as "illegal public protest" on criminal in nature, depending on the ways of protest. The term illegal raises many questions and it is a matter of interpretation of law and the Constitution. A particular action can be interpreted as illegal by those who are in authority or support the *status quo*, but the same action may be interpreted as legal by those who strive for change.

The phrase "new social movement" is in vogue in the contemporary discourse among social scientists and activists. Some use the term for those movements which according to them are new, such as women's, environmental, identity, peace movements. For some sociologists, the new social movements are the result of the issues of the post-modern society or it is after 1991, in the globalized era. These movements are not class based and they do not raise economic issues, nor they are concerned with state power. They raise the issue of humanity cutting across the interests of all classes. In the sense, "new social movements" are "social and not political". According to few authors, the objective of social movement is social transformation and social change. The political implications of the movement involve issues of justice and injustice. Politics does not mean political power not solely confined with the government, it is also located at various levels; so, the collective actions are not solely against the government, but at various levels against dominant culture, caste, class, and religion. According to few authors, the objective of social movement is social transformation. The people get mobilized for attaining social justice, of course, the society and the state are, therefore, socially and politically; are not one and the same. The political implications of the movement involve issues of justice and injustice.

Peace and Violence

Many of the research works done by social scientists and Anthropologists give a broad picture on peace and violence. The sociological perspective and the social work perspective, though similar in nature, but have their own uniqueness to scrutinize these areas. The concept of peace and violence with regard to tribals is a debatable area and since colonial period it has taken the interest of all. *Unbroken History of Broken Promises*[24] has given a total account of the assurances given by the state to tribals and their retaliation. The tribal quests in Bastar (the *Dandakaranya* region) in the post-independent India, what aspect agitates the tribals, and why; there is no answer through military solutions for the Naxal problem in the Bastar region. The various laws made for tribals and tribal development has always come to them as a bane and not as a boon. This gives the journey how the state has failed systematically in the tribal areas. Few authors who worked themselves with the government have firmly described how each of the provision and plan under the crux of *Panchasheela* has failed in its implementation. All the plans that came to the tribal region have added the stories of sorrow in the name of development of tribals. The miseries of tribal people piles up and form a calm-world. They are moving towards a blazing storm. This juncture of the tribal region where security forces are deployed and big corporates are ravaging the resources, again in the name of development. The Constitution with many provisions has led the tribals to criminalize.

Violence as understood by many researchers ranges from fighting and cruelty to brutality. The various types of violence does include from verbal violence, physical violence, direct violence, structural violence, cultural violence and political violence. It has different meanings and interpretations. In his book *Political Violence and the Police in India,* Subramaniam, K.S. (2007) has examined the selected patterns of increasing political violence in the country, the policies and the police response to it. It also suggests that the country need to be freed from their colonial past and restructure their institutional set up to address the issues and challenges[25]. This study focuses on selected patterns of political violence and enquires the roles of administration and police at local and national levels, but does not give any crime figures in details. It also explores the Indian police system and the crisis in it, as police structures need to be removed or else the police reforms will have no meaning. As the people are fighting for social and economic justice are often put down with brutality and human rights violations. This study examines the role of Intelligence Bureau and at the same time the deployment of force and their violence after the setback in late 1960s, re-emerged the development process/model in India. It also focuses on violence against women, tribals, dalits, and towards the minorities in Gujarat. The study suggests mainly reforming the police, revise strategy on naxalites and reforming the intelligence and defining security.

The study has defined the Indian state as an organized political community under one government and the other refers to an administered territory or entity such as Orissa, Tamil Nadu etc. The Union Ministry of Home Affairs, the Intelligence Bureau, the Central Paramilitary Force, Police and Intelligence of the State government in India referred here as police system. Political violence used here in describing large-scale violence and conflict which fall outside the traditional controversial crime. The term political violence is used in dual sense. Firstly, it refers to the violence which called for a political response from the State authorities rather than the police, and secondly, in a situation, where there is mis-governance, administration, and politics, takes an appetite for all spaces, private and public. In such situations the Indian state depends on police to collect information on social conflict and violence in their nature, causes and solutions rather from others. In case of Andhra Pradesh, the political class shifted its responsibility in responding for Naxalite movements to a non-state agency called grey hounds. The poor have to fight for social, and economic justice. All development struggles frequently collude with power structure and often bring them into conflict with police and force, which led to human rights violations. This study has focused on all the aspects into depth and how the Indian States have responded violence through police in all parts of the country addressing the social conflicts.

In India and the other Asian countries do face conflicts rising out of territory, for resources and for other reasons. But, the conflict situation among South and Central Asia are similar. Many of the agencies are devoted to bring peace among the region and how all the sections of the society can be included in the peace mission. These agencies are constantly making their efforts to bring all the stakeholders on a common platform for open discussion. Different projects are also taken up to study the issue, workshops are organized to debate. One such project by European Union which was published in a book form gives an overall picture of the *South Asia Searching for Peace in Central and South Asia*—An Overview of conflict prevention and peace building activities[26] has shown that large parts of the south Asia are affected by wars and violent conflicts and the main problem is that people who work for peace lack information about activities. This project gives the information to meet the challenges faced by the people. It is a collection of papers on conflict mapping, strategies, conflict over resources and their issues.

It is found that the world is moving towards development and also a desire for peaceful ways. But, there is always a chance that destruction looming the society. The matters like environmental concerns, human rights violations, conflict for resources and ward all this pervade over us all the time. There are issues related to conflict which remain unsolved. The powerful actors of the world like US has changed their notion to peace after the 11th September attack on US in 2001. So, it becomes tougher for the peace researchers to find out the real issues of violence, what causes violence, whether it is state sponsored and sponsored by non-state actors, and defining security are some of the possible challenges that peace and conflict researchers have. Barash, David and Webel, Charles have brought the 2nd edition, of their book *Peace and Conflict Studies*[27] (2009) has tried to get the attention of the scholars that peace is complicated and it is the beginning to get the consideration of the researchers.

There is no way to peace and peace is the way, wrote theologian and anti-war activist[28]. But peace researchers have tried to prove that there are many ways to reach peace. And in many ways we can approach towards peace. Guha, A., in his book *Peace Diplomacy*[29] also has suggested that peace has to be sustained with equity and equality. Peace has to be dealt with skills knowledge and with attitudinal changes. It has to understand from the perspective of conflict resolution, its root causes, the actors involved in it, the characteristics of the conflict, the biasness of the parties towards each other. Peace has to be viewed from a neutral angel with a mind-set that every positive has some negative particles and *vice versa* for a solution seeking process.

Other Forms of Violence, Conflict, Feud, Tension and Unrest

The other forms of the movement which are sporadic in nature, and few do continue for a longer period. Violence, conflict, feud, vendetta, unrest, social tension, uprising, though all these are used in similar terms with movement, but they do have their own characteristics, membership and boundaries. There is no definite pattern till now observed that one follows the other but majority do come to a point of conflict and take the shape of a movement. *Economy of Colonial Orissa (1866-1947)* by Samla, J.K.[30] (2000) discusses about the economy of the Orissa under the British which includes the princely states and hill tribes. The economic changes in the state and impact it has on the economic condition of the people. The state of Orissa was different in physical features from one part to the other part. The coastal plains were deltaic and fertile, densely populated, close to sea. The hilly tracts of the southern part where tribals like Sauras, Konds, Koyas etc. lived were rocky, with crops like maize was grown. The social system of the tribals were intact, they depend on forest. But with the network of rivers this area always showed prospect for irrigation projects, hydro-electric plants. Though, the region had natural resources but did not show a good agrarian economy. So, the southern region is rich in resources with poor people. Orissa was seen as a good place for revenue collection by different intruders and also by the Britishers who ruled from 1803 to 1857, the famine of 1866 implied the negligence by the British towards the state. After the state being administered in three provinces the Oriya speaking community had to live with other ethnic groups and were dominated by the socio-political structure. Besides 6 districts, a major part of Orissa was ruled by small chiefs who were obliged to British and continued exploitative practices.

Tribals mainly lived in all the princely states and their density was more in Koraput region. Their economy was primitive, barter oriented and they did not compete with the market, nor the government attended for it. They were only seen to collect revenues. Due to the extreme condition of the tribals, south Orissa witnessed several uprisings in the nineteenth century, but they were suppressed by the princely states with the help of British Police. With the passage of time many outsiders came into the tribal regions who worked with the agents of the princely state to cheat the tribals, and every class of intruder grabbed land from the tribals especially the Mahajans and the Sundhis (an exploiting caste as seen by tribals) caste people. Specials measures were necessary to protect the tribals. The majority of the tribals of Orissa became landless class and rest lived in the interiors of the forest and nothing was done to improve their living conditions. The tribals always rose in revolt whenever they felt that their culture and life style have been suppressed by alien activities. Their simplicity changed to uprising whenever they saw their economic resources including land, forest and labour is exploited. The policies of the British did not improve the agriculture and land systems in Orissa, rather in tribal regions it created disparity among the various regions. As the embedded caste structure and the exploitation could not be eliminated from the society.

The Unrest Axle (ed.) by Gautam Bera[31], (2008) is a compilation of the various papers of ethno-social movements under different names, like solidarity movements, social mobility movements etc. All these portray social change and social activity. Saints Simon in French first used the term social movement to characterize the social protest. Involvement of ethnic groups in changing the existing social structure may be said as ethno-social movement. Social movements among peasants (peasants are the section of people who are engaged in agricultural activities directly or indirectly or related to production and who surrender a part of their produce to landlord or to the agents of the State) are wide common in the Indian context in the past. This book has discussed the movements of eastern India which have been dominated by external influence over time. The strong feeling of ethnicity and identity have motivated and mobilized them to enter into social mobility. This book has presented the various types of social movements which has a theoretical interpretation. The movements among tribes have been both during the British and even after that. The tribes adopted plough culture and were linked to the market economy through governing colonial policies where survey and settlement processes were the main tools. Through all these tools and policies tribals entered into a process of peasantry which got intensified after independence. All the tribal movements after the independence of India are to defend their traditional rights over forest, land and resources. This book has presented through its various papers which are based on empirical study in understanding the socio-economic-politics-cultural factors which invoked the social movements. Papers related to the tribal movements in Chhotanagpur in colonial time for control of their resources, the Jharkhand movement which is an ethnic movement, the Jharkhand identity, the tribal unrest in Jharkhand in 1970s and after movements have been highlighted here.

As studies about other movements which have become active sometimes in the form of unrest, and sometimes took violent positions have also caught the scope of the research. The Kashmir movement which started in the early 70s with a momentum to gain the Kashmiri identity has failed in its own vision since it has taken a very brutal form. The main aim of the Kashmir Freedom Movement (KFM), which had actively campaigned for the freedom and independence of the State of Kashmir from all foreign occupation since 1972. It has been successful in mobilizing and activating people of Kashmir to know their culture, history and to understand the status of their struggle for freedom and its position in today's world.

Members of the Kashmir Freedom Movement (KFM) have been quoted as saying "To oppress and do injustice to others is sin, but to accept the life of oppression and injustice is an even greater sin".[32]

Members of KFM oppose the militarization of the Kashmir region and seek to regain their sovereignty and independence and re-establish their status as a nation-state in accordance with the Charter of the United Nations, so that, they can live in peace and harmony within the Community of Nations. The KFM believes that Kashmir belongs to all who live in it without distinction of religion, and that it is not territorial dispute between India and Pakistan, but is a question of the right of self-determination of all the people of the region.

The peace researchers have given a different viewpoint on the concept of conflict. They have not only defined the conflict but also have explained the various mechanisms of conflict, like *Conflict Resolution,*[33] conflict management and conflict transformation. Ramsbotham, Oliver *et al.* (2008) have given a broad account of conflict resolution, and its emergence as a field for academic enquiry, so that, it can be used to manage the conflict. The peace-building efforts, conflict prevention, if we see the backdrop of the conflict it has gone far beyond and has become the mandate of the many international organizations in the objectives, but the main streaming of agenda has favoured the powerful in the powerful structures. But at the same time new challenges have emerged. But this book has tried to use the terms conflict resolution, by not misusing them, e.g. if some who raise concepts like democracy, and freedom their actions and purposes should be in congruence with each other. The debate on peace and conflict is contributing to the global society in democratic norms and justice. It has a role to play for victims of conflict. With theories this has explained to bridge the gap between the practice and progress.

Feuds as understood by many Anthropologists and the quench their thirst they have deeper into the tribal life to find out how feuds rule and their role in community bond. *The Monograph on the Life of Dongria Kondhs* gives an analytical description of clan feuds. Nayak, P.K.[34] in his research *Blood, Women and Territory—An Analysis of Clan Feuds of Dongria Kondhs*, describes that the society is multi-cultural and in the post-colonial phase has many human conflicts. It has attempted to take such a clan feud as an example and analysed the feud derived from societal conflicts. The feud has been analysed from economic, social, political and religious contexts and how these can be ramified in the changing Indian society.

It is necessary to understand the different meanings of crime, and customs of the primitive societies. In this regard the field of anthropology has opened up a new world into crime, and penology. *Crime and Customs in Savage Society* by Malinowski, B.[35] gives a description of the fieldwork of the contacts with savages. The clear definition of crime and customs has widened the knowledge of human nature. The forces which form the order and cohesion in a savage tribe have been the guiding principles of colonial administration. But, the research has deserved the primitive law or it has exaggerated it. The community ownership of property which is oriented to community sentiments by them are made to surrender their rights and privileges. The binding force among the tribal societies for economic and social obligations is based on reciprocity. Going further profound the criminology and penology and their scientific studies have paved waves to get a picture of the systems of social control among the primitive societies. *Criminology and Penology*, by Korn, R. Richard and Corkle[36] prescribes which is need based on the standards on criminology and penology. It gives a body of knowledge on the nature of crime and conclusions where law is both social and political process and an instrument of social control. The discussion on penology where the basic premise is that, the problems arise from the problems confronting the agencies appointed to solve them.

Ethnic Movement and Insurgencies

To get an exact insight on ethnic movements and insurgency, it is required to understand what is meant by ethnicity when it is related to movements. Ethnicity indicates recognizing a group of people on the basis of strange standards or characteristics, which they are asked to share with each other. These are culture, race, language, religion, customs, history, economic experiences, social experiences, folklore, traditions etc. In order to contribute such features another necessary item is that they are keyed up into some collective activity for achievement of certain demands. The quantity relies on the selection of these demands by the ethnic group or its leadership. But, there are different opinions among scholars relating to the number of attributes, which hold an ethnic group. Indian scholars always regarded that mobilization as ethnic, which is dependent on the variety of qualities—language, religion, culture, history, economy etc. To illustrate, the mobilizations are based on language, on caste like *dalits*, or religion based.

Ethnicity, Movement and Social Structure Contested Cultural Identity, edited by Bhadra and Bhadra[37] (2007) describes, India a place of many ethnic and tribal groups and north-east is no exception to it. The cultural diversity and background portray this, is turn a large number of tribal communities in the region. The planning for economic development has created regional disparity in north-east region and has created poverty and backwardness in the area. The political processes have created discontentment among the people and this has brought all the ethnic groups to a unity and they continue to have conflict with the government on various issues. This is collection of papers which has tried to express the genesis, factors, causes and consequences of the movement and its impact on social structure. The role of economy policies has also been looked up with the relation of the movement.

Tribal Movements in India by Jitendra Prasad[38] focuses on how the tribal unrest in Bihar for a separate State has evolved from 1770s till at various periods and after independence in the 1970. The history has a strong interface between the tribals and the others which ultimately resulted in unrest events. This study has explored the dynamics of the power relations, socio-cultural relations between the tribls and the non-tribals, tribal exploitation, the attack of communal forces on tribals, the tribe-caste continuum and the assertion of pride in tribal identity. This study has probed all these structures into deep. The issue of exploitation lies with the economic-social-political system of the society. It is much embedded and core to any power relation. The study says the exploitation has two meanings, first is using an object for benefit and the second exploiting the natural resources. So, it is always important for the well-being of the people in the society and covers social inequality and struggle for justice. According to Marxian thought, one group produces surplus whose use is controlled by the other group. This is exploitation and it gives a class conflict in a later stage. The asymmetrical power relations is referred here as structures of deprivation. This study has attempted to use the political economy to understand the structures of deprivation at various levels such as economic, social and political. This study majorly focuses on the involvement of a major tribal group, viz. Santhals and Jharkhand movement in colonial and independent era the styles of protest by tirbals in relation to their structures of deprivation. Political economy refers to the social relation between people in the process of production, distribution and exchange and consumption of material. Whenever a social movement takes shape it is not just a theory of social structure, but a vision about future of the society. Social movement is the past experience of the people, the present social condition and the future creativity required.

During British rule they introduced land laws to exploit which was economic in nature. They also created structures like education, legal, administration systems to exploit the material and human resourcc and tribal were not exception in this paradigm. This study has also focused the mechanism of these exploitative systems and how they have affected the tribal communities over a period of time and especially what are the consequences on Santhals. This has been examined from DEO concept (discrimination, exploitation and oppression) all conflicts, movements generate from this model. This has explored the nature of exploitation of tribals in colonial and post-colonial phase. It is acute in case of tribals, though exploitation prevails everywhere. The style of protest/resistance by tribals in responding to the exploitation is analyzed from concepts like DEO.

Tribal movements in India are as old as other types of movements, they were considered to be rebellious and civilized rulers quelled them as they had superior aims. The tribals were in a position of confrontation both with the Hindu overlords and the British colonialists, as the latter seriously encroached on their rights and territories. Roy Burman identifies eight kinds of responses of the tribals to the different challenges that they field:

1. Response to threats to the privacy of habitats.
2. Response to threats to access to and control of resources.
3. Response to description of traditional roles in the total interaction set-up.

4. Search for new meanings of the relationships between man and nature.
5. Search for new meanings of the relationships between individual and society.
6. Search for new frontiers of identity.
7. Search for a more satisfactory system of control of resources.
8. Search for a more satisfactory system of organization of community power at all levels.

All these are mutually exclusive, but all did not turn to movements. Few went to the stage of revolt, rebellion and revolution. During British Rule, alienation from land, due to faulty legislation pertaining to forest lands and lack of understanding of the tribal social organization were responsible for tribal uprisings. Although they had diverse ideological overtones, the main there was the millions waiting for the day of deliverance from an acute situation of relative deprivation. Roy Burman points out that tribal movement, since Independence, has been characterized by two features. There is a strong tendency towards establishing tribal ethnic identities. They find new meanings regarding the relationships between man and nature and individual and society by reinterpreting their own traditions and myths. The second major trend is in the direction of agrarian and proletarian movements in the context of political ideologies (like Marxism, Leninism, Maoism) including the present Naxalite movement.

Naxalite Movements in Particular

The media has large coverage on the events of the Naxalites, be it the blasts, operations, their camps, interviews, any killings or encounters between the security forces and the Naxals. The Indian security forces deployed in the states of Orissa, Chhattisgarh and in other places have started a hateful mission against Naxalites. The interviews given in the local Oriya channel the retired Police high officials openly saying that if the Naxals kill them the security forces will kill more than that. The recent technology like using satellite large areas of India have been mapped. Altogether more than 80000 security forces are deployed by Centre, State and special to bring back Naxalite areas including their jungle bases in different states. Indian Government has ordered number of sophisticated UAVs (unmanned aerial vehicles) from US to head the operations.[39] Home Ministry has banned Communist Party (Maoist) in 2009 and called

Naxalites as the *biggest challenge to internal security*. During the recent elections in 2009, Naxalites called for a boycott and this was successful in number of villages in Eastern and Central states. Many studies show that Naxalites control nearly 25 per cent districts in the country.

Naxalite movement has its roots in a place called Naxalbari in West Bengal. On May 25th of 1967 a section of Communist Party (Marxist) (CPM) cadres started an uprising against the landlords in Naxalbari. This revolt was led by CPM leaders Charu Mazumdar and Kanu Sanyal. CPM which advocated electoral politics, did not extend hand to such an initiative. The revolutionaries were termed as Naxalites who separated themselves from CPM and formed a new party. They believed in the principles of Mao (Late leader of Chinese Communist Party), Marx and Lenin. The new form of Maoism in India is Naxalim and from 1967 till today it is showing its sparks and inviting masses to join them. During late 1960s, many university graduates joined the revolt which spread from West Bengal, Uttar Pradesh, Orissa and Kerala.

The Indian ruling class answered the rebellion with heavy arms. Government of India led by the Prime Minister, Indira Gandhi, employed the security forces in large numbers and by 1971 the Naxals were crushed. With the heavy state repression by the mid of 1970s the movement was literally dead. Many leaders were arrested and many went underground and many were killed in police encounters. The Naxalite revolt and their ideologies got fragmented and many groups raised their heads. Few went underground and into jungles and started working among *Adivasis* (tribals) and other oppressed castes.

In 1980s the naxalite groups in Andhra Pradesh were grouped under the banner of a party called People's War Group who were working among tribals. Their work got extended to other nearby states of Chhattisgarh and Orissa. Parallel another underground group which was working in the undivided Bihar and in West Bengal which was known as Maoist Communist Centre carried their activities against the police and in villages. During 2004 these two parties merged together and formed The Communist Party of India (Maoist).

Many studies and police sources put a figure that today Naxalites have approximately 20000 well armed cadres. In addition they have more than 30000 cadres committed to the movement active in the states mentioned above. They have also had sophisticated weapons including mortars, they run camps, and recruit people to their party. There have been many studies in other states than on Naxalite movement and many have studied their politics, their leadership, analysed their party documents, the conditions that give strength to naxalite movement. And few of the researches have been mentioned here.

As mentioned above that the initial Naxal revolt was stamped in the late 70s and many leaders were in jail, many surrendered and many went underground. The party had lost its directions and many did not know who can advise them to go further till they evolved into three different sects. During 1977, a book was published just at the right time when the party was under turmoil.. *Revolutionary Violence: Maoists Movement in India,* by Mohanty, Manoranjan[40] (1977) giving an account of the events occurring in the Communist Party and other events, when the party was marking the tenth years of their Naxalbari uprising. The repression of the government in late 1970s restrained the party from doing any celebration for the decennial period, but there was huge change in the Indian politics. The government was not only oppressive but did meet the challenges by bringing some reforms when the Congress Party was defeated. The Communist Party exposed many weak links of the then system. This book talks about the intimidating character of the government during the emergency period, the beginning of a new revolution, their party's re-structuring their major divisions and their strategies.

From the beginning of 1977 till the beginning of the 2000, there were not many studies on the Naxalite movement in the State of Orissa as there were no such incidents during the said period. Except few media reports no such research work was taken up until 2004, when their activities took violent form in Orissa. *Naxal Movement and State Power with Special Reference to Orissa*[41], where, the Naxalite movement is seen as a major internal security threat by the state and it is an issue of great concern. The different views of the two major parties involved here is the naxals and the state power; the former sees it as a socio-economic problem and the latter views as a law and order problem. But over a period of last five years the violence from naxals has reportedly increased in India and Orissa is not an exceptional case. The analysis of the development of the movement in the formative years in Orissa and subsequent occurrence of the movement in Orissa is a significant achievement. Though, Orissa was seen as a low intensity movement, yet the few incidents have proved that it has the potential to attach in a large scale. The official declaration of the movement in 1967 has spread into more than 13 states in India. This gives not only the initial years of movement in Orissa but also the violent activities in south Orissa, the strategies and tactics adopted by the Naxals to keep their violence. The analysis based on the talks of the Naxal leaders/ sympathizers with the Government of Orissa in 2004 which occurred parallel with the peace talks of Andhra Pradesh. Basing on all the legislative replies, the chronological activities by Naxals from newspaper sources, it gives a broad picture that their major issue is tribal land rights and socio-economic and reform policies would cease the conflict in the future.

The Naxalite Movement in India, by Singh, Prakash[42] (2006) is a narration of the whole movement from 1967 till now has gained strength like the Kashmir conflict. The ideology of Naxals has appealed the intellectual masses has sustained itself and increased its coverage, posing serious challenges as it did in the past. The movement showed its first spark in 1967 and many youth joined leaving their studies behind, after two decades in 1980s it was seen that the workers, peasants suffered the same as the political processes were diluted due to the powers of the vested interest groups and it was revisited that armed struggle is the only option. It ignites due to social injustice, economic inequality and failure of the system to redress the grievances of the people. Once Jaya Prakash Narayan while touring the Naxalite affected areas of Bhojpur (Bihar) on June 12-13, 1975, exhorted the people to shun the path of violence and work for total revolution. Addressing the crowd at Narayanpur he said if in five years from now nothing changes, I will not ask you to give up Naxalism. Naxalism is a much abused term as seen by few authors as the authorities fiddling with the term and use this to label anyone who is striving for social or economic justice and justify the repressive measures against him or her. The movement has not died besides all the efforts by the government and constantly draws its energy from the unaddressed grievances of the people. With this backdrop as seen within the party, the 1967 flash, the later Andhra Pradesh movement, the subsequent movements/uprisings which took place from 1967 to 1980, the new face of the Peoples War Group and the Maoist Communist centre. The various parties' different lines like the armed struggle, the mass line and the electoral politics. The Communist Party of Nepal evolved when the monarchy was exploiting the people. The Communist Party of Nepal adopted the path of violence when the demands were rejected. The Naxalite movement has many contours since its inception, it has setback, saw a phase of complete silence, and then a phase of growth. The People's War Group in Andhra Pradesh was in its peak during 1990s. The party re-organized itself constituting a military wing. The support base which was (as declared) 50,000 or little more through small but substantial, from the oppressed sections. The movement is strong in Orissa, Chhattisgarh, Andhra Pradesh, Bihar, Jharkhand and West Bengal, because these areas do have a history of struggles, and uprisings and the second being the dark side where the land reforms were not successful. Whatever the land laws were enacted could not be implemented. The problems because multiplied from land reform, exploitation, poverty, mis-governance, displacement and tribals rights, and a big mass of the population is living below the poverty line. The movement will be limited to certain areas or will spread over the country that will be decided by the changing times.

"Towards Naxalbari" (1953-1967),[43] is an account of the inner party ideological struggles by Pradip, Basu (2000) where the research has shown that the Communist history in India has witnessed various splits basing on the ideology and methods. Various studies do say that there have been 122 times spilt among which 22 have been inclined for armed struggle. The present Communist Party of India (Maoist) is the brain child of many debates and discourses in the Party since 1967. The Communist Party those who initially resort to violence have seen various setbacks in the party due to repression and fear. The work of Basu 2000, gives the inner-party struggles which yielded some uprisings like Naxalbari which had serious implications on the movement. But the two major thoughts which germinated from that one is the debatists and the other actionists, these two can be well said that the first group developed themselves as the critique of the second group. The inner-party debates are based on the party documents with academic point of view.

The Indian form of Maoism which is totally different from traditional left politics, which gave rise to the debates of radical Communism, which became Naxalism or Naxalites; though initially the Naxalites centred around the Communist Party of India and Community Party (Marxist). But its gave birth to a new party, i.e. Communist Party of India (Marxist and Leninist). The movement has been studied here from three aspects, first being the socio-economic structure and process which provide the backbone to it, second being the power structures and political relationships of the immediate political context and the third being the ideology and theory of the movement. These aspects combined together make small movements like Naxalbari, the Srikakulam movement more significant. The study of Basu focuses on the time span of 1953-1967, the 1953 as benchmark because by 1953, the very thought of parliamentary line of Communist movement has induced the minds and in 1952 they successfully participated in the general elections. This provoked the inner party struggle and dialogue to create lot of documents. This study has done an enquiry on two sets of documents, the primary material written during 1953 (included booklets, articles, pamphlets) and the secondary materials written during and after Naxalbari (include books, articles and interviews). This research focuses on two groups—debatists and actionists, the dabatists who concentrated on theoretical debate to expose the elected leaders and the actionists who believed in armed struggle and to create models of revolution.

Few authors have given their own journeys in the Naxal infested areas in a story form where interviews with different stakeholders have given their own opinion on the Naxalite movement. Even though this is not pure research studies but these are windows which open up new angles to view the movement. Chakravarti, Sudeep (2008) in his book called *Red Sun Travels in the Naxalite Country*,[44] has brought out the description of the other India. As he travels through the state of Chhattisgarh, the core Naxalite zone, he has explained that the Naxalite movement is not confined to one or two villages rather it has occupied more than 15 states in India and supported by the intelligentsia/intellectual class. Being a journalist by profession, he has taken interviews with sympathizers, bureaucrats, policemen, development workers, farmers (a cross-section of population) and incorporated in the book where he has shown that there is a deep and widening divide in our country and there are many more dangers/challenges which are ahead for the country due to this conflict.

Few researchers have worked on the politics of the Naxalite movement and their changing styles of operations. Very few studies have been done on the surrender of Naxalites and their policy implications. Rajat, Kujur and Bidyut Charobarty (2010) has mentioned in their research which is called *Maosim in India—Reincarnation of Ultra Left Wing Extremism in the Twenty First Century*[45], they have placed their views on the rise of Maoism and the contributing factors are the failure of the post- and pre-independence governments specially the failure of the government to implement the policies. The authors attempted to answer questions like is Maoism deep-rooted in the disappointment of the people or is it the outcome of the developmental models which are advocated by the planners? They consider Maosim is in its sprouting stages. They have analysed the documents to present the stages of Maoism and presented four issues to engage the masses: gain support from people who are aspiring for secession like north-east and Kashmir, attack on case system, fight for *Dalits* and gender equality. They have given an account of *salwa judum*, a civilian-Naxalite movement in Chhattisgarh to counter this problem along with the rehabilitation and surrender policy.

As in India, the nearby countries too have the issues like Naxalism and their challenges. Nepal and Bangladesh face a lot of problems with Maoism. The different parties who operate in Naxalite style do have a strong coordination among South Asia and South-East Asian region. A recent study on Maoists on Nepal has brought out their passage from the initiation till today where they are struggling to have a constitution. Maoists in Nepal from Insurgency to Political Mainstream, by B. Upreiti,[46] (2008) is a study which has attempted to locate the various components of the movement from the problems of Maoist insurgency, and how they shifted their focus to join the mainstream politics with drawing arms. This study has given a holistic angle to understand their support base, the human rights issues, the challenges and how they are trying to engage with the government. Overthrowing Monarchy was a biggest challenge and they have done it successfully, but still their journey is not over.

The Naxalites and their party is banned from 2009 and few of their activities have been compared as acts of terror. Their operations, ambush, killing of innocents, travelling in an Ambulance is a sheer case of human rights violations. After all the incidents, it is still found that they are able to spread with a smoother pace irrespective of their strategy. There are other instances and conflicts in India, especially in the north-east, where the country is having trouble with the neighbouring countries, especially China, to secure its borders. The comprehensive study on north-east is a significant one to note that the north-east problems will take still few more years to be solved. *Terrorism in India's North-East*, a Gathering Storm, by Ved Prakash[47] a detailed study. The democratic India though accommodated many tribals but till now has not been able to tackle their issues. This study aimed at understanding their problems and causes behind it. This book included all the struggles of north-eastern States.

Observer Research Foundation is an agency, which is an independent institution, has committed itself to develop policies and create knowledge on the issues of politics, security and governance. They conducted a two days national workshop on the Naxalite movement during January 2005 and all the papers were brought up in a volume called *The Naxal Challenges- Causes, Linkages and Policy Options*[48] where various papers were presented in different themes, social economic causes of the Naxalite movement, its political base, the strategies of the revolution, the linkages with other groups and few suggestions to tackle with the issue

The Naxalite movement has always attracted many Gandhians to rethink on their *gram swaraj* and reconstruction programme. It was found that many of the Gandhians in the South Orissa (the universe of the study)

did have a sympathetic attitude for them during the 1950s. And, similarly, many Naxalites who believed in Communist ideology had high regard for Gandhians like late Shri Biswanath Pattnaik who was known as Gandhi of Koraput region. This unique amalgamation of the ideologies has nicely been documented in a book called *Gandhi and Mao* (*in quest of analogy*)[49] by Dr. Ratan Das (2004) has tried to locate both Gandhi and Mao in today's circumstances. He has shown that the present culture has forgotten the plight of the poor and tribals. Culture comes as an offshoot of capitalism. And capitalism is fully engaged to swab out both the ideologies be it Gandhi or Mao. Both Gandhi and Mao are pioneers in their own fields, both had similar objectives but their ways of implementation were different. Mao's concept of dialectics and violence has saturated and total annihilation is fatal at this situation. The good aspects of Mao and Gandhi have to be synthesised, so that, it can be emerged as a way for social change and to get the best solutions.

The perspective on Maoism, its origin, its flaws, who will carry its legacy all these have brought out in *Economic Political Weekly*,[50] by D'mello, Bernard has shown that the initial thought about Communism is about freedom, freedom from the capitalistic exploitation. But the revolutionaries itself gelled with the system. What is needed is radical democracy to enjoy maximum participation. In the same volume the commentary is about who is responsible, the Communist Party or the Indian State, has highlighted the issues of human rights violations on *Adivasis*, the forceful eviction, the operation green hunt in the Naxal infested areas show a grim picture of the state. The tribals consider the Naxalites as their good friends as other doors for their solutions are closed. The security forces beats them, or label them as Naxalites, the political parties use them as vote banks and few of the parties does support the private operations like *salwa judum*.[51]

Journalistic Interpretation

The overall media highlights can be said in three ways, they highlight the points favouring the movement and why the Naxalite movement is on rise. Also there are some special features which covers the special operation and raids done by Naxalites. The interviews of the Naxalite leaders, and their questioning to the system of governance. But they cover largely on the incident part to a major extent, discussion on it, but they do not carry and give any direction to the appropriate solution of the issue. But the media's role is in deep appreciation as they have brought out and bringing out everyday's incidents of Naxalites, which is in way a caution check to the governments to think over the issue which is affecting a large section of the society.

The presence of the Naxalite/Maoist movement can be had on the World Wide Web.

Anyone who is interested to search the net on Naxal issues can find a number of sites and documents. There are numerous media reports, reports by research organizations, independent reports by magazines and other information available on the net. But the presence of Naxalite movement got recognition on net from the year 1998 when all the state capitals in India had internet access. A scanning of the net gives the following data on the presence: An unofficial but comprehensive website of: CPI (ML) (Peoples' War)

> A brief history of the pro-Maoist presence on the Internet (1997-2008)
> A brief history of the pro-Maoist presence on the Internet with reference
> In the Year 1997, Vara Vara Rao—The pro-Maoist poet appeared many times on live chat on rediff.com
> In the Year 1998, Com. Ganapathy, General Secretary of CPI(ML) People's War appeared on the internet on rediff.
> In the same year the Interview with Com. Prasad of Party Unity gave an appealing interview. All Revolutionary Ranks must Unite, i.e. November 1998.

In the year 2002 a pro-Naxalite sympathizer started http://www.geocities.com/cpimlpwg (Currently deleted).[52] The website can still be accessed at http://web.archive.org/web/*/ http://www.geocities.com/cpimlpwg.[53] In fact some of the original documents of the CPI (ML) PW can still be accessed online through the above website and other website[54] as http://web.archive.org/web/20021012230004/www.geocities.com/cpimlpwg/docu.html

In early 2005, it was believed that the website owner made the below provocative statement on his website.

Death Warrant: By the suppressive actions of the comprador State Governments of Andhra Pradesh, Jharkhand, West Bengal, Bihar, MP, Chhatisgarh the respective comprador Governments have virtually signed their own Death Warrants. Buddhadeb Bhattacharyya, Chandrababu Naidu, Babulal Marandi shall perish. People's War gives a call to all revolutionaries to take up arms and join the struggle for emancipation. Death to Buddhadeb Bhattacharyya, Chandrababu Naidu, Babulal Marandi. Long Live revolution. *Inquilab Zindabad.* This emotional outburst was stated as the reason for the State security forces that sent a notice to geocities.com to take down the website. Geocities was only too glad to oblige them.

The current status, background and origin of the webmaster of http://web.archive.org/*/http://www.geocities.com/cpimlpwg is not known[55], but it is likely he/she was from Andhra Pradesh as CPI (ML) PW had a strong presence there.

Year 2003 Peoplemarch.com (currently deleted) a pro-moist magazine[56] came online year 2003.

It was one of the most active online resources on the progressive revolutionary movement in India until May 2006 when according to the editor Com. Govindan Kutty the State Intelligence Bureau threatened the Website hosting provider who carved into State pressure and deleted peoplesmarch.com. The exact statement can be accessed at another website[57] and later another blog came into existence called peoples bulletin. Most of the back issue of peoples march can today be accessed at website.[58]

On February 14, 2008 the Ernakulam District Magistrate issued an order banning the publishing of the magazine in the district. The order was issued on the eve of Com. Kutty coming out of the jail on bail and he had been incarcerated on false charges. The real purpose for the arrest is now clear: to stifle freedom of expression in the country. *The People's March* is an independent magazine that fearlessly seeks to present the facts without facing any pressure from advertisers or the government to sing to any tune.

The editor, subsequently started people-truth.blogspot.com which some people believe the new profile of the people's march but it is not yet registered as a magazine. In the Year 2006—The Blogging Revolution By the year 2006, the Web 2.9 communication revolution had begun and blogs were an integral part of it.

Revolutionary Blogs: By doing a random search for certain key words, one can come across several defunct pro-Maoist and Naxal blogs[59] like http://springthunder.blogspot.com/ which seems to have started in 2003 and http://naxalnext.blogspot.com/[60] and http://cpimaoist.blogspot.com/ which started in 2006 some months before this blog[61], but most of them failed to garner an audience or make any impact and soon closed the shop.

Naxal Revolution: June 2006 Naxal revolution.blogspot.com. The blog was not the first pro-Naxalite blog, but it was the first to garner a dedicated following and was quite popular on the Internet getting almost 500 unique visitors and 1000 page views on a daily basis during its peak.

The blogger who ran Naxal revolution posted under the name of Abhay and claimed to live in Bangalore, in a post he that his intentions for starting this blog was mainly to protest against the censorship of peoples march and to counter disinformation against social workers and activists being carried out by some other blogs. Within a short time the blog started carrying some press releases that seemed to be from some Maoist organizations and which the blogger claimed he received through email. This contributed to the popularity of the blog. The blog mostly carried articles from mainstream media which were rehashed to suit the tastes of moist sympathizers along with media found online like videos, audio, pictures and the occasional official press release from Maoist organizations.

In October 2007, the blogger made an unexpected U-turn on his views on the Maoist movement in India and in this post, made the following observation. After following the Maoist movement closely for the last one year and a study of the prevailing conditions in the country I have come to the conclusion that the armed struggle waged by the Maoists may not be able to provide a lasting solution to the problems faced by this country and humanity in general, nor would I follow, endorse or recommend this path to anyone else as of today.

The blog eventually ceased publishing for more than 6 months after which some activity was observed in the months of August 2008, as of writing this post the blog was active again but it seems it is only temporary.

Resistance India[62] was started by a blogger who knew Com. Govindan Kutty the editor of Peoples March. Resistance India also became popular after it started carrying exclusive press release of Maoist parties.

The blogger posted under the name of Bimal and was based from Kozhikode, Kerala. Resistance India had a diverse following and as per the statistics displayed on its website it had received more than 15,000 unique visitors. In August 2007, the blog was hacked by unknown sources. He subsequently started Maoist resistance.

Having already set up a successful blog at resistance India[63] it was not at all difficult for Bimal to set up another one and within no time the new blog also started getting large number of visitors. As per the current statistics displayed on the website it has received more than 26,000 visitors till date.

Some Maoist/pro-Maoist organizations have their own blogs like

- http://rcpkarnataka.blogspot.com/[64]
- http://tamilporali.blogspot.com/[65]
- http://rdf-2005.blogspot.com/[66]
- http://rpfkeral.blogspot.com/[67]
- www.smwnews.com[68]
- www.writetokill.com[69]

It is impossible to recollect or post the entire list of all the International blogs but a large number of links appear on

http://mikeely.wordpress.com/, http://naxalrevolution.blogspot.com/search/label/Links[70]

Each blog contains a number of links to other blogs of similar content. All one has to do is follow the links and you will be amazed at the number of pro-Maoist blogs out there. New blogs can be found by searching for key terms like Naxal, Naxalite, Maoist on http://blogsearch.google.com/ but a lot of spam blogs make the process a little tiring. Pro-Maoist presence on Social Networking Websites. There are thousands of Maoist sympathizers of Indian origin present on social networking websites like orkut, face book who regularly interact and debate various issues.

The Conceptual Framework

While working on the topic "Naxalite Movement and participation of tribals in it, conceptual and theoretical inputs come from many sides. The most essential points emerge from the domains of Anthropology, Sociology and Social Work. Undoubtedly, all the conceptual matters discussed in social work are originally borrowed from both anthropological and sociological thoughts. Social work as understood is the art and science of helping individuals, so that, they help themselves. Many of the theories in social work give us a macro, micro and middle range theories focusing on a range of issues. Many times social work models, methods are termed as theories. *Theories* are the set of ideas which explain why things occur in a particular way, and how can one predict the outcomes in the future. They are the pulse of the subject which gives us a direction. Any movement or specifically Naxalite movement accrues to several conceptual discussions like differences, conflicts, quarrel, factions, disputes, feuds, violence, peace, social tension, war etc. which ultimately help to start the process of movement. Undoubtedly, this is explained as well as process where the factors like torture, bio-mental" torturing lie at the fundamental ground.

According people response, react and if continued for a grand period, go for a rebellion or movement. On this backdrop, I have tried to analyse the movement process, both theoretically/conceptually and practically (acting appropriate case studies) to take up a holistic view of the Naxalite movement. Therefore, without mentioning the theoretical or conceptual backdrop, the basis as well as purpose of the book will be incomplete and useless. In the previous discussions under "review of literature" though some of the basic points with reference to the rise and development of ovement have been discussed, under the conceptual framework, they are to be specifically highlighted with reference to theoretical understanding of the movement. A number of theoretical contributions may be presented with reference to conflict, peace, tension, violence, feud etc. to go up to the rise and continuity of a movement.

The tribe evokes different ideas and notions in peoples mind, for some it is a different utopian world, for some it is still the people who stay in forest away from civilization, for some it is a romantic world, for some they are matter of pity and concern and for most they are innocent living in culture of silence and can be exploited easily. The fact remains indebted that they represent a type of society which has failed to live with the advanced society so far. They are in different stages of our evolution, from hunting-gathering, shifting cultivation, settled cultivation, migrant workers, white collar jobs etc. of our civilization. Till now in the tribal society in the context of India and specifically to Orissa, the pre-agricultural society, can be found in the overall tribal society, who lives in isolation since ages. Though the government interventions did have brought few changes within them, but it is not that much when compared to the whole of the population.

Anthropology (study of mankind in general and tribals in particular) is still, to most laymen and too many specialists mainly an object of antiquarian interest. Savagery is still synonymous with absurd, cruel and eccentric customs, with superstitions, cannibalism and revolting practices, and what not. But certainly all of these aspects made us to probe into the tribal world scientifically with empirical ways. The tribals had their own kingdom, niche and independence. But the imperialistic paradigm of the British rule was responsible to make a whole in the tribal ozone layer, by disturbing their isolation. They not only broke the isolation but provided a scope and opportunity to plunder their tribal economy, their pride, their identity by outsiders the so called zamindars, money lenders, traders, merchants, and last but not the least, the systematized state actors.

History has witnessed in India that whenever there was an attempt to make a hole in the tribal ozone layer there were protests, resistance and movements.. The eighteenth, nineteenth and twentieth century tribal movements are a testimonial fact to this. All those movements continued and lived a life of one year to five years, but they were crushed by the powerful colonial state and now by the independent Indian State. As we know, that a hole in the tribal-atmospheric ozone layer emits harmful rays to all and affects the entire climate. Similarly, the hole which was made in the tribal ozone layer during the British has increased in its radius. There were no attempts to head the hole but rather the site of the whole increased during the independent Indian State. Now, the harmful emissions are seen, felt and well described as Naxalite movement. The form of the protest have changed, the style and the version of the movement have shifted, but the spirit remains the same, i.e. registering protest for autonomy, identity, spontaneous uprisings against the State, spontaneous violence against the exploitative structures, activity created by the State and nurtured by the State.

I have chosen here to explain the concepts and the ideas connected to such Naxal movements from sociological, social work, psychological angles to understand and present the work as mentioned below.

A. Law

No doubt, all types of movements start on the base-line of law. Law has several socio-cultural implications and connotations which anthropologists and sociologists usually study and document. In Anthropology laws have been articulated in a unique way to express not only the negative part of the human being but also the positive quality which enhances the human life and the collectiveness of any society. This acts as an instrument to nurture the society. In *Anthropology of Law, a Comparative Theory*, Leopold Pospisil[71] defines law as the property of the higher cultures and civilizations, and does not exist in the primitive tribal societies as claimed. Few have considered and adopted the Western definition of law which are governed by agencies of the State. For example, of there are no courts, then there is no law. But the tribal societies are not included in such a paradigm. But, Anthropologist's interpretations avoid such exclusions as it studies the societies irrespective of its primitiveness. It does not make any difference among the societies over the other. But studies culture as a whole in relation to another. So in this context, law should be studied as a part of the culture and not as a separate entity. It studies the social forces, society as a changing process, which has continuously disturbed by some elements and not as static. So, all laws are neither supported by people's feelings nor these emerged out of social change. But its science of law and, therefore, it is experiential.

In many of the claims feud constitutes the form of law in some tribal societies. The nature of feud in relation to law and classification of violence which human societies encounter is most striking characteristics of violence which varies from injury to killings, initiated from an earlier injured group and it is long in duration. Most tribal societies have war practices to a related group with whom friendship did exist or towards a new group. In this process the nature of the feud is to take revenge. Tribal societies do not have law, but have sanctions and ordeals. It does differ from the application of force for social control on politically organized societies. In many cases where the authority decides the law are less connected to the people and more for their actions representing the behaviour of the authority. In *Anthropology of Law, a Comparative Theory*[72], it is mentioned that the human nature and mind is same all over the world which has rationality, morality and regarded the most high human values. Traditionally, the "Europeans considered law as an absolute autonomous entity" which is independent of space and time, not related to in any particular way to the nature of the society in which it existed. Natural law was thought to consist of a body of principles which are inbuilt in the nature in its objects and all living beings which allows or allowed the complete development of all, so that, a concord can be maintained. As natural law defined, it gives the basic theory that it governed the human beings conduct and the way he related with the peer groups around him, and refers to all those principles which yield ethics that Judges were believed to utilize in their settlement of conflicts which is again irrespective of time and space. Law has to be incongruence with the culture of the society, and law of one culture cannot be added or imposed to another culture and dynamic in nature.

Law has different meanings and certainly law is a myth. Franks' definition[73] says law as sees of dispute. Redcliff Brown defines law as sanction. Roscoe Pounds remarks on law described as instrument of social control. Malinowski defines civil law as a body of binding obligations, regarded as a right by one party and acknowledged as a duty by the other. Few others have defined "law of a given community is the body of rules which are recognized as obligatory by its members." Seagle concludes that "test of law in the strict sense is the same for both primitive and civilized communities with the existence of courts." Frank defines that a number of definitions can be given for a law but there is no strict sense of the word law. A large number of communities have law but do not have legal institutions.

B. Feud

As generally understood feud is the bitter feeling of anger or enmity between two families or two groups. It is also the conflict shown by two enemy groups engaged in feud. The online oxford dictionary defined feud as the prolonged and bitter quarrel or dispute[74]. A feud sometimes a very long fight between parties, who are associated by families or clans. They begin because one of the parties involved in a feud believes or accepts that the other one is always attacking, insulting, or doing hurt to them. Feuds can last for many years or sometime even for generations. Feuds can be blood feud when they include punishment in return to take revenge or to give punishment. A vendetta is a blood feud between two families or groups where kinsmen of the victim intended to take revenge for his or her death by killing either those responsible for the killing. The practice has mostly disappeared with more societies getting organized ways, where criminal laws take the responsibility of punishing the deviant behaviour. Vendetta is still practiced where the local societies do not accept the local law enforcement authority as a form of justice. As in other continents the feuds continue to persist, in India caste feud is observed by various sociologists on which many conflicts germinate.

C. Social Tension

The general meaning of the word 'tension' is stress or pressure or anxiety. But at the same time if the same stress extends in the society it is connoted as social tension. After 1991 in our country the increase of private sector has squeezed the state's role to a greater extent and it only employs skilled people. But most of our population is tribal and other backward castes who are not skilled to handle such sophisticated jobs, so, this is creating a imbalanced picture and the gap between rich and poor is widening. There is a huge difference between the economic levels of the educated urban and they have not section that are tribals and other castes. The justice system is not working effectively as the cases are not solved in one's whole life time, rights are violated and all these aspects tend towards the rise of social tensions. The populist measures given to the voters are not acting in the proper ways rather the words are becoming like slow poison to the people. When the society is not stable how can we expect productive and equal growth for all? The 1950s Balwant Rai Mehta Committee reported to opt for multi-layered Panchayati Raj systems and the historic achievement of the 73rd and 75th Constitutional Amendments could not reach up to the expectations of the people; it acted as contrary to the people. The Nehuruvian vision and principles are yet to materialise, but many conflicts have moved ahead with different halting.

The democratization of the state or the democratic process of the Indian state could not penetrate into the social order and into the society it remained only with the few influential or few people, as a result there is a growing gap between the inner groups, inter-communities, inter-religion, or even inter-state. The social forces are acting negatively on many of the weaker sections of the society. But in all these categories poor cut across. Tensions or conflicts arise due to different situations, circumstances and due to different causes. If, we take a broad view of the inherent causes of these conflicts/tensions then it can be very well said that they are due to:

- Historical factors as between the Hindus and Muslims.
- Discrimination and exclusions.
- Linguistic factors.
- Gender inequality.
- Institutional factors which are the main pillars of democracy the legislative, executive and the judiciary have failed to give justice to people and have reduced their presence and importance.
- The governance system so far has not met the needs of the poor, the corruption is on rise, the instances of police oppression, violation of human rights, children dying of malnutrition and the continuing discrimination has washed the faith of the people on governance and its organs.
- Economic factors, as 70 per cent of the people in our country live below poverty line, the have-nots folk are dissatisfied and unhappy. The new economic policies have still added to their misery in terms of reducing the job opportunities due to industrialization.

So, there is constant tension among various groups, tension is a term which connotes the mental strain, stress, anxiety, excitement and the feeling of being stretched which causes some changes in the qualitative as well as quantitative aspects of individuals, groups, within the political, social and economic institutions. Why we are saying economic or social institutions as tension may explode due to economic deprivation, threat to economic deprivation, denial of rights, favouring a particular section of people over the other, due to conflicting interests and many more. Tensions are universal in any social life and can be present from the household level to the international sphere; tension is the aftermath of conflict and signifies to an open conflict.

According to Sociological thought, it brings in intergroup tensions in connection with his treatment on the topic of ethnic and racial groups and tells his readers that the phenomena of prejudice, tensions, and discrimination between groups are extremely variable.[75] Tension came from the field of psychology; it is a trait of living matter. Japanese sociologists have recognised nine distinct groups of tensions in their society. They are:

- Tension in family life,
- Tensions within communities,
- Tension between countries,
- Tension around the problem of outcastes,
- Racial tensions,
- Tensions in religious life,
- Tensions in economic life,
- Ideological tensions, and
- Tensions among young people.

Social tensions occur when there is a huge gap between the haves and the have-nots and synonymous to social conflict. The manifestations of tension could be very many. Social tension often characterises, or leads to conflict which has a bearing on the social relations, social position or the very endurance of some social groups.

D. Social Movement and Sociological Theories

Research on social movements began at the end of nineteenth century when all the focus was on revolutionary masses who had chosen different ideologies for their revolution. Since then the social scientists have noted the social movement as tool for social change along with, also tended consequently to see it as a disruptive social force, showing abnormal behaviour, and as a challenge to the *status quo*.[76] A social movement is viewed as a joint organized endeavour of a considerable group of persons in some way to change or alter the course of events by their joint activities[77]. The various sociological thoughts have advocated that, social movement basically depends on three aspects, viz. membership base of the organization, leadership of the organization and techniques to spread the message about the goal of the organization/movement. These techniques can be either through propaganda, through mass mobilization or through scientific research.[78]

As quoted by social psychologist the members and their collective impact, ideology, structural problems generated revolutionary activity. Sigmund Freud and his influence is reflected in three terms, viz. frustration of the individual, collective behaviour and neurotic or psychotic personality. As Freud sees, society controls an individual internally or externally which obstructs the achievement of certain drives of a human being which ultimately generate discontent. Individuals, who are obstructed by conditions which they cannot control normally, behave in two ways—first way where they adjust and think rationally, second way is showing their frustrations in aggressive activity. The second case always results in participating in a social movement. Sometimes, it may happen, so that, these individuals who show their aggression towards individuals or groups who are initially not responsible for their conditions. So, the support for such social movement comes from people who are part of a frustrated group. They show their anxiety by becoming the parts of other groups.

There are various kinds of social movements which can be initiated to get power, to monopoly or for territory. Politics does not mean political power nor is solely confined with the government, it is also located at various levels; so, the collective actions are not solely against the government, but at various levels against dominant culture, caste, class. While outlining the conceptual problems of social movements, Rao, M.S.A.[79] outlines in terms of definition and classifications, genesis, ideology, and identity, organization and leadership, internal dynamics and social consequences. He considers social movements as being characterized by three important features:

1. Collective mobilization,
2. Ideology, and
3. Orientation to change.

To explain the genesis of social movement, he examined three theories, viz. relative deprivation, the strain theory and revitalization.

He shows that, the last theories two do not adequately explain the ideological important aspects of a social movement and the social changes which will happen as a consequence. He suggests that theory of relative deprivation has a greater explanatory power as it places the perception of contradiction, conflict, conflict of interest and protest at the centre of social movements. Ideology is considered to be a crucial aspect of any social movement. As regards the problem of the organization of a social movement, Rao discusses the aspects of recruitment, commitment and leadership. He suggests that when a movement develops a high degree of formal organization with sanctions of rewards and punishment, it ceases to be a movement. M.S.A. Rao asserts that relative deprivation is necessary but not sufficient condition for protest movements. He argues, "A sufficient level of understanding and reflection, is required on the part of the participants and they must be able to observe and perceive the contrast between the social and cultural conditions of the privileged and those of the deprived and must realize that it is possible to do something about it.

Shah, G.[80] argues that the theory of relative deprivation ignores the importance of consciousness and the ideological aspects of the participants. It explains protests and movements of revolt, but does not analyse the revolutionary movements. The studies providing a conceptual framework have largely dealt with typologies of social movements during the 1970s. One of the classifying movements is their objectives or the quality of change they try to attain. Shah[81] classifies movements as "revolt, rebellion, reform and revolution to bring about charges in the political system. Reform does not challenge the political system *per se*. It attempts to bring about changes in the relations between the parts of the system in order to make it more efficient, responsive and workable. A revolt is a challenge to political authority, aimed at over-throwing the government. A rebellion is an attack on existing authority without any intention of seizing state power. In a revolution, a section or section of a society launches an organized struggle to overthrow not only the established government and regime but also the socio-economic structure which sustains it, and replace the structure by an alternative social order."

For Partha Mukharji[82], social movements are:

- Accumulative,
- Alternative, and
- Tranformatory.

Accumulative changes are changes within the given structure and system. M.S.A. Rao (1978) also suffers more or less similar typologies:

- Reformist,
- Transformatory, and
- Revolutionary.

All these types do not explain the changes of the movement which undergo over a period of time. It can be said that the typologies are not watertight compartments, they keep on moving from one type to another depending on the social structure, the structures of deprivation and the necessity of the situation. The social movements are also classified based on issues, some are forest rights, civil rights, un-touch ability, linguistic, etc. Naxalite movement can be said as the movement of proletarians or the subalterns who do not have any say in the system and structure. There can be the following types of movements[83]:

1. Peasant Movements,
2. Tribal Movements,
3. *Dalit* Movements,
4. Backward Caste Movements,
5. Women's Movements,
6. Student's Movements, and
7. Workers' Movements.

All the 7 types of movement can be separately discussed because a movement can be classified under the proletarian movement. Naxalite movement derives the name from where it started in West Bengal. The participants of the Naxalbari movement were peasants who were tribals. So, all this can come under the proletarian (Naxalite) movement, as above all sections do not have any say in the hegemony of the system as well as in the society. In this research I have indicated that the Naxalite movement can be well termed as proletarian movement or movement of the sublanterns, it is only for the understanding of the state that it is labelling the movement as Naxalite or Maoist, but the form and the version is slowly transforming into a movement of the marginalised, oppressed, and voiceless people which best suites as movement of the subalterns. Romanticizing the movement as Naxalite/Maoist is to satisfy the States ego which is trying not to disrupt its structures of hegemony and structural violence. It is very necessary to understand the relation between the peoples protest and how it develops, the relationship between the protest and social movement, the relation between social tension and social movement, and how they grow and decrease. It is not easy to capture the dynamics of the social movement as they do change according to the leaders and their approach. So, it is significant to understand the relations.

Sociology as a field of science is about 100 years old, but human culture has evolved before the recognition of sociology. Sociology is a continuous research field for academicians and continuously adds knowledge to our society. In simple term, sociology can be defined as study of society, but looking at the folk traditions and wisdom, it can be defined as a science of human life. The inter-human life occurs in any society, be it modern, primitive, simpler or tribal societies. Life is mixture of events, incidents, accidents and different encounters when people learn, develop insights, reflect and generalize. The folklore is interpreted by people in different ways, these are events of life work, amusement, cooperation and conflict, social production and reproduction, death etc. this amalgamation of things, makes knowledge. Many lose their near and dear ones; tragedies become a part of the life and sometimes it is very difficult to explain such feelings. Society has prescribed social orders for its members to attain the social goals. Few schools have claimed that no social orders gives equal privileges to all its members equally. So conflicts are a part of the society. So, conflicts are realities of society. And every society has to have the minimum realisation of its conflicts to survive. One of the sociological thoughts opines that humans in their earlier/wild state were beasts, but they struggled over a period of time and crossed the stage to modern civilization. This struggle with nature is also followed by inter-human struggles[84]. As the human beings are made good through punishments, rewards and law makes them work. Similarly, the purpose of law is to ensure justice and secure society.

(i) Conflict Theory of Polybius

The monarchy the first strongest rule of the human community and this is essentially concentrated on few power relations. From Monarch the society moved to kingship which was founded on the principles of justice and legal authority. Kingship is based on the ethics that is an obligation on one individual's part that is strong to prevail peace. The members follow the strongest even though they become physically weak and unhealthy. The next ruler of the king does not follow the peace rule and become unruly and forget to keep justice and peace. When this oppression becomes unbearable people unite to overthrow the monarchy. A few noble people who conspired to overthrow the monarchy are supported by the people.[85] The people slowly lose the mission with which they started and aristocracy takes over. The democracy still comes to the picture for a while, people gets suffocated paying bribe and government decided that it is time to restore the monarchy. It is the best solution to have government where there is a mixture of best aspects of kingship, aristocracy and democracy.

(ii) Conflict Theory of Ibn Khaldunte

Khaldun who was believed to be the first true sociologist trusted that social phenomena occurring in society obeys laws which operated on masses and thus cannot be modified or made by few individuals. The social laws can only be discovered with collection of data from a large number. The data must be from past and present events. As societies do evolve and change when they come in contact with other people or classes as a result of following or mixing. Each individual in the society cannot live alone and he or she has to mix up with others to acquire cooperation. So his concepts of social solidarity is a unique property of the society where the kingship, blood relations can be traced, all these aspects unite the smaller societies. But this blood tie has importance only when there is a mutual contact and they evoke the feeling of kinship. The tribal societies are nomadic in nature which require and demand social solidarity. All the places for the nomadic tribes are good and they are self-reliant. A state can be established when has the victory over the other in a process of conflict. The group who wins is move intact and organized religion is the most powerful tool to bring people together and it can be induced if there is a power social solidarity groups. In many cases it is found that it there is a single social solidarity group is present then a religion can be infused compared to a place where there are multiple tribal groups.[86] Similarly, a state must have a suitable solid base initially when it incepts. The authority is not questioned and the inactive life styles, luxurious lives of the few, powers in few hands; all these decay the solidarity of a state. The subjects or the members who were once obedient towards the authority start showing a divide between the rules and the others. The life styles of the rules as a result increase the taxes and as an outcome the state encounters aggression by the people.

(iii) Machiavelli's Conflict Theory

According to Machiavelli, who himself was in prison for 14 years, gave a notion that human beings are basically evil in nature and they show this character if they find an occasion or scope. The desire to win is the most quests for humans. They can be good if they are restricted by law. When people are poor they do hard labour. When human beings were residing at the beginning of the evolution, they were scattered and behaving as beast. But when the human race increased there was a felt need to defend others and to defend self. When few placed themselves at the height and others to obey him or her, then they started to distinguish between the good and bad, honest and dishonest. Machiavelli also agrees to the justice system by Polybius that law has to restrict the people who do badly for others. As long as the king is honest there is always justice. But, if anything goes wrong with the sovereignty then people start conspiring against the rulers. If ruler is not elected then there is no surety of justice. The extravagant rulers evoke a feeling of envy among people which leads to conspiracy. Fear of conspiracy makes the ruler more oppressive in nature. Increase of conspirators gave rise to a new form of rule called aristocracy. This, in turn, becomes corrupt and manipulative. And, it leads towards democracy, which steps into anarchy ultimately to dictatorship. Though Machiavelli was not considered a systematic theorist, his two books have two different political understandings, in first one, he sees all the aspects as political activities and, in the second, he sees them as political forces of a political society. If all the forces are balanced then a state will be stable and liberty is attained.

(iv) Conflict Theory of Bodin

Bodin was a lawyer. His analysis of society was through the lens of history. When his writing was taking shape in the society the French monarchy was weak due to conflict between the Catholic and others. He supported the monarchy against the religious divisions. He believed that family is the foundation of society which is the union of man and woman, where man rules the woman, whereas the state is an association of families with recognized sovereign power. In a state many class differences give rise to relation of superiors and subordinates giving rise to conflict. Bodin defined the power of sovereign as the crux of the civil society. But he never disassociated law from state. Law is treated as the command of sovereign. Customary law is valid only if it is recognized by State. He formulated theories showing the relation between law and custom.

(v) Hobbe's Conflict Theory

Hobbes accepted the concept of materialism between nature and human beings. The thoughts of human being begin with senses which come from memory, visions. All human kind has a desire for power, operating in two ways, in a king and in subjects. The natural relation of any human being is also competition, distrust and struggle. The state has all powers for war and peace and determines right and wrongs.

(vi) David Hume's Theory

Hume presents a picture of the state when many are ruled by few, where many resign and sacrifice their passions for the rulers. How it works, it is only the force which the state applies. State has the right to decide the rights of ownership, and property. The establishment of political society can led to justice and peace where public opinion is a must to involve.

(vii) Adam Ferguson's Conflict Theory

Adam Ferguson, a Professor in Psychology[87] tried to carry out the principles of Hume, and according to him, natural causes also determine the state's growth, sometimes these are external and not willed. He also believed that human beings never lived in isolation, but always lived in groups. And since being part of the society some institutions do come as a force. Conflict in human communities is for good of the human beings and it is meant for the development of the humans. If mankind do not struggle then it can never be aware of its fellows. Through struggles and wars only the mankind has evolved in a form. So, conflict and its various forms do appear in social, political and economic spheres and these forms and power do establish government with struggle. Like other theories, he does believe that consent should be major constituent in any government.

(viii) Turgot's Conflict Theory

Anne Robert Jaccues Turgot who worked in the French bureaucracy developed a concept of plurality which influenced mankind, viz. on customs, traditions, nature of soil, climate of the environment etc. He believed that human mind is same everywhere, but isolation does lead to barbarism. When culture developed, people thought to migrate to other places. This brings social change. During this mobility of people the nomadic and non-migrating cultures interact then a typical array is evolved. Over a period of time they try to rule over each other out of greed. But conflict is the major source of all progress.

(ix) Adam Smith's Theory

Physiocrates believed that society is based on natural order where human beings can think rationally and can control the processes. The characteristics of land is to produce, which is excess where other classes of the society thrive on it. The people engaged in agriculture can add value to it always. Other economic pursuits do come from the agriculture directly or indirectly. So, agriculture must be made free from any kind of obstruction. The state should do activities to protect the economy. This idea of natural order was much elaborated by Adam Smith where he made the agricultural class as the sole responsible for production. He gave two broad ideas: first, the competition in economic affairs should be free where by doing so the maximum productivity can be achieved. The second, the involvement of government should be reduced and natural forces will unite for the requirement of individuals and groups. The traditional conflict theories believe that state as the supreme object whereas physiocrates believed that it is the natural order and struggle for necessities of life[88].

(x) Thomas Malthus' Theory

Thomas Malthus, a Professor in History carried forward the work of Adam Smith and according to him competition can be positive if one sees this to increase accuracy. If we see with negativity the competition produces values where everyone cannot have that. According to Malthus, humankind is in want of more nourishment than what is available for them. In plant life few species prey on each other. Similarly, human population has an inclination to increase the means which support life. Every 25 years the population will double to itself and the soil has to produce in double. The only preventive can be birth control. In this all competitions one competition is to survive where the labour is just paid to live. So in economic terms the conflict rises for economy. As the powerful will always compete to keep their surplus and in way neglecting the other social classes.

E. Conflict

Basically conflict theories have been propounded by many conflict and peace researchers. I have chosen to use Edward Azar's Theory of Protracted Social Conflicts (PSC) as one of the main theories because it identifies causes of a conflict, particularly intrastate conflicts in developing state. I also used Hugh Miall's adaptation of Azar's Theory because it shows how conflicts interact with the government strategies and capabilities and its relevance to the Naxalite movement here. Apart from this two, the hour glass theory and approaches have been supplemented the content.

Conflict research could assume that the whole scenario of conflict is always directed towards the interests of the opposites and where two parties are involved. There can be many more involved in that, but always there are two major parties involved in that. These parties could be two communities, between the two powerful parties or between two opposites who are not in the same power and position. But generally, if we see, some communities are just incredible and fantastic, the people work together and respect each other. Various groups interact with each other and idea takes the shape of action. But some communities are different. People do not have the conducive atmosphere for everything; there is distrust, suspicions and dominance of one group on the other. Violence and crimes become a prevalent phenomenon, and takes the shape of the existing governance. It seems impossible to improve things.

We can separate these two communities in their capacity to face, deal, and resolve with conflicts. Conflicts are a part of life in any community. Conflicts can come out into the open through anger, words, hurtful actions, and ideologies. They can create a climate of fear, intimidation, despair and desperation. Conflicts generally have several layers to them the immediate conflict is often a dispute about some issues or events. That dispute is intensified by an underlying conflict, which involve a history of clashes in values, interests, needs and emotions. This underlying conflict may be intensified because of a deep rooted conflict which goes to the very identity of the people involved. Conflict describes a situation in which two or more actors pursue incompatible yet from their individual perspectives entirely just, goals. Here the perception of the state and the perception of the Naxalites are entirely different and they have their own mindsets on each other and as a result of this there is always an atmosphere of distrust and violence. The resultant factor is always seen as the structural violence by the state in various forms.

> "A conflict exists when two people wish to carry out acts which are mutually inconsistent. They may both want to do the same thing, such as eat the same apple, or they may want to do different things where the different things are mutually incompatible, such as when they both want to stay together, but one wants to go to the cinema and the other to stay at home. A conflict is resolved when some mutually compatible set of actions is worked out. The definition of conflict can be extended from individuals to groups (such as states or nations), and more than two parties can be involved in the conflict. The principles remain the same."[89]

The history of conflict in India can be traced back from the pre-independence period when the country was under the colonial British where there were struggles against the British imperialism in violent and non-violent ways. All the struggles which took place had a definite pattern, background, demographic, religious, socio-ethnic, political or economic structure which led to such kind of resistance and struggle. The conflicts are always seen and misunderstood as law and order problem which can be tackled or sorted out by police action. And at times they are taken with such intensity that they turn into conventional wars where there are few operations and use of weapons. But, it has to be also kept in mind that the conflicts are always people centred and can have the potential to convert an idea into an revolution. So, mere reliance upon arms under operations will only favour the situation towards revolution by people. And, it will not yield any effective results. There are several conflicts in our country where one can see how the idea or the ideology has changed the people and have shook up the conflict in case of Kashmir, Nagaland, Manipur, Darjeeling, and also in case of Naxalites where the idea has germinated in several states.

The definite pattern of conflict as earlier mentioned is always limited to a certain geographical boundary where there is the main thrust and the secondary derivatives and off shoots might exist in other places, but the main geographical area is the focus where tactics and strategies are made from. The main aspects of a conflict are:

- It has both a political and military struggle.

- The struggle to achieve political, social and economic power.
- It is protracted or long in nature.
- It is confined to a particular geographical area.
- The struggle is not a conventional war but it is like a war where the weapons are used.

These all aspects just give the idea of a conflict, but there could be more factors also which characterize a conflict. The struggle can be violent or non-violent, could be civil disobedience to mass destruction. Violent conflicts can be again classified depending on the nature and the degree of support base it gets from the people. The freedom struggle of India want for more than two centuries which was of mixed nature of violence and non-violence where the 1857 was a landmark. Always the conflict has some primary deep-rooted factors along with some secondary factors to act as the backbone of the whole conflict. Today, our country as well as the state of Orissa is undergoing lot of changes and transformations. The globalization has shaped our cultures in a ways that the whole society is going through economic, social and political transformation, where the role of the police is very visible. The society is becoming a volatile or unstable mixture of tribes, races, religion, where violence is playing a key role, be it the communal riots, struggle for state boundaries or the people's conflict over resources.

Various researches and studies have claimed that the Constitution of India is a visionary social document where it has created a conducive atmosphere for social equity. Our country's glory remains with the fact that it has the best document offered to the people. The magnificent principles which were enshrined in the Constitution by our social thinkers, visionaries and the Founding Fathers of it thought that the system will work democratically and the millions of poor people will benefit a lot from this. But the choices are not the same for everyone. The aspirations of the people remained bleak, the few "haves" those think that the market increases economic efficiency but the ground reality is that it has become the main cause of social tension as the deprivation is high. The developing society, like ours today, faces social tensions as due to the visible deprivation persisting. The basic philosophy of development justified the displacement of the people, leading to disruption of their production systems, social culture, and evicting from their resources. Taking into account of the tribal population, it tremendously affected them, impoverished them, dispossessed them, which mainly resulted into tensions.

Now, it cannot be assessed that whether conflict comes first or tension comes first. The various schools thoughts suggest that, these are all the steps of a same ladder resisting structural violence. The similar terminology which is used are grievances, disputes, complaints, conflicts, tension and all these direct towards a movement. Tension is a term which signifies the psychological strain, caused by the malfunctioning, like social, economic, political and other factors. Acute tensions leads to conflict among individuals, groups and it can be between nations.

(i) The Hour Glass Model

The process of conflict escalation is complex and unpredictable, as new issues and parties emerge which can change the struggle. Galtung's ideas on conflict and violence with escalation and de-escalation phases with the hour glass model of conflict.[90] The hour glass represents the narrowing of political space that characterizes the conflict escalation and widening of more space implies the conflict de-escalation. As in case of any conflict, roles of the people who raise voice, they feel that the political space given to them is very narrow. And whosoever to assert his or her rights is branded as a person who is conspiring against the state. So, it is like everyday squeezing their space and the more the space is narrowed the more is the violence. As shown in the figure below, the more it is narrowed, the options become less relevant. So, it is important to refer the phase of the conflict, the nature, the characteristics of the conflict, and the solution must include a comprehensive, and combination of many alternatives to resolve it.

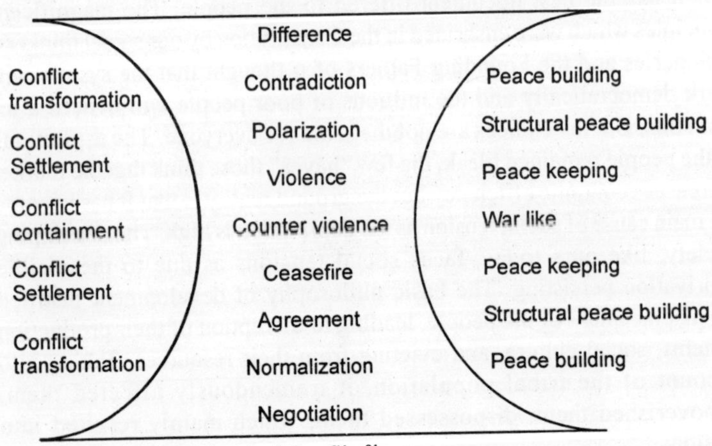

Fig. 1.1: Hour Glass Model of Conflict[91]

The above diagram suggests that if there is any conflict, the conflict ends with ceasefire and peace-keeping, and it increases if the space is less where polarized thoughts develop among the parties involved in the conflict.

(ii) Conflict Approaches

There are different approaches given by peace and conflict researchers but one of the approaches is very important to mention here. Thc below graph shows that, there can be 5 types of approaches to a conflict between the two parties.

(a) The contending (where there is a high concern for self and low concern for others).
(b) The yielding (more concern for others than self).
(c) Low concern for both hence they try to avoid the conflict.
(d) Balancing between the two which is compromising.
(e) A problem solving mode where there is high regard for both.

In any conflict it can be said that, the approaches go on shifting from (a) to (b) or (c) but at a saturated point of time they just oscillate between (a) or (c), but the appropriate would be (e).[92]

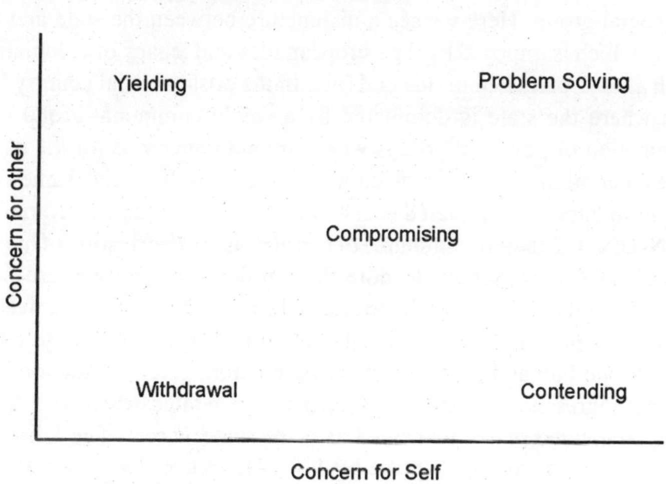

Fig. 1.2: Approaches to Conflict[93]

(iii) Edward Azar's Theory of Protracted Social Conflict (PSC)

According to him there needs to be an understanding of the conflicts through a rigid dichotomy of internal and external dimensions, analysis has to be done on the functional frameworks and always there is tendency seen to focus on the violence in the conflict and ignoring the underlying covert kind of conflicts. When we say this that there is ignorance of these kinds of conflicts, so the absence of violence is always seen as a state of peace or it is equated with state of peace. The term PSC contains that the main source of conflict basically lies within the state, with four variable, viz. communal content, needs, governance and international linkages. These four factors very well can or do contribute to intensify the conflict. These can be listed as follows[94]:

Communal content: Azar focused on identity groups like races, religious, ethnic groups and others. The main onus of the analysis remains on the identity of these groups; and the relationship between these groups with the state is the main focus. This is well said by Azar that the disarticulation between the state and society as a whole. The relationship between such groups and states are crucial to understand conflicts because the state machinery can become dominated by one or several communal groups that are unresponsive to the needs of other groups. Here the individual needs and interests such recognition, security, identity, mediated by a social group. Here we see a disjuncture between the state and the society which is imposed by the European idea and legacy of colonialism which always preached divide and rule. In the post-colonial country like India where the state is dominated by a single communal group or a combination of powerful groups which are not concerned for the needs of the other minor groups which ultimately weakens the social framework and germinates the protracted social conflict as a resultant outcome.

Needs: The underlying source of conflicts is the deprivation of human needs, and it is important to note that unlike interests they are non-negotiable; all human beings have certain basic needs which are universal and they are present or exceed in all cultures and they are not negotiable. Basically no human being is aggressive in nature given a situation they become aggressive and violent. Conflict is generated when their basic needs are denied or are perceived as being under threat. The failure to meet these needs forms the place for PSC. When needs are not satisfied the expression of the discontentment is usually expressed collectively. Malfunctioning by the state or authority to see to the satisfaction of these needs can eventually lead to a PSC. Azar lists security needs, development needs, political access needs and identity needs, the latter meaning in the form of cultural and religious expression.

Governance: State has the power to use force and it has the authority to regulate the force in the name of law and order, to protect its citizens and for good of all. The role of the State is very vital or becomes very vital in meeting the needs of the identity groups and their frustrations. According to Azar "most states which experience protracted social conflict tend to be characterized by incompetent, parochial, fragile and authoritarian governments that fail to satisfy basic human needs." There are three main arguments to this. First, many states are dominated by the largest identity groups, these groups are basically socially strong and the dominant/hegemonic groups and they maximize their interest at the expense of others by using the state. So, the communal content becomes the basis of PSC. Secondly, such monopolization of power and the exclusion or limited access of minor identity groups lead to a "crisis of legitimacy" for the identity group in power. Third, PSCs tend to take place in developing countries with fragile political institutions and authority structures, thus making it difficult for the state to meet the needs of all identity groups. These developing countries who have rigid socio-political structure and colonial legacy, and the society is hierarchical, feudal and in some ways obstruct the state to fulfil the needs.

International linkages: This term relates to the regional and global patterns of client age and cross-border interests. This is related to the economic interests of the state and also the economic dependency within the world economy. These hold significant power and influence over the domestic formation of social and political institutions in a country, particularly modern and weak states. They powerful states in fact control and regulate the weaker or developing country's economic interests to satisfy their own needs. So many developing countries within the framework of global economy are vulnerable to make changes in their state which ultimately affects the groups who are dissatisfied. All these four components have to be present in any PSC and it activates the conflict and this process of conflict is always dynamic with the actions taken by the groups, the actions taken by the state and the mechanisms of the conflict.

(iv) Adapted Framework for Edward Azar Protracted Social Conflict

Hugh Miall has developed on Azar's theory to produce a theory more suited to describe the direction of the conflict intensity, specifically how the patterns of a conflict interact with the satisfaction of human needs, adequate political and economic institutions as well as choices made by political actors[95]. According to the adaptation of Azar's theory a conflict arises from a historical context, from the denial of basic human needs, through suppressive and exploitative roles played by the state, international political and economic linkages and the military in politics[96]. This can be seen when reading the diagram below from left to right. When reading it the opposite direction, we can see how Miall argues that conflicts become destructive when the state and the communal groups base their respective strategies on suppression and violent rebellion. In this event, a conflict intensifies and can, therefore, be called destructive, potentially entering a negative cycle of escalating violence[97].

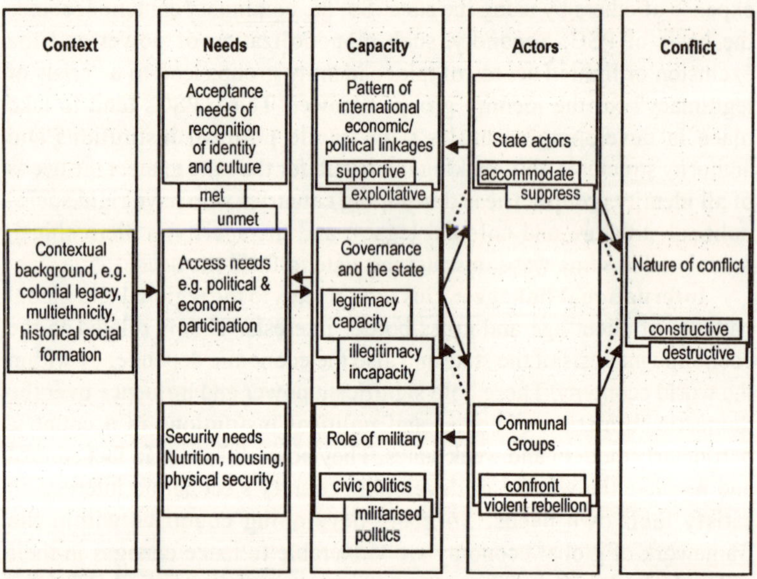

Source: Huge, Miall 2004: 6.

Fig. 1.3: Transformation of Protracted Social Conflict (Azar's Adaptation)[98]

F. Violence

The World Health Organization has defined Violence as the use of physical force with an intention. The use of force or power, could be towards a single individual or to a group, or could be a group. If the use of force results in injury, death, harm or deprivation then this act could be termed as violence. The definition given by WHO includes the death, physical harm and mal-development, which indicates the deprivation of the basic needs (like health, education etc.) is also termed as violence. There three basic types of violence, self-directed violence (which is caused by an individual to himself or herself), interpersonal violence (caused between the two individuals or groups) and collective violence (caused by the group of individuals towards the other group or party). There could be another typology of violence, like physical, psychological, domestic, neglect or deprivation, and sexual. Various schools of thought have broadly defined as social, ecological, and cultural as causes of violence.

Galtung's Theory of Violence

According to Galtung, all conflicts can be seen as a relationship between contradiction, attitudes and behaviours[99]. A contradiction refers to the actual or perceived incompatibility of goals of the conflicting parties. The attitudes include the conflicting parties' perceptions (both good and bad) of each other and themselves, the behaviour refers and reflects in action according to the attitude and contradiction. It can be cooperation or coercion. Furthermore, Galtung argues that all three components must be present for the conflict to deem a full conflict, and that a conflict is a dynamic process in which structure, attitudes and behaviour constantly change and influence one another.

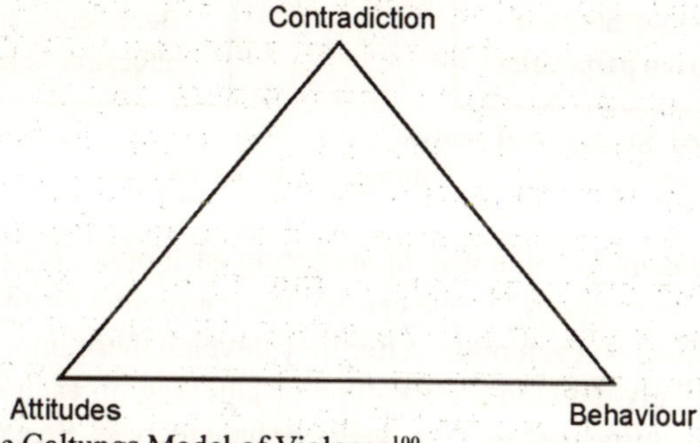

Fig. 1.4: The Galtungs Model of Violence[100]

In 1960s, Johan Galtung proposed this model of violence and conflict that consists of both symmetric and asymmetric relations, as shown in the above diagram that it can be seen as a triangle where C (contradiction), A (attitude) and B (behaviour). The C (contradiction) Mitchell still explains it as mis-match between social values and social structure; in a symmetric conflict, the contradictions are defined by the parties, their interests, and the clash of interests between them. Whereas in an asymmetric conflict, it is defined by the parties, their relationships and the conflict of interests inherent in the relationship[101].

Here Galtung refers that it is important to understand the conflict and violence oy

- How it was formed, who are the actors involved, what are their assumptions, what contradictions do they have and how do they behave with each other in the context of these contradictions. What are their goals and assumptions on each other? It is also important to see the time line/the history of conflict and how it has changed over a period of time.
- This model further can be explained as given the diagram 1.5 below:

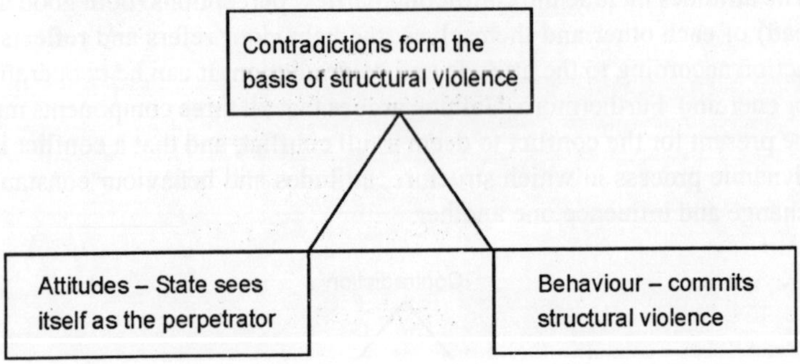

Source: Based on empirical study.

Fig. 1.5: Extension model of Galtungs Theory of Violence

Attitudes include the way of accepting each other, between the two parties, the perceptions, or one can say the impression on each other, the misperceptions on each other. After they develop these impressions they incline or likely develop a stereotype or labelling on each other. These attitudes are influenced by fear, anger, or hate redness. So each party has their own set of attitudes towards the other. These become very significant when the conflict is the violent one.

The bahaviour can be cooperative and can also be non-cooperative. In any conflict where violence is included it can start from threats to coercion, attacks, on each other. Galtung argues that in any conflict these three are to be present, ABC constantly influence each other and they also change over period of time. As this triangle is very dynamic the conflict is seen in their manifestations, the clash of interests is seen more visibly and they develop a particular kind of behaviour. The parties do organize around this interests and the conflict starts to grow and spreads its magnitude. In this process of conflict growing, there are some secondary conflicts which grow in relation to the original conflict. The secondary conflicts include the main parties but also other than that the outsiders who gets into it. So, the violence gets very complicated with full of twists and turns, and the original conflict is never addressed.

G. Social Work Theories

Social work is about dealing with the various problems that surrounds a society. A society is quite complex and has got many social problems which makes it even more complicated. To address such a problem through applying social work is to identify the problem, the source of the problem and then seek a solution for it. The social work theories are basically giving a systematic devise to understand the problem from various angles. Many theories of social work are borrowed from the psychology, sociology and from the field of development. The theories of social work in a way are a body of knowledge which is seen from economic, social and psychological point of view to a problem.

(a) Social Cognitive Theory of Social Work

This theory attempts to understand the social problems psychology of an individual. An individual behaviour affects the society also he or she is affected by the society. The antisocial behaviour, caused in many social problems occurs due to psychological problems. When an individual loses balance he or she shows deviant behaviour. Social cognitive theory aims at solving social problems through counselling at an individual level. It believes on the individual efficiency to power the change that one wants to see in a society.

(b) Conflict Theory of Social Work

Conflict theory aims at the structure of power distribution in a society, through which a major section of the society becomes oppressed. It seeks to improve social condition of the marginalized sections through unity.

Every society has two sides, the 'haves' and 'have-nots', where one section seeks to control power and resources into their hands making others poor. Conflict theory states that to achieve social equality, the marginalized sections should unite and struggle. It is influenced by socialist theory of Karl Marx and Engels and refers to social reform through shift in hierarchy of power.

(c) Social Constructivist Theory

This theory aims at studying how the beliefs, value structure and choices of individuals shape the behaviour of a society and how social dynamics affect individual behaviour. Social workers can devise strategies of bringing about positive changes in a society. Every socially accepted norm started out as a movement by one person and later it was adopted by society. This complex interrelationship of individual and society is studied and the analysis is used to make a difference.

(d) Feminist Social Work Theory

Feminist theories are aimed at studying the special problems of women in a society, who are often marginalized. Theory and practice are aimed at a singular objective of empowering women to take control of their life and restoring the gender imbalance. Of course, every problem in real world is different in itself and it is only through practical application that one can know whether a particular theory is sound or not. Social workers have to experiment a lot with different theories and approaches for a problem, before they can find a solution to a widespread social problem.[102] Social work is a practical job and it needs to make others understand why individuals got into the risk and how they can change their lives. The theories also do include about human growth and development in a society with reference to an individual or to a group. It also includes the theory of cultural change and empowerment theory. Basically, the social work theories encompass from different fields to analyze the problem from different sources.

H. Developmental Theories

The theories of development are a consolidation of various theories which explains on how to achieve the desired change in the society:

(a) *Modernization theory* of development analyzes the way in which modernization processes in societies do takes place. The theory looks at which aspects of countries are beneficial and which constitute obstacles for development.

(b) *Sociological and anthropological modernization theory:* The earliest principles of modernization theory can be derived from the idea of progress, which stated that people can develop and change their society themselves. This theory also states that technological advancements and economic changes can lead to changes in moral and cultural values. Many sociologists describe how social order is maintained in society and ways in which primitive societies can make the transition to more advanced societies. Other scientists argued that economic development leads to social changes which tend to lead to democracy;

(c) *Linear Stages of Growth Model:* Linear Stages of Growth Model is an economic model which is heavily inspired by plan which was used in Europe's economy after the Second World War. It assumes that the economic growth is only possible through industries and it is only restricted by social attitudes. Walt W. Rostow has identified five stages through which developing countries had to pass to reach an advanced economy status: (1) Traditional society, (2) Preconditions for take-off, (3) Take-off, (4) Drive to maturity, (5) Age of high mass consumption. He argued that economic development could be led by certain strong sectors; this is in contrast to for instance of Marxism which advocated that sectors should develop equally.

The Rostow model has serious flaws, of which the most serious are: (1) The model assumes that development can be achieved through a basic sequence of stages which are the same for all countries, a doubtful assumption; (2) The model measures development solely by means of the increase of Gross Domestic Product per capita; (3) The model focuses on characteristics of development, but does not identify the causal factors which lead development to occur. As such, it neglects the social structures which require being present to foster development.

(d) *Post-Development Theory:* This theory questions the idea of national economic development together. According to this theory, the goal of improving living standard leans on arbitrary claims against the desirability and possibility of that goal. Post-development theory came into picture during 1980s and 1990s, according to the idea of development is just a 'mental structure' which has resulted in a ladder of developed and underdeveloped nations, of which the latter desire to be like the before.

(e) *Human Development Theory:* It is a theory which uses the ideas from different origins, such as ecology, development and from the field of welfare. It avoids the norms and focuses on how the social capital is formed and it can be invested to maximize the overall economy of the human capital. Prof. Amartya Sen has worked on this human capital and emphasized on what people can do, the capabilities of people rather than on income or goods which will determine their well-being. This core idea also underlies the construction of the Human Development Index, a human-focused measure of development pioneered by the UNDP in its Human Development Reports.[103]

(f) *The Gandhian Theory of Development:* This theory advocates the rejection of the main stream theory of economics for development and focuses on giving an alternative to the people without emphasizing too much on materials, but also it does not compromise the human development indicators. Gandhi's philosophy of life is to understand Gandhian economics. Gandhi viewed life as a holistic being and not in isolation. According to the Indian scriptures, there are four aspects of an individual's life: *Dharma* (righteousness), *Artha* (money), *Kama* (desire), and *Moksha* (liberation). These aspects are interrelated, and, therefore, all of them should be harmoniously developed. Money is required to satisfy the basic requirements of life, but it is not the sole end in itself. Human's aim is not to increase the desires and to achieve this he or she has to engage whole life in acquiring wealth to satisfy the desires. The goal of life is to control desire and transform it, through righteousness, into liberation. He argues for the liberation of human being from this vicious cycle of *dharma, artha*, *kama* and *moksha*. According to him, true happiness lies in the all-round development of a human being's personality, and in living a full life. Gandhi's ideas on economics are a part of his general philosophy of life, which are as follows:

(1) *Humanism:* Man is both the means, and the end of all activity, and the measure of performance. Everything functions with a human face. All ideas, institutions, and actions are to be judged in terms of whether they help in building a better human being.

(2) *Simple Living*: Gandhi had faith in materialism without lust and passion. Material progress must be submissive to moral growth. The ultimate aim of man is not to accumulate wealth and enjoy luxuries of life, but to attain the higher values of life, and to lead a simple and full life. Simple living and high thinking should be the motto of life.

(3) *Social Justice*: Society is divided between rich and poor, between the **Gandhian Development** strong and the weak, between the privileged and unprivileged, and **Theory** between the elite and the masses. The principle of social justice requires that the former must help the latter in fulfilling their basic requirements. The ideal functioning of the society must aim at providing social justice and reducing inequalities.

(4) *Non-Violence:* Social change is to be brought about through nonviolent methods. Ends and means are inseparable in life, and only good means yield good results. An ideal society can only be established by adopting peaceful and nonviolent means, and not through hatred and war. In Gandhian economics, the principle of nonviolence means the following things: (a) the absence of capitalistic exploitation; (b) the decentralization of production units; (c) cheaper defence organization; (d) less inequality of income; and (e) self-sufficiency of communities.

(5) *Love and Cooperation*: An ideal society should be established on the principles of love and cooperation. In such a society, the love of others and not self-love; co-operation and not egocentric acts, pre-dominate. Relation between humans should be based on truth, love, and cooperation, and not on money and matter.

(6) *Harmony:* The ideal economic condition according to Gandhi is self-sufficiency of the economy. For this, the following harmonies should be maintained: (a) the requirements of the people must be in harmony with the resources of the economy; and (b) production technology should match the country's requirements.[104]

Galtung's Theory of Structured Imperialism

The foundation for Galtung's theory of structural imperialism is the following two facts: the inequality in all aspects of living standard within and between nations, including the inequality in power to decide over this living standard; and the resistance to change this inequality[105]. Galtung uses the term imperialism in a very wide sense, meaning that it can also encompass economic underdevelopment or injustice in general. Galtung argues that the world consists of centre and periphery nations, and that both of these in turn have their own centres and peripheries. The theory of structural imperialism aims to explain the discrepancy between these factions, especially between the centre of the centre and the periphery of the periphery. This relation very well becomes the foundation to derive the model of development.

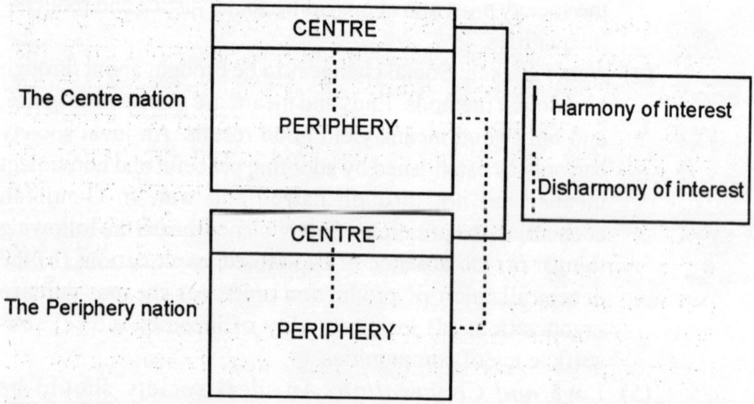

Fig. 1.6: Theory of Structural Imperialism[106]

As illustrated in the figure above, imperialism is a relation between a centre and a periphery nation with the following characteristics (Galtung, 1971: 43):

- There is a harmony of interest between the centre in the centre nation and the centre in the periphery nation.
- There is more disharmony of interest within the periphery nation than within the central nation.
- There is disharmony of interest between the periphery in the central nation and the periphery in the periphery nation.

I. Psychological Theories of Movement

Many of the sociologists have argued the social movements do occur when there is an amount of discontent among the social groups which develop as an insurgency. Sociologists have identified three factors critical to social movements: political opportunity, organizational capacity, and framing ability. They look at social movements as politics by other means, often the only means open to relatively powerless challenging groups. The theories have derived at few conditions which are required for the social movement:

Individual Psychology not so Important

Many works on social movements assumed that activism could be explained by examining the psychological motivations of individuals. Activism came from sensing a gap between what a person is entitled and what he is receiving. But these individual thinking is not sufficient for collection of others.

Prosperity

Poor or marginalised groups cannot afford to sustain the social movements and they only get involved in momentary insurgencies.

Physical Concentration

Bringing people into closer proximity in cities, increases the potentiality of social movement activity.[107]

The study of social problems and social behaviour has been limited by a lack of adequate conceptual tools. This limitation has been manifested in both psychology and sociology, although in different ways. Psychologists have been characteristically unable to deal with the fact of social organization and social structure. Societies and organizations consist of patterned behaviours, and the behaviour of each individual is determined to a considerable extent by the requirements of the larger pattern. This context is not often incorporated into psychological theories. Some such theories—the psychoanalytic, for example—deal with the influence of the family on the individual. Others take some account of the small group as the individual environment, and still others are concerned with the influence of culture, that most global of environmental concepts. Even social psychology, however, has neglected the organizational and institutional level. The basic aspect is to understand here the psychological point of view has never covered the large contexts which influence the behaviour of the individuals and groups which are very important to understand the psychology of social movements. On the other hand the sociological theories are always focused on the super organic or the collective behaviour leaving behind the individual behaviour and their interaction. They always stress on the outcome of such interactions but with the process through which such interactions takes place. To develop a comprehensive framework for predicting the effectiveness of behaviour required for organizational effectiveness, the different motive patterns to be understood.

Three categories of behaviour are required to achieve high levels of organizational effectiveness according to the psychological theories, people must join and remain in the organization; they must perform dependably the roles assigned to them; and they engage in occasional innovative and cooperative behaviour beyond the requirements of role but within the organizational objectives.

Four motive patterns are proposed to achieve the required behaviours in varying degrees. These are legal compliance, instrumental satisfaction, self-expression, and internalization of organizational goals.

Legal compliance is evoked by the use of clear-cut symbols of authority, backed by the use or threatened use of penalties. It tends to produce performance at the minimum acceptable level, and to generate no particular willingness to remain in the organization when alternatives are available.

Instrumental satisfaction is evoked by the use of rewards, and is more strongly evoked as the rewards are immediate, constant, and adequate. In general, system rewards hold people in the system, but do not necessarily encourage more than minimally acceptable performance and are ineffective for stimulating innovative behaviour. Individual rewards for performance are difficult to apply in large-scale organizations and many individual do behave differently as per own whims and pleasures. but under the proper conditions of immediacy, constancy, and adequacy can lead to increased productive effort. This occurs in any movements.

The motive of self-expression depends primarily on objective attributes of the job itself. As the job increases in complexity, variety, and responsibility, the individual has increased opportunity to express his skills and abilities through performance on the job. High productivity and strong attraction to the occupational system are characteristics of this motive pattern.

The internalization of organizational goals is at once the most effective of motive patterns and the most difficult to evoke within the limits of conventional organizational practice and policy. The extent of internalization depends upon the character of the organizational goals themselves, and their congruence with the needs and values of the individual. It depends also on the extent to which the individual shares actively in the determination of organizational decisions and in the rewards which accrue to the organization. Many times it is found that in movement organizations many members tend to internalize deeply and others only come for vested interests. (www.hrfolks.com)

J. War

War is a species of the genus of violence; more specifically, it is collective, direct, manifest, personal, intentional, organized, institutionalized, instrumental, sanctioned, and sometimes ritualized and regulated, violence.

"War is nothing but a continuation of political intercourse with a mixture of other means". Generally, war has been conceptualized as (1) a socio-political phenomenon; and (2) a judicial or legal phenomenon. According to the first conceptualization, war, in principle, can only take place between sovereign political entities (tribes, fiefs, nation-states, empires etc.). According to the judicial conception, war is "a legal condition which equally permits two or more hostile groups to carry on a conflict by armed force".

According to many cultural anthropologists, the difficulties of setting definitional boundaries around such concepts as 'war' and 'violence'. These difficulties are twofold. First, the terms express cultural categories; and, secondly, even as cultural categories warfare and violence are not phenomena they occur as part of many kinds of social relationships and cultural forms (Greenhouse, 1987). A number of anthropologists distinguish 'war' from 'warfare'.

While warfare refers specifically to the process or activity of battle, war refers more broadly to the institution (e.g., Nettleship, 1975), 'War' any series of events that meets the following three criteria:

(1) *Size*: It results in at least 1,000 battle deaths (not counting the indirect casualties);
(2) *Preparation*: It has been prepared in advance, and/or is being maintained by large-scale social organizations; and
(3) *Legitimation*: It is legitimized by an established governmental or quasi-governmental organization, so that, large-scale killing is viewed not as a crime, but as a duty[108].

For primitive war the figure may either be proportionally reduced or the criterion of size eliminated altogether as irrelevant. The most general, yet precise and delimiting, definition of primitive war has been presented by Prosterman (1972): "A group activity, carried on by members of one community against members of another community, in which it is the primary purpose to inflict serious injury or death on multiple non-specified members of that other community, or in which the primary purpose makes it highly likely that serious injury or death will be inflicted on multiple non-specified members of that community in the accomplishment of that primary purpose".

This definition thus identifies war as (1) a group enterprise; (2) directed not internally, but against a second community; (3) directed not against one individual or a specific family, but against any members of the opposing community—or at least any armed, adult, male members—who 'get in the way' or offer resistance; and (4) aimed either at killing members of the other community, or at some goal that makes it likely they have to be killed in accomplishing it.

This definition clearly excludes the murder of one man by another or a group attack on a specific individual or family, as in a blood feud or a revenge killing.

Malinowski's (1941) analysis of war is perhaps the best known example of this point of view.[109] Dividing the history of 'social fighting' into six stages, he reserves the term war for hostilities fought in the pursuit of national policies by organized forces. The presented stages are:

(1) Fighting, private and angry, within a group belongs to the type of breach of custom and law and is the prototype of criminal behaviour.
(2) Fighting, collective and organized, is a juridical mechanism for the adjustment of differences between constituent groups of the same larger cultural unit. Among the lowest savages these two types are the only forms of armed contest to be found.
(3) Armed raids, as a type of man hunting sport, for purposes of head-hunting, cannibalism, human sacrifices, and the collection of other trophies.
(4) Warfare as the political expression of early nationalism, that is, the tendency to make the tribulation and tribe-state coincide, and thus to form a primitive nation-state.
(5) Military expeditions of organized pillage, slave-raiding, and collective robbery.

(6) Wars between two culturally differentiated groups as an instrument of national policy.

This type of fighting, with which war in the fullest sense of the word began, leads to conquest, and, through this, to the creation of full-fledged military and political states, armed for internal control, for defence and aggression. The following conditions are necessary for true war: (1) Tactical operations; (2) Definite command and control: Without definite military authority in control throughout the action, there exists only a bloody brawl; (3) Ability to conduct a campaign for the reduction of enemy resistance if the first battle fails: This is a much higher condition than that of the mere raid, and implies more self-discipline and social organization; (4) The motive must have some clarity: The war must have a group motive rather than an individual one, or even one based on kinship. True war is above the plane of feuds; it is a political device; (5) An adequate supply.

The same theme was picked up by Hoebel (1949), who regards war as a complex institution that involves definite purpose and organized sustained assault. According to him, true war has four necessary conditions: (1) A group motive, (2) Leadership, (3) Tactical operations, and (4) Ability to sustain advisories of assaults until the aim of the war is attained.

In summary, the most important conclusions to be derived from the Wright study are the following:[110]

- War as a legitimate instrument for plunder or conquest is little known among primitive peoples.
- Primitive peoples only rarely conduct formal hostilities with the object of achieving a tangible economic or political result.
- Neither territorial conquest nor seizure of slaves nor plunder of economic goods is characteristic of primitive warfare.
- Wars for political domination, so important among civilized peoples, hardly exist among the primitive collectors.
- Wars of independence are unknown among the most primitive peoples because slavery, subjection, and class stratification are unknown.
- War to proselytize others to their religion is unknown among primitive people.
- The most primitive peoples, isolated and uncorrupted by contact with higher cultures, often have neither war nor brutality in their mores.

K. Peace

Peace has always been the highest form of human value which cannot be comprised at any cost. The most disadvantageous form of peace is also opted against the form of war. It is the opposite of conflict, war and violence. The concept of peace is very difficult to define. The simplest of articulating it in terms of harmony achieved by the absence of war or conflict. Applied to nations, this would mean the states that are not in conflict with the neighbouring states, have achieved a state of peace. This is what Johan Galtung defined as a "negative peace"—an absence of violence[111]. Peace can be of two types as per the conflict researchers—Positive and Negative. The absence of war is termed as negative peace. The concept of negative peace is immediately spontaneous and empirically measurable, and can be used as a starting point to elaborate its counterpart concept, "positive peace": having established what constitutes an absence of violence.

The *Global Peace Index* is a first step in this direction; a measurement of peace as the "absence of violence" that seeks to determine what cultural attributes and institutions are associated with states of peace. In 1999 the UN General Assembly launched a programme of action to build a "culture of peace" for the world's children, which envisaged working towards a positive peace of justice, tolerance and plenty. The UN defined a culture of peace as involving values, attitudes and behaviours that:

- Reject violence,
- Endeavour to prevent conflicts by addressing root causes, and
- Aim at solving problems through dialogue and negotiation.

It proposed that such a culture of peace would be furthered by actions promoting education for peace and sustainable.

Peace is also defined and approached as:

- Peace is a process—many sided, never ending struggle to transform violence.
- Peace is not mere absence of war. That is the first step towards peace. Sustainable peace is peace with justice, universal rights, economic well-being, ecological balance and other values.
- Absence of war is described as 'cold peace' and it is contrasted with 'warm peace'.
- Stable peace is a relatively rare state.

A sustained attempt by the main antagonists or who have a polarised view on each other in a conflict (including the government as party) to reach a stage on the main issues in a prolonged or protracted dispute. It is an attempt to lower the costs of the conflict, conflict management initially. The term 'peace process' suggests and opens to a new thought of diversified thinking in all dimensions more than an isolated peace initiative and the process should be able to withstand certain pressures. Stages of this process include conflict, pre-negotiation, confidence building and till it reaches to a stage of institutionalisation. The peace process can be seen as peace building, peace keeping and peace-making, the most important being the peace building,

Peace building process aims, at

- In addition to *humanitarian aid* or *emergency assistance,* designed to provide immediate means of survival for populations at risk, the UN's main categories of intervention are:
  - *Peace making*—to end hostilities and bring about agreement using diplomatic, political and military means.
  - *Peace keeping*—enforcing and monitoring an agreement and supervising confidence building activities.
  - *Peace building*—undertaking programmes designed to address the causes of conflict and grievances of the past and to promote long-term stability and justice.

Peace Building may contain the following:

- Peace Making
- Peace Keeping

This is an array of processes, for transforming conflicts, for peaceful relationships, more describes then defined. Like dealing with mediation, negotiation, building an atmosphere.

The process includes activities which releases from tension and violence, and resettlement, provision of security; reconstruction of infrastructure, rebuilding of economy, legal systems and bureaucracy reconciliation; civil society enablement and involvement, community empowerment, democratisation; reconstruction of relationships and many more innovative genuine thoughts and efforts.

- Cessation of direct violence is negative peace.

- Overcoming structural violence and cultural violence is positive peace.
- Structures oriented, actors oriented and culture oriented, who decides and who does whether vertical or horizontal, whether neutral timeline, the interests of various actors.
- Liberal peace as defined by different major actors…more securitized.
- Reconciliation.
- Reconciliation is a process through which a society moves from a divided past to a shared future, one mind and one heart, with humanity.

Aims and Objectives of the Study

As mentioned earlier in the area of study, the present research only focused on tribal participation and their role. This is an empirical study which emphasized on the following objectives:

1. To enquire and understand the socio-cultural and economic background of all the tribal communities associated with the Naxal movement.
2. To enquire about the socio-cultural forms of involvement and participation.
3. To explore the role of the pre-literate and elite tribals in the movement.
4. To investigate about the family support and opposition in the Naxal participation.
5. To collect data in detail on the economic grounds of Naxal participation on the following factors:
   (a) How much one earns by participation.
   (b) How much his or her family is taken care of in his or her absence (because of participation).
   (c) What is the ultimate gain or loss?
   (d) Political and other motivations behind the Naxal participation.
   (e) Role of various age groups (unmarried youth, married, traditional leaders) of the tribals in Naxal participation.
   (f) To reveal the role of women in movement on process.
   (g) Situations favouring and encouraging tribals for joining Naxal movement.
6. To enquire about the stand of State and Central Governments in controlling the Naxal movement.

7. To enquire about other ancillary bodies (other organizations, institutions, registered or not registered) of Naxal movement.
8. To know about the support of the inter-tribal and intra-tribal institutions in the Naxal movement.
9. To suggest alternatives for the Naxalite movement and how to bring back them into the main stream.

Methods and Techniques of Data Collection

The present piece of study is empirical in nature to be conducted in a holistic manner. Review of literature has been done to have a deeper understanding of the situation both at the national and state levels. Attempts have been also made to have an understanding the international scenario. This research includes samples from Naxal rebellions/activists and villagers where the activities of Naxalites are more. The Universe of the study is South Orissa, comprising four districts, namely Koraput, Malkangiri, Rayagada and Gajapati for the research.

As per the various reports, the following blocks are Naxal affected which are mentioned as follows (wherefrom the data have been collected):

Table 1.1: Universe of the Research

Sl. No.	*Name of the Districts*	*Name of the Blocks*
1.	Koraput	Bandhugaon Narayanpatna Pottangi Nandapur Lamtaput Boipariguda
2.	Rayagada	Gudari Padampur Chandrapur Muniguda
3.	Malkangiri	Kalimela Motu Mathili
4.	Gajapati	Mohana R. Udayagiri Nuagaon.

The research has been defined into two broad major classifications as far as participation is considered—active and passive participation. As shown in Fig. 1.7.

Under Active participation jailed activists (38 no.), underground activists (36 no.) and open activists were taken as sample size. Under Passive participation persons were interviewed from their frontal organizations and others who sympathized with the Naxals. So, the last category which included respondents from three major sections as per the diagram, the open activists, members of the frontal organizations and others who were old members which constitute 128 in number (the interview schedules are given in Annexures 1 and 2).

The major 4 District Jails, viz. Koraput, Malkangiri, Gajapati and Rayagada were taken. The researcher obtained permission from I.G. (Prisons), Orissa to interview the under trial jailed Naxalites for the research. Except in Rayagada there were no cases as on, when the researcher went for her data collection. In Koraput, Malkangiri and Gajapati (Parlakhemundi) District Headquarters Jail, the researcher could interview around 38 jailed Naxalites.

The study also included the interviews with the spokesperson of Orissa state committee of CPI (Maoist) and his views. Apart from the Naxalites in Jail the researcher could venture into the forests of the universe and interviewed 36 rebellions inside the forest. Data were also collected from villagers where the activities are more. Case study material was applied while collecting data from individual naxal rebellions (both inside the Jail and Forest). Whenever necessary focus group discussion and participatory observation techniques was applied. Apart from the above, data were collected from a cross-section of population from government officers which included police department also, members of civil society organization, students, teachers, advocates, and media to know their opinion on the issue.

At the outset, I extensively used the method of observation to note down peoples day-to-day living, pattern in order to understand their culture. I prepared schedules, and interview guides to enquire about the basic grounds of their involvement in the naxal movement. I also formulated 12 working hypothesis for the systematic progress of the research work.

Key informant interview schedules were developed for the case studies, and interview guidelines were used for the cross-section of population. Eight interviews were taken from those people in the universe who actively participated in the Naxalite movement which was parallel to the Naxalbari movement in the south Orissa during 1966-1970. All these eight persons were from Koraput, Rayagada, Gajapati and Malkangiri. It was very unfortunate that the two respondents comrade

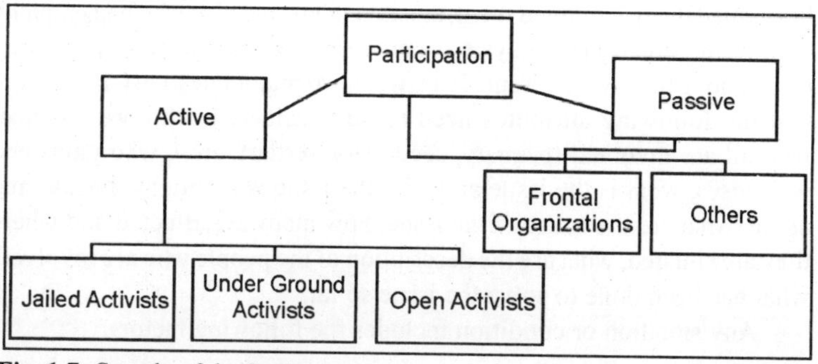

Fig. 1.7: Sample of the Study

Bhuban Mohan Pattnaik passed away in 2009 and Shri Biswanath Pattnaik popularly known as Gandhi of Koraput also departed from the world in 2010. All total 120 sample size have been taken for the study and analysis. All the case studies have been taken from only tribals who belong to Halva, Bhumia, Saora, Jatapu, Kondha, Paraja and Gond. Observation technique was used to capture the daily lives of the naxal activists in the camps. Case studies of the jailed Naxalites and the Naxal activists who surrendered were also included.

Apart from the primary data, lot of party/organization literature has been collected from Communist Party of India (Maoist) and from their frontal organizations which are banned from May 2006. Lot of articles from various sources, librarians, CDs of the Naxal activities where collected for the study. Few interviews were recorded during the data collection, as taking photographs were not allowed to the researcher. Few reports from the government and also from the civil society organizations were collected. The researchers to the maximum extent collected the new clippings of the local media in the universe. This whole gamut of the data was generated for the research.

In this, piece of research keeping in view the specific tribal situations in south Orissa, I have used situational analysis both extensively and intensively. **Situational analysis** of the south Orissa with regard to Naxalite movement in general, and tribals participation in particular can be seen from two sides from the potential factors of participating and also from the negative aspect of why there is so much involvement of the tribals in it. The situation not only depends on the tribals but also the other factors, viz. social, economic, environmental factors which influence them or has impacted them to do so. When I say other factors like social etc. I also say that the past history of the Koraput region, people who have ruled them, exploited them, agitated them, and also who had empathy with them. Situational analysis is a process to identify the issue and what can be done to solve the issue. It answers two major questions. But before that the following attributes need to be considered, who are affected, who all are involved (primary, secondary, tertiary etc.), who gains and who loses, what is the issue and why the issue is highlighted again and again, what are the cause of the issue, how many are affected and where they are situated, what are the description of the people who are involved, what has been done to solve the issue so far.

Any situation or condition includes the following factors:

1. An examination of the state, and status of the people and environment. It does not limit to only eco-systems but also the pattern in which it was developed and how the external factors acted on it to gear up these patterns.
2. It is also important to identify the problems of the region and how they have affected their lives and what requires immediate notice.
3. When we see the past history of a region, their patterns of influencing the ecosystem by outsiders, and how the external factors influenced the people. Then it is also needed to analyse how the external factors have violated their rights, and needs of the people and how these external factors manage the conflict and solve them. Along with this, it's significant to see that how the people have appealed, and solved their issues.[112]

Situational analysis is seen through strengths, weaknesses, opportunities and threats where few responses are empirically used to view the issue in a unique manner. In a conflicting situation it is seen from different perspectives. Here when I say different perspectives I mean,

- How different people view the same situation differently?
- How different people think about the root causes of the issue?
- How different people give a sense or meaning, or define the issue?
- How different people think what are important for the issue?
- How different groups think that can be done for the issue?

And what can be done to solve the issue or what can be adopted to solve the issue as different groups believe.

Working Hypothesis

Even though I took up all the scientific methods and techniques usually adopted in a social science research, the formulation of hypotheses always works like a gear box which increases the pace of the research on a systematic path. Therefore, after getting into the problems of the tribal people who are both active and passive participants, I could be able to gather some fundamental issues both indigenous and exogenous. Basin on these I shall be able to formulate the hypotheses in the following manner, keeping in mind the theoretical inputs:

(1) Naxal movement, like any other movement never had sudden rise from the people's grievances and sufferings to the battle field of movement. It takes up all the basic steps in a long run basis like people's sufferings due to exploitation, crossing the limit of their tolerance, the long term awaiting for the justice and solutions, the extent of exploitation by the outsiders (mostly officials) and then motivation by the activist leaders and finally, leading to the enforcement for joining the Naxal force.

(2) Even though the tribals are illiterate or pre-literate, in the face of suffering, exploitation and prolonged economic backwardness, they are compelled to accept the naxal ideology with immediate effect.

(3) Tribals as per their cultural standards accept readily and comfortably the matters which are served at their door step. Whereas government officials hardly reach the tribal people face to face, naxal leaders reach people at their door step and able to convince them comfortably to join Naxalite movement.

(4) The exploitation of money lenders, landlords and other opportunist migrant population (in addition to government officials) are most often taken as clue and supportive cause for motivating the tribals to join Naxalite movement.

(5) Primary and subsequent observations in the tribal area confirm that most of the tribals after joining the movement are so much so red-marked that they fear to come back to normal life even if they realise their breaching of law and order of the State. In case of extreme torture only, they take a drastic decision to come back and surrender.

(6) Even though Naxalite movement proceeds on a single track basing on a single ideology it has not been able to maintain

consistency and uniformity because of variable strategic operations of the government and variations in the local cultures (economic as well as cultural backwardness). Like Naxal ideology, the participation of people especially the tribals never accept the movement in a similar manner, variations emerge as a result of their economic backwardness and cultural variations.

(7) As regards, the inclusion of the tribals in the movement process, it is verified that tribals everywhere in south Orissa are more or less from similar or uniform cultural bases. In some districts, tribals accept and support the movement in order to take revenge on the exploiting population and come forward to join in some districts the movement without any choice; in some districts they see it as an alternative way to ventilate their anger. It is also true that in some areas where government activities are satisfactory, people hesitate to join the movement.

(8) Besides the cultural and other local variations, the participation in the movement always takes a bi-fold path; firstly, some people because of the surrounding problems remain as active participant and others who are not very much affected, only ideologically remain as passive participant of the movement.

(9) From ideological point of view, the Naxal movement had attracted the attentions of the economically backward tribals, but as observed from different incidences (as published in the media), the ideology is noticed to be diluted due to the incorporation of personnel's vested interests of some leading Naxal ideologues and their activists.

(10) As known at the international, national and at the state level, the sovereign governments most often follow the incidences of movement, whereas the movement makers always take a strategically superior stand by following an offensive role in the whole process.

(11) As observed anthropologically, the solutions to such an undesired movement process seem to be far reaching mainly because, there is no absolute solution—seeking dialogues, compromises and compromising attitudes between the two parties involved, so far.

(12) The conflicting and confronting attitudes of both sides are ought to create bloody fights and loss of human lives. In fact, the two parties involved in the conflict (leading to movement) are at fault, which they never realise. Therefore, unless both the parties sincerely desire for a solution, no solution would be possible.

Difficulties Faced

The first and foremost hurdle was to select such a topic and to probe into the tribal factors in it. It took more than one and half years for data collection which is of little deviation from the work plan as mentioned in my synopsis. This was due to the various operations and blasts conducted by the Naxalites which stopped my fieldwork. Whenever I used to visit the affected areas people never responded me. They used to think that I am a police informer. I want to quote very strongly that I almost became a person who is in between the Naxal and their supporter and the administration. When I used to approach the police or the government for my research they used to brand me a Naxal sympathizer. I had to explain them time and again that I am an independent researcher who is doing Ph.D. on the subject. They were very much doubtful about the credibility of such a research work. During one of the interaction with an academician who is in a very good position in Education Department, addressed me as Naxal because I am doing research on Naxalite Movement. It was very awkward and very much irritating situation for me before others, though I argued with him. But, inside my heart I was very angry and sad. When I working with the people, the government authorities very much eager to know my findings. Similarly, experiences I faced where the Naxalites also doubted my integrity and often feel reluctant to tell the crucial factors. However, I had to take a big time to convince both sides to trust me and allow me to at least finish the work as per the scientific procedures.

When I was interviewing one of the very high police officials, he asked me.... Tell me the names of those with whom you are talking and taking their interviews. I told him I am doing research and as per the research ethics I can't disclose the identity of my respondents, if I do so it would be unethical. I think still in Orissa, people need to understand the essence and importance of research on such conflicting issues.

Whenever I used to go for interviews to Jails, the official used to ask me what they said, what is their opinion. Time and again I was explaining the officials that after the submission of my book only I can disclose its and not before that. The main difficulty I faced is the branding me as a Naxal sympathizer which was very hard on my part to accept. As I believe in principles of non-violence, which was coined by the Mahatma Gandhi to all the coming generations of our country. Due to various operations / attacks by CPI (Maoist) in Rayagada, and Malkangiri I could not extend my fieldwork after July 2008 due to interstate combing operations, it was very difficult on my part to meet the activists. But again continued after the situation was normal. But the fieldwork had halts at different times due to the operations by the state and the operations by Naxals. So, it took me more than two and half years to complete my data collection in the four districts. It was indeed a splendid experience.

Rapport Established

It is very difficult to name on label who is a Naxal looking at the reports and media notes. Everyday there is somebody who is arrested and he or she is branded as Naxal ideologue. A person who is talking against the system is a Naxalise, a person who is anti-industries is a Naxalite, and a person who is moving with guns in the forest is also a Naxalite according to the various sources. And if a person shows sympathy towards the movement is also a Naxalite, a person if keeps their literature by chance is a Naxalite, if a person has links with them is also Naxalite. This is a whole preview of Naxalite definition in our Orissa State as on today.

So far me it was very difficult to identify who can at least help me to reach out to those people who are inside the forest. And it is a topic that one cannot discuss with anyone and everyone. I had to be very cautious in the process. But during my pilot study I visited the affected blocks as mentioned earlier and asked the people about the areas in that block from where the activists come. I took them into my confidence and they helped me a lot in providing me data on the area, their location, the timings of their visit and also about their support base in big cities like Bhubaneswar, Rourkela, Cuttack, Puri. It was surprising for me to know that few people who work with the government but do extend a heart for the movement. It was interesting to note that rich people in big cities do extend support for the movement. So, everything is very secret and underground in this movement. But my main source of help is the villagers, also one really suffering everyday and very angry on the system, they paved my wave into the areas where I could go and collect my data.

References

1. *Yojana*, February 2007, p. 3.
2. Bante, A. and Otero, G., 2000, *Yojana*, February 2007.
3. *Harijan* (18-01-1942).
4. Party Documents 2004.

5. Party document on formation of the united communist party 2004.
6. Banerjee, Sumanta (2005). *Hobsons Choice for Indian Communist EPW*, Vol. XL, No. 19.
7. Banerjee, Sumanta (2005). All quest on the Maosim Fornt. *EPW*, Vol. XL, No. 6.
8. Banerjee, Sumanta (2006). Beyond Naxalbari: *EPW*, Vol. XLI, No. 29.
9. Banerjee, Sumanta (2006). Peasant Haves and Capitalist Hounds of Singur, *EPW*, Vol. XLI, No. 52.
10. *EPW Commentary*, June 01, 2002, Naxalbari: Between Past and Future Banerjee, Sumanta.
11. *EPW*, Feb 18, 2006, Under Development and Naxal Movement, Kujur, Rajat.
12. *Jungle ku Rasta*, Abhay Mohapatra, 1960 (its a Oriya book based on Gandhi of Koraput, Late Biswanath Pattnaik).
13. Propaganda of 1963-64 in Oriya (which was used in Orissa and Koraput by the then Communist party. Scanned and given).
14. Merger Party documents.
15. *Social Movements in India*, A Review of Literature, G. Shah, 2006.
16. "Social Movement". (http://www.shvoong.com/social-sciences).
17. *Social Movements in India* (ed., by M.S.A. Rao, 2000).
18. *Social Movement in Orissa* by Subash Ch. Padhy (2008).
19. *The Oriya Movement* by Niranjan Pattnaik (1919).
20. *Intelligentsia as a Ruling Class*, Ashok Rudra, (*Indian Economic Review*, XXIV, 2006, pp. 2 to 6).
21. T.K. Oommen published in 1972; with the title *Charisma, Stability and Change*.
22. Examining different issues in movement was started. S.C. Malik (1977).
23. Clarifying concepts relevant in the study of movement, in a special number of *Sociological Bulletin* (1977), T.K. Oommen & P.N. Mukherji.
24. *Unbroken History of Broken Promises* (2010) by B.D. Sharma.
25. *Political Violence and the Police in India,* Subramaniam, K.S. (2007).
26. *Searching for Peace in Central and South Asia*—an overview of conflict prevention and peace building activities (ed., 2003, p. 5).
27. Barash, David and Webel, Charles have brought the 2nd ed., of their book *Peace and Conflict studies* (2009).
28. There is no to way to peace and peace is the way, wrote theologian and antiwar activist, A.J. Muste (2005, p. 4).
29. Guha, A., in his book *Peace Diplomacy* (http://www.vedamsbooks.in/no48384/peace-diplomacy-amalendu-guha)
30. *Economy of Colonial Orissa (1866-1947)* by Samla, J.K. (2000).
31. *The Unrest Axle* ed., by Gautam Bera, (2008).
32. (http://www.rediff.com/news/slide-show/slide-show-1-kashmiri-freedom-movement-has-been-derailed/20100906.htm)
33. C*onflict Resolution,* conflict management and conflict transformation. Ramsbotham, Oliver *et al.* (2nd ed., 2008).

34. *The monograph on the life of Dongria Kondhs* gives an analytical description of clan feuds. Nayak, P.K. in his research *Blood, Women and Territory*—An analysis of Clan feuds of Dongria Kondhs (Reliance Publishing House, 1989).
35. *Crime and Customs in Savage Society* by Malinowski, B. (1925, pp. 4 to 8).
36. *Criminology and Penology*, by Korn, R. Richard and Corkle (1960, pp. 10 to 16).
37. *Ethnicity, Movement and Social Structure contested Cultural Identity*, edited by Bhadra and Bhadra (2007).
38. *Tribal Movements in India* by Jitendra Prasad, (2005. pp. 15 to 30).
39. (http://www.worldliveevents.com/naxalite-movement-in-india).
40. *Revolutionary Violence: Maoists Movement in India,* by Mohanty, Manoranjan (1977).
41. *Naxal Movement and State Power with Special Reference to Orissa*, (Dash, Satya Prakash, 2006).
42. *The Naxalite Movement in India*, by Singh, Prakash (2006).
43. *Towards Naxalbari* (1953-1967), is an account of the inner party ideological struggles by Pradip Basu (2000).
44. Chakravarti, Sudeep (2008), *Red Sun Travels in the Naxalite Country.*
45. *Maosim in India—Reincarnation of Ultra Left wing extremism in the Twenty First Century,* Rajat, Kujur and Bidyut Chakrobarty (2010).
46. Maoists in Nepal from Insurgency to Political main Stream, by B. Upreiti, (2008).
47. *Terrorism in India's North-East*, a gathering storm, by Ved Prakash (2008 in three volumes).
48. *The Naxal Challenges—Causes, Linkages and Policy Options* (ed., P.V. Ramana, 2008).
49. Gandhi and *Mao* (in quest of analogy) by Dr Ratan Das (2004).
50. *Economic and Political Weekly*, November 21, 2009 (Vol. XLIV, No. 47) by D'mello, Bernard.
51. Oriya Local Newspapers of Jeypore edition from 2008, 2009 and 2010.
52. In the year 2002 a Pro-Naxalite sympathizer started http://www.geocities.com/cpimlpwg (Currently deleted).
53. http://web.archive.org/web/*/ http://www.geocities.com/cpimlpwg.
54. http://web.archive.org/web/20021012230004/www.geocities.com/cpimlpwg/docu.html
55. http://web.archive.org/*/http://www.geocities.com/cpimlpwg
56. http://webarchive.org/web/20030823153035/http://peoplesmarch.com/
57. http://peoplesmarch.googlepages.com/ 58. http://www.bannedthought.net/India/
58. http://www.bannedthought.net/india
59. http://springthunder.blogspot.com/
60. http://naxalnext.blogspot.com/

61. http://cpimaoist.blogspot.com/
62. http://resistanceindia.blogspot.com/
63. http://maoistresistance.blogspot.com/
64. http://rcpkarnataka.blogspot.com/
65. http://tamilporali.blogspot.com/
66. http://rdf-2005.blogspot.com/
67. http://rpikeral.blogspot.com/
68. www.smwnews.com
69. www.writetokill.com
70. http://mikeely.wordpress.com/; http://naxalrevolution;.blogspot.com/search/label/Links
71. In *Anthropology of Law, a Comparative Theory* (1971, p. 5) Leopold Pospisil.
72. *Ibid.* (1971, p. 128).
73. Franks (*Politics of Law and Ritual in Tribal Society*, by Gluckman, Max 1971, p. 181).
74. www.oxforddictionaries.com
75. *Social Tensions/Conflicts and their Functions*, Vol. XLVIII, No. 3, July-Sept., 2002.
76. Bush, Gary and Serge. R, *Social and Political Movements*, 1971, p. 2.
77. *Ibid.*, p. 3.
78. *Ibid.*, p. 121.
79. Rao. M.S.A., *Social Movement in India,* 2006, p. xvii.
80. Shah, G., *A Review of Literature*, 2001, p. 28.
81. *Ibid.*
82. Partha Mukharji (1977), in *A Review of Literature*, Sage 2001, p. 29.
83. Shah, G., *A Review of Literature*, 2001, p. 30.
84. Martindale, Don, *The Nature and Type of Sociological Theories,* 1961, p. 130.
85. *Ibid.*
86. *Ibid.*, p. 131.
87. *Ibid.*, p. 140.
88. *Ibid.*, p. 143.
89. M. Nicholson: *Rationality and the Analysis of International Conflict.* 1992:11) http://www.slideshare.net/lauramoya/conflict1
90. Ramsbotham & Woodhouse, *Contemporary Conflict Resolution*, Polity Press, 1999, p. 12.
91. *Ibid.*
92. *Ibid.*, p. 15.
93. *Ibid.*
94. *Ibid.*, p. 85.
95. Huge, Miall, 2004, p. 5.
96. *Ibid.*
97. *Ibid.*

98. *Ibid.*, p. 6.
99. Ramsbotham, 2005, p. 9.
100. *Ibid.*, p. 10.
101. *Ibid.*, p. 9.
102. www.buzzle.com/articles/socialwork
103. www.wikipedia.org
104. [PDF] UNIT 4 *GANDHIAN DEVELOPMENT THEORY*, www.egyankosh.ac.in/bitstream/123456789/34911/1/Unit4.pdf)
105. Galtung 1971: p. 42.
106. Approach to peace Ed. by David Barash, 2000, pp. 43 to 46.
107. Galtung 1971: 43.
The Citizen's Handbook: A Guide to Building Community in Vancouver. http://www.vcn.bc.ca/citizens-handbook August 2001
108. http://rossbishop.com/blog/2011/08/26/war/).
109. www.jstor.org/stable/2769922
110. http://www.press.uchicago.edu
111. *Global Peace index, 2010, Methodology and Findings*, p. 4.
112. http://cmsdata.iucn.org

2
People and their Culture

"A nation's culture resides in the hearts and in the soul of its people." —*Mahatma Gandhi*

Cultural and Ethnic Identity of Different Groups

A comprehensive account of the socio-economic, political and cultural heritage of the present research being discussed in this chapter. In south Orissa, Koraput is the most ancient territorial entity which is the habitat of *Adivasis*, the first settlers. This region is endowed with rich ethnic diversity, biodiversity and natural resources and a treasure of the tribal folklore which always resisted the invaders in the history. Their culture always showed a political power to resist any intrusions. The past Koraput region which was under Madras Presidency during the British and the present Koraput region where 76 per cent of tribals feel that the developmental process is paralysed. The development process is a contradiction to their culture and tribal values. Until 1992, undivided Koraput consisted of 4 districts and after 1992 it was divided into four districts, namely, Koraput, Rayagada, Malkangiri and Nabarangpur. The history of this region from pre- and proto-historic ages where it formed a part of Kalinga, it was also under Nalas, Somvanshis and Suryavanshi Gajapatis. The Madras Presidency has an extended area up to undivided Ganjam district. The present research focuses on this contiguous path of four districts looking at its geographical location, tribal diversity and the issues, these districts are Koraput, Rayagada, Malkangiri and Gajapati. Geographically, this area is a land of mountains, waterfalls, streams and tribal hamlets. The term Scheduled Tribes as per Constitution, Article 342, says that:

1. The President, by the Constitution (First Amendment) Act, 1951 {may with respect to any state [by the Constitution (Seventh

Amendment) Act, 1956, and the Scheduled Castes and Scheduled Tribes Orders (Amendment) Act, 1976] [on Union territory], and where it is a state…., after consultation with the Governor…., thereof}, by public notification specify the tribes or tribal communities or parts of or groups within tribes or tribal communities which shall for the purposes of this Constitution be deemed to be scheduled tribes in relation to train state [or Union territory, as the case may be].

2. Parliament may [the Scheduled Castes and Scheduled Tribes Orders (Amendment) Act, 1976] by law include in or exclude from the list of Scheduled Tribes specified in a notification issued under clause (i) any tribe or tribal community or part of one group within any tribe or tribal community, but save as aforesaid a notification issued under the said clause shall not be varied by any subsequent notification.

The term Scheduled Tribes has not been defined in the Constitution. However, as per Government of India stipulations, since decades, the following criteria have been in use in order to identify and declare a particular community or parts of one group. These are primitive traits, distinctive culture, geographical isolation, shyness of contact and backwardness. It may be mentioned that, in this context the Draft National Tribal Policy[1] envisages replacement of certain pejorative criteria which does not hold true.

The term tribe, as a colonial jargon, was introduced by British by their policies of assimilation, integration and isolations, during pre-Independence the tribal communities often referred as *Adivasi*, *Adimajatis*, *Girijan-Vanavasi*, *Vanyajati* which identified them as early settlers, forest dwellers, hill dwellers. But during the post-Independence period their ethno-socio-economic-cultural identities have been redefined after the promulgation of Constitution of India of scheduled tribe on *Anusuchita Janajati*.[2] According to Behura and Mohanty, "Tribal societies are small scale, simple in character, with contiguous populations and socio-cultural homogeneity; there less complex divisions of labour, apart from those necessitated by age and sex factors. The term tribe as a structural and cultural concept connotes a social type in the evolutionary stage. In the civilization context the tribal communities represent the folk society; Indian population has three broad segments, such as,

1. The folk (tribal),

2. The peasants (rural caste communities), and
3. The urban (town/city dwellers).[3]

The first segment interacts with the second and both first and second interact with the third, and they form the tribal rural urban community Though the tribal, are economically backward, but have rich cultural heritage, relatively isolated, marginalized and represents the weaker section of our Indian state. Their rich culture provides them to deal with the outside physical environment, and to develop the coping mechanisms to survive. This study analyses their participation in the Naxalite movement, in the contiguous part of Koraput region, where it is the area of red-rebel as per the government reports. It may be remembered that society is dynamic and not static, where resistance and change are cardinal principles. For that matter this tribal society has witnessed several processes of changes such as colonization, social movement freedom movements, tribal revolts and uprising, *Bhoo-satyagraha* for land, de-tribalization, Christianization, ethnic revitalization, democratization and also revolutionary phases.

The Administrative Set-Up of the Study Area

The study area has four districts which is a contiguous patch starting from Gajapati district till Malkangiri district in the extreme south of Orissa. The number of blocks and number of villagers are given in the table below :

Table 2.1: The Administrative Profile of the Study Area

Sl. No.	*Name of the districts*	*Block*	*GP*	*Villages*	*Subdivision*	*Assembly constituency*
1.	Gajapati	7	129	1619	1	3
2.	Koraput	14	226	2,028	2	4
3.	Malkangiri	7	108	1,045	1	2
4.	Rayagada	11	171	2.667	2	4

Source: Status of Agriculture in Orissa, 2008, Directorate of Agriculture and Food Production, Orissa, Bhubaneswar.

The Sex Ratio Among the Tribals

Population of women in the Orissa as per Census 2001 is 1.8 crore, which is an increase of 145 per cent from 1951 census. The rural women population have increased by 115 per cent surprisingly its 840 per cent increase in urban areas. However, Orissa sex ratio is always appreciated as it is higher than the national average. Sex ratio of total population in Orissa and districts in 1951-2001 is given in Table 2.2.

Table 2.2: Sex Ratio of the Study Area

State/District	*1951*	*1961*	*1971*	*1981*	*1991*	*2001*
India	946	941	930	934	927	933
Orissa	1,022	1,001	988	981	971	972
Gajapati	1,041	1,027	1,026	1,023	1,027	1,031
Rayagada	1,008	1,010	1,004	1,020	1,012	1,028
Koraput	981	981	978	988	991	999
Malkangiri	1,015	998	936	962	985	997

Gajapati district has the highest rank since last two decades. (Census of India).

Geographical Location

The four districts of the study area are located in the extreme south of Orissa. The geographical location of the four districts is given below:

Malkangiri District

The district is named after its headquarters town Malkanagiri. During formation of Orissa Province in 1936 Malkangiri was a "Taluk" of Nabarangpur Sub-division of Koraput District of Orissa. In 1962 it was upgraded to a subdivision of Korapurt District. The present Malkangiri got its identity as an independent district due to reorganization of districts of Orissa as per notification on 1st October, 1992 with effect from 2nd October, 1992, an area of 5,791 sq. kms and lies between 81.8825279E longitude and 18.3435863N latitude.[4] Oriya is the main spoken language. The district is divided into two district physical divisions. The eastern part is covered with steep Ghats, Platues, valleys sparsely inhabited by primitive tribes notable among whom are Bondas, Koyas, Porajas and Didayis. The rest of the district is comparatively flat plain broken by a number of rocky wooden hills. Almost the whole of the district is a vast dense jungle. Potteru, Saberik, Sileru, Kolab and Machhakund are the main rivers flowing in the district. Malkangiri District is bounded by Andhra Pradesh and Chhattisgarh. In the East Malkangiri is bounded by Koraput (a portion) of Orissa, Visakhapatnam and East Godavari district of Andhra Pradesh. In the East Malkangiri is bounded by Bastar district of Chhattisgarh. In the North Malkangiri is bounded by Koraput district of Orissa. In the South Malkangiri is bounded by East Godavari and Khammam district of Andhra Pradesh. This district is spread over an area of 5,791 sq. kms [as per Census of India—2001 (Provisional)]. Maximum North-South Elongation is 137 kms. Maximum East-West Elongation is 76 kms.

Koraput District

The history of Koraput goes back as far as third century BC. It originally belonged to the valiant and dreaded Atvika people who fought the Kalinga war to restore the empire's glory. The region successively came to be ruled by several dynasties: Satavahans, Ikshvakus, Nalas Ganga kings and kings of Suryavansha. Finally, becoming a district of Orissa state on 1st April, 1936.

The origin of the name "Koraput" is obscure. But theories abound. According to Mr. R.S. Bell, former Collector of Koraput the name derives from Kora-Putti meaning "the hamlet of the nux-vomica" a tree that has once prevalent in the region. Another theory suggests Koraput is the corrupted form of "Koraka pento", literally meaning "Hail-stone". While folklore says Koraput is name after Khora Naiko—a valiant warrior of Nandapur kingdom. Koraput abounds in the imprints of Orissa's glorious past. Temples, monasteries and other historical monuments from the medieval period, breath taking in their beauty and of incalculable historical importance, stands as footprints of telling the story of the ears bygone. It falls at latitude of 18.813487N and longitude of 82.7123327E with an area of 8379 sq. km, 2900 ft. above sea level.[5]

Gajapati District

Gajapati District is named after Maharaja Sri Krishna Chandra Gajapati Narayan Deb, the Ex-Raja Sahib of Paralakhemundi estate. The region has a hilly terrain inhabited mostly by tribal people. Headquartered at Parlakhemundi, Gajapati has an area of 3,056 sq. km. and is home to over half a million people. This district is lying between 19.1912221 North latitude and 84.1857115 East longitude. The area is abutting the state boundary, i.e. Andhra Pradesh towards South. Ganjam district bound

Table 2.3: Geographical Area (block-wise) of the Study Area (showing blocks, number of Gram Panchayats, and literacy rate of the three districts of Universe)

Sl. No.	Name of the District	Name of the Blocks	Geographical Area in sq. kms	No. of Gram Panchayats	Literacy Rate (%)
1.	Rayagada	Gunupur	952.83	17	16.28
		Ramnaguda	642.30	12	14.98
		K. Singhpur	418.21	13	12.19
		Muniguda	648.39	16	18.83
		Chandrapur	433.31	7	6.45
		Gudari	766.89	9	8.85
		Padampur	856.23	12	18.05
		Kolnara	366.56	15	18.95
		Bissamcuttack	615.82	21	16.06
		Kashipur	484.82	18	23.18
		Rayagada	525.53	26	2.23
2.	Koraput	Nandapur	685.60	22	28.38
		Narayanpatna	157.00	9	16.24
		Jeypore	510.09	18	27.19
		Laxmipur	310.33	13	22.84
		Borigumma	606.48	30	27.23
		Semeliguda	314.65	16	19.95
		Boipariguda	1026.55	16	17.18
		Bondhugoan	223.14	12	16.18
		Kotpad	422.48	16	23.82
		Kundura	359.86	12	21.06
		Dasmanthpur	663.96	16	17.75
		Pottangi	258.02	14	17.19
		Lamtaput	576.99	16	25.05
		Koraput	420.89	13	30.18
3.	Malkangiri	Khairput	443.97	9	19.28
		Kudumulugumma	568.95	16	13.43
		Kalimela	440.18	16	28.60
		Korkunda	726.66	22	25.54
		Podia	452.76	11	22.43
		Mathili	609.23	22	19.98
		Malkangiri	418.12	14	45.75
4.	Gajapati	Paralekhmundi	494.53	21	43.44
		Kasinagar	478.03	12	33.62
		Gumma	1054.78	19	29.49
		Rayagad	967.99	18	35.94
		Mohana	658.47	32	40.68
		R. Udayagiri	462.30	13	41.15
		Nuagoan	439.68	14	34.54

this direct on the East, Rayagada district on the West, Ganjam and Phulbani districts on the North.[6]

Rayagada District

The district with 7584.7 sq. km. as geographical area falls on longitude degree 83.4163226 east and latitude degree 19.171209 north. The district Rayagada was carved out of the erstwhile Koraput district on 2.10.1992, as part of the extension plan of district in the state. The district has a population of 832019, out of which 473379 are tribals. In other words, the district has a predominantly a tribal populated district with 57.52 per cent of tribal population. Keeping this in view, all the 11 blocks of the district have been covered under tribal sub-plan with 3 micro-projects in operation for the pre-literate indigenous tribal communities.

The physiographic of Rayagada gives a prefect platform for the tribals in sustaining their ethno-cultural identity in the district.

The consolidated figures of the blockwise geographical area are given below in tabular form of the study area.[7]

Climate, Rain Fall and Census Analysis

The average annual rainfall is about 1700 mm in Malkangiri. Relative humidity is generally high especially in the monsoon and post-monsoon months. During the rainy season it becomes impassably swampy and heavy floods isolate it from the out world. It lies within the malaria pronc belt: The average rainfall in Koraput is 1522 mm (average). The minimum temperature is 12°C and maximum being the 38° C. The climate and the terrain are ideal for horticulture. Average rainfall is 1,284 mm, Gajapati is also noted for its cane and bamboo handicraft works. The Rayagada district has a normal rain fall of 1521.8 mm.

Census Analysis

The state of Orissa has seen rapid change of population, during 1951-2001; the population saw an increase to the effect of almost 151 per cent, but decadal trends do show that the rate of growth has slowed down considerably since 1991.

Table 2.4 indicates a growth in the population; but Gajapati shows a low population growth rate over decades. The Malkangiri district is a very extraordinary case as during 1960-1970 there is sudden rise of 89

Table 2.4: Population Growth rate of Orissa, and Tribal Population of the study area

State/ Districts	*1951*	*1951-61*	*1961-71*	*1971-81*	*1981-91*	*1991-2001*	*Growth rate*	*Overall growth rate*
Orissa	1,46,45,946	20%	25%	20%	20%	3,68,04,660	16	151
Koraput	5,44,286	9%	21%	20%	20%	11,80,637	15	117
Rayagada	3,41,241	18%	27%	19%	17%	8,31,109	16	144
Gajapati	2,62,998	8%	22%	15%	13%	5,18,837	14	97
Malkangiri	1,06,637	33%	89%	25%	26%	5,04,198	19	373

Source: Census of India.

per cent due to the Bangladeshi refugees who were rehabilitated in the district. Rayagada has a steady growth rate along with Koraput district.

Social Organization

According to Article 242 of the Constitution of India, Orissa is rich with 62 tribal groups in the tribal map. The population is very high in Koraput, Rayagada, Malkangiri, Gajapati and Mayurbhanj. The decadal growth rate of ST during 1981-1991 is 18.89 per cent and that of the state is 20.06 per cent. Tribes such as Konds, Gonds, Souar and Sandals are high in number. But each of the tribe has their own cultural identity which is manifested in their language, social organizations, festivals, dress, arts and crafts. The Orissa tribes are broadly divided into three ethno-linguistic groups, Mundari (Austro-Asiatic), Dravidian and Oriya (Indo-Aryan). The study area tribals majorly fall in Mundari groups like Bondo, Paraja, Didayi, Gadaba, Desia, Saora; the Dravidian tribals of the study area are Koya, Paraja, Jatapu and Konda Dora, the Oriya tribals of the study area are Bhumia, Halwa, and Kotia.

The tribals have retained their systems to manage their internal affairs like from village council and dormitory. Though dormitory system is not seen but they do have places where the unmarried boys and girls sleep in a particular place among tribals like Paraja, Gadaba, Didayi and Bondo. The Paraja boys do sleep in a particular place in the verandah of the house. In few interior villages it is still seen. It is not compulsory, but they do it as a norm. The festivals of the tribals are at different level which is for self/individual and the other is for the village. For self its child birth, marriage and death; for the village it is related to agricultural cycle, hunting etc. the famous festivals of the study area are "Chiata Parab", "Gotar" by Gadaba, "Meriah" by Kondhs and "Guar" by Lanjia

Soara. To highlight the social organizations of tribals few examples are give below to given a thought on the tribals.

Bhumia

Bhumias mostly concentrated in Nabrangpur and Koraput districts. According to 1991 census their total population in Orissa was 1,09,538 of which 56,657 are males and 52,881 are females. (*Tribes of Orissa*, 2004). Within a decade of 1981 to 1991 there was an increase of 45.62 per cent in their growth. Their main occupation of is settled cultivation and also agricultural wage.

Bondo

The uphills of Malkangiri inhabited by Bondo, they have retained their identity in respect of the geographical classification, language. According to 1981 census the total population of the Bondo was 5,895 which increased to 7,315 in 1991 with a growth rate of 24.09 per cent[8]. They practice shifting cultivation. These hillocks are now used for shelter base by Naxals. But so far Bondos are not that much visible in Naxalism. The Bondo kingdom has 33 NGOs on pen and paper (who officially working there as per their registration) it also includes Hindu temple and churches. Many Bondos have converted into themselves and following Christianity. In the sheer confusion more than 60 per cent Bondos did not want to respond to any of the questions which was asked to them.

The social organizations among the tribals in south Orissa are in a state of confusion due to the influx of Naxals into their area. The traditional social organizations are no more in tact. The tribals are in various stages of development ranging from shifting cultivation, hunting, settled cultivation and white collar jobs. The infusion of naxals using the base of these organizations and these organizations becoming an eyesore to the police. Any organizational activity is seen as a Naxal activity in the study area. The recent killings in Bijapur is an example of such organizations which are becoming fatal for the tribals.

Political Organization

The harmonious relation of tribals with the natural environment is beyond anybody's understood and their societies are organized on egalitarian basis.

Their distribution of resources among them was also done in democratic way. They have governed their territories with their local organizations.

According to IFAD, Indigenous People suffer higher rates of poverty, landlessness, malnutrition, human rights violation, unemployment and internal displacement than other sects of the society, and they have lower level of literacy and less access to health services.

Situation of Adivasis in India[9]

40.1 per cent of the *Adivasis* are displaced.
55.2 per cent of the *Adivasis* are under below poverty line.
64 per cent of the *Adivasis* are the poorest of the poor.
63.5 per cent of the *Adivasi* households do not have electricity.
53.1 per cent of the *Adivasi* households do not have drinking water source.
83 per cent of the *Adivasi* households do not have access to toilet facility.
56 per cent of the *Adivasi* children are undernourished.
53 per cent of the *Adivasis* are illiterate.
76 per cent of the *Adivasis* do not have permanent houses.

(www.ifad.org)

The harmonious and symbiotic relationship with the natural environment and their societies tend to be organized on an egalitarian and communitarian basis, with their own systems of knowledge, self-governance and nationhood. They have governed their ancestral territories and natural resources as a participatory community based on democratic processes. They have a collective dependency to the natural resources in their habitats and territories. They also have a historical and unique relationship with their ancestral territories. They have developed particular cultures, life styles, traditions and belief systems according to their territories and natural resources.

Economic Organization

The tribals of south Orissa have undergone a remarkable change during the last five decades, though the signs of these changes were visible during the contact with the British administration. Tribes can be implied as a social entity and also as a community of people with unique cultural values. These tribes as per the study area they are not conscious of the upcoming needs and challenges of the globalized world. The globalized world is always between two unequal partners where the economic activities of tribals have no place. The tribals who resists to these changes are seen as barriers to fall in capital investments.

The tribals in the study area are still in different stages of economic activities. Few are in the stage of practicing hunting and gathering; few are in shifting cultivation, few still collect forest produce and engage themselves in barter. In many parts of Koraput, Rayagada and Malkangiri districts tribals exchange their produce to get the household item. The country had 67.8 million (1991 census) of ST population, a substantial part lives in Orissa, Andhra Pradesh, Jharkhand undivided Madhya Pradesh etc. As per 1991 census 87.19 per cent of St. population depended on agriculture either in settled or shifting cultivation. These statistics do mean the economic association of tribals with land and forest. The study area tribals with land and forest (almost 80% of them). The new economic policy has changed their land use pattern and it has been put into commercial use squeegeeing the acquisition by tribals. Land and forest is seen as revenue. One of the tribal in Rayagada district opined "The hill contained minerals which is a mother to us, but this is money and profit for companies like Vendanta and Utkal Alumina. So, if the lands are taken away from us then we no way have no way to go. We are very insecure now in our own territory. So, if the state feels that the naxals through tribals is escalating and it is creating internal threat, then I would say that people who are insure socially, economically and politically we only create threat for others."

In the tribal areas of South Orissa, statistics give a glaring picture of the socio-economic indicators:

- 37 per cent of the tribal household's income is less than Rs. 700 per month.
- 24 per cent of household's income is between Rs. 301-400 per month.
- 26 per cent of household's income is Rs. 600-700 per month.
- But 72 per cent of the tribals are under below poverty line.
- Among the 72 per cent, 37 per cent are unskilled labourers, 20 per cent are agricultural labouers.
- 23 per cent of tribals do not have any sustained income and they entirely depend on forest produce.
- Due to poverty 66 per cent of tribal female and male children are illiterate, 32 per cent only attend school to learn how to sign and after that they never see the school.
- In the Koraput region only 2 to 3 per cent of tribal students who attend colleges.

- Moreover, the area is famous for starvation deaths and diarrhoea deaths.
- Study conducted by KBK round table in 2009 in KBK region.[10]
- These factors do motivate and bring a revolutionary thinking among some tribal youth who see violence as an option.

A trend in the figures, which is decreased form, 1961-68.18 per cent of ST cultivators to 54.05 per cent in 1991; also an increase of agricultural labourers from 19.71 per cent to 32.69 per cent from 1961 to 1991.[11] This indicated the alienation of tribals from their land, where land is acquired for dams, mining, projects and etc. The Planning Commission Report (2000) gives the official figure as 9,17,590 acres of land has been alienated from tribals in all states and 21.2 lakhs have been displaced between 1951-1990. The country's 80 per cent of mineral and forest resources are located in scheduled area, particularly in Western Ghats and Eastern Ghats (study area). These resources attracted two major interest groups, the non-tribals who want to settle in the area and the state which made the region a laboratory to experiment the planned development projects like dams, mines for national interest, where the interests of the tribals were just sacrificed. The perception of utilization of the resources is completely opposed to the utilization as the state puts it. Slowly, the area saw the influx of migrant population like expansion of tertiary sectors like shopping centre, big townships, real estates, trade which are the new economics activities where the tribals still pushed to perform domestic service and vending.

Land-use Pattern

This explains the way the land has been put to use for various purposes like agriculture, residential, industrial, commercial, rural etc. The natural use such as pasture lands, waste lands, forest lands are classified in this way. According, 2001 Census, 68 per cent total workforce in Orissa is engaged in agriculture, forestry and fishery sectors, where 76 per cent rural workforce is engaged in this activities. If the cottage industries will be included in agricultural land use pattern then the number would go up to 80 per cent of the total workforce.

Religion

India is a country of different faiths, and religions. People give different names to their beliefs these can be well known by ism, faiths, cults and religion. The individual relation with god and in connection to god varies. Besides all this religion is considers as the strongest socio-cultural aspect of human civilization. It has given rise to tradition, rites, rituals; festivals and the existence of the supreme god who is present everywhere. There are divisions of beliefs but as a whole people do believe that there is one almighty, the divine power who is the creator of this universe. Everyone prays the god but the way its manifested and expressed is different from person to person. India is an amalgamation of different religions, viz. Hinduism, Buddhism, Sikhism, Jainism, Christianity, Zorastrians and also the tribal religion has survived under the influence of other religions since ages. Many keep their religion as confidential and population census is the only means to collect the data on religion. It has both positive and negative effects on the lives of the individuals. Food habits, cultural practices, connection with nature, health, rituals, celebrations, life cycle rituals all have positive and negative effect. But, it plays an important part in the life. In the tribal areas their beliefs are attributed towards nature and worshipping nature. Anything hindering the growth of the nature which disturbances them and their entire life cycle (This meaning is a derived from a Kondh song, the person sung and explained the meaning, the relation of tribals and their beliefs with environment).

As per 2001 Census the following table shows the number of STs to each major religion in Orissa and their percentage to total population.

Table 2.5: Distribution of ST population by Religion

Sl. No.	*Name of the religion*	*Population*	*% total population of the state*
1.	Hinduism	71,80819	88.16
2.	Muslims	13,782	0.17
3.	Christianity	60,5880	7.44
4.	Sikhism	251	Negligible
5.	Buddhism	175	Negligible
6.	Jainism	196	Negligible
7.	Other Religions and persuasions	3,40,532	4.19
8.	Religions not stated	3446	0.04
	All religions total	81,45,081	100.00

Source: Census of India, 2001.

From Table 2.5 it can be seen that 88.16 per cent tribals practicing Hinduism. If we see the number of ST person in each of these six religions between 1961-2001 Census then we see that there is an increase in Christianity religion among tribals.

Table 2.6: Trends in Religious Distribution of Tribals from 1961 to 2001

Name of religion	*2001*	*1991*	*1981*	*1971*	*1961*
Hinduism	7180819	6244474	5302256	4761000	4118134
Muslims	13782	1609	231	22	—
Christianity	605880	411346	326952	218677	104125
Sikhism	251	408	69	29	—
Buddhism	175	178	111	08	—
Jainsim	196	763	03	12	—
Other religions and persuasions	340532	371839	174703	—	1498
Religions not stated	3446	1597	—	332	—
All religions total	8145081	7032214	5915071	5071937	4223757

Source: Ota, A.B., *Analysis of Scheduled Tribe Population in Orissa*, 1961-2001, SCSTRTI, 2009.

Table 2.6 shows an increasing trend of followers among tribals towards Christianity. Still breaking down to rural and urban setting, the rural areas have a sharp rise to Christianity then in urban. Among the districts have maximum number of population in each religion on 2001. Gajapati District has maximum followers of Christianity as far as the study area is concerned. In the study area it portrayed a peculiar feature regarding the religion and religious beliefs when the respondents were asked and observed:

- When the question was asked to the respondents 100 per cent said they don't practice any religion in the camps.
- But 100 per cent opine and identify themselves as tribals who have a strong connection with nature gods.
- The respondents of Gajapati district parts of Gunpur subdivision of Rayagada District parts of Jeypore subdivision of Koraput district are followers of Christianity though introduce themselves as tribals.
- More than 92 per cent of the respondents in Gajapati district follow Christianity.
- Sixty per cent of the respondents of Rayagada and Koraput follow Christianity.
- In Malkangiri district the respondents did stick to tribal religions which are about 80 per cent.

But all the tribals strongly emphasise their connection with nature god though their faiths are Hindu or Christianity.

The study area is a mixture of different religions from tribal religion. Buddhism, Jainism, Christianity, Hinduism and Islam. One finds a synthesis of all religions in the study area. Buddhism is seen in few pockets of Koraput district and Rayagada district; and largely in Gajapati district. There is a large community of people following Islam in Nandapur block of Koraput district, especially Christianity is present in all the four districts. This area being the part of the Eastern Ghats share a natural assimilation of religions. 62 tribal groups inhabit in the state of Orissa. And almost more than 50 tribes are inhabitants of this region[12].

The respondents from the study area do show a clear picture of the various religions that they follow:

- Though no religion is followed in the camps, but it is an individual affair.
- 50 per cent of the respondents in Gajapati and Rayagada districts follow Christianity though they belong to tribal groups.
- The respondents in Koraput and Malkangiri did not give a clear picture of their religious practices but most of them belong to tribal groups.
- There are incidents as questioned by the Naxal Leader that few of the underground activists who were not allowed for the Christmas holidays. It is not compulsory to follow any religion.
- In one such village it was found that (in the borders of Koraput district and Malkangiri district) the villagers are at cross roads as they receive different messages. The Hindu fundamentalists advocate for Hinduism, the Christian pastors advocate for Christianity, but the Naxals do preach that don't follow any religion except tribalism. In this process the villagers get confused with many actors involved in religion.

Economic Condition and Poverty

Orissa is one of the poorest provinces in India, with 47.15 per cent of its people below the poverty line, as against a national figure of 26.10 per cent worse. The incidence and persistence of poverty is even higher in Southern Orissa, which comprises Gajapati, Koraput, Malkangiri, Rayagada, Nabrangpur and parts of Kalahandi. The State's Per Capita Income is below the national average. The gap between the State Per Capita Income and the corresponding National Per Capita Income is alarmingly increasing from Rs. 2,901 during 1993-94 to Rs. 5,067 during 2000-01 as per quick estimates. The incidence of poverty is greater in the southern and western regions of the State. Furthermore, the percentage of rural families living below the poverty line is substantially higher in the State (66.37%, as per estimate made by the Panchayati Raj Department, Government of Orissa, in 1997) as compared to the rest of the country (34%). The Southern districts have remained under-developed largely because of a lack of political involvement and bureaucratic apathy. Past government laws and policies made these people's lives impoverished, as the tribals were forced to give their resources either to the Government or to private companies living themselves to a nowhere situation. So, it was a good breeding ground for the movement in the rising stage.[13]

Table 2.7: Occupational Distribution in the Study Area

Name of the District	*Small Farmers*	*Marginal Farmers*	*Agricultural Labourers*	*Rural Artisans*
Gajapati	4.96	5.86	22.51	0.72
Koraput	14.85	22.84	35.69	1.14
Malkangiri	24.68	30.17	23.68	3.34
Rayagada	7.97	18.99	34.81	3.41

Source: Atlas of Development Trends, FES, 2009.

The above table shows the district-wise rural BPL families on the basis of their occupation as per 1997 survey.[14] The Orissa state has some significant progress in reducing the poverty figures. The table also indicates that about 85.61 per cent of the rural poor in Orissa comprises agriculture labourers, marginal farmers, small farms. From these groups largest number of BPL rural families comes under the category of marginal farmers and agricultural labourers. The poverty conditions are highlighted by the two following information:

Villages without Power

Eighty five per cent of the villages in Malkangiri are without power supply. In Rayagada and Koraput more than 60 per cent of the villages are without power. 48 per cent of the villages are without electricity in the district of Gajapati.

Drinking Water

The data about drinking water for the undivided Koraput and Ganjam district are as follows:

Table 2.8: Drinking water facilities in Koraput and Ganjam Districts (undivided)

Undivided	*1991*			*2001*		
	VH	*VDWF*	*HP+TW*	*VH*	*VDWF*	*HP+TW*
Koraput	5983	5976	3422	6244	6190	5852
Ganjam	4187	4166	1814	4324	4313	3697

Note: VH—villages with hand pumps
VDWF—villages with drinking water facility
HP+TW—hand pumps and tube well

Table 2.8 indicates that there is an increase in drinking water facilities, but it is found that in many villages these pumps do not work.

Poverty by Hunger and Acute Distress

By the end of 2001, it was found that with 23.4 per cent of houses in Rayagada were going hungry, between 2002-03 it witnessed 12 starvation deaths, followed by Koraput 32. Child sales were higher in Gajapati district between 2000 to 2003. Also it witnessed 22 number of starvation deaths within the same period.

Table 2.9: Economic Condition of Distress in the Study Area

Districts	*2001*	*2002-2003*	*No. of Child Sale*
	Houses Going Hungry	*No. of Starvation Deaths*	
Gajapati	7.8%	22	7
Koraput	5.1%	32	0
Malkangiri	—	1	—
Rayagada	23.4%	72	—

Source: *Legislative Assembly Debates*, Vol. XII, No. 11 and *District Level Deprivation in the New Millennium*, Bibek Debroy and Laveesh Bhandari.[15]

The houses not able to afford two square meals a day shows the magnitude of poverty of the study area.

Table 2.10: Land Holding status of the respondent families

Sl. No.	*Communities*	*Land Holding (%)*				
		No. Land	*0-2 Acres*	*2-5 Acres*	*Above 5 Acres*	*Total*
1.	SC	7.1	1.4	0	0	8.5
2.	ST	32.9	18.6	27.1	4.3	82.9
3.	Others	8.6	—	—	—	8.6
	Total	48.6	20	27.1	4.3	100

Table 2.10 shows us that nearly 49 per cent of the respondents' families do not own any land, and only 20 per cent of them own less than 2 acres; 27.1 per cent own between 2 to 5 acres. The whole pattern of the respondents in the party gives a clear picture that why certain sections of the society are only going into such kind of movements and armed resistance and not others. The poor are only into this conflict.

Table 2.11: Quality of the Land owned by the Respondent Families

Sl. No.	*Name of the Study Districts*	*Land Quality (%)*		*Total*
		Rainfed	*Irrigated*	
1.	Gajapati	23.26	2.33	25.59
2.	Rayagada	20.93	2.33	23.26
3.	Koraput	27.91	4.65	32.56
4.	Malkangiri	18.60	—	18.60
	Total	90.70	9.31	100

The above table shows that 90.7 per cent of the land is rain-fed. The basic topography of the study area is hilly where the most so-called technology will not work. Though the study contains enormous amount of water resources but it is not used for the tribal purposes rather harnessed for big dams, factories leaving the tribals homeless and with no irrigation facilities. Whatever irrigation facility that has been crated goes to the rich farmers and not the poor tribals.

Table 2.12: Housing Patterns of Respondents

Sl. No.	*Communities*	*Types of Housing (%)*			*Total*
		Katcha	*Pacca*	*Other Type*	
1.	SC	2.94	1.47	—	4.41
2.	ST	55.88	19.12	13.24	88.24
3.	OC	1.47	5.88	—	7.35
	Total	60.29	26.47	13.24	100

The above table shows that 60.29 per cent of the houses are katcha, whereas 26.47 per cent are pacca and rest 13.24 per cent are either tiled or roof house. From the 60.29 per cent, 55.88 per cent houses belong to tribals which are katcha houses. It again indicates greater poverty.

Migration

It is the budding issue which the study area is facing. According to 2001 Census, about 9,37,148 people have migrated from Orissa to other states for many reasons. These reasons include for work as no opportunity available. It was found that from Gajapati district tribals do migrate till north-eastern India for wage work. In Rayagada and Koraput the migration number is escalating every year. Especially, from Dasmanthput and Nandpur blocks the people are migrating for wage work more. From Malkangiri district the tribals migrate to Andhra Pradesh and Chhattisgarh mostly. The inter-state migration is rampant in search of work to places like Berhampur and Bhubaneswar as shown in other tables that the tribals are alienated from their land, home and hearths.

It has been mentioned in the conceptual framework that needs are not negotiable and people feel more insecure when the felt needs are not met. In the workshop for IAP (Integrated Action Plan) the State is taking ample activities to meet these basic needs. It is also discussed that when there is a potential present to have all good facilities but certain sections of the society; on the other hand the tribals in the study area are not receiving even the actual ones. When this state occurs it is an indication that violence is present in the system which is in a way provoking people for counter violence. For example when children in the study area are dying out of diarrhoea without receiving the actual by the state at the same time children who are enjoying the facilities at its best. So, this situation one has to vouch for future better action. What are the needs? The basic needs for any person or individual involve the access to minimum consumption, education and health. But according to Global Hunger Index, India stands as 67 out of 81 countries, much below the neighbouring countries like Nepal and Sri Lanka. So, there exists deprivation by major chunk of people in the country as well as in the study area. According to Planning Commission, 100 most backward districts in the country, Koraput, Rayagada and Malkangiri are such districts that fall in the study area.

Basing on six indicators, viz.

- Income poverty (poverty ratios),
- Hunger,
- IMR (infant mortality rate),
- Immunization, and
- Literacy rate and enrolment ratio.

Three districts of the study come under India's most 69 backward districts, viz. Gajapati, Koraput and Rayagada. These 6 indicators as mentioned above are specific goals shows in the eight millennium development goals. Tables 2.12, 2.13, 2.14 and 2.15 show the Human Development Indicators of the Gajapati, Koraput, Rayagada and Malkangiri districts as per the 69 backward districts criteria:

Table 2.13: Characteristics of Backwardness in Gajapati District

Characteristic	*Ratio*	*Characteristic*	*Ratio*	*Characteristic*	*Ratio*
Percentage of population below poverty line	43.9	0-6 sex ratio (females per 1000 males)	962.6	Urbanization	10.2
Percentage of households going hungry	7.8	Female literacy rate	52.4	Population density (per sq. km)	119.9
IMR (per 1000 births)	92.0	Female work participation	35.1	Flood prone area (%)	3.5
Percentage of children getting complete immunization	62.0	Percentage of women receive skilled attention during pregnancy	24.7	Drought affected area (% in 2000)	—
Literacy rate	41.7	Crude birth rate	27.6	Percentage of safe drinking water habitations	86.3
Gross enrollment ratio (elementary)	80.6	Total fertility rate	3.3	Percentage of villages connected with pacca roads in the district	21.5

These figures show the situation of poverty in the study area directly connected to the needs perspective.

Literacy

Since 1951, the State of Orissa has seen a growth in its literacy rate to 21 per cent, but below the national literacy rate of 65 per cent. In spite of the programmes undertaken by the state still the regional disparity between the districts prevail.

During 1971 and 1981 the literacy rates among men and women in rural and urban area are as shown below.

The figures are given here for undivided Koraput and Ganjam.

Table 2.14: Characteristics of Backwardness in Koraput District

Characteristic	*Ratio*	*Characteristic*	*Ratio*	*Characteristic*	*Ratio*
Percentage of population below poverty line	80.1	0-6 sex ratio (females per 1000 males)	993.1	Urbanization	16.8
Percentage of households going hungry	5.1	Female literacy rate	52.2	Population density (per sq. km)	133.8
IMR (per 1000 births)	125.0	Female work participation	25.2	Flood prone area (%)	—
Percentage of children getting complete immunization	55.5	Percentage of women receive skilled attention during pregnancy	20.4	Drought affected area (% in 2000)	—
Literacy rate	36.2	Crude birth rate	27.3	Percentage of safe drinking water habitations	100.0
Gross enrollment ratio (elementary)	175.1	Total fertility rate	3.1	Percentage of villages connected with pacca roads in the district	10.8

Table 2.15: Characteristics of Backwardness in Rayagada District

Characteristic	*Ratio*	*Characteristic*	*Ratio*	*Characteristic*	*Ratio*
Percentage of population below poverty line	80.1	0-6 sex ratio (females per 1000 males)	982.9	Urbanization	14.0
Percentage of households going hungry	23.1	Female literacy rate	51.3	Population density (per sq. km)	116.4
IMR (per 1000 births)	125.0	Female work participation	27.9	Flood prone area (%)	—
Percentage of children getting complete immunization	55.2	Percentage of women receive skilled attention during pregnancy	28.8	Drought affected area (% in 2000)	—
Literacy rate	35.6	Crude birth rate	28.5	Percentage of safe drinking water habitations	100.0
Gross enrollment ratio (lementary)	175.1	Total fertility rate	3.3	Percentage of villages connected with pacca roads in the district	10.8

Table 2.16: Characteristics of Backwardness in Malkangiri District (though it's not counted in the 69 backward list, few indicators are highlighted)

Characteristic	*Ratio*	*Characteristic*	*Ratio*
Percentage of population below poverty line	80.1	0-6 sex ratio (females per 1000 males)	989.7
Percentage of households going hungry	0.0	Female literacy rate	51.6
IMR (per 1000 births)	125.0	Female work participation	25.0
Percentage of children getting complete immunization	50.2	Percentage of women receive skilled attention during pregnancy	10.7
Literacy rate	31.3	0.6 year old in the total population	34.6
Gross enrollment ratio (elementary)	100	Pupil teacher ratio	83.0

Table 2.17: Literacy Rates (in %) of undivided Ganjam and Koraput Districts

Districts	*1971 (%)*						*1981 (%)*					
	Rural			*Urban*			*Rural*			*Urban*		
	Person	*M*	*F*	*Person*	*M*	*F*	*Person*	*M*	*F*	*Person*	*M*	*F*
Koraput	8	13	3	39	50	28	12	19	5	46	57	35
Ganjam	22	35	9	47	59	34	28	48	13	53	64	40

Source: Census of India.

The literacy rates among men and women in rural and urban areas for 1991 and 2001:

Table 2.18: Literacy Rates of the Study Area

Districts	*1991 (%)*						*2001 (%)*					
	Rural			*Urban*			*Rural*			*Urban*		
	Person	*M*	*F*	*Person*	*M*	*F*	*Person*	*M*	*F*	*Person*	*M*	*F*
Gajapati	21	30	11	53	64	42	31	42	20	63	71	54
Koraput	13	20	6	56	66	46	22	32	13	65	73	58
Malkangiri	4	20	7	45	55	35	23	31	15	56	64	47
Rayagada	17	25	9	52	62	42	24	34	15	63	72	55

These above figures indicate that the urban areas women have fairly increased in literacy rate for better facilities.

Literacy among STs

The state of literacy though showed a significant growth over last few decades, but there has not been any considerable growth as far as the literacy rate among STs are taken into account. The ST who nearly constitutes about 22.13 per cent of the total population of the country but there literacy growth was almost behind prior to the independence. According to 1931 Census, percentage of literacy rate among STs was lower than the general literacy which was 9.50 per cent. The literacy rate among ST women during 1931 was 0.2 per cent compared to general female literacy rate which was 2.93 per cent. The reasons behind such low literacy rate depend on many factors such as the areas being very remote and forested the lack of interest by the British. Despite many efforts by the independent India, the literacy rate according to 2001 remained as 37.4 per cent among STs.

Drift of Literacy among STs

The Table 2.19 below explains the literacy rate of Orissa and India between the years 1961 to 2001.

Table 2.19: Tribal Literacy Rate in Orissa and India from 1961 to 2001

Census years	*Orissa (%)*			*India (%)*		
	Literacy of Person in Total	*Male*	*Female*	*Literacy of Person in Total*	*Male*	*Female*
1961	7.4	13.0	1.8	7.99	13.04	2.89
1971	9.5	16.4	2.6	10.89	17.09	4.58
1981	14.0	23.3	4.8	16.35	24.52	8.04
1991	22.31	34.44	10.21	29.6	40.65	18.19
2001	37.4	51.5	23.4	47.1	59.2	34.8

Source: Census of India, 1961-2001.

Table 2.19 explains the literacy rate among total and ST population of Orissa by sex (1961-2001).

Table 2.20 shows the literacy rate of the study area (ST population by sex): Census 1991 and 2001.

The literacy component is still a blot in the tribal development as in

Table 2.20: Sex-wise Literacy of Tribal Population and Total Population

Census years	Total population (%)			ST population (%)		
	Male	Female	Total	Male	Female	Total
1961	34.70	8.65	21.66	13.04	1.77	7.36
1971	38.29	13.92	26.18	16.30	2.58	9.46
1981	47.10	21.10	34.20	23.27	4.76	13.96
1991	63.09	34.68	49.09	34.44	10.21	22.31
2001	75.35	50.51	63.08	51.48	23.37	37.37

Source: Census of India, 1961-2001.

Table 2.21: Literacy Rate of Tribals of Study Area in 1991 and 2001

Sl. No.	Districts	Literacy Rate of ST population					
		1991			2001		
		Total	Male	Female	Total	Male	Female
1.	Gajapati	15.88	25.66	6.75	27.77	41.60	14.83
2.	Rayagada	10.39	17.73	3.40	20.23	31.16	10.07
3.	Koraput	8.34	14.61	2.14	18.68	29.25	8.38
4.	Malkangiri	6.77	11.21	2.32	14.69	22.05	7.50

spite of all programmes the growth is not that visible. The Naxal conflict and the violence have created a fear among the teachers and they don't go to attend schools in the interior pockets of the study area. Many schools are occupied by security forces, for which the Naxal activists blast these schools. During the last five years a total of 260 schools have been cracked in India according to the report of the Ministry of Home Affairs. UNESCO has cited instances of damage which includes 11 schools in Jharkhand, 9 in Bihar, till July 2009. The Home Ministry also puts facts as the most hit district in schools is Chhattisgarh which is 131, followed by other states like Andhra Pradesh, Maharashtra and Orissa. This is a vicious circle of trap and entrap, as once there is any blast, or murder or display of posters by the Naxals in an area suddenly get a sanction of being Naxalite affected though actually its not. After it gets label of being affected all the services by the state is paralyzed under the shadow of this label. Nothing reaches the people and unwontedly the area goes into the Naxal net. Almost 58 per cent of the people living in the rural areas of universe strongly say that the state should take immediate steps to stop this kind of intrusion rather declaring it as an affected area. The whole politics behind declaring the area as affected is unknown to the people.

Extent of Exploitation and Sufferings of the People

Indian tribes constitute roughly 8 per cent of the nation's total population, nearly 68 million people according to the 1991 Census. One concentration lives in a belt along the Himalayas stretching through Jammu & Kashmir, Himachal Pradesh, and Uttar Pradesh in the west, to Assam, Meghalaya, Tripura, Arunachal Pradesh, Mizoram, Manipur, and Nagaland in the north-east. Various studies do point out that the exploitation in the tribal areas mainly include in land, labour and in livelihood sectors. Land exploitation is being the highest where the land is not only taken for developmental projects by the government, but also land is encroached and falsely encroached by the outsiders which has become the budding issue in the tribal areas as well as in the universe. The universe of the study has witnessed several land struggles from the end of 1990s mainly through the following:

- Ceiling land occupied,
- Land occupied by the re-settlers, and
- Land taken by the companies.

The land became the main issue which motivated the tribals to join, was the basis of their sufferings.

Active and Passive Participation of the Tribals

The following few tables indicate the factors of motivation, the opinion regarding the right path of the naxal (active and passive) supporters at large for which tribals participate either passively or actively. The acceptance level by the respondents gives a picture that the Naxalism is some way has a place in many of the people.

Twenty four per cent of the respondents do feel that this is required for our country and rest 30 per cent of the people in some or the other do show their support for the movement and show their affinity. They feel that this is the best strategy for the present time and hope that this will increase, but on the whole the opinion is very strong that there is a necessity of some kind of revolution which should be ultimatum. 18 per cent of the people also feel that this is not the right path.

People have accepted them because of their thinking, teaching, their deed towards the poor, and their closeness to the villages. 17 per cent of the people accept them without any condition. As they feel that a stratified

Table 2.22: Opinions Regarding the Sufferings

Sl. No.	*Responses*	*%age*
1.	Due to the LPG the gap between the rich and poor is more, so unless there is a revolution nothing is going to change	1.4
2.	Violence is an effective weapon for radical changes	1.4
3.	Revolution but without arms	1.4
4.	Violence is not the way	2.7
5.	It is time for triblas to stand and be counted	1.4
6.	It is not, but they have met the aspirations of the tribals to some extent	1.4
7.	To some extent tribals get moral encouragement	4.1
8.	Yes	32.4
9.	No	24.3
10.	To some extent, it's the right path as this is a social problem	9.5
11.	No idea	4.1
12.	That is the ultimatum	8.1
13.	Right or wrong it suits the condition	4.1
14.	Revolution is necessary may be or may not through naxalism	92.7
15.	It's good as an opposition	91.4
16.	There should be class annihilation and not person annihilation	1.4

Table 2.23: Acceptance Level – The Responsible factors for tribal participation

Sl. No.	*Responses*	*%age*
1.	No comments	5.33
2.	Yes, it has the force to make people conscious	1.33
3.	I do empathize as their national patriots	1.33
4.	No	29.3
5.	Not exactly, but the movement makes me happy and sad	2.67
6.	Yes	22.7
7.	Yes, accept their thinking	5.33
8.	Yes, believe in armed struggle	5.33
9.	Yes, they are close to people	2.67
10.	Yes, they have reached the un reached areas	2.67
11.	Their teachings are good so accepted	8
12.	To some extent	6.67
13.	Accept their way of thinking and not their means, but heart is with them but not the killing part of it	6.67

class structure where the proletariat is with the petty bourgeoisie consciousness is lumping. According to the Newton's second law of motion "a body continues to be in state of rest or continuous motion unless an external force acts on it". The proletarian surroundings are is paranoiac about future. And may be the movement is acting as a force to change their present position of rest as every exploited person is a potential revolutionary. 2.67 per cent of the people do derive happiness and sadness from the movement; as they opine the Naxals kill the poor informers, police rather they should kill big corrupt political leader. And they sometimes do feel that the naxals are killing the poor informers and other village level people, but they should go and kill the big actors as they opined. The Kandhamal incident where by mistake they blasted a land mine where a hospital ambulance carrying patients including women and infants all died. The party did express their grief over a press statement but all these incidents do affect the credibility of the Naxals over the general public at large.

Table 2.24: Suffering and Participation—The Tribal Linkage

Sl. No.	*Responses*	*%age*
1.	Don't know	4.2
2.	They free the tirbals from their immediate exploiter	4.2
3.	At village level they endure good governance for tribals in getting wages, PDS etc.	1.1
4.	Make aware, conduct meetings	7.4
5.	Their struggle is maturing through tribals	4.2
6.	It instills hope and courage among tribals	1.1
7.	They have been able to take out fear from tribals	1.1
8.	They help the tribals in getting land	6.3
9.	They organize tribals to unite and fight	13.7
10.	Mobilize tribals to raise issues	3.2
11.	Train them politically, bringing cultural revolution within them, give good teachings	10.5
12.	Tribals see them as rescuers, a way to ventilate their anger	7.4
13.	No	5.3
14.	Tribals like them as they mix with them in the village, close to their hearts, their interactions are very heart touching and help in getting minimum requirements	2.1
15.	Fight against all kinds of exploitation	4.2
16.	Its visible process of change	4.2
17.	Use tribals as luggage carriers	11.6
18.	Anyway tirbals are dying so why not die with an ism	1.1
19.	Preparing tribals for future	5.3
20.	Made the tribals to resist which they didn't do for since ages	1.1

They are not doing any good to the tribal communities and using them as to carry their luggage carrier, to guide them in the forest, ask for food, and they are taking shelter in their tribal hamlet as a result tribals are suffering from this. Many tribals in the border areas of Koraput-Malkangiri, Gajapati-Rayagada have been to jail repeatedly and are released. They say even though they are not associated in any activity but since they stay in those places they have to pay a price for that but 7.4 per cent feel that they are the rescuers of tribals, and they mingle with them by speaking their language and mobilize them, 4.2 per cent feel that their struggle in ultimately maturing through tribals and in a way indicated the tribals are well participating in it. There is no leadership among tribals in the movement from south Orissa and the leaders come from Andhra Pradesh and Chhattisgarh who are directing in these districts of south Orissa. So, 5 per cent of the respondents do feel that they don't do any good to them. And they are killing the gram pedas who are very poor and impoverished thinking that they are police informers. It is just to terrorize them and this is not the real ideology.

But, 7 per cent do opine that the tribals see them as rescuers as they help them in eliminating their immediate enemies and free them from his or her exploitation. And they are well accepted in the villages as they look like them, talk their language, stay with them and make them aware to raise their voice democratically. And their struggle is maturing through the tribals. 4 per cent of the people do feel that this process of revolution is very visible but they also say that they are doing good work in Chhattisgarh and not in south Orissa.

References

1. *A Policy for the Scheduled Tribes in India*, circulated by Government of India, Ministry of Tribal Affairs (No. F 20025/3/2003 – R P) (part-IV) dated 5th July, 2006.
2. *Constitution of India.*
3. *Cultural Heritage of Orissa*, vol. XI, Koraput district, State Level Vyasa Kabi Fakir Mohan Smruti Sansad, BBSR, 2008, p. 22.
4. www.malkangiri.nic.in
5. www.koraput.nic.in
6. www.gajapati.nic.in
7. www.rayagada.nic.in
8. *Tribes of Orissa*, 2004.
9. www.ifad.org
10. Study conducted by KBK round table in 2009 in KBK region.
11. *Scheduled Tribes and Development*, edited by H.S. Sakheran, Serials Publications, 2006.
12. *Tribes of Koraput*, COATS 2006.
13. Party documents.
14. *Orissa Development Report* 2002.
15. *District Level Deprivation in the New Millennium*, Bibek Debroy and Laveesh Bhandari.

3
The Genesis of Naxalite Movement

> "Whenever people with money have power over people with less money, you have the potential for exploitation."
>
> —*Jennifer Weiner*

As per the ethics of the research, the actual names of the informants have not been cited here. All the names mentioned here are fictitious. But the facts and information's are expressed as explained by the informants. In few places the information's are given in italics and in other places they are anonyms.[1]

The most basic manifestations of the Naxalite movement can be traced with the Telengana movement in Andhra Pradesh during 1948-1950, where embedded dissent against the government over incompetent land distribution rules had provided an appropriate place for Communist ideologues to experiment with the experiences and inspirations from the Chinese Peasant revolutions. The movement caught fire in more than 2000 villages in Andhra Pradesh against the state. Wikipedia explains the word *Naxal*, *Naxalite* or *Naksalvadi* is a general reference to various Communist groups who believe in armed struggle or militant groups operating in different parts of India with different organizations outfits, they are refer to themselves as *Maoists* or *Maovadis*. The term *'Naxal'* derives from the name of the village Naxalbari in the state of West Bengal where the movement had foundation.

The Historical Background

Our Honourable Prime Minister has opined that Naxalism (Naxalite Movement) is the biggest internal security for the country. The *Naxalite* Movement which is believed to follow the philosophy from Marx, Lenin and Mao's (*Marx, Engels, Lenin, Stalin and Mao's Philosophy*) philosophy to capture power through armed struggle. The scope of Communism may be no longer worry the Europe, but it continues to worry the Indian State and its ruling powers from its vast rural tribal hinterland. The (*2nd Armed Communist Movement*) movement started in May 1967 from a small village called Naxalbari, when three share croppers supported by Communist Party of India (Marxist) {The Communist Party of India was founded in the 1920s to create an alternative mass movement to the existing Congress anti-imperialist movement. The Communist movement grew out of economic causes and was rooted against the classes whether British or Indian. The "revolt" was not against the colonial government and the ruling Congress as much as it was against the capitalist system} *(The Communist party was formed in abroad in 1920, but it was formed in India in 1925. So, it is correct to say 1925 as formation year. The movement was against both colonial masters and Indian capitalists and landlord exploiters. Its aim was to establish an exploitation free socialist system in India. The party was split into two, as CPI and CPI(M), popularly known as pro- and anti-Congress Communists respectively. Actually both parties follow basically same parliamentary line and not seriously tried to build revolution in India. Again another division occurred in CPI(M) party and revolutionary ranks came out of it to form CPI(ML) party and Naxalbari type movement. This happened after the repression of the CPI(M) collision government on struggling peasants of Naxalbari.* These hungry peasants lifted the grains from a granary of a landlord without giving any share. A small village yet it gave name to the all kinds of revolutions against the powerful classes in the future. Three police stations Naxalbari, Kharibari and Phansidewa, where an armed struggle was ignited not only for land, but for state power according to Communist leaders. Why did they start this uprising, the share croppers were exploited by the landlords and the fear of getting evicted from the land was always haunting the tribals and the landless.

The uprising was under the leadership of their ideologue, a 49 year old Communist Late comrade Charu Mazumdar, who defined the objective of the new movement as 'seizure of power through an agrarian revolution'. The strategy was to elimination of the feudal order in the Indian countryside to free the poor from the clutches of the exploitative landlords and replace alternative land reforms. The tactics was guerrilla warfare by the peasants to eliminate the landlords and build up resistance against the state's police force which came to help the landlords, and gradually set up 'liberated zones' in different parts of the country that would ultimately joining together into a territorial unit of the proletarian power. The uprising at Naxalbari was crushed by the police within a few months, the movement spread over March to till the end of May 1967, caught like fire in other parts of the country, but it did bring changes in the Indian socio-cultural scenario. (*The movement was started in May 1967 and continued till July 1972, till the martyrdom of Charu Majumdar. Then the movement was set backed.*)

The Cross Border Impact

The inception and development of the *Naxalite* movement under the leadership of the CPI (Marxist-Leninist) should also be positioned in the modern-day global context of the 1960s. During this phase in Europe, Asia and America, there were eruptions of radical struggles according to the readings of Marx, the literature which inspired individual courage and the willingness to sacrifice for a cause. These trends were well reflected in the national liberation struggle of the Vietnamese; in the civil rights movement of USA; students' agitations in Western Europe; in Che Guevara's sacrifice in the jungles of Bolivia, and China's cultural revolutions, all were the quest to go for some new dream of international solidarity of all revolutionaries. Today, it had affinity from the neighbouring country Nepal and from the South Asian network of *Maoist/ Naxal* organizations.

The Naxalite movement is a political movement which ignited in India in 1967, when there was an armed uprise of peasants and labourers against the local landlords in a place called Naxalbari in West Bengal, the peasants storm the granaries of the landlords, forcibly harvested standing crops, burnt records of outstanding debts etc. This new upsurge gave rise to formation of a major party in 1969 called Communist Party of India (Marxist-Leninist). As the name suggests, this new party believed that the Indian revolution would be achieved by following the Marxist-Leninist ideology and Mao Tse-Tung's thought. The *Naxalbari* movement became very popular amongst youth in late 1960s and early 1970s, thousands were killed, arrested and imprisoned on a scale exceptionally in the post-Independence history of India, the movement spread to significant parts of rural and tribal India, wherever the people were poor and the most exploited. Unfortunately, from early years and in the following decades, for various reasons, the CPI (ML) heavily got divided. According to one estimate, there are as many as 60 *Naxalite* factions operating in different parts of the country.

The other left groups in India do not advocate violence. The Communist Party of India (CPI), which was the parent Communist Party, broke into two factions after the 1962 Sino-Indian War, because of differing interpretations of the War, and unstable implications, especially on the Communist movement in India. (*CPI Party had divided in 1964. Along with International debate the approach towards ruling Congress was also the issue of difference inside the party.*) Three trends emerged which are well articulated by different Communist groups as revisionists. (*Revisionist CPI and Modern revisionists like CPI(M) were following, parliamentary path and revolutionary CPI(ML) advocated armed revolution—these are three trends at that time.*), people who believe in armed struggle and the other who follow the parliamentary form of democracy. Beginning with the elections in 1967 in Kerala and West Bengal, it slowly adapted itself to work within the Indian state, (*Beginning with 1952 election after Telengana armed struggle and 1967 United Front government of CPI(M) and Bangla Congress, a splinter group of Congress in West Bengal....*), preferring to work for a communist cause within a bourgeoisie state. In fact, the Naxalbari and Naxalbari type of uprisings were required to be crushed by the very government that came to power in West Bengal in 1967, a coalition of the CPI-Marxist and the Congress.

In this context electoral politics, it is interesting to note on how the Maoists of Nepal have actively and successfully managed the shift from guerrilla warfare against the state (represented by the monarchy) to electoral politics. After 10 long years of 'People's War', witnessing deaths of 12000 of cadre, the Communist Party of Nepal-Maoist finally entered the political field. While this paradigm shifts, seems to be against the basic doctrines of Mao, but it was sensible and suited the Maoists in Nepal. Many debates and discourses are taking place among the Indian Naxal believers that is the right time to enter into electoral politics. But looking at the size of the country it is not possible to go for the political stadium. But in the study area the electoral profile is controlled by the party and influenced. In a way the impact of Nepal's role is slowly inducing some sense for open fight. But they do agree that this is not the right time to do so. (*Like the Indian parties CPI and CPI (M), the ultra-modern revisionist CPI (ML) parliamentary fractions, Nepal Maoists also surrendered before the imperialism and their home ruling classes through parliamentary path.*)

Even in India, while the Naxalbari uprising occurred with the unspoken consent with active participation of peasants, the recent incidents of violence, such as the Jehanabad Jailbreak (2005), the Chhattisgarh attack on police forces (2007) and stray incidents like blasting of train tracks, police stations etc. are increasingly disjointed with the interests of the masses. In this context, it is easy to understand the Communist Party of Nepal-Maoist's actions. It undertook violent measures till they had the consent of the majority, and abjured violence when the people's interests (favoured by a turn from monarchy towards republican democracy) became antagonistic to further violence. In India on the other hand, the Maoists have not yet followed this direction and continue to campaign for violence. However, as these acts of armed uprising against the state become more and more separated from people's interests, the movement may lose popular support.

Initiation in India and Orissa

The Naxalbari uprising or any kind of revolution that sparked in different places of India, parallel in spite of being derailed by excesses, arrest, errors and crimes committed in the name of 'class-struggle' which initially began as a campaign for putting an end to bureaucratic authoritarianism and transforming the nature of the system. But the Naxalite movement was a part of this contemporary, worldwide urge among radicals to return to the roots of revolutionary idealism. In the Indian context, it took the source of all revolutions in the Third World—the peasants, which had a tradition of fighting against the British imperialism and feudalism. The Naxalite leaders drew inspiration from the Indian peasant uprisings of the eighteenth and nineteenth centuries and the more modern organized armed peasants' struggles led by Communists in Telengana of south India in the late 1940s, as well from the other global demonstrations of protest.

After the death of the Russian Communist leader Stalin, there was a revisionism which was flowing within the communist revolutionaries. As a result there was a major faction in the party during the 1964 and the communist party got divided into two. This can be termed as the first major division in the party. The newly formed communist party of India (Marxist) could not give the right direction to the revolution, was unable to question the nature of the state and the policies which affect the poor peasants. There was lot of internal differences among the party members during that phase.

The Naxalbari

To solve these issues the newly formed CPI (Marxist) deviated from the revolution/people's struggles and adopted the electoral politics, and in this process lot of people got divided from the party. Members who were not in favour of the electoral politics they in fact started a new phase of ideological revolution, among these, main pioneers were Charu Mazumdar, Saroj Dutt, Amulya Sen, Kanhai Chaterjee and Sushital Ray Choudhury. With this background Charu Mazumdar presented the eight historic documents for revolution before the revolutionary powers *(not powers but caders)* of our country in 1965, the documents known as the historic documents in Indian Communism (*Communist struggle*). Basing on these documents there were arguments and counter-arguments in the country within Communist Party. As an outcome of this series of arguments the armed Naxalbari uprising blossomed with the new version of Marxism, Leninism and Mao's thought to seize the political power. To direct and manage the Naxalbari revolution lot of leaders separated them from CPI (M) and formed AICCR (All India Coordination Committee of Communist Revolutionary) and later from this platform of AICCR, the Communist Party of India (Marxist-Leninist) came into existence on dated 22-4-1969.

On 18th March, 1967 there was a peasant's conference which was organized at Darjeeling when the ruling government in West Bengal was in coalition with the leadership of CPI (Marxist), during this convention, the following major proposals were agreed upon:

- To eradicate monopoly over the rights on land.
- (*For*) land distribution through peasant's committee among the landless.
- To developing a sustainable resistance against the feudalism more than 20,000 landless, middle farmers and poor people who were involved in the struggle from 1951 took a pledge to accomplish the above three tasks to end exploitation under the communist revolutionary leaders. The struggle which started during 1951 was at its peak during May 1967, and the poor peasants took up arms against the state repression which was in full-fledge operation to suppress the struggle. During that time the main three formulas which had a positive impact on the whole country were people's awakening, people's uprisings, and people's resistance. Using these formulae the poor struggled against the feudalism-capitalism and colonialism to acquire the political power. From these three formulas the revolutionaries formed the people's guerrilla's army for resistance.

As per the Census of 1961 there were 3 crore of *adivasis* in India and the level of exploitation was very high on them. The Santhals of

West Bengal got united with the communist revolutionaries and fought against the state in Naxalbari, Jalpaigudi and Karibai which was an armed struggle. The impact of this armed struggle spread over the areas of Srikakulum and Parthipuram of Andhra Pradesh, south Orissa border areas, Medinipur and Gopibalavpur of West Bengal, Lakshmipur of Uttar Pradesh, *Dandakaranya* regions of undivided Madhya Pradesh; [*In Dandkaranya the movement was started only after 1980, following the self-critical review of old Naxalite movement by Andhra Pradesh state committee and formation of CPI(ML)-PW*].

The Srikakulum and Parvatipuram

In all the areas, similar struggles were seen, but the spark was more intense in Andhra Pradesh in Parvathipuram and Srikakulam bordering of South Orissa. The problems of the tribals in South Orissa and the Girijans of Srikakulum were similar as both the groups were fighting against the oppressed system, the region mainly consists of Jatapus and Konda Doras (*kuvies and souras*), who got united and rise to the occasion. The main leaders who were spreading the message of revolution in Andhra Pradesh were Subarao Panigrahy, Adibatla Kailasam and Vemtapu Satyam who were whistle blowers of the movement. There were simultaneous strenuous efforts seen all over the country. To accelerate this movement against the feudalism, Charu Mazumdar visited Andhra Pradesh and bordering areas of South Orissa on March 29th, 1969, after his visit in bordering areas of South Orissa which is adjacent to Andhra Pradesh the activities of the movement caught fire and increased momentum. The Srikakulam movement which was basically led by two teachers was very much in news during those days and it impacted to a large extent to the Koraput region. There were lot of differences observed among the Communist leaders in India in their ideology for which the four long years of Telengana struggle got collapsed which was against the Hyderabad Nizams.

Srikakulum movement could mobilize lot of educated youth, and the movement increased reaches to the Girijans of that area. The 300 sq. miles area of Parvatipuram was mainly inhabited by Jatapu and Konda Dora, whose main enemies were the money lenders, Forest officials, Police and Revenue officials. The Girijans got united against this injustice done to them. The movement which started by P. Ramulu in 1951 in this area got the right pace during the Naxalbari period, using the tri-formula, around 300 villages were mobilized for this struggle. V. Satyam was organizing people. A. Kailasam who was from a rich family donated all his land to tribals and joined the Communist Party had full dedication to the ideology. It can't be said that the Communist Party in the Srikakulam and Parvatipuram area only opted for armed struggle. During the Panchayat elections of 1962 they participated, and won most of the seats in the area. After winning they felt that the rich are creating obstacles in the governance process which provoked lot of dissatisfaction among the Girijans and they started a food raid movement by organizing themselves during the famine. The leaders were arrested between 24th June, 1967 and 25th August, 1967, section 144 (**Section 144** is a section of Indian Code of Criminal Procedure, which prohibits assembly of five or more persons, holding of public meetings, and carrying of firearms and can be invoked for up to two months, www.wikipedia.org) was active in the 200 villages in the area. By breaking this law people resisted and called a public meeting to show their aggression. When the police and their agents started attacking the innocent tribals who came for the meeting, two people died on the spot and they abused the women who came to participate in the meeting.

The message was spread to the people in the whole of Andhra Pradesh, against the repression by the police and also by the landlord's goons. After the killing of two tribals, the case was reported in the police station, the landlords who were key persons in killings of those two were put behind the bars. But they were released through money power. The police repression increased, people were harassed looting their belongings.[2] All these incidents of the movement occurred, simultaneously in India during the phase. During this phase the wing of AICCR started in Andhra Pradesh on 29th June, 1968. Armed squads were prepared in all these areas to raise voices. There were raids on the Zamindar houses, distribution of food grains to poor people from the godowns of landlords, distribution of household articles, attacks on police camps, Jan Adalats were organized, and debt papers were burnt. The tribals were got influenced more by these activities. By the end of 1969 there were 86 people's courts/Jan adalats were organized in 86 places to solve the people's issues. When the property of the rich was distributed among the poor became the main crux by which the tribal's got united more in number. The series of events continued to occur in the movement, the repression of the government got intensified and in May 1969 the Chief Minister of Andhra Pradesh sent 15,000 Central protection forces to Parvatipuram agency area.

The central force as usual started their role with looting, fake encounters and illegal detention, torturing women became the regular feature in the area. The leaders were killed in encounters by the police in 1970, and after the extreme repression of the police the movement lost its pace. When Charu Mazumdar was arrested in West Bengal and was killed in police custody on 28th July, 1972, the whole movement completely lost direction and the passion it had. Many leaders surrendered, many changed their line of revolution and many shifted their ideological tracks, many went underground, many became informers to the Police, and many were behind bars.

The Orissa (Naxalbari Type) Revolution

The Communist Party in Orissa was successful to a large extent in mass mobilization. (*The party was formed with the help of WB party in 1936. Bhagbati Panigrahy was the first leader. Under his leadership anti-colonial and anti-feudal struggle had developed in costal districts,* viz. *undivided Balasore, Cuttack, Puri, Ganjam etc. and to some extent in Koraput, Nilagiri, Dhenkanal and in Ranpur anti-colonial Praja Andolan party played a major role.*) The party grew under the influence of the Telengana armed struggle and the ideology on the party was spread across the state of Orissa. Under the leadership of the party the Nilagiri struggle, the Paraja Andolan of Ranpur, fight against *Muthadar* in Ganjam, fight against the systems like *Bethi* in Koraput, rights over Podu land were the main achievements of the party in uniting people. As a result of this people's resistance, the tenant's rights law was passed. The ideological difference which started earlier did not have much impact on the Orissa Communist leaders. *[Major party leaders and cadres had remained with CPI. Only leaders and cadres of Nilagiri, Ranpur, Koraput and few from old Puri district had joined CPI(M). During Naxalbari movement the leaders and cadres of Koraput and few students of Ganjam, along with some intellectuals joined CPI(ML)].* The force was only limited to Koraput and Gajapati regions. The leaders of the contiguous patch (Gajapati and undivided Koraput) D. Bhuban Mohan Pattnaik, Nagbhusana Pattnaik, Jagannath Mishra were in constant touch with the Srikakulam leaders. Among the tribal communist leaders Purusottam Palli, Purnachandra Gomango, were the front-liners. The commitment of these leaders the *Adivasis* were organized for people's movement. The food movement in Gunpur during the famine time in 1962 was a biggest landmark in the Orissa Communist history. The Parvatipuram and Srikakulam struggles had a major impact on the Koraput region the bordering areas. D. Bhuban Mohan Pattnaik and Nagabhusan Pattnaik took main roles in fighting the *Adivasis* land related dispute case in the courts of Jeypore, Parlakhemundi and in other areas.

These two leaders became very close to the people of this region. By 1964 Harish Chandra Baxipatra was elected as the Koraput District Secretary of the *Communist Party of India (Marxist),* but he was sent to jail under different cases, later he kept himself away from the party. After that Purusottam Palli became the Secretary of Koraput the leaders were mainly emphasizing on the people's issues on land and worker's rights. (A pamphlet of the then Communist party is given in Annexure-4). When the pressure was more on the government to release the political prisoners few leaders came out of the jail and started organizing the workers of JK Paper Mill in Rayagada, Jeypore Motor Sangha, Balimela Power Project worker to strengthen the Communist movement. The workers movement and the Adivasi movement were imbibed with Communist ideology. All the south Orissa leaders joined the Communist Party of India (Marxist), this leader from the beginning supported the Srikakulam movement and together they formed Andhra Orissa border committee, and then they joined in AICCR as earlier mentioned.

In 1967 Balimela workers movement, the Gunpur food raid movement, created waves all over Orissa including the workers of the iron mine (Biramitrapur) in Sundergarh also was shaking the government. Student leaders like Ramesh Sahu, Santosh Mohapatra *(SCB Medical college student Gopi Mishra, Khadagpur IIT student Narayan Kundu)* believed in armed struggle and joined the movement. They pioneered in organizing students. The intellectual like Rabi Singh, Jaladhar Nanda played significant role in the movement. On May 1st, 1968 around 5000 workers *gheraoed* the Chitrakonda Police Station and looted the arms. The then Chief Minister of Orissa Sri Rajendra Narayana Singh Deo while answering to a question in the Vidhan Sabha, informed that only 32 guerrilla squads are functioning in Gunupur region, and to suppress them, Orissa Government has asked police force from Andhra Pradesh, and from the Central Government.

Nabina Subudhi and Sadashiv Das from Balugaon used to publish two revolutionary thought magazines called *Bela* and *Abha.* These two magazines were pro-movement and police used to arrest people if they were found reading these magazines. Ganonath Patro who was working as a Lecturer from Parlakhemundi College, left the job and joined the movement. When the big and small initiatives were rising in Odisha, there was a secret meeting in Kapilpur of Gunupur from 23rd January 1969 to 28th January 1969 to expedite the tempo of the movement. The state showed its repressive actions, all leaders were arrested and were sent to jail under the Chitrakonda police station looting case. The leaders were in Jail till 1972, few were still behind the bars till to 1977; the ideological difference which cropped at the national level had a strong effect on Orissa, by which the leaders got divided basing on the armed revolution and electoral politics. After a long break from 1977 to 1984, the new face of the movement was visualized with proper direction and confidence. After several divisions in the party the only visible party which trusted the armed struggle was the Communist Party of India (Marxist-Leninist) peoples war, *[CPI(ML) party unity and MCCI all three groups were leading the armed struggle. The Liberation group had quit armed struggle line slowly from 1980, and had come out over ground in 1992. Other groups like 2nd Cc were also leading armed struggle in few pockets. Except Liberation, all parties together with has formed Maoist party. The PW started its work in AP and Dandkaranya. Party Unity and MCCI both were working in Bihar, Jharkhand and Bengal, Punjab etc. mainly.]* which revived the pace in the Abujmadh areas of the undivided Madhya Pradesh in the early 1980s.

In 1984 *(as part of DK movement in 1980, sent to Malkangiri, which was situated in between DK and East Godavari of AP.)* the Communist Party of India (Marxist-Leninist) people's war sent its members to re-visit Gajapati, Rayagada, Koraput and Malkangiri areas. The party came here with an agenda of land grab, increase in wages, rights for bamboo cutters, price hike for Kendu leaf workers, and this heated the pulse of the government by 1996. Sabyasachi Panda who was in Communist Party of India (Marxist-Leninist) Liberation, left the party in 1995 and started working with the same agenda, parallel to people's war group which was working in the interior hilly areas of Gajapati, Rayagada. and Kandhamal. He started organizing the tribals of Rayagada and Gajapati under the banner of Chasi Mulia Sangha, Kui Lawenga Sangha and believed in raising voices in democratic way but they had full support of people's war group who believed in armed struggle. (*This group had some differences with the then PWG regarding developing people's consciousness through mass movements, and not to give over emphasis on isolated armed actions. Armed struggle should develop as per people's movement and development; this was the opinion of this group. The group was close to CPI (ML) Party Unity, to which PWG thought a party of right deviation. The group started its work in 1995 and had developed one mass base in 1997 and was able to influence Orissa politics to some extent. This group joined Unified CPI(ML) PW in end of 1998. The third group MCCI had also started its work in Jagatsingpur in 1995 under the leadership of one Majdur leader, who had worked in West Bengal. Their work was mainly to propagate revolutionary ideology among selected cadres and recruit them as per need. In 2004 they had started their work under the leadership of Orissa SOC of MCCI in Sambalpur-Deogad-Sundargad area by directly sending one armed group from Bihar-Jharkhand, in which some cadres of Jagatsingpur joined. Jagatsingpur remained as the main recruiting centre till 2008 until there were many arrests by the State.)*

Responsible Factors in its Favour

India as a country was a major agricultural civilizations, and the world's first revolution was the agricultural revolution. In the early age, human was a hunter gatherer who kept moving from place to place in search of food, this was the tribal stage of Indian history. With the beginning of the agricultural revolution, permanent human settlements first appeared in the smaller river valleys where the soil was lighter, e.g. the Chambal, Godavari rivers etc. But still few were semi-migrant tribal cultures. Bronze and later Iron implements were produced, human civilization migrated to the alluvial flood plains of the major river valleys where the soil was heavier and required domesticated draught animals (like Bulls, Buffaloes) to till the soil. This brought the human settlements size to much bigger and more permanent in nature. The emerging industries of brick making, pottery and other subsidiaries were established. Soon big villages started evolving which were converted into prosperous cities accumulating capital. Then cities became states and later empires. *(In India, first agricultural civilization had emerged in big tree less desert lands in the river banks, like Mohenjodaro and Harappa this is also worldwide phenomena of first agricultural civilization. The jhum cultivation was done in forest areas with crude methods. Then after discovery of Iron or any other metal, surplus produced permanent agriculture developed in big river banks. Aryans had captured the home lands and agricultural land of Indian tribals. Assimilate some tribes in their cast system; those were defeated by them in war. Those refused to surrender had fled to forest and other areas to survive them from Aryans attack. Gradually, these tribal areas also came under non-tribal rule, directly or indirectly.)*

With the development of States, soon two parallel civilizations were well noticeable in the Indian subcontinent. The main agricultural civilizations were cantred along the major river valleys and the tribal cultures in the smaller river valleys. The less developed civilization still followed the nomadic culture, hunter-gathering and practiced *jhoom* (slash and burn) form of primitive cultivation. The empire that arises in the agricultural civilization found it best to marginalize the tribal civilization. The agricultural economy was based on the principles to generate a surplus through land revenue. The tribal regions were unproductive—as they did not generate an economic surplus and communication/infrastructural infiltration was too costly and not considered value the attempt. As a result, three successive rulers that unified India—the Mauryan, the Mughal and the British, were comfortable to marginalize the forest/ nomadic tribal societies and left them in fine isolation. In the isolation of the forests, the tribal had little notion of scarcity, surplus and hence, little motivation for loot. As a result the Indian subcontinent, therefore, simply marginalized its tribal societies and left them isolation.

Today, India is in the process of going beyond the agricultural to the Industrial revolution in tribal areas, some of the poorest and least developed regions. Ironically, these regions are richest in mineral deposits of Coal, Iron, Aluminum and many other industrial minerals. 85 per cent of Indian coal reserves are in Chhattisgarh, Andhra Pradesh, West Bengal, Orissa and Jharkhand. These are also areas with huge reserves of Iron ore and Bauxite (Aluminium). As such these tribal areas can no longer be left in complete isolation. Still, (the study area) the Koraput region located in different stages of tribal society who practice hunting, gathering food from the forest, jhumming, terraced cultivation and settles cultivation, which gives ample scope for fighting with each other. The society has not evolved to compete with the industrialization. As infrastructural intrusion takes place in these mineral rich tribal areas, the two cultures as stated above are bound to have conflicts with each other. The establishment of industrial townships, mining settlements and Special Economic Zones (SEZs) is bound to disturb the tribal way of life. The exclusion of tribals from the forest by the Forest Act is already an axis of violent confrontation between the two stages of human civilization. Naxalism needs to be viewed in the prism of a clash between the agricultural and industrial civilization in India. The tribal lens has to be kept as priority when we talk about Naxalite movement.

In February 2008, the Indian Prime Minister had felt compelled to highlight Naxalism as the most significant threat to India's internal security. Stating from a minor clash in 1967 (Naxalbari) the movement had taken a long journey into a serious security concern. What was significant, that the firmness of the ideology in the rural and tribal areas despite of being defeated by all Government. In spite of the Government's concerted efforts, the movement had continued to grow and escalate in the degree of violence and extent of spread. The following table charts the spatial growth of LWE from 2001-2008 in the first decade of this century:

Table 3.1: Statistics of the Naxal Affected District

Year	*No. of States*	*No. of Districts Affected*
2001	9	53 Districts
2004	13	105 Districts
2008	17	180 Districts

Note: 2009, also the figure remained as 180 districts.
Source: *Journal of Defense Studies*, 2008.

If we see the human development index of the study area; (Human development index is based on three dimensions of human development that are considered to be fundamental, namely longevity, knowledge, and a measure of necessary income) the values of Human Development Index of the State as a whole turns out to be 0.579, this is regarded as somewhat medium level Human Development Index). The human development index of the study area.[3]

Table 3.2: HDI of the Study Area Districts

Indicators	*Districts*			
	Gajapati	*Koraput*	*Malkangiri*	*Rayagada*
Infant Mortality Rate	143	136	151	131
Health Index	0.173	0.218	0.122	0.250
DDP per capita in 1998-99, (in Rs.) (at 1993-1994 prices)	5.498	5.148	4.436	5,300
Income index	0.558	0.539	0.497	0.547
Combined Gross enrolment ratio (6-14 years (2003-04)	84.82	88.12	84.73	88.21
Overall literacy rate index	41.73	36.2	31.26	35.61
Combined gross enrollment ratio (6-14 years) index	0.848	0.881	0.847	0.883
Education index	0.561	0.535	0.491	0.531
HDI value	0.431	0.431	0.370	0.443
HDI index	28	27	30	25

Source: Human Development Report, Odisha.

Table 3.2 shows that the Human Development Indices do give a glaring picture which becomes an important factor for multiplying the Naxalite ideology in the tribal pockets of the south Orissa. India's present venture into various investments in industries, opening of markets and "resources" to foreign companies, especially the resources of land, mines, forest and water has made the tribal life chaotic. This present explosion is hiking the markets by uprooting indigenous tribal communities all over central India, and the study area which is also causing damage to India's environment. The extraction of minerals not only affects the immediate and long-term environment but has also lead to mass dispossession. *Adivasis* now are showing a determination in refusing to get displaced. Even the most generous "Resettlement and Rehabilitation packages" offer only cash and promises of jobs which in practice are rarely kept, land for land is not mandatory (as required by international standards set by the International Labour Organization etc.). The backdrop of NALCO displaces and the other victims of dam displaces have lost their culture and food basket which they were once owners. This is what the main cause behind the police killing of 14 *Adivasis* at Kalinganagar on 2nd January, while protesting against a steel plant about to be constructed on their land—the most high profile story. This factor is also connected to the spread of Naxalite influence in these areas, and recent escalation.

One needs to understand the qualities of tribal society, the reasons why displacement and loss of their land, livelihood, dignity and self-sufficiency lead to a cultural genocide, and their struggle to keep it intact. Another role is to analyse the power structures which impose these changes on *Adivasis*, including the mining companies themselves, the officials of the government, a strong nexus works and this power the changes the whole tribal society. What is need to understand is the factors responsible and how they impact? How do these companies use such power? In the name of development nothing can be imposed on tribals. Tribals have resisted since ages and they have faced lot of repression from the colonial government and also from the Independent Indian democratic government. Be it anywhere in India and Orissa the tribals have shown up their concerns through uprisings, revolts and rebellions. If you take the case of south Orissa it has major water resources projects and also the region is full of mineral wealth, but the region is famous for backwardness and termed as Koraput-Bolangir-Kalahandi (KBK) region which is covered under a special regional plan.

The big dams like Indravati displaced about 40,000 people. As in all of Orissa's big dams, no proper record was kept of those displaced, and compensation at the rate of Rs. 14,000 per acre of land taken has never been paid. Surrounding villages that were promised electricity from the huge hydro-power to be generated are still in dark. The loss of forest alone has been huge and most of it has been felled. The project was funded by loans from the World Bank. A tribal woman said to a World Bank official visiting the site to be affected in April 1993, *"If we starve, you also bear a responsibility"*. A movement against the dam had been crushed by mass arrests in April 1992. For Orissa's indigenous tribal population all these projects have absolute poverty destroying their culture and People's Movements in India. From a tribal point of view, the company is essentially invading their territory, taking over their land and common space, and bringing outsiders who serve the company or set-up many businesses. To quote Bhagwan Majhi, one of the leaders of the Kashipur movement against Utkal Alumina:

> "We ask one fundamental question: How can we survive if our lands are taken away from us? We are tribal farmers. We are Earth Worms. Like fishes that die when taken out of water, a farmer dies when his land is taken away from him. So, we won't leave our land. We want permanent development. Provide us with irrigation to our lands. Give us hospitals. Give us medicines. Give us schools and teachers. Provide us with lands and forest. The forests we want. We don't need the company. Get rid of the company. We do not oppose development. In fact we all want development. But what we need is stable development. We won't allow our billions of years old water and land to go to ruin just to pander to the greed of some officers. We ask them not to get engaged in these destructive works. Stop this work, give us what we want if you really mean development. We tell this to our leaders. But the government has not even agreed to talk to us. They should think that nature is not only for just one or two, or three or four generations. Nature has created us, it helps us survive. The people, for whom development is meant, should reap benefits. After them, the succeeding generations should reap the benefit. That is development. It should not be merely to cater to the greed of a few officers. To destroy the age-old resources is not development" (from an interview in A.S. Das' film, *Matiro Puko*).[4]

First the British adopted isolation approach, then the charity approach by the Independent Government of India and now they are killed in the name of development and nobody has seen their emic and etic views. Ultimately day will come when we will end up seeing tribals in museums only where they are made to stay as exhibits without any life. To preserve their fight for the environment the *Adivasis* are risking their lives, the main factor be it Kashipur, be it the land struggle of Gudari in Rayagada district, the struggle against the *Sundhis* in Koraput, the fight against the miss-governance in Malkangiri, the land struggle of Gajapati or be it movement like POSCO or Kalinganagar. The Naxalite movement which is a movement of people's struggle, just supplementing the tribals energy to fight and that is favouring for participation in raising their voices. The question is, that the tribals today have in their mind that how do they help to build up a consensus in favour of them which will allow their land and separate identity? And how will they build an authoritative critique of the genocide policies still being imposed on indigenous people, is forcing them to opt for violence. Who will fill the vacuum that is created by the age old governance by Kings, landlords, by British and by the independent country.

The ethnic poor peoples of this region express that—"our goodness that after so many times of displaced but still we didn't revolted all these years, otherwise we should have done it two decades before. We got displaced for others benefit, spreading lights for others but living in total darkness under the roof of the false promised of the leaders as people of nowhere. Few of us are living in camps without even a name and identity, we called as Displaces camp 1, 2 or 3 the government even do not have proper records how many of us got displaced. It is democracy that we are aiming at?" Gisu from village Gudaguda: This village is a bordering of Malkangiri and Koraput says with suppressed anger that..."now, the contractor has been killed in Govindapalli by the Naxals, the government will never go in a fair means to find out the root cause of the killings rather it will deploy one company of CRPF or any other force who will harass poor villagers on a routine basis, all the government structures will be renovated and repaired here in the area... but what about people like us....? Will the state think about us and why this naxal movement is propagating in a macro way. The state only thinks that it can solve this problem with law and order and with minimum developmental initiatives. But it is not true...it should first accept that a major percentage of people live with less than Rs 12 per day after 68 years of Independence. Is it justice that we are talking? Certainly not, the so called democracy has not reached the people for which the movement is quite appealing for us. Rather we don't have any choice before us than to rebel. Will the state accept all this facts that the poor, the major chunk of people are unhappy, they are harassed and every day they are marginalized in all aspects of life? They are frustrated with the eyewash activities of the government. When will the government reflect on its own system and its behaviour ?"

"Today whoever is fighting for their rights is branded as Naxalite. If we raise our voice we are killed in encounters, if we question we have to face illegal detention and in the coming years we will be languishing in jails for years waiting for bails. The state has a complete nexus to prove that it's right by all means and we have to face the consequences if at all we stand to the occasion. So, what can we do.... Take up arms and fight. Sona, a soura tribal person of Gajapati district says very happily that their way of talking (referring to the Naxals) is so touching; no government person has ever talked to me like the way they approach. It gives us confidence, knowledge and information. It gives to understand our own condition and it gives to go deep to understand and analyse why we are poor. The Naxals are also in desperate to kill but we tribals have no choice."

Patronization by the Political Parties and Foreign Agencies

It is worth saying that the Naxalites do take advantage of mis-governance, corrupt bureaucracy and politicians and spread intolerance among tribal areas against the functioning of the system and to further their cause, which is true in many parts of Koraput district. Many quotes have been heard from the different political parties that they do appreciate their ideology, but not the means. Among the communist parties who don't believe in armed revolution do justify the ideology preached by Naxalism. There have been media highlights that the Naxalites do get training from former armed group LTTE (Liberation Tigers of Tamil Eelam), both the groups have affinity towards each other. The coordination committee of Maoist Parties and organizations of South Asia usually goes by abbreviation, CCOMPOSA, a federation of various South Asian Maoist parties and movements, and basic purpose is to coordinate all activities in South Asia[5]. This is very strong party with a South Asian affiliation supports the Indian Naxalite movement. It is hard to say who supports and who is not, as everybody is afraid of being labelled as a Naxalite sympathizer in the eyes of the government. But many civil liberty groups though they don't have any political affiliation do support the movement. It is explained by the informants that all the political parties do patronize by giving money even though they do not like it.

Different Stages of Development

Formative stage (Structural Foundation: 1950-1952)

Before discussing the formation stage of the movement one of the major event that history of South Orissa witnessed is the Land *Satyagraha* by a veteran Gandhian is well known as Gandhi of Koraput region, Late Biswanath Pattnaik. From the pages of his own narration, *Before Naxalbari-Bhoo-Satyagraha*:

"The Koraput region, blessed with natural resources, hilly terrains and rich ethnic diversity, still a laboratory for many experiments from dams to schemes. Biswanath Pattnaik, born in Kumrada village of Ganjam district in 1916, May 11, was 8th child of his parents. Biswanathji who was basically interested to become a saint (*sannyasi*) twice attempted, but failed. During 1930-1947 which was the crucial period for India, where whole country was going through the freedom struggle, he could not stop himself and started his way for social service. He got trained in Bari, Jajpur in Gopabandhu Choudhuri Ashram. As a part of the freedom struggle people of India were encouraged for hand weaving, and cotton cultivation. It was decided that Sri Biswanath Pattnaik will start his work in Koraput Region after his training. Koraput had different social dynamics. The people of Koraput were very much loyal to the King, they used to pay tax, it had systems like Bethi, Gudum, and exploitation by Sundhi's. Though the British used to address the kings as *zamindars*, but people considered them as kings. The kings were not directly interacting with people, and *Amins* and *Muthadars* were the intermediaries who were the main tax collectors, who had the full autonomy of working and exploiting the people.

Gudum system is just like the present days Revenue circle. Few villages were considered as one *Gudum* and *Muthadar* used to be the main in charge of the area for revenue collection. Whereas in case of *Bethi* system the labour was compulsory, and sometimes free obligation to the king (landlord). Tribals used to go to Jeypore from Gunupur, walking all the miles to offer free (compulsory) service. The other most inhumane torture was: other forest government officials during their field visits, tribals used to carry them if the terrains were difficult. This carrying work had no payment. Mostly Amin/tax collections were forcing the tribals to carry them along with their belongings. If tribals will not carry them they had fear that the Amin might play some mischief and they might lose their land.

These are few forms of exploitation that was in the Koraput society in 1941. Sri Biswanath Pattnaik came to Kujendri (6 miles away from Gunupur) in 1941, with a vision to start development work among tribals and understand the world from their point of view. He stayed in the house of the village head, he was Bairu Gomango, who later became his main support in mobilizing the tribals of Gunupur region. Biswanathji started living like a tribal person's life and adopted their lifestyles to observe them closely. He started teaching them literacy, organized women for village sanitation, organizing them for freedom struggle. In organizing women when Sandi Sabar (Bairu Gomango's daughter) took the key role. Twice Biswanathji went to Jail for freedom struggle along with his *adivasi* associates, but this never stopped his spirit and he didn't deviate from his mission.

After lot of efforts from all over the country India got Independence in 1947; and the tribals of Gunupur Region as well as others thought that now our government will not act as the British and will surely take radical reforms for poor people. There were programmes which introduced, but it could not protect the interests of the tribals. For tribals the independence became like an elephant which was seen and felt by four blind people. The money meant for tribals did not reach them, a major chunk of the money was siphoned by the officials, whoever genuinely worked for tribal development were not successful in achieving their aim. All these events disturbed the mind of Sri Biswanathji. He felt that, if tribals, and the development done by the government are two parallel lines who will never meet with each other. During 1951, the Andhra Pradesh state was burning with the Telengana struggle; looking at the scenario he thought it is necessary that a "society without exploitation and equal rights to all is essential". Since he was very much accepted by the tribal society, he appealed them: "if you want to free yourself from exploitation then prepare yourself, raise your voice, don't wait for others to address your problems". He also preached Mahatmaji's economic equality for all. But to bring economic equality in India the governance did not took any steps towards fulfilling this objective. Even Late Gopabandhu Choudhury also had mentioned that:

- In Koraput region, the question of exploitation is not between tribals and non-tribals. Even tribals do exploit tribals. It is the question of rich and poor and it is the question of power.
- It can't be said that only Telugu, Kumuti are exploiting tribals many Oriya's are also exploiting the tribals.

- The tribals are dependent on laws to get their lands, but the law meant for tribal land has many loopholes through which one can easily escape. So, stringent laws are required to check and regulate.
- After a long self-analysis and reflection Biswanathji started *Bhoo-Satyagraha.* He always considered Gopabandhu Choudhury as his teacher and guide, he wrote to him about his idea of *Bhoo-Satyagraha*, but he did not get any reply from his Guru, without wasting time he started organizing tribals in the 30-35 villages of Gunupur region, and a committee was formed.

> The District Gazetteer of Koraput 1945 (R.C.S. Bell) has stated that in 1848 the people of Gunupur raised their voice against the king and his systems as a result of which the officers of the king had to leave the area. When in 1855 the British took over the Koraput region and appointed his own agents in 1863 when one Saura person was arrested fakely the tribals killed the Inspector of Puttasinghi and 4 constables. They set fire the Police Station.

To quote these two incidents, implies that the tribals are against the state power, and if sometimes the harassment was too much unbearable for them; they used to retaliate with their own capacities and ideas. Within 1851-1951 the outsiders have made the tribal landless in their own land, within that 100 years the tribal already could feel that no government or any government official will not be able to solve their problems, as they are the main instruments of the exploitation process. Though they listen to the government officials but do not take them seriously as they know nothing will change their lives and only false promises will remain. Biswanathji called for a Public Peasants Sabha, which was not based on any "ism" or philosophy. Biswanathji only believed in *Ahimsa*—non-violence. He though to state *Bhoo-Satyagraha* to put moral pressure on the government, so that the government will realize its duties. And *Bhoo-Satyagraha samaja* was inaugurated. The concept of the *bhoo-satyagraha* is given on page 136[6].

The translation of the above Oriya newspaper has been given here.

(Koraput is tribal dominated region. The tribals once were owing land but in a process with intrusion of outsiders they have lost their lands. Many have become landless and are starving for food. The tribals are falsely implicated in many cases and the powerful people are holding the land and other resources. Land issue is very crucial and the tribals may divert themselves to opt for violent ways. But they are aware now they

ଭୂ-ସତ୍ୟାଗ୍ରହୀ ସମାଜର ପ୍ରଚାରପତ୍ର :

ଭାଇ ଓ ଭଉଣୀମାନେ !

ଆପଣମାନେ ଜାଣନ୍ତି ଯେ କୋରାପୁଟ ଜିଲ୍ଲାର ସମସ୍ତ ବାସିନ୍ଦା ହେଉଛନ୍ତି ଆଦିବାସୀ । ଏ ଅଞ୍ଚଳର ସମସ୍ତ ଜମିଜମା ଦିନେ ଆଦିବାସୀ ମାନଙ୍କର ଥିଲା । ସେମାନେ ହିଁ ଥିଲେ ଏ ସମସ୍ତ ଜମିଜମାର ପ୍ରକୃତ ସତ୍ତ୍ୱାଧିକାରୀ । କାଳକ୍ରମେ ବାହାରୁ ଲୋକେ ଆସି ଆଦିବାସୀମାନଙ୍କର ସରଳତା ଓ ନିର୍ବୋଧତାର ସୁଯୋଗନେଇ ଅନ୍ୟାୟ ଓ ଅସତ୍ ଉପାୟରେ ସେମାନଙ୍କ ଠାରୁ ସମସ୍ତ ଜମି ଅପହରଣ କରି ନେଇଛନ୍ତି ଏବଂ ଆଜି ଆଦିବାସୀଙ୍କ ପରିବର୍ତ୍ତରେ ବାହାରୁ ଆସିଥିବା ଲୋକେ ହିଁ ହେଉଛନ୍ତି ସମସ୍ତ ଜମିର ମାଲିକ । ଫଳରେ ଏ ଅଞ୍ଚଳରେ ଆଦିବାସୀମାନେ ଆଜି ଭୂମିହୀନ । ନିଜ ଅଞ୍ଚଳରେ ଫସଲ ଆମଦାନି କରିସୁଦ୍ଧା ସେହି ଫସଲକୁ ଭୋଗ କରିବାର ଅଧିକାର ସେମାନଙ୍କର ନାହିଁ । ସେମାନଙ୍କ ମଧ୍ୟରୁ ଅନେକ ଯେ ଖାଇବାକୁ ନପାଇ ମରିଛନ୍ତି ଓ ମରୁଛନ୍ତି ଏକଥା କାହାରିକୁ ଅଛପା ନାହିଁ । ପ୍ରଧାନତଃ ବଣର ଫଳ ଓ କନ୍ଦା ଖାଇ ସେମାନେ ଜୀବିକା ନିର୍ବାହ କରୁଛନ୍ତି ଅଥଚ ଏଣେ ପୋଡୁଚାଷ କରିବା ଅପରାଧରେ ଆଦିବାସୀମାନଙ୍କ ଉପରେ ପ୍ରତ୍ୟେକ ବର୍ଷ ହଜାର ହଜାର ମକଦ୍ଦମା ଦାଏର କରାହେଉଛି ଏବଂ ସେଥିପାଇଁ ସେମାନେ ଜେଲ ମଧ୍ୟ ଭୋଗୁଛନ୍ତି । ତାହା ସହିତ ପୋଡୁଚାଷରୁ ଆମଦାନୀ କରୁଥିବା ଫସଲକୁ ଜୋରିମାନ ସ୍ୱରୂପ ଦେଇ

୧୪୬

ସର୍ବସ୍ୱାନ୍ତ ହୋଇ ପୁଣି ସେହି ବଣୁଆ କନ୍ଦାର ଆଶ୍ରୟ ନେଉଛନ୍ତି । କିନ୍ତୁ କାହିଁକି ଯେ ସେମାନେ ନିର୍ବୋଧଭାବରେ ପୋଡୁଚାଷ କରୁଛନ୍ତି ତା'ର ମୂଳକାରଣ କେହି ଅନୁସନ୍ଧାନ କରୁନାହାନ୍ତି । ଏହାର ଏକମାତ୍ର କାରଣ ହେଉଛି ଯେ ସେମାନେ ଭୂମିହୀନ । ସେମାନେ କୋରାପୁଟ ଜିଲ୍ଲାର ସମସ୍ତ ଜମିର ମାଲିକ ହୋଇ ମଧ୍ୟ ନିଜର ସମସ୍ତ ସତ୍ତ୍ୱାଧିକାରରୁ ବଞ୍ଚିତ । ସେମାନଙ୍କ ପାଖରେ ବଞ୍ଚିବା ପାଇଁ ଆଜି ଜମିଥିଲେ ସେମାନେ ପୋଡୁଚାଷ କରନ୍ତେ ନାହିଁ ବା ଖାଇବାକୁ ନପାଇ ମରନ୍ତେ ନାହିଁ ।

ବଡ଼ ସୁଖର କଥା, ଏତେ ବର୍ଷକାଳ ଅତ୍ୟାଚାର, ନିର୍ଯାତନା ଓ ଅନଟନରେ ସଢ଼ି ସଢ଼ି ଏବେ ସେମାନଙ୍କର ବୋଧଶକ୍ତି ଫେରିଆସିଛି । ସେମାନେ ଆଜି ସେମାନଙ୍କର ନ୍ୟାଯ୍ୟ ଦାବି ହାସଲ କରିବା ପାଇଁ ବଦ୍ଧ ପରିକର ହୋଇଛନ୍ତି । ଏହି ଘୋର ଅନ୍ୟାୟର ପ୍ରତିରୋଧ କରିବାର ଚେତନା ଆଜି ସେମାନଙ୍କ ପ୍ରାଣରେ ଏବଂ ଏଥିପାଇଁ ସେମାନେ ବିପ୍ଳବ ଲୋଡୁଛନ୍ତି । ଏହି ଚେତନାର ବଳରେ ସେମାନଙ୍କର ନ୍ୟାଯ୍ୟ ଦାବି. ହାସଲ କରିବା ପାଇଁ ସେମାନେ ଆଜି ହିଂସାର ଆଶ୍ରୟ ନେବାକୁ ଯାଉଛନ୍ତି । ବେଳ ଥାଉଁ ଥାଉଁ ଆମେ (ଯେଉଁମାନେ କି ସେମାନଙ୍କର ଅବସ୍ଥା ବୁଝିଛୁ) ଯଦି ସେମାନଙ୍କୁ କୌଣସି ପନ୍ଥା ନଦେଖାଉ, ତେବେ ନିକଟ ଭବିଷ୍ୟତରେ ସେମାନେ ଯେ ହିଂସାର ଆଶ୍ରୟ ନେବେ ଏଥିରେ କୌଣସି ସନ୍ଦେହ ନାହିଁ । ଫଳରେ ସାରା ଦେଶରେ ବିଶୃଙ୍ଖଳା ଓ ଅଶାନ୍ତି ବ୍ୟାପିଯିବ ।

ବହୁଚିନ୍ତା ଓ ଗବେଷଣାପରେ ମନେହେଉଛି ଯେ, ଏହି ବିପ୍ଳବର ଏକାନ୍ତ ହିଁ ପ୍ରୟୋଜନ । କିନ୍ତୁ ହିଂସାକୁ ଏଡାଇବା ପାଇଁ ଏ ଧାରାକୁ ପରିବର୍ତ୍ତନ କରିବା ଦରକାର । ଏ ଯୁଗର ମହାମାନବ ମହାତ୍ମାଗାନ୍ଧୀ ସତ୍ୟାଗ୍ରହର ଯେଉଁ ପନ୍ଥା ଦେଖାଇଛନ୍ତି ତାକୁ ଅନୁସରଣ କରିବା ଫଳରେ ହିଁ ଏହି ଅହିଂସାତ୍ମକ ବିପ୍ଳବ ଓ ସତ୍ୟାଗ୍ରହ ସଫଳ ହୋଇପାରିବ । ଅନ୍ୟାୟର ବିରୋଧ କରିବା ଓ ଜମିର ପ୍ରକୃତ ସତ୍ତ୍ୱାଧିକାରୀଙ୍କୁ ତା'ର ଜମି ଫେରସ୍ତ କରିଦେବାର ଦାବି ନେଇ ଆମେ ଗୋଟିଏ ସତ୍ୟାଗ୍ରହର ଆୟୋଜନ କରୁଛୁ । ଏଣୁ ନିବେଦନ କରୁଯେ ଆପଣ ଜାତିବର୍ଣ୍ଣ ନିର୍ବିଶେଷରେ ଏଥିରେ ପୂର୍ଣ୍ଣପ୍ରାଣରେ ସହଯୋଗ କରି ଆମର ଏ ସତ୍ କାର୍ଯ୍ୟକୁ ସାଫଲ୍ୟ ମଣ୍ଡିତ କରନ୍ତୁ ।

ତା ୨୭-୧୧-୯୧ ନିବେଦକ

ଭୂ-ସତ୍ୟାଗ୍ରହୀ ସମାଜ

ପୋ.ଅ. : କୁନ୍ଦୁରା ଜି. : କୋରାପୁଟ

୧୪୭

are inclined to solve their problems with non-violence means as preached by Gandhiji. So, we all appeal please help to fulfil our mission.

A letter about the *satyagraha* was distributed among 50 villages of Gunupur Region. Many Sabha's were organized in the villages. There were few conditions prescribed for people who will join the *Bhoo-satyagraha*. That was known as Pratingya Patra on Oath taking letter. The village list was prepared for *Bhoo-satyagraha*, in and around Gunupur Region, where first *Bhoo-satyagraha* was initiated are: Ulikona, Khariguda, Dibirisingi, Araini, Khasakam Padar, Kenduguda, Kaita Padar, Khilinggirai, Pandrapalli, Birsa, Pendli, Budaguda, Suchalipanga, Tarla, Perupang, Ambababi, Rengam, Asada, Siriguda, Lakshmipur, Hukumaguda, Laba, Kadma, Kujendri, Khilapadam, Sorisapadar, Godiyabandha, Bamunidangar, Salimi, Gojiguda, Siruguda, Badigam etc. During this *Bhoo-satyagraha*, the *satyagrahis* used to request the people who have occupied their land, file cases against them, made the whole list of encroached land; if the case was not solved within two to three hearings the tribals used to make a declaration in the public and occupy their land. This was a creative civil disobedience. (Such a letter to the landlord is given which was written in 1951-1952 is given below.)

ନିବେଦନ ପତ୍ର :

ଶ୍ରୀଯୁକ୍ତ ବୈଶ୍ୟରାଜୁ ଲକ୍ଷ୍ମୀନାରାୟଣା, କୁଜେନ୍ଦ୍ରୀଙ୍କ ସମୀପେଷୁ,

ମହାଶୟ,

ଆପଣଙ୍କ ଆଖି ଆଗରେ ବର୍ଷ ବର୍ଷ ଧରି ଭୋକ ଉପାସରେ ନାନା ଅଖାଦ୍ୟ ଖାଇ ଆପଣଙ୍କୁ ତଥା ସରକାରଙ୍କୁ ମୋର ପେଟ ଦୁଃଖ କଥା ଓ ଜମିହୀନ ଅବସ୍ଥା କଥା ବାରମ୍ବାର ଜଣାଇ ନିରାଶ ହେଲି । ବର୍ଷ ବର୍ଷ ଧରି ସବୁ ପ୍ରକାର ମାଡ଼ଗୋଳ ଓ ଅତ୍ୟାଚାର ସହି ଆପଣମାନଙ୍କ ସୁଖ ସୁବିଧା ପାଇଁ ବ୍ୟବସ୍ଥା କରି ଆସିବା ସତ୍ତ୍ୱେ ମୋର ଏ ଦରମଲା ଦେହ, ଭୋକିଲା ପେଟ ଓ ମୋ ଛୁଆପିଲାମାନଙ୍କର କଷ୍ଟ କାନ୍ଦଣା ଆପଣମାନଙ୍କ କାନରେ ବାଜିଲା ନାହିଁ । ବାରମ୍ବାର ନିବେଦନ ସତ୍ତ୍ୱେ ଆପଣ ଯେତେବେଳେ ମୋର ଦୁଃଖ ଗୁହାରୀ ନଶୁଣିଲେ, ସେତେବେଳେ ଏଭଳି ଅନ୍ୟାୟର ବିରୋଧ ପାଇଁ ଭଗବାନଙ୍କର ଆଶ୍ରୟ ନେଇ ମୁଁ ମୋ ନିଜ ସତ୍ୱ ଜମିରେ ଚାଷ କରିବାକୁ ଠିକ୍ କରୁଛି । ଏ ଜମି ଆଜି ଆପଣଙ୍କ

୧୬୩

The translation of the above letter is given here:

Dear (Name of the Landlord)

We the tribals are helpless as none of our efforts are heard by the government. The grievances are not heard by anyone in the system or outside the system. The land which is occupied by you it belongs to our forefathers. They worked for this land but by some notorious means it has gone to your hands. So, to get back my land we are entering into our lands with all non-violent means.

When the events of *Bhoo-satyagraha* started occurring in different places of Gunupur region from 24th November, 1951 to 10th June, 1952; the daily *Samaj* (local newspaper) highlighted the issue as Dacoity dispute in Koraput by Savara's. It was written that the Savara's are creating troubles, and a law and order situation.

The Savara's who completely followed the path of Mahatma Gandhiji non-violence ways, became an eye-sore to the government, viewed as law and order problem. After going through the newspaper the then Lok Sabha representative (MP) T. Sanngana condemned the incidents and told the media that *Bhoo-satyagraha samaj* is the creation of the whole problem. He appealed the tribals to keep away from the *satyagraha*, his statement was published on 1.7.1952 in *Prajatantra*. He said the outsiders who are not part of the Congress, those who have come from outside the Gunupur are using the tribals to get recognition and leadership. The problems can't be solved by taking law in hands. He appealed the tribals to leave the path of *satyagraha*. The Congress Party is trying to do the best for tribals. During the assembly session in June 1952, the question was raised on the same issue and the then Chief Minister Sri Nabakishore Choudhury answered that: Savara's tried to occupy their lands but they went without arms. Since nobody heard their grievances on land matter they have formed on *Bhoo-satyagraha* Committee to get their land back. For this no political party has provoked them. Few social workers have made them aware. Government has decided to send a special officer to Gunupur Region to study and solve the land problems of the area. Revenue Board officials will be sent to the place to end the dispute by mutual discussion. Few *Bhoo-satyagrahis* have been arrested and cases have been already filed against them. The social workers of Gunupur Region feel that it Savara's would not adopt this way then they would have adopted the violence way."

As per the orders of the Chief Minister, Revenue Commissioner, District Magistrate, and other visited Kujendri to discuss the matter with

Biswanathji. They tried to discuss with the Committee members, landlords to solve the issue with mutual understanding. If the government will not solve the issue within four months then again they will continue their *satyagraha*, was opinion. Biswanathji felt that the government machinery is not interested for radical changes, and does not want to do something truly for the poor and it seemed there was lack of political will. The country got independence, but it could not change the character of the leaders and of the government. In the meantime Vinobaji entered Orissa with his *Bhoodan* concept, but much could not be done. Nobody supported Biswanathji, the land problems did not solve. By the end of 1951, the Communist ideology had started capturing the minds of the poor. Biswanathji often opined and till his death if the problems would have been solved with genuineness then tribals would have never adopted the violent way. And the *Bhoo-satyagraha* saw its own end.

Pre-Constructive Stage

On 15th August, 1947, India got its independence; tri-colours were visible with great hope and aspirations, when everybody aspired for a better life in an independent country. A life with equality, justice and rights promised by the new Constitution. Few years passed, with Nehruian vision of socialism, and building secular temples in India in the name of national interest, Shastri's "Jai Jawan, Jai Kisan" and Indira Gandhiji's "Garibi Hatao", washed all the hopes. The poor were frustrated, and on 18th March, 1967 the frustrations are ventilated with the red flag. The peasant convention of the Siligudi sub-division, five hundred (some) armed with traditional weapons chalk out a new path for their future, for seizure of political power with a revolution model.

The Naxalbari—A New Chapter (1967-1972)

In 1966 the groundwork took place and during 1965-66 the "Siliguri Group" (of the newly formed CPI (Marxist) called for the immediate commencement of armed revolution. The Party workers started organizing the people, collecting weapons, forming peasant cells. On March 3rd, 1967, a group of Kissan/peasants surrounded a plot of land in Naxalbari region, making a boundary of Red flags around began to harvest it. The first clash was ignited when a share-cropper, Bigul Kissan, was beaten by armed agents of a local landlord. This was followed by violent clashes, the forcible seizure of land and confiscation of foodgrains, by the landlords and their gangs was smashed and a few were killed. By end of May the situation reached the level of an armed uprising. On July 19th the paramilitary force were deployed, and thousands were arrested, beaten the leaders like Charu Mazumdar, Jangal Santhal and others went underground. Many became martyrs. Few weeks later Charu Mazumdar wrote "Naxalbari has not died and will never die".

The spark of Naxalbari gets peoples recognition all over India. The oppressed started identifying themselves with the Naxalbari uprisings. The Naxalbari set aflame in Srikakulam, Birbhum, Debra, Gopiballavpur, Mushahonil, and Lakhmipur Kheri. The States of West Bengal, Andhra Pradesh, Bihar, Punjab, Uttar Pradesh, Tamil Nadu, and south of Orissa draws inspiration from its and Naxalbari has taken the armed struggle on the revolution agenda. Naxalbari took place when the poor masses of India got disappointed from its independence which was then 20 years old. It was the loss of patience and loss of trust in the leaders, Naxalbari restored the revolutionary essence of revolution among the Indians. It gave answers both practically and ideologically. It analyzed that, India is a semi-feudal country, the ruling bourgeoisie is comprador, and the independence is not real. It outlined for new democratic revolution against forces like feudalism, imperialism and capitalism. The friends of revolution are peasants, middle class and working class. It adopted the strategy of protracted people's war, building army for guerrilla warfare. It rejected elections. These were the main principles, but later the movement evolved against the multi-national companies who were to loot the tribal resources.

When the Naxalbari Movement was crushed the Naxalbari peasants Aid Committee held a conference on November 12th and 13th, 1967 and decided to form "All India Coordination Committee of Revolutionaries of the CPI (M), which undertook the macro-propagation of Marxism-Leninism Mao Zedong thought, trying to unite all Communists, the revolutionaries and the Naxalbari type struggles. During 1968 it was renewed as AICCCR —All India Coordination Committee of Communist Revolutionaries. The Naxalbari type of revolutions were catching like fire and on February 8th, 1969, AICCCR decided to form a party and CPI (Marxist-Leninist) was formed. By mid of 1969, the party movement fully went underground.

Constructive Stage (1967-1980 and 1980-2004)

This stage is very crucial which paved the ways of Naxalite movement for the next generations. This stage saw many ups and downs, but after ideological churning very few remained with the armed action of revolution. When Comrade, Charu Mazumdar died in police custody in 1972, by that time the movement was on its dust stage, with one hand there was heavy repressive actions conducted by the State and on the other hand the rise of inter-conflicts among the Communist party taking the struggle into a different mode. Many of the leaders started blaming each other for the failure of the movement. Many of them were in jail by that time and many were also surrendered before the police. After 1972 three lines of thinking emerged from the Communist Party.

1. One of the segments considered themselves to be revisionists came under platform of Communist Party of India (Marxist-Leninist) and the other Communist Party of India (Marxist-Leninist) Liberation who deviated from the main principles of the party. (*Source*: *The Naxalite Movement in India*, Singh, Prakash, Rupa & Co.) *(Revisionists mean those who are deviated from main principles of rèvolution.)*
2. The other section of the leader who surrendered before the government *(Politically by their activity and joined in the stream of CPI and CPI(M)'s electoral way...)* joined the Communist Party of India and with the Communist Party of India (Marxist) and obtained the electoral way of politics. They formed parties like Communist Party of India (new democracy) and other parties *[like CPI (ML)-red flag, CPI(ML) Kanu Sanyal, CPI(ML) Ramchandran and CPI (ML) Liberation etc.]*[7]
3. The third section of the leaders who followed the original principles of the Communist Party of India (Marxist-Leninist) and remained with the revolution ideology believed in the armed struggle. From this thought a new party emerged called Communist Party of India (Marxist-Leninist) people war under the leadership of Kondapalli Sitaramaiah. CPI (ML) people's war came into existence with the revolution leaders of Andhra Pradesh, Maharashtra and Tamil Nadu. Similarly, in West Bengal and in undivided Bihar the leaders who believed in armed struggle united and formed Maoist Communist Centre (MCCI). Few other leaders of Punjab, West Bengal and Bihar who also aimed for armed struggle formed Communist Party of India (Marxist-Leninist) party unity.

During 1998 the two parties Communist Party of India (Marxist-Leninist) party unity and Communist Party of India (Marxist-Leninist) peoples war merged and formed Communist Party of India (Marxist-Leninist) people war. Then later during 2004 these two parties Communist Party of India (Marxist-Leninist) peoples war and Maoist Communist Centre (MCC merged and formed the present active party; the Communist Party of India (Maoist).[8] Those who call themselves irrespective of their parties; call the first category as revisionists, the second category as opportunists and the third category as the adventurists. The unification is the most developed stage as far as the politics of the movements; the strategy is concerned, where they are able to move forward into newer areas and also recruiting more youth in the movement.

The Second Phase of Constructive Stage

The Unification in 2004

Since 1980, the Communist Party of India (Marxist-Leninist) [Peoples War] and the Maoist Communist Centre India had close relations with each other, respect for each other, deep faith in revolutionary character of the other organization, and a strong desire to unite as a single revolutionary organization has been the well spring of this long and enduring friendship. Both parties have reviewed their own failings in effecting this unification in the respective political and organization reports. The long strained relationship between the two parties witnessed loss of lot of precious lives, they passed also through conflicts, but the realization started from both the parties from February 2003. Talks between the two parties helped both sides to realize their errors. And on September 21st, 2004 these two parties merged to form the Communist Party of India (Maoist). CPI (Maoist) is presenting the self-criticism of the CPI (ML) PW and the MCCI on the eve of merger to the Indian proletariat, the revolutionary masse, the various revolutionary parties within and outside the country, the sympathizers and well-wishers of the Indian revolution. The unified party has also pardoned before the masses for its mistakes (from the party documents).

The Self-Criticism of MCCI

- The tense relations between MCCI & CPI (ML) PU started in

1990s. After the CPI (ML) PU & CPI (ML) PW merged together the relations continued to be so.

- This conflicts and differences assumed over the shape of beatings, killings, snatchings of weapons etc. between each other in the wider scale. It became a deep concern for all the genuine revolutionary forces within the country.
- The South Asian Regional Committee of the Revolutionary Internationalist Movement (RIM) and some other revolutionary organizations sent letters and appeals to stop clashes.
- The Central Committee of MCCI had on important meeting in January 2000, where they discussed to stop the clashes and adopting Maoism instead of Mao's thought. And on January 7th, 2000, the CC of MCCI issued an open declaration to stop the clashes. Responding MCCI, the CPI (ML) PW also came forward with a declaration in March to stop these clashes.
- With the exchange of letters, in August 2001 a joint meeting was organized at the central level, issuing an appeal to stop the internal clashes. As a result coordinal relations began to grow.
- In 2002, November, the MCCI had a strong evaluation of their approaches and perceptions with CPI ML (PU) since 1978 and with CPI (ML) PW since 1981 and concluded that:
  (a) It was a black chapter of our history.
  (b) We take the responsibility of the action that we made against them.
  (c) We discarded the earlier political positions as they were wrong.
  (d) We considered the other parties as revolutionary in words, but not in practice.
  (e) We always focused to counter them and we never adopted any method for talks.
  (f) All these occurred as we lacked the required spirit of honesty and flexibility, which was needed to solve the serious matter of mutual clashes.
- Therefore, we humbly express our sense of grief to all who lost live for our period of clashes[9].

Hence, on 23.5.2004, we promise to conclude that we will not only continue to try our best to become the benefiting disciples of the founder leaders of the MCCI, but we will also continue to strive hard for becoming able heirs of all our teachers including com. Karai Chartarjee and Com. Charu Mazumdar. At the same we promise to remain firm in rectifying our mistakes through criticism and self-criticism and continuing in advancing forward in the light of and on the basis of Marxism-Leninism-Maoism.

Self-Criticism of CPI (ML) PW

The main reasons for the genesis and growth of tensions in Bihar, Jharkhand states between the MCCI and PWG was primarily on the following issues:

First, while working in the same area the approach and outlook in handling contradictions among the people and dealing with problems that arose in the course of practice. Second, the ideological and political difference between the two parties that were reflected in different practices.

- The central committee owns its share of responsibility for the lapses that had taken place on its part by not resolving the conflict with MCCI, which was a dark chapter, and hereafter never resort to such fratricidal onslaught against our own class brothers.
- The killings of each other in 1990, contributed more to the serving relations, which was a political weakness.
- We also regret for our slogan in 1995 "wipe out MCC". The root cause of this lies in our impetuosity and sectarian approach.
- We always showed accruing finger towards MCCI, this was our sectarianism and non-proletarian approach to resolve the problem.
- We got involved in the contradictions among the village masses. Basing on one group we used to attack the local MCCI's support base. Instead of solving the contradictions with a class approach with the aim of achieving the unity among the people, and solving the contradictions in a non-antagonistic manner, we adopted a parochial and non-proletarian approach.
- Due to lack of political vision on the part of the leadership we tried behind the arguments of the rank and file. We pledge to rectify our mistakes and remould ourselves as genuine proletarian revolutionaries (party document).

The Merger

The unified party—the CPI (Maoist)—pledges itself that it will continue the revolutionary legacy and always hold high the Red Flag for the liberation of the country from the clutches of imperialism, comprador bureaucrat capitalism and feudalism for the realization of socialism and communism on a world scale. The unified Party assures the vast oppressed masses of India—the working class, the peasantry, women, *Dalit* masses, the religious minorities, *Adivasis*, oppressed nationalities, students, youth and intellectuals—that it will stand steadfast by them at all times, lead them to liberate themselves from all types of inhuman oppression, suppression and exploitation and build a new Democratic India and pass on to socialism and communism thereby achieving free and unhindered development of one and all.

We also hereby declare that the two guerrilla armies of the CPI (ML) [PW] and MCCI—the PGA and the PLGA—have been merged into the unified PLGA (People's Liberation Guerrilla Army). Hereafter, the most urgent task, i.e. principal task of the party is to develop the unified PLGA into a fall-fledged People's Liberation Army (PLA) and transforming the existing guerrilla zones into base areas thereby advancing wave upon wave towards completing the new democratic revolution. The formation day of the PLGA is to be December 2nd, the day when a people's army was formed in 2000 for the first time ever in our country, on the 1st anniversary of the martyrdom of three comrades Shyam, Mahesh and Murali. (from the Press statement October 14th 2004)[10].

After the merger of the party Orissa state committee was formed in July 2005. As per the newly formed structure Orissa has been covered by three broad based committees.

- Orissa State Committee (Consisting of a part of Rayagada, undivided Ganjam and Phulbani, undivided Dhenkanal, Puri, (*undivided Cuttack, Sambalpur, Sundargarh, Deogarh, Kendujhar, etc.*)
- Andhra Orissa Border Committee (Part of Rayagada, undivided Koraput).
- Bihar Orissa Jharkhand committee (undivided Sambalpur and Mayurbhanj). (*Source*: Party Documents) *(Only part of Kendujhar and Sundargarh, in Bihar-Jharkhand-Bengal special Area cmt and in West Bengal–Orissa border cmt part of Mayurbhanj is included*).

Development Stage (Continuing Stage from 1998 to 2008 and 2008-2012)

The development stage gas seen several contours in Orissa Naxal history which can be again categorized into three sub-phases, one phase which can be dedicated to the period when the movement was active in Gajapati and Rayagada districts with no or minimum violence (1995-1998); the second phase when the frontal organizations were active with the support of PWG during 1998 to 2008; and the third phase, when there was a serious difference between the party from 2008 to 2012. After the differences were visible in the unified party due to the sectarian thinking on violent killings and mass mobilization a new party came into existence in the Gajapati and Rayagada and parts of Kandhmal districts known as Orissa Maoist Party. But the foundation of these development stages in south Orissa will always remain as Bansadhara land struggle as the main stone.

Bansadhara Land Struggle

The tribals who were once the owners of their land became slaves to their own land by several means. In our country 8 per cent is the *adivasi* population and in Orissa 22 per cent belong to *adivasis* which is next to undivided Madhya Pradesh. *Adivasis* have community ownership of the resources wherever they had their habitations. They were completely cut off from the outsiders and didn't allow any intruders unto their land. There have been resistance episodes against British by the tribals. Primarily, they were dependent on shifting cultivation, from which they travelled to settled cultivation and to the collection of minor forest produce. They had their own customary laws and rules, in their own independent niche. The outsiders entered the *adivasi* lands through developmental roads. Though it was difficult from the kings and rulers to visit the forested hilly areas, but they wanted to control this isolated tribal population through appointing non-*adivasi* cult *(non-adibashi agents)*. This process introduced lot of non-*adivasis* cults like Pana, Paika, Sundhi, Rana, Gouda to the undivided Koraput region by the Jeypore and Parlekhemundi rulers. Those areas were under the then Madras Presidency by the British. During the second phase of intrusion the list of non-*adivasis* those were Kumutis, Kampa, Brahmins, Karana the so called higher castes belonging to Andhra Pradesh, Orissa and Madhya Pradesh entered the area with small business and other were working with the kings.

The first seed of exploitation started by all these non-*adivasis* and slowly they acquired the lands of the *adivasis*. Not only these intruders, but also many other people joined these who came in search of jobs from the plain areas to these hilly areas. It has been observed that the non-*adivasis* do not wish to come to the hilly areas, but once they came they settled by increasing their wealth. *Adivasis* never could compete with them. The refugees from east Bengal *(and the Tamilies of Sri Lanka)* became settlers in Malkangiri and Umerkote. The Telugu Kumutis who also came *(fled to Koraput region out of fear of Srikakulam revolt)* to Koraput region during the Srikakulam uprisings are now the settlers here.

Many have come here to introduce cash crops like tobacco and cotton for profit; they have acquired all lands which are close to the riverbanks. These are the different dimensions through which *adivasis* have lost their resources. Once Tripura was the totally a tribal dominated state, but now the population has reduced to 33 per cent which is minority. In Orissa the statistics shows that there have been declining from 83 per cent of tribal in 1941, to 22 per cent of tribals in 2001. But why the figures are reducing and what are the main reasons behind it, is difficult to ascertain. But the main is through the infiltration of the migrant population and the opportunist population who came here. Not only, the outsiders have looted the resources, but also the culture, identity and their tribal dialects have been attacked in various ways. So, in this way tribal have become slaves in their own land.

First time the British started with the survey and settlement approach in the hilly area after declaring the forest as a state property. In 1865 the tribals lost their rights over the forests. After that, there was an excise law; restrictions were laid on the preparation and consumption of country liquor on *adivasis*. Then tax was laid on the land after the introduction of the new settlement rules. The *adivasis* had community ownership of land, when the survey was done it was recorded in the name of the chief or the *Mukhia*. The *mukhias* are the head of the land distribution in the tribal villagers, so it was suggested by the tribal villages to record the land in the name of the *mukhia* (village head). They didn't know as they were illiterate and ignorant of law. So, the lands were recorded in their *mukhias* and in some villages if the *mukhia* was good there he divided the lands and distributed among the villagers and where the *mukhia* was manipulative in nature there the villagers suffered. Few *mukhias* also harassed their own people by joining hands with the government officials.

From other castes people also became *zamjindars*. Most of the non-*adivasis* in Gunupur, Gudari, Remanaguda and in Padmapur block of Rayagada they have become the landlords. Many of the tribals lost their land due to indebtness. Though there was ceiling law, but the *zamindars* manipulated by showing it in various names. It is not that only the non-*adivasis* have exploited, but also the *adivasis* have exploited the *adivasis* too, the number may be small. On the other hand the non-*adivasis* have acquired the property through the help of the Inamdars and Muthadars in the Koraput region. The *adivasis* had to pay for the liquour due to the restrictions of the law, which took away all their belongings. The situation is same all over the country. Few of the names of the *adivasi* villages have been changed as per the non-*adivasis* wishes.

The Struggle for Land

This was the backdrop information by which the frontal organization started preparing the tribal to struggle for land. The laws introduced in 1951 and 1955, viz. the *zamindari* state abolition act, and the tenancy act, the land reforms act in 1960 could not end the plight of the tribals. The case was similar in all the states of India. Though the country got independence, but the tribal could not get their lands back. When the tribals were resisting against the British for the resources they were diverted towards the independence struggle, but after the country was independent the state of the tribal never improved rather it was deteriorated. For the first time in 1967 the tribal peasant's uprisings in the Naxalabri, the Srikakulam movement, and the land struggle in Gunupur, Padmapur in Koraput regions was some of the evidence of the tribal's unrests. But all these movements could not reach its positive end as they had some hiccups in the leadership.

Land Movement by Chasi Mullia Samiti in South Orissa (Gajapati and Rayagada Districts)

The Gudari, Gunupur and Gajapati region was chosen for the movement as this area had several promises from for land to be given to the people, but nothing was done. This area also had a solid background of Naxalbari type of revolution and *bhoo-satyagraha*. People who cultivated the land get a very less output and with the help of the government machinery the *Zamindars* had filed several cases against the tribals. The political leaders always take the case of the land under ceiling law during the election manifesto to use poor tribals as vote banks, but they don't exactly don't do anything concrete for the people after they win. Since this area is very needy and dominated by tribals this areas was selected for the first step of the movement in the development stage. Looking the growth of the *(Telengana and)* Naxalite Movement in India it can be well said that the first phase of the movement stated during 1950 onwards and ended in 1972, the second phase started from 1977 till 1990 where the basic ground work was done in Orissa, and the third and the current phase that everyone is witnessing in 1990 and thereafter. The movement has changed its strategy, direction, and approach and looking into their surroundings.

The movement started in Gunupur region which comprises the Rayagada district and Gajapati district in 1995, under the banner of Chasi Mulia Samiti. They started mobilizing the people in Gudari block and by the end of 1998 they built a base in the area. By the end of the 2000 the organization took a decision to work on the ceiling land *(and also non-ceiling lands)* which is still acquired by the *zamindars* and other people *(forcefully or by manipulating the laws may be they have patas legally)* illegally. The organization took out all the names of the *zamindars*, the area acquired and the place of the land. Most of the *zamindars* were residing in town areas like Padmapur, Naira and Gudari, but their agricultural lands are located in the tribal areas.

The land movement which was initiated by Sabyasachi Panda during the mid of 1990, by the end of 2000 it gained a good momentum. It is very interesting to note that the movement started in the same place where earlier Sri Biswanath Pattnaikji had initiated the *Bhoo-satyagraha* in 1951. As the problems of the land could not be solved, so, the movement which lost its energy in 1951 got fresh air from the new face of revolution and tribals started their agitation. First they selected 5 villages to forcefully acquire land, and the decision took place on 2001, November 2nd in a village level meeting. The *zamindars* not only took the land of the tribals by all means but also they use the tribal women as their sex slaves. The villages were the first spark began are Dimiriguda, Boroda, Gummi, Luhagumma, Siriguda, Burlendi, Ramluguda, Asada, Bamunidongor Birapanga, Adda, Rengam, Balipanga, Bhitarpur, Parakupuda, Bijapur, Guluguda and Khamriguda. These are the names of the 27 villages were the *zamindars* had occupied lands of tribals.

The 5 villages which was selected for the forceful harvesting, other 12 villages joined hand with them as the Chasi Mulia Sangathan had a strong hold in the area. They were successful in harvesting the crops, then slowly it spread over 32 villages. As a result of which, each village people organized themselves into revolutionary Chasi Mulia Sangathan. Then it spread over 100 villages in the area. For example Siriguda is one such village where only two people supported the organization, all of them in Siriguda are landless, but the movement could turn the direction of the entire village and everyone in Siriguda joined the movement and started harvesting the crops. In every village more than 400 people participated in the harvesting. The people knew from before that there will be police repression so, they had created all kinds of barriers to keep away the police from the place. The villages who participated in harvesting crops are:

- Bhitarpur
- Sidaguda
- Dimiriguda
- Luhamunda
- Rekapankala
- Burkadi
- Dhepaguda
- Gajiguda
- Balipanga
- Siriguda
- Arjunguda
- Barda
- Titimiri
- Titimiriguda
- Parakupuda
- Rangam
- Kardang
- Sagiguda
- Adda
- Ramnagar
- Jigidibata
- Brahmanidanagar
- Anuguruti
- Silimi
- Luhaguma
- Burlendi
- Bijapuir
- Jalanidhi
- Muliput
- Laxmanguda

During this phase Government of Orissa deployed 25 platoons of police in the area, and all total 72 persons were arrested including 23 women were sent to jail from 10 villages. Peoples tried to resist the police but they were badly injured. There was a meeting conducted by Chasi Mulia Samiti in Dimirugda were 4000 people congregated to witness the police harassment. Even the Tahasildar and Revenue Inspector were made captive for two days, but the tribals freed them when they promised to take action, which never happened. Section 144 was declared in Gudari. Though people went to meet the Collector by breaking the 144, but they had to return with false promises. To protest, there was a meeting in Chandrapur and also in Bhubaneswar.

The police, CRPF and the Andhra Pradesh grey hounds started searching the villages and also started checking the vehicles, harassing the villagers. The district administration though started to measure the land for a short time as an eye wash but nothing concrete came to the people. This attempt by the administration though diverted the people from the movement for a short time, but in 2002, the people again got involved in the *phasala kata andolan* (crop harvesting movement) could not convert it into land movement. Few *zamindars* also didn't dare to enter their lands and the lands were laid fallow. But few *zamindars* started cultivating land through *bhagachasi* system. Except two to three *zamindars* most of the *zamindars* left their lands, and with the help of police force they started cultivating lands with tractors. Though the people could not take the possession of the land but they organized themselves and again in 2002, for crop harvesting (*phasala kata andolan*) in few villages, viz. Rengam, Balipanga, Dimriguda, Badabhuin, Sanraijhola in these 5 villages took place. The poor farmers were able to acquire around 400 acres in Ramnaguda and Kolnara region.

The repression was greater than before and there were attempts to divide the people who were involved in the movement. Revolutionary tribe poet Dasuram Maleka got arrested from Rayagada by Andhra Police, he was tortured till 16 days and then handed over to Odisha Police. The Gram Panchayats like Mandimera in Gajapati, Dhepaguda, Katragada, Sanraijhola, Gulanda, Padapadu, Dimiriguda, Parakuguda, Bhitarpur, Balipanga, Rangam, of Gudari were everyday people were arrested. But the movement organized tribal people of the region, still went one step ahead and started taking possession of their lands in 2002 and 2003. The tribal enter the land with a red flag and the flag used to be there on the land. As the possession of the lands started increasing, the repression also increased. Similar incidents took place in Narayanpatna block of Koraput district from 2004 to 2009 where the organized tribals occupied their lands. But after the killing of two tribal youth in November 2009 the local movement got into violence by taking the shelter of the Naxals and the direction of the movement changed.

Few *zamindars* left the places and few surrendered before the people in Gudari and Gajapati. In 2003 in 20 villages the movement geared up. The poor farmers cultivated the lands in Gulanda, Dahani and in Belamguda. The *zamindars* surrendered before the people the lands were distributed in 2004, around 100 acres land was distributed in villages of Katrgada, Tubuni, Jigidibata, Ludri, Horu Gamberi, Sukuduwaju, and Bonda. During the interviews with the villagers of this Gudari area, they said that few *zamindars* surrendered before the movement and collectively it was decided to distribute the lands equally among the people. The then Communist Party of India (Marxist-Leninist) people war has always showed their concern towards the tribals land movement which didn't involve any violence in the early stage.

The Development Stage—The Dandakaranya Region, A New Face of the Movement

With the new face coming in Odisha during 1990, which had its stepping stone in DK region as mentioned earlier. The PWG has started working in DK to show a model of alternative democratic system. *Dandakaranya* (DK), that vast forest expanse of Central India, is home to a large number of tribals. Living for centuries in backwardness, they were looted through feudal, pre-feudal and colonial forms of exploitation, more than half century has not given much to these tribals and has worsened their situation by causing damage to them by the public purpose capitalist projects. With this background the guerriilas of the CPI (ML) peoples war entered to the hearts of the tribals with ideals of Marxism-Leninism and Maos thought, illuminated a new path of protracted people war, for building a new democratic society towards socialism and communism. *Dandakaranya*, covering an extensive area of central India, is spread over four states. It encompasses thick forests, hills, rivers and rivulets and is the abode of several tribes.

It is spread over 11 districts in the States of Andhra Pradesh, Orissa, Maharashtra and Undivided Madhya Pradesh. It covers a vast area of over one lakh ten thousand square kilometres comprising parts of Adiliabad, Khamam, East Godavari, Visakhapatnam districts of Andhra Pradesh, Gadchioli, Chandrapur and Bhandra district of Maharashtra; undivided Baster of Chhattisgarh; Balaghat districts of Madhya Pradesh, Koraput and Malkangiri of Orissa.[11]

The liberated Guerrilla Zone (GZ) of *Dandakaranya* comprises parts of the eight districts; Gadchiroli and Bhandra in Maharashtra; Balaghat in MP, Kanker, Dantewada, Bastar and Rajanandagaon district in the new State of Chhattisgarh and Malkangiri of Koraput region in Orissa. Here in this zone they created an alternative development model by giving all power to *gram rajya* committees where, education, health, cooperatives, women empowerment, agricultural development, and other works are taken by true people's participation. The model which is shown by the DK GZ is one of self-reliance, growth and increase well-being of the masses.

The recipient of the first Ramnath Goenka, C. Vanja, [award of Excellence in Journalism (2006) in the category of Uncovering India invisible] who went to the jungles of the Chhattisgarh (the part of the *Dandakaranya* region) and stayed there for more than 10 days and interacted with the party members, and *adivasis*. Her work was published in *Andhra Jyoti*, daily on April 10, 2005 called *Dandakarantamlo Janatana Sarkar* means a parallel peoples government in *Dandakaranya*. During her stay in the region she could gather lot of information about the developmental activities by the CPI (ML) people's war in the area which was neglected since ages after independence. After her visit she wrote her experience where she mentioned that the *adivasis* are inspired ideologically and politically with training. Withstanding all the repressive measures from the government this region is a model for the revolutionary movements which has built mass base, people's organizations, created awareness and progressed a lot. Where the power is with the people with the coalitions of peasants and workers, with special emphasis on women. The developmental activities are done on a cooperative basis and want to liberate the area.

Why the Dandakaranya Region as a Model?

By the end of 1979 it became apparent that the government and landlords would resort to much more brutal repression for snuffing out the peasant struggles. The movement had reached a critical stage by the mid of the 70s. To advance the movement necessary preparations were started to revive the whole movement by training people on military aspects and on the political ideology. After several discourses and debates it was reflected that the party leadership betrayed the movement in the Telengana struggle and the numerous Naxalbari type of resistances were crushed by the government repressive measures. *(Actually the party's method of struggle do not suit to all regions and all types of economic zones of India like plane and semi-forest area. Movement in urban and the source of revolutionary cadres is too weak and non-continuous. We lack a rear for our PW. It lacks a proper democratic and non-sectarian line, i.e., mass line could not implemented in all places. Even in DK we could mobilize consolidated one-third of total masses instead of 80 or 90 per cent of people. In the name of class struggle the party targeted middle class tribal and gave one base for government to launch salwa zudum. Similar tactics in Rayagada-Gajapati also helped the government to start one counter revolutionary santi sena like organization and the movement had suffered loss. Killing of any left party cadres like Biswanath Madi, Arjun Kendruka etc. are reflection of sectarian line in the name of revolution. Before building a number of guerrilla bases in all India level hastily it has been intensifying the armed struggle to establish a base area. Moreover, there is not sufficient infrastructural preparation including supply, arm ammunitions sources, doctors and technicians which are needed for an armed struggle. Also there is lack of organizing people who can engage with enemies such as government-intelligence. These are the cause of failure of earlier movement from which the movement is not trying to learn and repeating the mistakes.*). So, in this context the party prepares a perspective for guerrilla zone which has lot of importance, where the north Telengana. Adilabad, Karimnagar, Warangal, Khamam district of Andhra Pradesh, which was continuous patch of forest was included. It focused that the party has to build the village level cells and squads. Village level organizations to make the foundation stronger.

The perspective document foresees that when the repression increases on its cadres it has to have a safe area to face the eventualities. The other side of the Godavari river was the *Dandakaranya* region. The document outlined the major tasks as:

- To provide protection to squads that temporarily retreat from the four district of the guerrilla zone to help them to counter attack the enemy.
- To organize the tribals in the forest areas and to extend the struggle building the Party and revolution army among them.

Many issues were taken by the party in this region and it was also successful, to name a few are distribution of lands, struggle for increase in agricultural wage rates, increases in tendu leaf plucking rates, demand for irrigation tanks in the area, etc. the tribals were organized, women were organized and they fought against the age old patriarchy. They have a total system of administration starting from the village development committee, range level committees (with 30 to 40 villagers) and divisional level committees (10 to 20 ranges). The children are also organized for the future revolution. The party claims that the *Dandakaranya* region has become a liberated zone with the party revolutionary movement where the guerilla squad numbers more than 1,00,000 and that is their strength.

Once the PWG declared their strength in the DK region as 40,000 armed caders and sometimes it was declared to be more than one lakh. The interview by the central committee members says it is more than that. All these creating confusions about the exact number of armed caders. On an average if the 3 Gram Panchayat in a block support the movement in that case it is huge. So, the numbers only give us the magnitude, but the intensity of the movement is much more than this.

The Post-Development Stage in Odisha (2008-2012)

As mentioned in 3.8 first paragraph the development stage has witnessed various waves in the Naxalite history in south Odisha. The data from research also showed a deviance in the two regions with the study area. The Gajapati and Rayagada districts had different notions on the movement, whereas the Malkangiri and Koraput districts had a different one. The levels of influence, association of the movement in the tribal regions are different as derived by the field data. The field data reveals six levels of participants in the tribal areas as follows:

1. The first level where there is a mutual cooperation of the tribals and the naxalites to work healthy as in Gajapati and part of Rayagada district.
2. The second level where there is a vacuum created by the system and to fulfil this gap the tribal opting for this path, as it observed in parts of Rayagada and Malkangiri districts.
3. There are various democratic movements by the tribal against the landlords and against the companies. These democratic movements though are not violent in nature but they do get a strong support from the Naxalites. This can also be explained in either way, that the Naxalites who only think on a single track blaming the government when they see voices of dissent then they try to capture these movements. In this process the third level becomes very vulnerable where the tribals are targeted by the government as Naxalites. When they are labelled they have no choice but to join the Naxals. This is seen in parts of Rayagada and Koraput district.
4. The fourth level is very significant where people want to achieve something so, they join the movement. But when the tribal see that there is huge gap between the ideology and the action they leave the organization and some get killed in encounters as it happened in Basangmali in 2011.
5. There is other level where the area is very suitable for the naxal hideouts, where the tribal are force to join them, carry their bags and have to obey their orders. This is largely seen in Pottangi, Nandapur, Lamtaput, Kudura and Boipariguda blocks of Koraput district. The government is active and the tribals are not interested to participate in the process but they are sandwiched between the naxals and the police force.
6. There is another interesting level where the tribals see them as an alternative as in case of Malkangiri where they have been displaces and completely cut off from the mainstream. During 1980s the naxals visited them and advocated their ideology and occupied the area. The tribals have no other way than to accept

it, as they are at crossroads, whether which way to go. Whichever they go they will be targeted as naxals.

These levels show that there is a huge difference emerging in the party. After the killing of a Hindu saint Swami Laxmananda in Kandhamal the differences started. The differences were so intense that the inner party disputes went up to watching the members within the party itself. The differences were on some burning issues:

- Killing innocents in the name of police informers without any proper investigation, killing of children and handicap people.
- Making the organization more involved in the religious issues and creating riots in the tribal areas.
- Harassing women.
- Exploiting people for money.
- More influence of cadres from Andhra Pradesh.
- Unnecessary kidnappings.
- Not focusing on mass mobilization, trade union movements and not consolidating the democratic movements experience rather working on isolated gun culture.
- Killing police in raids and in villages. This violence without any sense.
- Not deriving a proper plan of the alternative model rather creating base area for own protection.
- On one hand the Naxals are against the companies who are displacing tribals and on the other hand they collect money which is a big contradiction.
- Asking the tribals to participant with force has no meaning.

These differences has divided the unified party into two, namely CPI (Maoist) and the Odisha Maovadi Party. This is latest faction that has emerged in April 2012.

References

1. Most of the chapter 3 is based on interviews with Naxal ideologues from AP and Orissa. And also from a special interview with CPI (Maoist) Orissa commander Sunil (name changed). They corrected the chapter and wanted that these things should be highlighted. This whole chapter was written in field.

2. 39 years of Naxalbari by Dandapani Mohanty (in Oriya a booklet).
3. *Human Development Report.*
4. A.S. Das' film, Matiro Puko.
5. *People's March*, Vol. 2, September 9, 2001.
6. *Samaj* (Oriya news paper, 1951).
7. 40 years of Naxalbari by Dandapani Mohanty (a booklet in Oriya).
8. *A Naxal Profile,* Kujur Rajat, 2008, IPCS.
9. From the Party Documents.
10. *Peoples March Supplement*, Nov.-Dec., 2004.
11. Party Documents (in Oriya).

4

Naxal Movement in India and Orissa in General

An Overview

"Weapons are an important factor in war, but not the decisive one; it is man and not materials that counts".—*Mao Tse-Tung*

The Naxalite Movement and Inception is described in the previous chapter. To iterate again an overview is given here. The movement which was first incepted in 1967, ignited and the flames spread around India. Initially, it had very intelligent people in the movement, including educated youth. The movement which was just limited to one village in 1967 and now estimated that it has widened it base in 13 states. One of the estimates shows that, out of 640 districts in India, 200 districts are affected by Naxal conflict. The revolutionary party the Communist Party of India (Maoist) claims that they are spreading their wings even more than what is estimated by government and from other sources. Decades passed and the form of exploitation remained the same, the peasants, workers and tribals became more victims of modernity and development, the embedded violence in the society remained where the structures of deprivation escalated along with the structural violence. *One of the tribal respondents advocated that, "we need not to understand the huge volumes of Marx, Lenin, and Mao, as we have experienced it all through our lives what is written in the book. We may be illiterate but we do have emotions to understand the politics of our exploitation. And today without our wish we feel that armed struggle is the only path at this juncture of our evolution."*

Motivational Factors

There can be many motivational factors to join the movement and they differ a lot in study area. There are individual differences and also there are variations found in the geographical situation. The intensity of these motivations also different as the responses was recorded. The places where the Naxals used it for hideout the motivation is different and in other places where the tribals were forces there the motivation was different. The Naxals used a high rate to achieve their target in creating a base area wherever they introduced their agenda. In some places they used their gun power to motivate the people. In some places their relationship with the people was so strong that the tribals got motivated. So through achieving, through power and through relationship were the main three tactics that is used by the Naxals.

The following few tables indicate the factors of motivation, the opinion regarding the right path of both active and passive members at large for which tribals participate either passively or actively. This table gives a picture that the Naxalism is some way created a space for itself.

Table 4.1: Opinion Regarding the Right Path (What do you think is it the right path to establish equity and equality in the society?)

Sl. No.	*Responses*	*%age*
1.	Due to the LPG the gap between the rich and poor is more, so unless there is a revolution nothing is going to change	1.4
2.	Violence is an effective weapon for radical changes	1.4
3.	Revolution but without arms	1.4
4.	Violence in not the way	2.7
5.	It is time for tribal to stand and be counted	1.4
6.	It's not, but they have met the aspirations of the tribals to some extent	1.4
7.	To some extent tribals get moral encouragement	4.1
8.	Yes	32.4
9.	No	24.3
10.	To some extent, it is the right path as this is a social problem	9.5
11.	No idea	4.1
12.	That is the ultimatum	8.1
13.	Right or wrong it suits the condition	4.1
14.	Revolution is necessary may be or may not through Naxalism	2.7
15.	It's good as an opposition	1.4
16.	There should be class annihilation and not person annihilation	1.4

Twenty four per cent of the respondents do feel that this is required for our country and rest 30 per cent of the people in some or the other do show their motivation for the movement and show their affinity. They feel that this is the best strategy for the present time and with a hope to expand, but there is a strong sense of motivation which says that there is a necessity of some kind of revolution which should be the ultimatum. 18 per cent of the people also feel that this is not the right path.

To suffice Table 4.1, the secondary sources do give a picture in the light of above motivational factors: Shri Jaya Prakash Narayan, while touring the Naxalite affected areas of Bhojpur (Bihar) on June 12th to 13th, 1975, exhorted the people to shun the path of the violence and work for total revolution. Addressing the crowd at Narayanpur, he said: "if in five years from now if nothing changes, I will not ask you to give up Naxalism"[1]. Had been he alive today, everybody would listen to him for his reaction. What motivates a person to opt for arms is a real challenging question. The passive members opine that it is easy to say that the tribals have discontent so, they are going for arms, but does it suffice the question of participation in the armed struggle? The movement refuses to uproot itself despite all the repressive measures taken by the government including the recent green hunt. Because it gains getting energy for its sustenance from the following factors:

- Growing discontent, and not just discontent,
- The unheard grievances,
- Unaddressed problems,
- Insecurity about lives and livelihood, and
- Squeezing the political space, since all these remained unanswered.

There is trust deficit among tribal towards the government which could be motivating them as a whole to opt for arms. The motivational factors do differ from area to area, as we can in a graph it in two variables; trust *verses* the areas under the universe of the study. Where there is more trust there is less participation and *vice versa.* In Gajapati district of the universe the armed revolution is considerably visible. In Koraput district except in two blocks (Narayanapatna and Bandhugoan) it is intense, in rest of the areas though the movement is present, but is unable to gain momentum due to better governance by the state.

There is very good cycle which is adopted in the participation. First to destroy the government establishments than to make their presence felt.

When such violent activities take place, it is a common tendency by Government to deploy force in those areas.

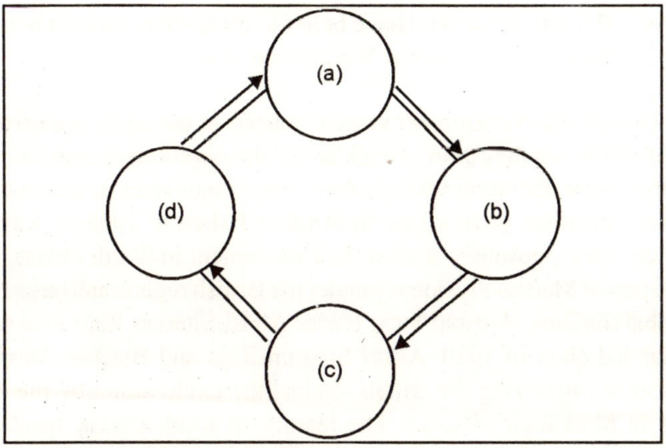

Developed as per the Empirical Research. So, the pattern follows:

(a) Destruction of establishments by the armed group, to show their presence and grabbing the area by the Naxals,

(b) Deployment of the force, harassment by the force to the innocent tribals,

(c) The tribals get anger and this state of anger is very well en-cashed against the government by the Naxals, and

(d) Tribals opt for arms and participate in the movement.

Fig. 4.1: The Cycle of Participation

The field data give a grim picture regarding participation, more than 50 per cent of the tribal youth in Lamtaput, Nandapur, Boipariguda blocks of Koraput district; 30 per cent of tribal youth in Rayagada district are in a state of vacuum as no one believes them. If they don't attend the meetings of the armed group they are blamed as police informers, they are beaten, and intimidated. If they come and seek help from the government they are labelled as Naxalites. They are in dire state of confusion, as no one is helping them. Some even cannot live their villages to work outside when the armed groups conduct meetings and camps. The tribals in a sandwiched state, and explain that either way they end up in jail. Four distinct patterns that emerge from the field, regarding the motivational aspect:

(i) Tribals those who believe that this is the only way,

(ii) Second group of tribals who believe that as there is no option this is last resort,

(iii) Third group who have strong faith in the system, and use all constitutional provisions to raise their voices, but labelled as Naxalites, and have finally opted, and

(iv) The last group who have belief in the system, located in the war between the state and Naxalite conflict.

Though the Naxalite Movement started in the study area from the end of 1980s, but they didn't attack any of the government establishments, and they were operating through their protest movements, but when four women Naxalites were killed by Andhra Police in 1998 in Rayagada district[2], they rigorously started their movement in South Orissa. South was a part of Madras Presidency under the British regime and has a history of tribal uprising. A tribal local leader Alluri Sitaram Raju rose against the landed class in 1920. Alluri Sitaram Raju and Bangara Devi were pioneer in organizing the tribals against the exploitation by the landed class in Malkangiri district. The history of south Orissa speaks that, whenever the exploitation was persistent in tribals, it became a motivation for uprising.

The three following Tables 4.2, 4.3 and 4.4 give the motivational factors with the justification for the participation in the movement.

Table 4.2: Factors Motivating for Participation

Sl. No.	*Communities*	*Circumstances which pushed them for this way*		
		Social	*Village*	*Others*
1.	ST	37.70%	25.41%	22.13%
2.	SC	5.74%	4.10%	—
3.	Others	1.64%	1.64%	1.64%
	Total	45.08%	31.15%	23.77%

The different circumstances which compel or force the tribals to participate in both ways is personal (social) level, when they see the exploitation which occurs towards them since the childhood, finally makes them so, hard that they are ready to kill the other person without any mercy. The whole village faces severe situation with abject poverty, their issues are not heard. So, when they see Naxals do come and help them in mitigating their problem by threatening the immediate oppressor they join them. During the explanation of the factors they also said "the tribals participate not because they will get something overnight but they are taking part in the sense some good will happen."

Table 4.3: Significant Persons or aspects behind the Motivation

Sl. No.	*Communities*	*Motivation behind*					
		Self	*Family*	*Friends*	*Villagers*	*Naxal leaders*	*Others*
1.	ST	17.93%	1.38%	6.90%	11.72%	22.67%	17.93%
2.	SC	3.24%	—	—	4.14%	4.14%	3.45%
3.	Others	1.38%	—	—	1.38%	2.76%	1.38%
	Total	22.55%	1.38%	6.90%	17.24%	29.57%	22.76%

The communities mostly get motivated by the Naxal leaders who often visit the villages and conduct meeting. Their meetings are powerful and trigger the tribal mind, in breaking the silence. But silence is converted into violence rather being ventilated in a democratic way they will be put behind the bars or get killed, so, they should have the power of arms to counter the structural violence existing in the society. Villagers, friends and other factors do help to motivate them to par take in this.

Table 4.4: Justification of the Motivation

Sl. No.	*Communities*	*Justification*	*It is the best way*	*Condition may change*	*Others*
		This can give justification			
1.	ST	34.17%	17.5%	20	10.83%
2.	SC	5%	4.17%	0.83%	0.83%
3.	Others	1.67%	—	2.50%	2.50%
	Total	40.84%	21.67%	23.33%	14.16%

Table 4.4 shows the justifications of the motivating factors behind joining the contributing factor, as the respondents opine that the democratic movements are always viewed as having links with Naxals. Though Naxals trying to extend support to democratic movement taking place today in Orissa as well as in the study area. But when state bans the democratic movement and tries to repress it by bullets, it is automatic generating a war in which the tribals are taking up arms. Squeezing political space creating a conflicting situation among the tribals. In case of war (as defined by the dictionary[3]) that is an organized, armed, prolonged conflict between two parties who are part of extreme aggression, social disturbance and high mortality. The techniques use by

the group in the war is warfare. But this is a structural war as the structures (political, and economical) are engaged which is a critical phase.

Active and Passive Membership

The History of Naxalite Movement is almost five decades old now with changing human Indian society. Throughout history it is seen that whenever dissatisfaction has prevailed with the existing socio-cultural-political-economic circumstances that has motivated individuals and tribal groups to arbitrate, question, challenge, confront and change the state. Ironically, it can be said that, conditions have changed but within the same situation the contradictions do exist as the interests of the tribals are not met and the needs unmet. On the other hand the movement is continuously changing its tactics, innovating new idea, to increase the membership base. The data shows that, there are two major ways to increase the membership. First through collective action when members influence the new members, secondly through alliance building has been a major strategy of the armed groups. The merger in 2004 was a step ahead in this direction. It is important to say here that, there are 27 Marxist and Leninist groups in India who believed in armed struggle directly or indirectly. There are about 10 revolutionary groups in India who are influenced by Maoism for example, United Liberation front of Assam and Jharkhand liberation front. There are about 25 communist organizations which are historical, but defunct now.[4] The Communist Party of India (Maoist) is the largest group, but Janashakti is also active. At the international level two visible networks those are RIM and CCOMPOSA are active. This is the overview of the membership of the armed groups.

There are frontal organizations who are passive members of the movement but do fall under the purview of their collective Mobilization, which has given them an identity. This collective identity has given them the strength of solidarity and a common goal in their struggle. Their solidarity groups are in different form and they do change their identity on a regular basis. There are also cases where the communities get organized to raise voice as it happened in Narayanpatna block of Koraput district, and later due to the less intervention of the government it became an active extension of the membership of the Naxal constituency. All the village level organizations as articulated Biplabi Committees are the passive members of the party. There are many intellectuals in the capital city of Orissa, advocates, business men, writers, media personnel's and individuals who are the passive members.

Table 4.5: Membership base

Sl. No.	*Active Membership*	*Passive Membership*
1.	Underground Naxal caders	Activists of the democratic organizations
2.	Over ground sympathizers	Jailed Naxals
3.	Other sympathizers who believe in the ideology	Individual HR activists
4.	Other armed organizations	Teaching Faculty
5.	Tribal members at the village and Panchyat level	Members from the civil liberty groups and organizations
6.	Frontal organizations of the Naxalite base	Few Media persons
7.	Advocates, HR activists	

The above Table 4.5 explains the active and passive members of the study area.

Support by the Non-member Groups/Persons

From the history of the Naxal conflict it has been witnessed time and again that the movement derives constant strong support from the non-tribals groups and members. The earlier episodes of the resistance were supported by Comrade Charu Mazumdar, Kanu Sanyal and others. One of the main leaders in Naxal movement in Orissa was Comrade Nagabusan Pattnaik who was inspired by the ideology of Marx and who fought for the peasants and was actively involved in the 1960s. 30 per cent of the respondents in the study area were from the non-tribals and from other groups. But it is difficult to point out who are active groups supporting the movement as these groups often change their identities and profiles which change over a period of time. The duration of the support groups also changes and new members start replacing them. It is a cycle that the movement gets an invariable support from the groups who are fighting for rights, but so far it is seen that there is no support from the non-governmental organizations. But the party forcibly extorts money from the non-governmental organizations in the study area, especially in Malkangiri district and to some extent in Koraput district.

The non-group members accepted them because of their thinking, teaching, their deeds towards the poor, and their closeness to the villages. 17 per cent of the people accept them without any condition, as they feel that a stratified class structure where the proletariat is with the petty bourgeoisie consciousness is lumping. According to the Newton's 2nd

Table 4.6: Reasons of Acceptance Level by the Non-group members

Sl. No.	*Responses*	*%age*
1.	No comments	5.33
2.	Yes, it has the force to make people conscious	1.33
3.	I do empathize as their national patriots	1.33
4.	No	29.3
5.	Not exactly, but the movement makes me happy and sad	2.67
6.	Yes	22.7
7.	Yes, accept their thinking	5.33
8.	Yes, believe in armed struggle	5.33
9.	Yes, they are close to people	2.67
10.	Yes, they have reached the unreached areas	2.67
11.	Their teachings are good so accepted	8
12.	To some extent	6.67
13.	Accept their way of thinking and not their means, but heart is with them, but not the killing part of it	6.67

law of motion: "a body continues to be in state of rest or continuous motion unless an external force acts on it". The proletarian surroundings are paranoiac about future. And the movement is acting as a force to change their present position of rest as every exploited person is a potential revolutionary. 2.67 per cent of the people do derive happiness and sadness from the movement; as they opine the Naxals kill the poor informers, police rather than they should kill big corrupt political leader. And they sometimes do feel that the Naxals are killing the poor informers and other village level people, instead they should go and kill the big actors as they opined. In Kandhamal incident they blasted a land mine in which ambulance carrying patients including women and infants were killed. The party did express their grief over a press statement, but all this incidents does affect the credibility of the Naxal over the non-member support.

The non-member support is showing a decline over the last five years, mainly because of two reasons, the fear of police repression, and due to the ideological dilutions of the Naxals.

References

1. Singh, Prakash, *The Naxalite Movement in India*, Rupa & Co. 1995, p. 3.
2. Das, Satya Prakash, *Naxal Movement and State Power*, Sawrup & Sons, 2006.
3. http://en.wikipedia.org
4. www. Massline.info, update as on November 25th, 2008.

5
Tribal Members of Naxalite Movement in Orissa

"Let a hundred flowers bloom, let a hundred schools of thought contend."
—*Mao Tse-Tung*

The Naxalite movement is showing a strong hold of the tribal areas in the recent past. Various studies do show that these areas fall in the central India, in the states of Chhattisgarh, Jharkhand and south Orissa. The three tribal dominated states in India accounts for 70 per cent of the India's coal reserves, 80 per cent of its high grade iron ore, and 60 per cent of its bauxite and all most all the chromites reserves. Orissa is one such tribal dominated state along with Chhattisgarh and Jharkhand[1]. Taking the only case of Orissa, it contains 51 per cent of bauxite reserves which are mostly located in south Orissa. Generally speaking, the major mineral producing districts of the country including Orissa do share common characteristics like forest cover, tribal population, incidence of poverty and backwardness. The mineral map of the country overlaps with the tribal and forest map of south Orissa is famous for its tribal population, for its tribal revolts in the past, for its poverty indicators, and, off late, the growing Naxalism in the study area (Gajapati, Rayagada, Koraput, and Malkangiri) of south Orissa is strategically located, sharing borders with two other states which are Andhra Pradesh and Chhattisgarh.

All the four districts especially share major border with Andhra Pradesh. Now, the research shows that it has become the epicentre of the rapid rise of violence. Until very recently it was renowned for its inclusion in the popular regional planning KBK (Koraput-Bolangir-Kalahandi), now it has shifted to the growing facets of Naxalism. Violence since the early 2000 and end of 1990 reached peak here in 2004 when the Naxals raided the district armoury, and killed one person. Not only the district arms were looted, but around 5 police stations were blasted the same day. It is one of the most memorable incidents in Naxal history. South Orissa was also the locus of experiment for the Neheruvian vision of secular temples when the first Machhkund dam was built here in 1950, displacing thousands of tribals of Koraput region. Many industries came here which displaced the native tribals and other weaker sections of this region that were voiceless and became citizens of nowhere land without any identity. A Paraja tribal in Kotpad resettlement camp opines while sharing his own life history, "Naxalism is the only answer for tribals. As no one is taking up the tribal agenda at this juncture of privatization." He says "we were just thrown rather everyone calls us DP camp (Displaced camp people). The government has given no facility to us; it not only took only land and livelihood from us, but left us to lead a degrading quality of life. So, we all had to stay in these camps without any other choice."

As per the ethics of the research, the actual names of the informants have not been cited here. All the names mentioned here are fictitious. But the facts and informations are expressed as explained by the informants. In few places the informations are given in italics and in other places they are anonymous.

To explain the tribal members of the Naxalite movement there are two case studies given below. Kudu and Judu belonging to Kotia and Paraja tribal have lost lands in Upper Kolab Multipurpose Dam Project and also in Sunabeda Naval Armament Depot. They were not educated to get jobs. So, without any choice just to take shelter forcefully came to the camps, they lost their common property resources, became landless and jobless. Their social ties got disintegrated and now they are just living in distress condition. Each person has a story to share in the rehabilitation and resettlement colonies. After so many years of staying in the camp, their plight continues. As per the Census 2001, this region has the maximum tribal population, as per the government records from the home department all the blocks in this district of Koraput are fully or partially affected by Naxalism. The members of this movement are primarily tribals followed by other poor sections who constitute *Dalits* and other backward castes.

Table 5.1 gives the profile of the Naxalite members present in different blocks of Koraput, Malakangiri, Rayagada and Gajapati districts along with their extent, represents as presence, partially affected, affected and intensely affected. The name of the blocks shown in the table do not indicate, that the total Gram Panchayats present under the block are affected but few of the GPs are affected in that particular block. It also shows the growing momentum of the Naxalite conflict. In few of the blocks it is mentioned in both columns like in presence and going to be affected, this indicates that their presence is felt with few killings, blasts and it is going to escalate in the coming five years.

Table 5.1: The Intensity of the Naxalite Movement in the Study Area

Sl. No.	Name of the district	Name of the block	Only presence	Partially affected	Affected	Intensely affected	Going to be affected
1.	Rayagada	Rayagada	✓				
		Kashipur		✓			
		Kolnara	✓				
		Kalyansinghpur	✓	✓			
		Gunupur	✓				
		Gudari			✓		
		Padampur	✓	✓			
		Ramnaguda		✓			
		Bissamcuttack					✓
		Muniguda			✓		
		Chandrapur				✓	
2.	Gajpati	Parlekhmundi	✓				✓
		Nuagad		✓			
		Mohana			✓		
		R. Udaygiri			✓		
		Kasinagar	✓				✓
3.	Koraput	Koraput					✓
		Semeliguda	✓	✓			
		Pottangi	✓	✓			
		Nandapur	✓				✓
		Lamtaput	✓				✓
		Laxmipur	✓				✓
		Narayanpatna			✓	✓	
		Bandhugoan		✓			
		Dasmanthpur					✓
		Jeypore	✓				
		Kotpad	✓				✓
		Boipariguda	✓				✓
		Kundr	✓				
		Borigumma	✓				✓
4.	Malkangiri	Malkangiri	✓				
		Podia			✓		
		Kudumulugumma		✓			✓
		Khairput	✓				
		Kalimela				✓	
		Korukunda		✓			
		Mathili		✓			

Table 5.1 shows the growth of the Naxalite movement in the study area, where the tribal groups are involved in it. The basic difference here

Table 5.2: Tribal Members of the Naxalite Movement

Sl. No.	Name of the District	Tribal Groups	Leadership Dominance
1.	Gajapati	Saora, Kui	Orissa,
2.	Rayagada	Saora, Kui, Jatapu, Kondha	Orissa and Andhra Pradesh
3.	Koraput	Paraja, Bhumia, Gadaba, Jatapu, Duruva, Kotia	Andhra Pradesh
4.	Malkangiri	Koya, Halwa, Paraja	Andhra Pradesh and Chhattisgarh

is though the tribal groups are involved, the leadership is mainly maintained from outside the state. There are no tribal leaders as such in south Orissa. Nachika Linga who was closely associated with Chasi Mulia Adivasi Sangh which strived for tribal land has taken shelter of Naxals. In a way the tribal groups opine that he has been used by them, but not effectively.

Tribal Perception of Naxalite Movement

Perceptions as explained by many theorists, generally as the way we accept things, accept the other people, events, and their life. It includes a wide range of things from person to culture. The perception often connects to reality who perceives it. Often things as perceived as realities may not be true. Beautiful things can be perceived as ugly and *vice versa.* Accepting things depends on observation and it is based on certain facts and events. This observation of events is related to with our environment. Human being is a socio-eco-psycho-biological being. The relationship between the human beings and the environment is very important as she or he fulfils the needs from this environment. Needs are fulfilled when human beings participate in the observation process and how creatively they participate is also important. When human beings undergo such a process of observation where they cannot participant what is happening around them they remain silent for certain period of time. During this phase lot of waves are generated, when a thought comes that some collective action is needed to break the silence, some kind of eruptions takes place. Many of our inventions have gone through such kind of phases. Our mind contains systems which has emotions. Promoting to take actions, which could be revenge or reaction, movement or conflict. The most primitive portion of the brain is responsible for the survival of the human beings, where human beings have portrayed certain ways of behaviour. Basing on the biological grounds human culture has developed, with lot of diversities, though many things in common.

Authors like Edward Wilson have proposed that the tribal mind is common, by which warfare has been a common phenomenon in the evolution of human society. Competition has always been there and genocide too. The human culture is the interaction between the genes and the environment, both are responsible for human behaviour. The nature and the nurture both contribute towards our behaviour. This behaviour has always shown the concepts like (MY) which are the root cause of many movements. All human beings with whatever behaviour, do have some kind of specific perception. All human beings are born with some needs which are non-negotiable, if these needs are not fulfilled, till certain period they remain silent, later they develop a particular perception on the environment, and react in a certain way. The Naxalite movement portrays all characters of these unmet needs. The tribals in south Orissa have unmet needs from the environment, which is showing some kind of typical behaviour.

When we say the tribal perception, it includes how they see themselves, how they see others, how do they perceive the officials, the outsiders, all the events that has taken place or taking place in their life. The perception of the members includes their life journey, experiences in the village, with government officials, their traditions and their aspirations. Their democratic movement is often seen as a violent movement in any form, be it the *Bhoo-satyagraha* (Land *Satyagraha*) in 1951, under the leadership of late Biswanath Pattnaik, veteran Gandhian who opted *Satyagraha* mode to give the land rights to tribals. The Mandravaju land struggle, the Chitrakonda people struggle for good governance, the Gudari Land struggle, and the Narayanpatna land struggle have been viewed a lens of violence. When we say about the unmet needs of the tribals the informants explain that:

- 67 per cent of tribals feel that they have unmet needs.
- 68 per cent of tribals do feel that in whatever they want to engage with the state for demanding their rights, they are seen as Naxalites.
- 53 per cent of tribals feel that, by all means they will end up in jail, whether speaking about their injustice against the system, if they take a rally for their demands and entitlements, or for any reason. So, it is better to join hands with the Naxals, and in that case they will end up in jail.

- On the other hand 72 per cent of the government officials do strongly feel that all tribals are Naxalites in the study area. This is their strong perception. But de-attaching themselves from their administrative posts 80 per cent of them strongly opine that because of the discontentment within the tribals they are entering into this path.
- The other dimension is, Naxal conflict has taken the advantage of this discontent to a greater extent which is persisting in the form of poverty and alienation can be ventilated only through armed struggle by taking revenge. 87 per cent of the tribals have perceived that violence is the last resort for solutions of the problems as there is no other way to get rid of their plethora of issues.

The escalation of Naxalite conflict in 2005 has taken 669 lives[2] and an increase of 18 per cent rise in the casualties compared to 2004. August 15th, 2006, while addressing to the Nation, Prime Minister Manmohan Singh termed the Naxalite conflict as the single biggest threat to country's internal security. After 15 days of this view, the previous Prime Minister, V.P. Singh, came up with a different angle and said no option, but to embrace Naxalism in the present model of development, where there is forceful land acquisition by the state. As mentioned earlier the non-negotiable unmet needs of tribals, their agony could have put them into this vicious circle of movement and conflict. They have no other way rather to opt for arms.

Every human being or social group derives its sources of energy from the environment; this ecology is the relation between the species and environment. In terms of social groups it is the interaction between the different groups, and it has to be looked basing on inter-dependencies of the groups and the environment. The ecology of groups[3] considers the influences that extra-group variables have on group activity. These variables are structural (embedded in the systems of the society) and deal with the influences that the position of the group has *vis-à-vis* other groups. Groups also get influenced from their socio-geographical location, the same group being member of many groups which is a potential side; also it creates conflict between the groups. The perception of tribals with respect to the socio-cultural-political environment has become a reality as they have been getting the same kind of treatment since ages through the various social, political structures of the society.

The study area has spread over four districts, has a rich ethnic diversity, Table 5.1 has shown where the Naxalism is extending its wings. The major tribes of the study area are Koyas, Parajas, Duruva, Matia, Halwa, Bhumia, Bondo, Kondha, Didayee, Saura, Jatapu, Benia kui, and Kotia. Table 5.3 shows the representative sample of the tribal population involved in Naxalism from the study area.

Table 5.3: District-wise and Section-wise Distribution of Respondents

Sl. No	*Name of the districts*	*Communities*		
		SC	*ST*	*Others*
1.	Gajapati	—	25.7	1.4
2.	Rayagada	—	21.4	2.9
3.	Koraput	8.6	15.7	1.4
4.	Malkangiri	1.4	81.04	2.9

The above Table 5.3 shows the percentage of respondents in the four districts, which clearly indicates that the tribals are more participating followed by other sections of the society. The Naxalism first started in south Orissa during 1965-67. And later it was re-defined in a newer way during 1990s under the banner of Kuilavanga Sangha and Chasi Mulia Sangha, till now Gajapati district remains the core area of Naxalism with maximum tribal participation.

Table 5.4: Age-wise and Section-wise Distribution of Respondents

Sl. No.	*Age of the Respondents*	*Communities*		
		SC	*ST*	*Others*
1.	10-20	—	12.9	—
2.	21-30	5.7	40	7.1
3.	31-40	4.3	20	1.4
4.	Above 40	—	8.6	8.6

The age-wise respondents across community show that the percentage within the age ranges of 21-30 is high in all sections of the society. The youth are more into this Naxalism as they feel that they do not have any direction to follow nor have a good leader to idealize. They have a big vacuum and no one is there to fill this gap. The movement might reward them or not they do not have foresight as it is going to take time. But it is helping them in taking out the anger from them. This age group is basically engages as their people liberation guerrilla army, and the next age group do engage themselves in other auxiliary activities. When asked that many

NGOs are working for them, so why do they adopt the violence path. They replied that NGOs though do some work but they cannot take drastic steps as the organization CPI (Maoist) does.

- 87 per cent of the Naxal activists feel that the NGOs take government funds and they are in nexus with the state machinery, so, they cannot be so active in the empowerment process and cannot make the tribals empowered to take part in the political process.
- 82 per cent of the respondents do not appreciate the NGO style of functioning.
- 90 per cent of the revolutionaries do not want any kind of interference or interruption in their acquired areas which include NGOs. If anyone wants to do any activity then they have to seek their cooperation. Even if they are conducting a meeting an outsider cannot even attend it without the party's permission. There are two reasons for this, first, they have the fear of being police informer and second, no interruption by a new comer. But situation is changing now, it is opined by the respondents in Orissa they do take help of NGOs and other organizations, but not in south Orissa so much as of now.
- Media personnels, sometimes, do some favours to them to take their interviews, but limited to only few media and not all media.
- More than 50 per cent of the respondents say that, they have their network systems in the government machinery and in other related institutions from where they get information about their enemy's movement. Sometimes, they get correct information and sometimes not.
- While sharing this, they said that the state has an impression that NGOs do support us, but it is not true, as the NGOs ideology do not match with the conflict ideology. Off late, they started collected money from NGOs too as they do it from other stake holders like contractors and other officials.

As mentioned earlier the extra variables which are present in the social, economic, cultural and political structures of the society which always influences one group over the other. The tribal groups have so far alienated from the main groups and their perception has turned to be real where they have started questioning, their lives pertaining to issues and how the inter-connections between the power relations in the political, social and economic manifested in making the tribals suffer. So, all these have in a way acted as an ideology of the tribals, though they are not literate, but they have understood the meaning of empowerment *vis-à-vis* tribals. So, this process of growing conscience it has become so necessary that they are moving for disempowered (with no choices) to empowerment demanding choices. As their democratic space is squeezed, so armed revolution is a sufficient condition. The paradigm shift of tribals from silence to realizing the awareness on themselves, their capacities and competencies is a sense of empowerment, where the Naxal movement has acted as a catalyst. So, the tribal ideology remaining from empowerment perspective is to change the oppressive system by throwing it, all social and political structures and to have control on their own lives which is preventing them from accessing their own needed resources.

Specific Tribes Entering into

As mentioned in the above two Tables (5.4 and 5.5), the percentage of tribals in the study area is high, Koraput being 49.62 per cent, Gajapati being 50.78, Malakangiri 57.43. and Rayagada is having 55.76 per cent of tribal population. The participation of tribal in the movement is high with the major tribes participating are Koyas, Bondas to a smaller extern, Bhumia, Sauras to a greater extent, Jatapus, Paraja, Gadabas, Halwas, Benia kuis, and Kondhs in the study area. There are no specific characteristics which portray that only certain tribes are into this movement. But certain sections with revolutionary thought process are getting into it from all tribal communities. As it is mentioned in the theories of ABC triangle in the Galtungs Theory in Chapter-1, when a tribe observes and reflects that the interest of state is only to protect a few sections of the society and not the others, they feel, violence is the only way to get justice. The following two Tables 5.5 and 5.6 show us factors because of which the tribals entering into this movement.

Table 5.5: Reasons for Membership

Sl. No.	*Communities*	*Reasons of membership*				
		Through compulsion	*By choice*	*As an alternate way*	*To get some benefit*	*Others*
1.	ST	2.56%	35.04%	29.06%	2.56%	10.26%
2.	SC	4.27%	4.27%	5.98%	—	
3.	Others	1.71%	2.56%	1.71%	—	

Table 5.5 shows that 35.04 per cent of tribals are entering into this by choice, whereas 29.06 per cent of them are viewing this as an alternative which can give some healing effect to their issues. As a whole, 36.75 per cent of the communities have felt that, this is the only alternative left for them to get justice. The informants explain that the country is going through a crucial phase of politics, though we have elections at regular intervals the peoples representatives are elected, the legislators are made but still no concrete results as far as tribal issues are concerned. Whichever may be the party, they are protecting the interests of the rich and not of the poor. Not only the tribals, there are urban folk who believe in this path and sympathize with them to a greater extent, may be youth, political leaders, government employees, advocates, teachers, and few business people. As history witnessed the Naxalbari revolt, more than 40 years ago, till today the peasants, disadvantaged poor tribals believe that this is the only way to get justice is a shameful remark to our democracy. The LPG (liberalization, privatization, and globalization) has made the poor tribals life a hell and there is a systematic attempt by the state to crush their democratic movement, and to corroborate this there are various examples in the study are a like the Mandrvaju land struggle, the Gudari land struggle, the Narayanpatna Chasi Mulia Adivasi Sangha, the Kashipur struggle against the mining, the struggle of the Dongrias against mining, the struggle for good effective governance by the cut off area people of Malkangiri district.

And in future, there are many more such struggles are yet to come. When it was asked to the passive supporters a larger public on the awareness of the movement, and why tribals are entering into it, the study derived 23 responses from other sections of population ranging from advocates, teachers, human right activists, civil liberty groups etc. The responses are given in Table 5.6.

It is a fact that 10 per cent of the people do perceive that the ism is on rise and due to the gap between the rich and the poor and it will continue in the future. They also feel that they do well to tribal people and tribal people in fact do see them as helpers, as and when they do not get any legitimate benefits from the existing governance system, they report to the Naxals and they in order threaten the contractor, forest official or anybody who is not helping the poor. So, Naxals are seen as friends, helpers in the villages.

The various explanations of the responses as interpreted by the respondent, this movement is more in the south Orissa districts, there are specific reasons for it. The age long deprivation of tirbals in these places,

Table 5.6: The awareness of the movement with regard to tribal participation

Sl. No.	*Responses*	*%age*
1.	It's a budding issue	4.9
2.	Humbled by their sacrifices for Tribals	2.0
3.	Know a general account of it from books	1.0
4.	The movement is active in South Orissa	7.8
5.	Very little knowledge	1.0
6.	Get to know from my professional circle	1.0
7.	Was a sympathizer in past and agree with their path	4.9
8.	Tribals don't get justice and Naxals take advantage of the situation	3.9
9.	Left the movement due to the fear of police	2.9
10.	It's a rebellion	1.0
11.	Tribals are exploited and naxals are giving them a party to fight, and they do have fighting spirits	11.8
12.	Movement without any ideology	2.9
13.	It's going through ups and downs	2.9
14.	The ism is on rise due to the gap between rich and poor	9.8
15.	Their teachings are good	7.8
16.	No idea	1.0
17.	During their visits to the villages we come to know	5.9
18.	They do good to poor tribals	3.9
19.	This is a socio-economic problem	7.8
20.	This is a political problem to capture power	2.9
21.	Tribals join out of fear	3.9
22.	We report to Naxals if we don't get our wages, PDs and other facilities	2.0
23.	This is a law and order problem	6.9

the level of exploitation is so high that the State never treated them as human beings, the movement here started in early 1990, and later, it picked up through a revolutionary awareness among the tribals. The Naxals are not against the development of roads, but they are certainly against those developments which make the poor tribals of the area poorer. As the roads come in, they pave new roads to mines, industries and various other institutions which make the tribals displaced and more marginalized. The tribals join as they do well to them and there is no other way for the tirbals to ventilate their anger and outrage.

The society is so made that, in the process of development, major chunks of the people have been deprived and they are paying the price of national interest. And there is enough amount of discontent within the tribals to join the movement. But still 7 per cent of the people feel that it can be solved through police and it is a law and order problem. The above Table 5.6 shows that only 7 per cent of the population feels that it is a law and order problem whereas the rest 71 per cent feels that it is justified in someway or the other to keep the fight. Every leader who is elected opines that the Naxalism is growing for exploitation, unemployment, high economic disparity between rich and poor, no justice for poor in the system. But there is no radical reforms have taken place so far. 80 per cent of the people do live a life for Rs. 20 a day. Potable drinking water and primary health care is a dream for many in south Orissa. The recent cholera deaths have proved that. Children are barred to get education as their parents cannot afford it. The PROBE survey shows that it takes Rs. 315 per child to afford for education[4]. The National ST Commission has suggested the government of Orissa to fill all the vacant posts in the scheduled areas, it has also suggested to give opportunity for education to tribal children, more residential facilities to tribal children, and mobile health facilities. The Commission suggested that the development of STs to be accelerated. The tribals are dissatisfied, they are victims of displacement.

When the belief on the system was explored, the tribal respondents came out with answers as Yes or No. The following table shows that how the contradictions between the state and the tribals have brought patterns of specific perspective towards each other which reflects in their direct violence in the form of killing each.

Table 5.7: Acceptance of the movement

Sl. No.	Communities	Do you believe such revolution will reward you			
		Yes	No	Yes in future	Others
1.	SC	100%			
2.	ST	100%			
3.	Others	100%			

The contradictions between the state and the Naxals have reached a stage of movement to intensity with conflict where both are completely antagonistic to each other. They identify with each other with violent ways only. Everyone participating in the conflict believes that this will reward them justice but in future. As state is showing violence by making it as vehicle for law and order, similarly they do firmly believe that through violence they can get justice.

Active and Passive Participation of the Tribals

As mentioned earlier about the active and passive membership base of the movement, the research probed in knowing the tribal linkage with the movement in study areas, whether their linkage yield any results and there 20 different responses came out as follows:

Table 5.8: The Tribal Linkage (What do they do the Tribal Communities/People)

Sl. No.	*Responses*	*%age*
1.	Don't know	4.2
2.	They free the tirbals from their immediate exploiter	4.2
3.	At village level they endure good governance for tribals in getting wages, PDS etc.	1.1
4.	Make aware, conduct meetings	7.4
5.	Their struggle is maturing through tribals	4.2
6.	It instills hope and courage among tribals	1.1
7.	They have been able to take out fear from tribals	1.1
8.	They help the tribals in getting land	6.3
9.	They organize tribals to unite and fight	13.7
10.	Mobilize tribals to raise issues	3.2
11.	Train them politically, bringing cultural revolution within them, give good teachings	10.5
12.	Tribals see them as rescuers, a way to ventilate their anger	7.4
13.	No	5.3
14.	Tribals like them as they mix with them in the village, close to their hearts, their interactions are very heart touching and help in getting minimum requirements	2.1
15.	Fight against all kinds of exploitation	4.2
16.	Its visible process of change	4.2
17.	Use tribals as luggage carriers	11.6
18.	Anyway tirbals are dying so why not die with a ism	1.1
19.	Preparing tribals for future	6.3
20.	Made the tribals to resist which they didn't do for since ages	1.1

They are not doing any good to the tribal communities and using them as to carry their luggage carrier, to guide them in the forest, ask for food, and they are taking shelter in their tribal hamlets as a result tribals are suffering from this. Many tribals in the border areas of Koraput-Malkangiri, Gajapati-Rayagada have been to jail repeatedly and are released. They say, even though they are not associated in any activity, but since they stay in those places they have to pay a price for that, but 7.4 per cent feel that they are the rescuers of tribals, and they mingle with them by speaking their language and mobilize them, 4.2 per cent feel that their struggle is ultimately maturing through tribals and in a way indicated the tribals are well participating in it. There is no leadership among tribals in the movement from south Orissa and the leaders come from Andhra Pradesh and Chhattisgarh who are directing in these districts of south

Orissa. So, 5 per cent of the respondents do feel that they do not do any good to them. And they are killing the Gram Pedas or village security person who is very poor and impoverished thinking that they are police informers. It is just to terrorize them and this is not the real ideology.

But 7 per cent do opine that the tribals see them as rescuers as they help them in eliminating their immediate enemies and free them from his or her exploitation. And they are well accepted in the villages as they look like them, talk their language, stay with them and make them aware to raise their voice democratically. And their struggle is maturing through the tribals. 4 per cent of the people do feel that this process of revolution is very visible, but they also say that they are doing good work in Chhạttisgarh and not in south Orissa.

The tribals as they do enter in the movement, but they have very strong reason which shows different factors of not relying on administrative/legislative/judicial system which makes them active in the movement process.

Table 5.9: Reasons behind and the Disbelief the System (Why they are against the system, why they do not believe in government machinery)

Sl. No.	*Responses*	*%age*
1.	No comments	5.6
2.	Faulty system	0.8
3.	As they say, naxalism is a social problem, it's a farce, the system is good	0.8
4.	System is meant for the rich, and the poor are always exploited and the system is not sensitive to the real issues and the system do not address the real issues	64.8
5.	The system has not given an effective tribal leader or leader of the poor who is genuinely addressing the issues	4.8
6.	System has no justice for tribals, they are uses as only vote banks	1.6
7.	The system has created the gap between the rich and the poor, the have and have-nots	5.6
8.	The system is against the movement and its *vice versa*	2.4
9.	This is a bourgeoisie state pro-capitalist, colonial set-up and it's a hypocrisy	11.2
10.	No system is 100% right, it has to be practical in addressing the issues	2.4

The explanations of the responses are given here as—81 per cent of the respondents do feel that the system has not done anything for the tribals—poor sections of the Indian State who constitute 8 per cent of the population, and in Orissa they constitute 22 per cent and in the study area they constitute more than 60 per cent of the population. The Naxal forces are a natural off-shoot of the saturated discontent in these tribal pockets, which have lost their land, livelihood, identity, and their resources for the developmental projects. The present system has a pyramid with the ruling class on the top, followed by political leaders, new rich, and last the proletarian. The Naxal forces just dream to change the pyramid in a reverse direction. How far it is true it has to be tested by time. And these forces are acting in the normally needy areas which are quite natural. Where the tribals have lost their own identity, their lands, their resources, where they are made to fight within themselves in the name of religion, where they do not have any directions and it is very easy for the movement to breed their where they are welcomed.

They have their own version of the system and they want to change the whole pyramid of present where the ruling class is at the first, but the poor should come first. Their aim is to change the structures. 3 per cent of the respondents do feel that no system is perfect and we cannot talk of as system which is completely utopian, as the system and structures complement and supplement with each. The structures are crated to protect the system and *vice versa*. So, it is necessary to be practical and not radical.

Economic Package for the Tribal Members (in the Naxal Organisation)

The movement has seen many faces during these 60-70 years starting from Telengana movement, the Parvatipuram, the Naxalbari, the Chhattisgarh, Abujmad intervention, the later sparked in south Orissa, in the early 1990s. The episodes show that it has gone a long way. Due to ideological differences many have formed new fractions, so there are very few fragmentations of the revolutionaries who believe in armed struggle. The previous leaders who were associated with the movement in south Orissa said that they really did not had any package as such, and were totally dependent on the people. The case study and the viewpoint of the Comrades (who was in the movement in 1960s, now open ground but still in the non-armed party of the Communist) are given here to understand the situation.

On the economic package there are various different viewpoints of the previous leaders who are now open and it is extremely difficult to get information from the party as they were highly secretive. Few of the respondents who are frontline leaders did opine that their families are helped during illness of any members. Few said that their cost of the legal cases—if they go to jail is always borne by the party.

Few also opined that all the monthly requirements are met by the party, like shoes, cloths, soap, oil, special provisions for females participants etc., but very few shared that their families do receive a monthly finance package between Rs. 2000 to 5000. So, it depends on the kind of association with the party. It is difficult to arrive at an inference with this data available from the field. But it is a fact that they do receive some money. The old leaders do say that, the movement has changed in the course of time, they change from contractors, from business class people, from public representatives, and also people give it in the form of cash and kind. The members of the people liberation guerrilla army do get some money which is sent to their army respective houses, but it is the minimum amount. The party decides as to how it will supply the essential items to its members. The people working underground are supported by their sympathizers in the forest and also in the jail. During one such data collected the researcher saw that the underground activists got a bag full of rice and dozens of soaps for them. They have developed certain mechanism which fulfils their needs.

There are few quotes from the respondents which are given to understand the situation and the factors involved in it. "*A person from Gajapati who was in movement in the 1960s, an old leader involved in the movement during 1967-1972, later he left the movement, now he is an active member of the Communist Party of India Marxist-Leninist liberation. He explains Gurandi in Gajapati was the hotspot of the movement during the 1960s under the influence of the Srikakulam movement and also with the Koraput movement. This place was quite safe, a good hide out and was used as a shelter by all the revolutionaries. There was one ashram in the Paralekhemundi town where most of the time they used to take shelter. His brother was also involved in the movement so, he got his ideological orientations from his family on Communism. And he was automatically motivated to join the movement.*"

During 1960s, the government could not make much difference in the lives of the people after almost two decades of independence, so, there was a political upsurge as there were no radical reforms for the poor people. So, violence was adopted by the people with a slogan "land to the tiller". That was the first time the whole country saw revolution among peasants after independence. On April 22nd, 1969, the Communist Party of India (Marxist-Leninist) was formed, as for revolution, a revolutionary party is required. I was a student at that time and as per party orders I was directed to go to Chitrakonda to organize the workers there. He believes in left revisionism and in mass mobilization and the time will come when the people will take up arms to fight for their rights. Where the political power will go to the deprived sections of the society. The leftists who believed in the parliamentary path and came to power in the early 1960s, but could not fulfil the promises of the people and they had to dace the outrage of the tribals in a village called Naxalbari, where the tribals fought with a violence method to get back their lands and it was a resistance movement. This was the revolutionary phase in the Indian Communist history for the first time after independence. The struggles before the independence were also fought bit due to the failure of the left government in India the movement took place becomes much significant for the history of communists.

When we observed that that was the time when we had to prepare for an armed stage of revolution. The dream became true to some extent through Naxalbari. The party witnessed various splits in 1964, 1969, and later in 1972 and so on and so forth. I was student and my lecturer also went underground. He left his job and joined the movement and I also left my studies and joined the movement. The Communist Party also did experiments at few places, in organizing the tribals, taking the small areas the making it as units, liberating them and finally covering the urban areas. This has been the thought of Mao. But looking at the Indian conditions the party could not succeed as the stage of revolution was different. But we are under a process of a total revolution. If I say that the Nepal experiment was successful, but the time will prove that whether they are able to change the system or not. We being the largest party among the Marxist and Leninist groups [CPI (ML) liberation], also adopting the path of parliament, changing the tactical lines and our political thoughts. What we thought during the Naxalbari period was that India is an agricultural country and agriculture is the key to development, and if we want to fight for liberation then it will be through peasantry liberation struggle to seize the political power. But after losing our cadres due to police repression we changed the style and thought that gun is not the only means, legal struggle is much more important for which arms are not required, armed squad is not the way. So, there were different line of thinking among us and we divided basing on the ideological differences.

But we believe in armed struggle, but it has to be through an agrarian revolution by exposing the inequalities of the system and it should be a people's resistance movement. But I do not accept the present CPI Maoist style of people's mobilization as they are far away from the masses. As the tribals are recruited without any political sharpness and, there is no movement as such among the tribals. But without understanding the issues of the tribals, the government says that the tribals are Naxalites. Now, what I feel that no one should preach or teach the tribals that they should take up arms, but rather the tribals should sense it that this system is not ours and we should not take up arms for our liberation. There is need to a great deal to prepare mentally and psychologically.

I feel that the success through the present movement is very less and we have to prepare the masses by bringing them to the main stream and we need to review our Constitution also and focus more on the mobilization of the peasants and emphasyze on the agrarian problems. As I feel that two aspects are directly proportional to each, i.e. the more the problems are unsolved the more will be the preparation by the people. I also do not accept the present party the way they collect money through extortion. But this was not the way in 1960, but now, the cadres are paid. The revolutionary cannot be paid job. Ultimately, we have to depend on the peoples resources and we cannot make ourselves sustainable though looting, destroying the government establishments, and collecting money by force. But I feel that we still need minimum 20 to 30 years to reach that stage of people's mobilization. Though, we also adopted the line of annihilation for some time, but that will not solve the problem as attacks and counter attacks will follow and the very idea of struggle will be diluted. Media does not have a proper understanding of the issue. The democracy of our system is limited to few and it is only for the rich and influential people. Most of the people depend on labour and the disparity is very and is high the growing everyday. So, the only option is revolution for a new democratic system. I do not support the path of negotiation and I feel that Naxaliam is a theory and it will be proved along with the time. It is not a law and order situation, by making some roads, and giving support to tribals will not solve the issue, there has to be changes in the system.

Another Case Study from old leaders also points out that the economic package in the past and now has a huge difference. *"A worker who is retired from the Chitrakonda Dam Project leads a life of isolation in Koraput district as till today he fears police repression. He was in jail for a long time during the 1970s and his wife was in an ashram during his jail tenure. The Naxalite movement in Koraput district started under the influence of the Srikakulam movement. But the foundation can be traced from the background of Chitrakonda Power Project trade union movement. The trade union movement started with the leaders who had connections with leaders of Naxalbari, but till 1968, Koraput region did not had any violent incidents. But many people like intellectuals, and advocates participated in the underground movement for a short phase among them the famous leaders were D. Bhuvan Mohan Pattnaik, Naga Bhusan Pattnaik, Purusottam Palli and others. Comrade Palli and others were already a part of the Communist Party. But the Naxalbari call made their actions very visible and the spark was very lightening all over the areas."*

The Chitrakonda Dam project had different rules for the labourers. They had a system of retrenchment where they had systems like 8 months of work and 4 months of off, where the workers did not receive any benefit. So, the trade union had a demand charter… "they organized a rally and demanded for same facilities to the contractual staff as it was for the regular staff, go home allowances, retrenchment allowances, unhealthy allowances. All the Communist leaders came and organized the trade union movement in Chitrakonda. But during the strike many of us got arrested including him. But after the strike we have succeeded in getting few demands. We got faith in the leaders and the workers movement was the first significant achievement by the Communist Party of Koraput in 1966, but as workers we did not know the line of struggle and the politics, we fought for our rights. The new leaders gave us strength and belief to trust the mass mobilization. We all workers thought that since we are not so educated, so leadership was needed from outside and Naga Bhusan Pattnaik was elected as our president, as he was also an advocate by profession.

When the arrests were more the leaders went underground, but we had a tremendous support from outside intellectuals and they used to keep contact with us and inform us how to proceed further. The other members escaped from the police, we the workers always helped the leaders to escape. I used to give shelter to the leaders and supply them food and medicines, but when we were in jail we had regular classes on Communism. We had two sections in jail, Communists and non-Communists. Prurusottam Palli was one of the most active tribal leaders and he had the whole map of Koraput district on his finger tips and he was like a wisdom pool. Being a tribal he was an ideal for many."

There were regular demonstrations till 1970s, the slogans created environment for action. Many students also joined the movement and supported, and since the Naxalbari movement was on peak. *"So, we the workers told the leaders that we cannot support them directly but we will be their sympathizers. The police was torturing the people like anything. I feel the people who were harassed by the police in those days are now completely active in the movement. The main emphasis of the movement was mass mobilization.*"

There were differences among the leaders, few wanted to boycott the court and few wanted that they should use court to expose the laws to the public, as the people will hear the court arguments and will know the exact face of the laws and the system. The harassment in jail was to such an extent that the juveniles were kept along with the adults and not separately. *"I was there in the jail for 5 years and released in 1974, after my release I used to take part in the rallies and demonstrations and was threatened by police and started working in the dam project again. I saw there were lot of fractions in the party and few started believing in Parliamentary path and I do not believe in the path, but I believe in mass mobilization path and not in violence way. There is brutal torture in the democratic system. Still feudalism exists and the exploitation continues. If the line of Naxalbari is wrong then why the people still adopting it? Today there is no education, no facilities for the people and there is discontentment within the people. Till now we have done opposition* (pratirodh). *I feel the masses are not ready to take up arms and if they are ready then there should not be any problem. Why the people are joining in such a large number from the cut off area in Malkangiri because they have faced ages of police torture and they are taking revenge. But the movement has become a paid job; getting money from the companies will not suit the path of the revolution."*

Sex and Social Status of the Respondents

This section explains the sex, the education, the land holding by the respondent family, their quality of land, their housing pattern, the marital status and the family size of the respondents to give a picture of their social profile.

Table 5.10: Sex of the respondents

(in %age)

Sl. No.	*Sex of the respondents*	*SC*	*ST*	*Others*	*Total*
1.	Male	10	70	4.3	84.7
2.	Female	0	11.4	4.3	15.3
	Total	10	81.4	8.6	100

Table 5.10 shows the percentage of gender in the movement, and is

seen that the percentage of male is more, but there is a gradual increase of women participation in the movement as they share. Most of the raids are led by women, like the Nayagarh raid, the Koraput armoury raid were led by women. The female want to revolt against the all odds of the society. The party celebrates the International Women's Day inside the forest to mark the importance of women and women's movement. The party has different frontal women wings in the state level and as well as national level.

Table 5.11: Educational Status of the Respondents

Sl. No.	*Communities*	*Educational status (%)*				
		Illiterate	*0-5th std*	*6-10th std*	*Above 7th std*	*Total*
1.	SC	0	0	1.4	14.3	15.7
2.	ST	17.2	30	25.7	4.3	71.2
3.	Others	0	0	1.4	5.7	7.1
	Total	17.2	30	28.5	24.3	94

The above table shows that the educational status (basic school education) of the respondents is hardly between 10th standard and 17.2 per cent are illiterate among tribals. But, though they join as illiterates into the party, but they got enough political education there to understand, the social structure, social analysis, distribution of resources among the society. So, they believe that for any resistance education is not necessary but what is necessary is courage to raise voice.

Table 5.12: Land holding status of the Families of the Respondents

Sl. No.	*Communities*	*Land holding (%)*				
		No land	*0-2 acres*	*2-5 acres*	*Above 5 acres*	*Total*
1.	SC	7.1	1.4	0	0	8.5
2.	ST	32.9	18.6	27.1	4.3	82.9
3.	Others	8.6	—	—	—	8.6
	Total	48.6	20	27.1	4.3	100

Table 5.12 shows us that nearly 49 per cent of the respondent's families do not own any land, and only 20 per cent of them own less than 2 acres; 27.1 per cent own between 2 to 5 acres. The whole pattern of the respondents in the party gives a clear picture that why certain sections of the society are only going into such kind of movements and armed resistance and not others. The poor only got into this movement.

Table 5.13: Quality of the land owned by the respondent families

Sl. No.	Name of the study districts	Land quality (%)		Total
		Rain fed	irrigated	
1.	Gajapati	23.26	2.33	25.59
2.	Rayagada	20.93	2.33	23.26
3.	Koraput	27.91	4.65	32.56
4.	Malkangiri	18.60	—	18.60
	Total	90.70	9.31	100

Table shows that 90.7 per cent of the lands are rain-fed. The basic topography of the study area is hilly where the most so-called technology will not work. Though the study area contains enormous amount of water resources, but it is not used for the tribal purposes rather harnessed for big dams, factories, leaving the tribals homeless and with no irrigation facilities. Whatever irrigation facility has been provided goes to the rich farmers and not the poor tribals.

Table 5.14: Housing Patterns of Respondents

Sl. No.	Communities	Types of housing (%)			Total
		Katcha	Pacca	Other type	
1.	SC	2.94	1.47	—	4.41
2.	ST	55.88	19.12	13.24	88.24
3.	Other	1.47	5.88	—	7.35
	Total	60.29	26.47	13.24	100

Table 5.14 shows that 60.29 per cent of the houses are *katcha*, whereas 26.47 per cent are *pacca* and rest 13.24 per cent are either tiled or roof house. From the 60.29 per cent, 55.88 per cent houses belong to tribals which are *katcha* houses. It again indicates more poverty.

Table 5.15: Marital Status of the Respondents

Sl. No.	Community	Marital status (%)		Total
		Married	Unmarried	
1.	SC	5.71	4.29	10
2.	ST	70	11.43	81.43
3.	Others	2.86	5.71	8.57
	Total	78.57	21.43	100

Table 5.16 portrays that most of the tribal respondents are married components to other communities. If somebody chooses someone within the party, that is welcomed by all. Most of these respondents do work in particular vicinity and where they can meet their family at a regular interval. Most of the spouses are also in the same party in different positions.

Table 5.16: Family size of the Respondents

Sl. No.	*Communities*	*Family size (%)*			*Total*
		0-4	*4-6*	*Above 6*	
1.	SC	5.71	2.86	1.43	10
2.	ST	28.57	38.57	14.29	81.43
3.	Others	1.43	4.29	2.86	8.57
	Total	35.71	45.72	18.58	100

Table 5.16 shows that the average family size of the respondents is 4 to 6 which comprises 45.71 per cent. The largest family size is also a factor where the younger ones go out to work with the parents and serve the society and nature closely. It is very easy to motivate young minds. So, during the data collection it was found that a 12 to 13 years old girl had joined the movement. It is true that out of compulsion and frustration with the traditions minors do join the party and do surrender for many reasons, either they are caught or by fear they surrender. During August 2, 2011, girls who were minor surrendered before the Koraput police who were working in Narayanpatna area.

Teaching and Training of Naxalism

Any institution or movement would have its own norms and rules for the propaganda. The rules are followed in their system and they are imbibed in the geographical area. These do come in the various forms, such as rules, approaches, their teaching. The opinion of the membership was taken to understand the teaching and training aspect of the Naxal movement. Table 5.17 shows what their pamphlet contains manifesto/propaganda:

What actually is preached by Naxal is found in their posters, leaflets and pamphlets which are seen at different places of south Orissa, which are against the exploiters like the *sahukars*, moneylenders, contractors, injustice done towards the people. It also against the corrupted officials, advocates, police repression and the actions of the police and they appeal

Table 5.17: Their Manifesto/Propaganda

Sl. No.	Responses	%age
1.	Not so clear	21.8
2.	People to people type basically speaks their problems	1.3
3.	They talk on imperialistic role of government in taking away the resources from tribals	1.3
4.	Against liquor vendors	2.6
5.	On declared bandhs, weeks	5.1
6.	Demand on land to poor tribals	5.1
7.	Against exploitation system, injustice	10.3
8.	Against system	5.1
9.	Against police repression	6.4
10.	Against *sahukars*	3.8
11.	Against corruption and government officials, and other corrupted people like advocates	3.8
12.	Appeal to public to join the movement	3.8
13.	Appeal to boycott elections	9.0
14.	Against corrupted contractors	9.0
15.	Against forest and revenue officials	6.4
16.	They are all imaginary constructions and useless	1.3
17.	Against capitalistic attitude of the government and MNCs, displacement	3.8

the people to join the movement. While the respondents opined these facts they also shared that it may be difficult for the government to accept these facts but they are true. Now-a-days the government has adopted a policy of escapism and anything they see they immediately point out that this is done by the Naxals before going to the roots of the problem, and in this process the Naxals have become the scapegoat for everything. All the responses indicate the injustice for the poor.

Their pamphlets, posters only are against the exploiters like contractors, government officials, and companies. 1.3 per cent of them do feel that these facts are not true and everything is perfect, but a majority have shared that their teachings are on this. What they distribute outside, also the same training manual is imbibed for the party workers. They conduct classes everyday for their cadres, there are special classes, seminars, on issues but political awareness teachings are a part of their routine. This is related to the armed cadre of the party, but there are different approaches and strategies for different sets of the people. When they enter a new area, they survey the area and collect all the informations regarding exploiters of that village and Gram Panchayat and then they conduct mass meeting and slowly take that area into their clutches. Normally, this process varies from one month to two years. A community teaching process is given here as to how they can impart training to the whole community using those methods.

The Approach Rules (From their Party Documents)[5]

As mentioned earlier, every movement of the process has some definite rules and regulations by which they spread their message. The Naxalite movement does have certain rules by which they enter into new area and implement their ideology. These responses came from a village Praja Court (local courts that are organized by the Naxal cadres where they address village issues), where they also explain and teach about their rules. When they intervene in new area, the information is collected on the area, based on caste, economic status, social dynamics and about the exploiters. After that, the first seed which is sown in the area is in the form of a small organization called Biplabi Chasi Mulia Samiti, Revolutionary Peasants and Labourers Committee and/or it can have any name which symbolizes the people's power in the village. Making this committee as a base they have a clear cut policy through which they build up the base which are as follows:

- This is the backbone of the new democratic revolution. This is also a fighting committee (Ladhua Sangathan). This will work for the alternative governance at the village level.
- Anybody who is above the age of 16 years can become a member of this *Samiti*, irrespective of caste, religion, sex etc. Women representation will be given importance. The people who are touts informers will not be included in this. And an open election will be conducted where landless, and poor peasants will be given opportunity to become leaders. There are no restriction as such for men and women.
- Every year this Committee will collect a minimum membership fees and also during the harvest period they will collect a certain amount towards the *sangathan* which will be used for the village during the crisis in the future.
- To avoid any vigilance of the government, all the papers and documents related to the *Sangha* will be kept secret. This is to save the *sangha* from the attacks of police. This *sangha* which is the alternative government of the people have to protect its own identity and presence; for this purpose the *sangha* will form a "*Gram Raksha Dal*", consisting of youth (both male and

female) of fighting spirit, to fight the enemy. This "*Dal*" will create barriers for the enemies from entering into the village. As the alternative government will start functioning in the village, it is obvious that there will be repression from the outside enemy especially the police. This Raksha Dal will protect the village from all sorts of external obstacles.

- It is believed that the so called democratic rule of our country help the exploitation process to sustain by any means. This present system always protects the interests of the rich, the vested interest groups, and other influential people, but the system has always failed to give justice to the ordinary common people. So, it is quite impossible for the poor to take the help of this system to fight for their rights or to revolt. So, the *sangha* will reject the present system of governance and will form its own alternative system under the leadership of the poor peasants. So, this *sangha* is the primary step towards the direction of formation of the alternative government.
- So, any member of the *sangha* will not be involved in the present electoral system directly or indirectly. Rather, it will appeal to the people to boycott the election system. So, the emphasis will be given to strengthen the *Sangha* and to build their capacities to function effectively the village level governance system.
- As the *sangha* grows, it will not pay any type of *sistu*/tax to any government department in any form. So, the *Sangha* will be trained in this direction.
- Though the present democratic system has created a three tier decentralized Panchayati Raj system, yet it is just an eye wash. The elected Panchayat representations ultimately become the agents of the system. And in their process there is lot of corruption, the fundamental issue of the people are not solved, the plans which are made are just to make the people silent; it is just throwing peanuts to monkey. The government wants to give something to save its face. So, the *Sangha* will stop people from accepting those plans, as the plans are very luring to the people for a short period, but they do not adhere the basic issues of the people.
- Gradually, the *sangha* will prepare the people not to accept any provision from the present government system.
- This *sangha* will take up new developmental schemes for the village. All the schemes will be alternative models of development.

- The Biplabi Chasi Mulia Samiti/Sangha is secular in nature. It does not believe in any particular religion, belief on any cult. People have to decide and they have the full right and freedom to adopt any religion. As the present government politics provokes people for communal riots. But the *Sangha* which is the alternative government is completely against of all this communal issue.
- The *Sangha* do not believe in the traditions of casteism, so, it fights against the caste system. The *Sangha* is also against the system of untouchability and any other form of discrimination.
- It believes in gender equality. It fights for the rights of women and also for all kinds of oppressions against women. It is against the patriarchy system of thinking and strives for equality in society between male and female.
- The families who will take leadership in this *Sangha,* will be helped by other. The families, who are tortured by police, will also be helped by the *Sangha.*
- The surrounding natural resources (such as land, water and forest) of the village will be taken care of by the *Sangha* and no outsider (like any company or government) will have any right over the resources. For this purpose, people will acquire the lands of *zamindars* (who are absentee landlords) and also from other landlords, (who do not labour on their land, but engage others).
- The landlords who stay in towns but have lands in scheduled areas, all this agricultural land will be acquired. And it will be re-distributed among the poor, tribals, *dalits* (both men and women).
- The landlords who act as police informers, or who leave the area and go elsewhere to reside, his or her land will also be acquired, and will be distributed among the poor tribals. The ceiling surplus land will also be acquired and distributed. The forest lands, *patita* lands, *anabadi* lands, the land which is under the control of any religious institution will also be acquired and distributed among the people. The village *Sangha* will not only distribute the land, but will also maintain whether the person is able to cultivate the land or not.
- This *Sangha* will fight against the money lending or any type of this system. And it will try to form a people's cooperative. It will stop the land leasing to outside money lenders who take land for cash crops.
- This *Sangha* will fight against all kinds and forms of exploitation like Bethi system, bonded labour, forced labour, etc. *Sangha*

will fight for the enhancement of wages to the labourers and equal wages for male and female.

- The *Sangha* will fight for the good support price for the agricultural harvest and also for the minor forest produce.
- The people will not allow the forest department to enter into the forest as the natural resources belong to them, (as mentioned earlier). They will protect the forests and use its benefits as per their requirements. For this purpose, they will form a Forest Protection Committee. The people will be made aware not to cut the fruit bearing trees for timber use. The people will protect their forest from contractors who go for illegal falling. The *Sangha* will prepare the people to protest against industrialism, mining and displacement.
- The *Sangha* will encourage the people to reject the present problem solving institutions like police departments, courts etc. rather, it will encourage the people to go for their traditional system of conflict resolution. The land disputes between the villagers, disputes regarding marriage etc. will be solved within the village with the help of this *Sangha*.
- Inter-village disputes will also be solved through this *Sangha*. Justice will be delivered to the people irrespective of their socio-economic status.
- The *Sangha* will concentrate to improve the lifestyles of the people. For this purpose, it will set up a hospital to cater the leader serious to people. It will stress on safe drinking water and sanitation. The *Sangha* will form an education committee through which it will take up literacy programmes for illiterates. The *Sangha* will also give political education to the people.
- The *Sangha* will focus on use of organic manure and effective technologies for agriculture. And it will train the people in this regard. The *Sangha* will educate the people on how to minimize the use of chemical fertilizers. The *Sangha* will also form an Agricultural Cooperative Society to solve the peasant problems.
- Vegetable cultivation, horticulture, and livestock development programmes will be taken up to improve the standards of living of the people.
- The *Sangha* will oppose any kind of communication with people which will destroy their culture like vulgar films or any forms of entertainment which is vulgar in nature. The *Sangha* will work to eradicate the orthodox beliefs of the people. The *Sangha* will

form a cultural committee who will try to prevent their own culture in progressive ways and thoughts.

- The Cultural Committee will try to spread the message to recognize own cultural values. The Committee will take the help of those films, and documentaries which are meant to educate people in this direction. The Committee will also use the traditional folk media as songs, music and lullabies.
- The *Sangha* will oppose and fight against any kind of intoxication, habits and indulgences of the people. The *Sangha* will build the capacities of the people in order to prepare organic food products from Sago Palm, Dates, Mahua; instead of preparing liquor from those.

All these above mentioned and highlighted points are the duties and rules of Biplabi Chasi Mulia Samiti at the village level. The first step to enter into a village or any area, the CPI (Maoist) party [which is an underground/secret party] is to form an alternative peoples governance system. They also appeal all the villagers to reject the present governance system and have their own governance systems.

Training Aspect—Glimpses from the Camp Life

The paragraphs have explained foregoing their rules and regulations which are also distributed in the local language in their operational areas. Apart from their teaching, they do have a policy for training their cadres starting from the village to the higher level. Their teachings are very intense and the life of revolutionary party workers is very difficult. The life in the camp is much disciplined, where they get very less sleep. The sentry job is on rotation basis 24 hours all 365 days. During important party events like seminars, special camps, conferences they depute four layers of sentries. Both male and female equally share this responsibility, wherever they organize a temporary or permanent camp in those areas where they have a very strong hold of the masses. They have strong networking and they have their special informers in all levels, which alert them about the movement of the State Security Forces.

Early in the morning they have a roll call, after finishing the morning chores the armed squad goes for physical training which is very hard. The sentries go for their respective jobs, in four directions to guard the camp. Few go to the nearby markets to buy necessary things as per the need. Few are engaged in cooking, bringing water, so there is a perfect division of labour. Before breakfast there is roll call and after that there are political classes, combined studies and special classes. They are also given notes; they got note books and other stationary from the party. In evening, they go to villages to conduct meetings, and conduct cultural songs which are a strong medium for intellectual stimulation. The camps are normally mobile which carry all the utensils and plastic sheets with them. Each one carries almost a load of more than 15 kgs irrespective of their gender. They do not waste anything and derive their own measures to save water for the camp life. They carry plastic sheets which is everything for them. Everyone is always armed all the time, they are extremely alert. They maintain the weapons daily like cleaning and greasing them. While cleaning everyone faces at one direction. Their physical education classes are very tedious. Radio is the main source to get information from outside. Few media people do help them in giving some essential items; they even get newspapers some time. Few also leave the struggle as they cannot cope with the hard life. But they take care of their health, drink water after boiling. Few nearby doctors and religious institutions do help them. They do take precautions for malaria.

They have separate sectors like survey wing, research wing, although the polity bureau is the highest body to take all decisions. At times, it has been seen that few members out of ego clash are taking their own decisions without informing the higher body in terms of killing of some important people like Swami Laxmanananda at Kandhamal. They do rotate their functions as per situation demands. Everyone get the basic armed training for self-defence.

It is also found that in few camps higher cadres harass the females and get indulged in drinks. They also compel the villagers to arrange food for the whole party members. These are mostly found in Koraput districts in Pottangi and Lamtaput blocks. They do compel the tribals to carry their luggage and cook for them. These patterns of behaviour have shown a negative effect now on the tribal cadres in the past two years. But their rules as indicated are very clear in the early intervention.

References

1. *Rich Lands and Poor People, CSE*, 2008.
2. *MHA*, 2005 reports.
3. *Handbook of Social Work with Groups*, 2004, pp. 32-35.
4. *Dhartri*, 17th June 2008.
5. *Their Approach to a Village* (party document in Oriya).

6
Philosophy of Naxalite Movement and its Constituted Principles of Action

"Political power grows out of the barrel of a gun."

—*Mao Tse-Tung*

Making of the Constitution

The constitution of the Naxalite movement draws its grounding principles from its past struggle and from the present state in the country. Their constitution has principles which talks about the membership, special section for the women, their deviation rules if some members act on their own wishes. The backdrop of the constitution is based on polices of the government. Today, India has opened markets and resources to foreign companies, which has only one clear policy to uproot the indigenous communities primarily from central India. The minerals lying in these regions of Orissa, Chhattisgarh, Andhra Pradesh and Jharkhand are open for foreign companies. The extraction of minerals leads to mass dispossession of the people, especially, tribals in this area. They are showing a strong resistance not to be displaced. The most so called good Rehabilitation and Resettlement (R and R) packages only offer cash compensation and not land for land policy (as set by ILO).

This is due to the contradictions between the interests of the *adivasis* and the companies. Conflict of interests have very well manifested in terms of violence. After losing life, culture, land and livelihood *adivasis* are ultimately taking the shelter of Naxalism to revolt. This discontent among the *adivasis* is a good ground for Naxalite intervention and to fuel the conflict. In order to understand the current phase of Naxal movement-conflict, their constitution, party programme and the guerrilla perspective have to be viewed with the changing phases, and the various transformations that have occurred in them. Though the Naxalite movement (taken its origin, name from the Naxlbari revolution) shares most of the characteristics with social movements, but the genesis of it has to be seen in the context of communist movement in India. To describe in a nutshell the timeline goes as follows:

- The Communist Party first split into two, Communist Party of India (CPI) and Communist Party of India (Marxist) [CPI(M)] in 1964.
- The Naxalbari revolution took place in 1967.
- The eight historic documents were dedicated by Comrade Charu Mazumdar to the proletarian world.
- The Naxalbari uprising blossomed with the new version of Marxism, Leninism and Maosim.
- After that, to manage such uprisings the joint platform AICCR (All India Coordination Committee of Communist Revolutionaries) came up in 1969.
- By the beginning of 1970s, similar struggles were witnesses in Uttar Pradesh, Andhra Pradesh, Orissa, Bihar with greater intensity.
- By the mid of 1970s, there were many splits in the party due to ideological differences, few leaders went underground, few surrendered and very few even restricted to the armed resistance.
- By 1977, many accepted the parliamentary path of democracy Peoples War Group was incepted in 1980s.
- A similar group MCCI (Maoist Community Centre India) also incepted in northern part of India.
- There was a conference held on 15th to 30th of November, 1995 by the CPI (ML) people's war where they asserted right to self-determination, their support to similar struggles in Nagas, Kashmiris, Assamese etc. And these all struggles are integrated part for the new democratic revolution. The conference unanimously declared to fight against economic policies, establish people's authority at grassroots level, build urban movement, fight for women's oppression, against caste-discrimination etc.
- The unification of MCCI and PWG was a historical event in the movement.
- The present split in the unified party during May, 2012.
- The eight historic documents dedicated by comrade Charu Mazumdar (CM-works blog) gives the first founding principle

as to work towards a new democratic revolution. He has emphasized on the flood crisis, rising prices, depends on imperialism by the government will give rise to more conflict. The discontent among public will grow and will take the form of struggle in future. The country cannot follow the policy of repression with its growing population. For this, the revolutionary party has to establish with revolutionary cadre with activists group at the local level, with peasant organization and trade unions as their frontal organization.

The ultimate aim should be seizure of political power, area-wise seizure and then occupy the central power. Working class have to be involved more, to take arms, form armed units for confrontation, politically educate every armed unit. There will be spontaneous movement by youth, or any affected mass, this will open the source of the revolutionary parties.

- The unification process of MCCI and PWG took more than two years with intense discussion and conferences. Many documents were prepared and the constitution was made for the Indian revolution with various international developments actors as a backdrop database.[1]

The Constitution—An Overview

The constitution formed after the unification of two revolutionary parties in 2004, has 13 chapters stating the general programme, objectives, membership, funds, rights of the member, organization principles, discipline in the party, deviation of the rules and punishment therefor offered, debates and a detailed rules how to function at different levels.

Adherence to the Constitution

The constitution is the synthesis of the idea, documents, debates and discourse between the two parties, with their experiences to wage peoples war. The unified party organizes congress once in every two years. So, this 2004 constitution might have undergone with few additions to enrich the document. But this stands as essential weapon in the hands of the party for solving the fundamental problems of the Indian revolution for its victory. The general programme of the party is to establish communist society. New democratic revolution will be carried out through armed wars, with area-wise seizure of power, from country side moving to the cities and then to the Centre. The army and the united front are the two important organs of the revolution. As per the constitution, the main task is to establish people's liberation, army base areas and then transforming them to people's liberation guerrilla army. Every member should work tough as the road to revolution is very tough and dedicate them for long revolution.

Deviation from the Constitution

As per the constitution, there have been some practical rules for the members who work for the party. If any member or unit of function violates the objectives of the party, programme or structure they will be subjected to indiscipline and will be liable to disciplinary action. The disciplinary action ranges from warning, suspension, cancelling membership, expelling from the party with the approval of the higher committee. Sometimes, the units of function are against reconstituted. If any member of the central committee violates the constitution provisions or indulge himself or herself in any anti-party activity, then with two-thirds approval he or she can be removed or expelled from the rank. If anyone wants to leave the party by his or her own choice they can do. Some leave the party without informing too. Some even surrenders before the State, some leave the party due to ego clashes with others, some leave because of leadership crisis, some leave to extend their families, some leave due to misappropriation of funds. But the party cannot take any action as they are not in the catch of the party procedure once they over ground.

Administrative Set-up

The highest body is the central committee, the polity bureau (which has members from military commission and other wings), the administrative diagram of the party is shown in Fig. 6.1.

Primary unit of the party will be a cell which consists of a minimum 3 and maximum 5. All committees elect their respective secretaries. The party congress is the supreme authority of the entire party. The Central Committee elected by the Congress is the highest authority in between two congresses.

In the study area, in south Orissa, for example, the structure is more or less as follows (this Fig. 6.1 is just to understand work at large, but this changes too when required).

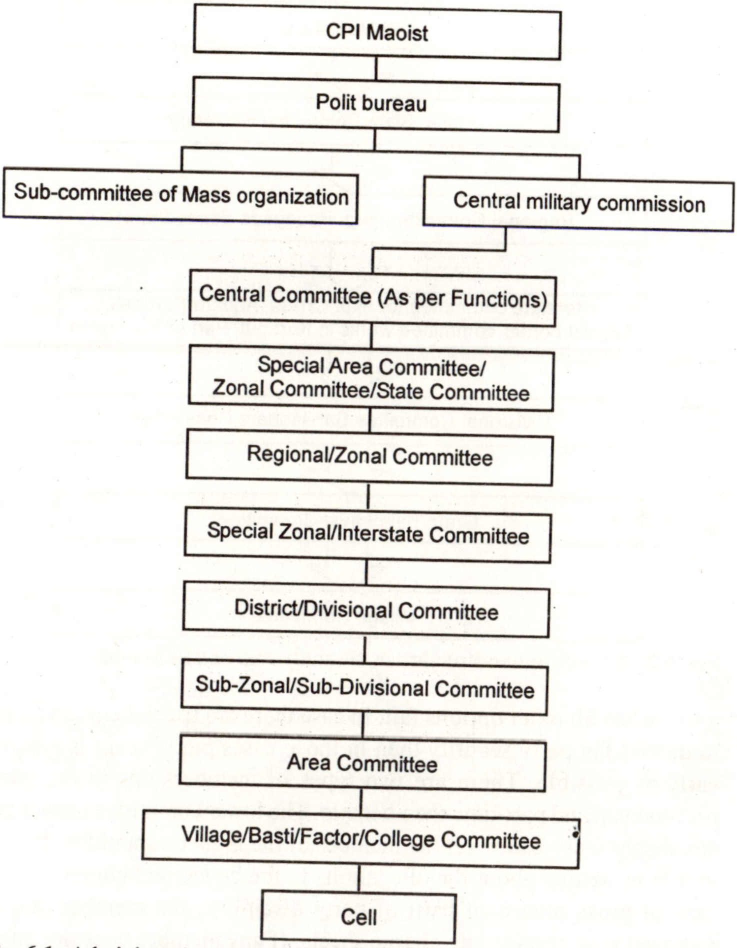

Fig. 6.1: Administrative set-up of CPI Maoist

Orissa State Committee (works directly in Gajapati and Rayagada Districts). The committee is extremely secretive and it is difficult to decode their structure as it keeps changing depending on their enemies strategy towards them.

Regulation of Deviation from Behaviour

Article 28 of the Constitution describes that to regulate any deviant behaviour of the member punishment is not the last option; it is only

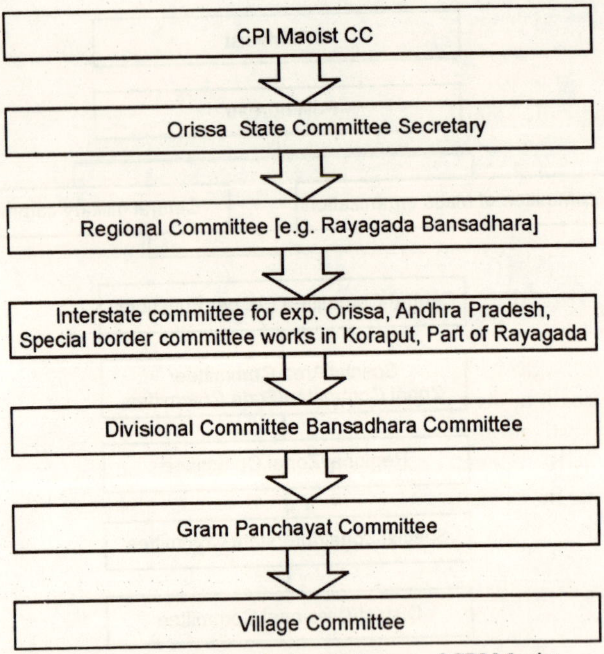

Fig. 6.2: Administrative structure in the study area of CPI Maoist

given when all other options fail. In case there are special circumstances to defend the party security then in those cases punishment is given as early as possible. There are two types of memberships in the party; professional and part-time membership. The lower committee cannot take any disciplinary action on the member of the higher committee, but can give it in writing about the allegations to the concerned committees. In case of gross breach of trust of party discipline, the member may be removed with appropriate charge sheets. If any member does not attend the meetings for a continuous period of six months without showing any justifiable convincing reasons, she or he will be withdrawn from it. If anyone is corrupt, becomes characterless, practices illegality, then only shall be liable to punishment. If a member is arrested, then there will be no responsibility on him or her, and membership will be under observation for six months time. After the imprisonment, party will take the decision later. Due to the current pressure on the party, there are also people who work for the party as part time members, but their names are not mentioned anywhere in their documents. A few were arrested in the recent past within 3 to 4 years. But these people are indirectly connected to some of the organization which has some similarity with them or talk of some similar agenda as the party has. Though, they are not connected in any way with the CPI (Maoist), yet they approach to these organizations and individuals to help them in some way or the other.

Maintenance of Order and Discipline in the Group (Reward and Punishment)

Any resident of India who has reached the age of 16, associated with any toiling class obeying the constitution can become a member. The membership is recommended by two members, and the referees must have thorough knowledge about him or her. The applicant should submit an application, then the concerned primary unit will secretly conduct a joint investigation with the villages/masses and party members; then he or she is recommended. Once the application is submitted there is a candidate membership is received. And the observation period varies to get the new membership depending on to which she or he belongs.

(a) 6 months—working class, landless, poor peasant, agricultural labourer.
(b) 1 year—middle peasants, petty business and urban middle classes.
(c) 2 years—other classes and other parties.

The same method is followed from the area committee level to all other levels. If they are not satisfied it is extended to six more months, if the review is not satisfactory. As mentioned in 6.5 and 6.4, the punishment is the same to defend the party's interest, respect and secrecy at top priority. But apart from all these rules and articles in the constitution there are individual cases where the party members have misappropriated the party funds during collection, there are cases where the members have sexually harassed the girls (as one case in Jharkhand), as this is not the nature of the party to harass the female members and to misuse the funds. There are also people who enter by seeing the underground glamour of the party but cannot adhere to the hardest conditions of the party and leave the party before the review period.

Cadres in Naxalite Movement

As mentioned in the administrative set-up the Central Military

Commission is basically looks after warfare, large operations, raids, train people and build capacities on weapons. There are State Military Commissions too. But the party is extremely secretive and did not want to give any other detailed information. As it is very difficult to ascertain how many members are there in the Central Committee and in respective State Committee. But all the members do not take up arms, only the People's Liberation Guerrilla Army (PLGA) takes exclusively. At the time of need during big operations few other members in addition to the PLGA, may also join to help them. But to distinguish the PLGA: the people who are under the district committees with arms are designated as PLGA members. The people who are above and in same ladder of district committee though carry weapons, but are not compelled to be PLGAs. They carry weapons for self-resistance only. The PGA force is again divided into 3 types of force, main force, secondary force and base force. The base force is the village Militia which is the civil army. So, it is an army of the village which looks after the village affairs and protects it. The secondary force is restricted and concentrated on area. It is the first crude force to fight for any simple operations. The main force are engaged in mobile warfare, propaganda of the party, raids, operation, attacking the enemy etc. Their primary role is to fight against the enemy. They annihilate the enemies, take part in big raids like Koraput armoury raid, Nayagarh raid, Alampaka ambush, and such blasts. They concentrate on war. The party has formations like platoon (consisting of 25 to 30 members, sometimes up to 60), company (with 60 to 100 members) and battalion (it is more than 100). These forces help other wings in conducting meetings, conducting cultural awareness etc. It was known as guerrilla squad. Now, it is divided into local organizations squad, (like women organization, Chasi Sangthan to make the people politically aware) and LGS—local guerrilla squad (work with district level or area committee level and fight). Normally in the study area the party moves in the form of platoon and company. Sometimes, they move in a company number too depending on the situation the presence of the force.

They do not want to share how much strength they have in the study area. But during 2005-06 they declared and accepted that there is 40,000 PLGA/base is present in Dandakaranya region which consist of few parts of Malkangiri and parts of Chhattisgarh and few parts of Andhra Pradesh and Maharashtra. The reason they do not want to share is, they do not want to give any scope to the state which consider as their enemy to know the number which helps them in modernizing the police force to repress them. But it is found that the few blocks of the study area as mentioned have area committee. The whole of the study area is at different levels, like in Gajapati the level of intervention is different where they have formed semi-liberated zones. So, there are different cadres at different levels, some work as PLGA members, some as couriers, some as village organization members and at the same time same person may act at all levels.

As explained above the roles and responsibilities of the Naxal cadres are shown in the following two tables to understand their activities and their definite jobs.

Table 6.1: Role and Responsibility of the Cadres

Sl. No.	*Communities*	*What role he or she is playing*		
		Fighting	*Organizing tribals*	*Others*
1.	ST	20.18%	37.61%	19.27%
2.	SC	4.59%	5.5%	5.55%
3.	Others	0.92%	2.75%	3.67%
	Total	25.69%	45.86%	28.49%

Table 6.1 shows the roles played by the different members in the party, few play specific roles and few play multiple roles. Few are there who collect letters and newspapers from their linked persons all most every day. 37.61 per cent of tribals play a major role in organizing the masses which is very important for the movement process. They are also assigned to fight with the enemy which is 20.18 per cent. The others category includes the leader roles which is played by the other communities. But at the village level the leadership is by tribals controlled by outsiders.

Table 6.2: Specific Role of the Respondents/Cadres

Sl. No.	*Community*	*Roles*						
		Informer	*Village Leader*	*Service Provider*	*PLGA Member*	*Senior Leader*	*Member of the frontal Organization*	*Others*
1.	ST	11.54%	12.18%	14.10%	17.31%	1.92%	8.33%	5.38%
2.	SC	0.64%	—	0.64%	3.21%	3.20%	3.21%	1.28%
3.	Others	1.28%	1.28%	1.28%	1.28%	0.64%	—	1.28%
	Total	13.46%	13.46%	16.02%	21.80%	5.76%	11.54%	7.94%

Table 6.2 shows the specific roles at different roles, it is found the PLGA membership is high compared to others which show that at the time of need everyone joins as the PLGA force, followed by service providers, informers and village organization members and leaders. 11.54 per cent of tribals act as informers in the study area, and only 1.92 per cent are leaders, which indicate that the tribals are only in the ground level mobilization and are not promoted to the leadership levels.

Financial Management of the Movement and Strategy of Adoption

Article 60, Chapter 13 of the party constitution[2] says that the funds are obtained through the membership fees, levies, donations, taxes and penalties to different classes like contractor, companies and money lenders. They are also collecting money from Non-governmental Organizations (NGOs). The NGOs who are working in the area where the party has some presence or has any connection or likely to increase their presence, are paying some amount to them on yearly basis. Here there are some distinctions also, like

(a) The NGOs who do not work efficiently and do manipulate funds do pay certain amount.
(b) Some NGOs in Gajapati and Malkangiri do give annual form of cash or kind to the party and the party shares that as these NGOs are not working and exist only on pen and paper they have to pay like other contractors.
(c) Few NGOs who work properly become enemy to the party as the masses do not attend meetings of the party and are well mobilized by the NGOs. During late 1990s in Gajapati and in 2010 in Koraput the party put posters in the local language in remote villages naming some NGOs to leave the area and work elsewhere. There is a constant war to save their territory not only from the security forces but also from the NGOs.
(d) Few NGOs who work in consultation with the party in paying them and though they do not do any work at the grassroots, but have offices and all establishments in the area where the party works. They pay regularly to the party.
(e) In the recent history of Naxals in the study area, 3 to 4 cadres run away with the money, but no action was taken against them.

So, there are different cases in relation to NGOs. Similarly, for companies and other contractors same rules apply. The one who are honest are against them and cannot make their presence if the party comes there. The party threatened them and wanted to go out of the area. They do demand ration from public representatives. Few villages which are under the liberated and semi-liberated zone collect grains and money on yearly basis and donate to the party. Few sympathizers in the city donate them. The party has got a major share from intellectual working class. Public buses running in the study area do donate forcefully without their wish or else they cannot run their services. The big shops in the study towns do give money on monthly, quarterly or yearly basis.

The Panchayat representatives, the other local representatives, the colleges, the government departments all the stakeholders working in the area where the party has a high presence give money. It happens so that some time they force the tribals hamlets to give food to them. And the tribals do so with fear. It is nexus but publicly no one agrees as they have the fear of caught by the police department. Sometimes, they seize the ration meant for the force and sometimes, in the cut off area of the study area the police force do supply ration to the party. It is like an open secret, but everything is brushed under the carpet. The people who collect money from the shops do maintain a high secret channel. But the party has their own financial audit once in 2 to 3 years to see the income and expenditure.

Organizing Principles in the Beginning and Now—A Comparison

Crisis in leadership, continuous political debate among the party, difference between action and impact, not too much presence in the urban area, creating curriculum for the cadres for training has been some of the main concerns of the present face of the party. But one cannot really compare the old principles with new to validate the situation as the party documents are extremely confidential and secretive. But few changes which were articulate are:

- The politics has remained un-changed whether it should be pro-Chinese or pro-Russian, but it should be based on Constitution of India. The Indian Maoism is Naxalism. But still deriving an Indian form of armed struggles needs lot of intellectual exercise and the party has no time as most of their time is utilized to safeguard themselves from the enemy, no time for mass mobilization.

- When they take money from the corrupted contractors and other corrupt officials they are also watched by the mass with whom they claim of having presence. But ultimately, the masses feel that no work has been done for them, and in this process they lose their trust and support from the people. This is happening in many places in the study area, especially in Koraput district where people are reaping the fruits from the government and other NGOs in non-violent ways. They do not have the faith on the party. So, the party is undergoing the tussle for trust.
- The idea of a base area should be based on Indian condition taking into consideration of the local caste and class dynamics. But it cannot be done to a larger extent.
- The army was prepared in 1967, in 1974 it was recognized as guerrilla squad, but during 1998 a new army was created. In 2000, People's Guerrilla Army (PGA) was formed with the main force, secondary force and base force. The three main weapons as party, army and united front were reframed. Scientific progress was emphasized with division of work.
- State level people revolutionary committee was formed by modified people's war.
- The main landmark change was the unification of all the major armed resistance parties as one single large party, gave immense strength to the party organization.
- The detailed village plans to form alternate governments with peoples power is a systematic approach.
- The new formations in the PLGA have helped to open new vistas in the study area to show strength to the enemy in mobile warfare.
- They have been able to associate and identify their struggle with various mass organizations, civil liberty groups, and other democratic movements. Whenever they see some democratic movement where they connect with the party. But on the other hand the presence of the party in democratic movements has been a big problem for the democratic open activists. They are targeted as Naxalites and ultimately even though they do not want but forced in a way to adopt their ways and means. If we take the example of Nachika Linga of Narayanpatna, who was leading an open democratic movement for tribal land had to take the shelter of the party. He is the bright example how things are changing.
- But they are able to create a lot of support from intellectual backing in case of legal support which was not present in earlier days.

- The work has been started in urban areas to question the power structures, developed a cadre policy to recruit more youth. Party is not only emphasizing on political education, but also on minimum literacy.

References

1. Unification documents of the party.
2. Party constitution.

7
Role of Tribal Women

"Being a woman is a terribly difficult task, since it consists principally in dealing with men." — *Joseph Conrad*

Inclusion of Women's Wings in the Organization

The movement has widened and deepened its roots in the tribal area of Orissa, as the data reveal. These areas are strategic as per the states negligence is concerned. The participation of the women is gradually increasing its scale with formation of more women's organizations and forums. The growing sexual violence on women is becoming a push factor for them to be a part of the guerrilla army. The more number of women going into the movement is on higher side than the men. The development indicators for women are very less in tribal areas. The so called development temples like dams, and other big projects have even made women's life more miserable than before. In few tribal pockets of Malkangiri where the dams has submerged few GPs and more than 12 GPs in three blocks have virtually become islands marooned through the year, where women have less mobility and no access to the key social indicators like markets and hospitals. They have to be dependent on the male counterparts. Their agony does not stop here, they have to face more assault from the outsiders who have settled in the districts of Gajapati, and Malkangiri.

These settlers have taken the control of their economy and also their social lives. In Gajapati, big landlords have forcefully kept the tribal women as keeps. One such incident points out that a woman who complained in the Praja Court of Gajapati district to kill his husband as he was mis-behaving with other tribal women. These are all sparks that we see a new face of women. In Malkangiri district each Koya village woman has a story to tell where the settlers from outside have kidnapped them, forcefully married them, looted their land. Many Koya women have not returned to their village since years out of shame. The outsiders engage in such kind of activities to acquire tribal land and to get tribal status.

The research could cover only 11 female activists, from which most of them are from other caste, but dedicated to work for the tribals. In Gajapati, Malkangiri, and in few parts of Rayagada it was found surprisingly that, wherever the Naxalites have intervened, that particular village had an incident which was related to women. The story had a background of tribal woman kidnapped by the contractors, or they are sexually abused by local business men, or outside settlers. But it is important to note that wherever tribals have revolted, one of the main causes behind that is their women have been abused. A link can be found between the entrance of the party and the abuse of the women in the area. The constitution of the CPI (Maoist) has always addressed both she and he in all their articles. The party strongly feels that without women there will be no revolution. No women no revolution is their slogan. The party programme of the CPI (Maoist) point no. 25, sub-headings 8 and 10 clearly state that: it will ensure reservation for women, *dalits*, *adivasis*, in order to make them par with others, based on their degree of oppression they face. It also states that it will abolish all types of discrimination against women in the patriarchal male dominated society, liberate women from the so called clutches of domestic work, ensuring their participation in social production, provide them with 50 per cent job reservation and in education to achieve the real equality with men and do guarantee equal rights over property.

The All India Special Conference which was held on 15th to 30th November, 1995 by the then CPI (ML) people's war has some special slogan as their major tasks, for which they committed to fight upon. These were 14 important slogans on various issues, but No. 12 was mainly dedicated to fight against oppressions of women and develop women's movement. All the above indicators show that the gradual inclusion of women into the movement is remarkable. The party has dedicated a special

small book called "*Women Martyrs of Dandakaranya*"[1] to salute all women who came forward to be the part of this revolution.

Women have proved themselves to be brave, committed at all fronts as the secondary sources reveal. During the last 25 to 30 years of the historic struggle, Krantikari Mahila Sangathan and Dandakaranya Mahila Sangathan are the two pioneering organizations in this direction. There are special sections in the constitution which are dedicated to the women. Women have been in the army, mass organizations, as party members of the central committee. In all organs of the party they have proved their ability. Many qualified women have come to the party and sacrificed their lives for the sake of the movement.

Tribal women have basically entered into the movement to break the barriers of clan authority, sexual exploitation, domestic violence, hard economic exploitation and the various forms of structural violence.

- 62 per cent of tribal women feel that the police force always torture them.
- 78 per cent of young women even do not like the way the police/ security stare at them.
- 80 per cent of tribal women feel that they are the worst sufferers since the security forces are deployed. So, only answer is get into the movement. As the movement gives them confidence, to involve themselves in struggle of land, in rasing their wages, their role in governance. The oppressive tribal traditions which always victimize women, the party has well identified and addressed it. In any meeting the women sing, dance and celebrate the joy of freedom. The party does celebrate the International Women's Day on March 8th to mark the significance of women's movement in the study area.

The Naxal leaders sincerely believe that the women population is half in the world, so women has to equally participate in all phases to transform the lives of women in the coming future. Several women have lost their lives in the *Dandakaranya* region fighting against the enemy in raids, ambushes, and in other types of blasts. These are some special sections dedicated for women. During the field visits it was found that in any squad of 6-7 members, at least 3 are female members. Many case stories of women martyrs have shown the way for others. Two such women cadres fought bravely with the enemy and gave their lives. Comrade Durgi and Comrade Meena who are real examples for others. Till now more than 40 Naxal female cadres have given their lives in fighting with the enemies or killed in police encounters.

Motivation and Participation of the Local Tribal Women

Table 7.1 shows the percentage of participation of women in the study area. The participation of tribal women is 22.27 per cent which is under all categories ranging from frontal organizations, PLGA, their mass organizations. As the data reveal that 72.73 per cent of women are from other communities do work in the study area as member of cultural troops, member of PLGA. These 72.73 per cent are basically from their liberated zone of Dandakaranya region, and other coastal parts of Orissa. They are strongly motivated by spirit of the party. Few have been married to their fellow party members, but many are unmarried. They opine that media which spread misinformation that the girls are harassed in the party are not based on facts. There are individual cases of marriage and they wanted personal freedom in the forest which was not possible for the party to approve.

Table 7.1: Female Participation in the Movement

Sl. No.	*Communities*	*%age*
1.	ST	22.27
2.	SC	—
3.	Others	72.73

There are individual cases but the research could not found out any systematic sexual harassment case against women. The party also is much sensitive toward the women's needs like if someone is having some health problems they advise her to surrender before the police. It happened so in the recent past where a woman member of a senior leader surrendered before the Koraput Police in April, 2011 as she was facing severe gynaecological problems. After several discussions and negotiations with the party she surrendered. There is a friendly atmosphere in the camp life and in a day-to-day life, with equal division of labour among male and female. In a posting by Xavier on May-June 8th, 2009, 5:09 am (PDT[2]) to it where it was an interview with a polit bureau member who said that the party does not support the idea of children. The women are sensitized after marriage in order to comprise their political careers. But, if someone wants they can go for children. In one of the interview the central committee member Kishenji said that the party advise them for family planning, but if any couple wishes to go for children the party welcomes it and there is no restriction for this.

The case stories from the field give an idea about the background of the female cadres, Itul, who can make good handicraft and feels that she is a very creative and that creativity helps the party in forest. Her family gets financial assistance during her sickness. From the age of 13 she does not believe the police force and strong heartedness for them as she has seen police misbehaving with other women. Her father works in the fields and mother in the frontal organization and she was educated in the meetings by the party. She explains that though the tribals stay in a good environment, yet they have to sleep empty stomachs, and without solving their problems, the state advocates for industrialization. The schools do not function as teachers do not go. As teachers have good nexus to bribe their own circle and stay out of their job. Children go to these *bal sanghams* to get education, where they are exposed to the realities of the role of the state, revolutionary politics and structures of deprivation.

Table 7.2: Age group of the Female Cadres

Sl. No.	*Communities*	*Age (in%)*			
		10-20	*21-30*	*31-40*	*Above 40*
1.	ST	9.09	54.55	9.09	72.73
2.	SC	—	—	—	—
3.	Others	—	27.27	—	27.27
	Total	9.09	81.82	9.09	100

Table 7.2 shows the age group of the female members in the party. As it indicates the female members come from the age range of 21-30 years where they want to question the unequal power relations. Among tribals, girl is married by the age of 14 or 15, and sometimes she is abandoned at the age of 18, these are the questions that the tribal traditions have set before them. The social disabilities that a tribal women faces. Liquor consumption by men is another tragedy in the lives of tribal women. Party will be addressing these issues when they enter into a new area, so women in the potential age group join their village committee and also in their army at a later stage.

It is significant to note that the women participation from other communities is also high within the same age group of 21-30 and it is 27.27 per cent. As these women are so much frustrated by the systems no direction for them as youth group, no ideal leader in front of them whom they can follow, they get lured by revolutionary thoughts and want to change the system. A 10th standard Koya girl who has only seen the harassment of her own fellow tribes since childhood is a potential leader of the revolution and later she has joined the party. She explains this is the government does not want real and genuine development of the tribals, this is the reason the tribals are kept as un-educated, politically weak, easily thrown and displaced at the mercy of others.

She describes since the tribals faced long marginalization process it is time now against structural violence measures. The special police officers harass and rape them in the undivided Koraput region. The similar incidents have already started in many places of India like in Chhattisgarh, Jharkhand, West Bengal. 62 per cent of women in the study area strongly feel that women are harassed and raped in south Orissa. If the violence continues to increase, more women are likely to take the shelter of the party.

There are also media reports where the Maoist leaders have blamed their female cadres for indulging in marriage and affairs. Still the women cadres have to evolve as they explain.

Table 7.3: Marital Status of the Female Cadres

Sl. No.	*Communities*	*Marital status in (%)*			*Total*
		Married	*unmarried*	*Others*	
1.	ST	9.09	63.64	—	72.73
2.	SC	—	—	—	—
3.	Others	—	27.27	—	27.27
	Total	9.09	90.91	—	100

Table 7.3 shows the marital status of the female members in the party. 63.64 per cent of the members are unmarried among tribal community whereas 27.27 per cent of the females are unmarried among other communities. Though few are married they have been deserted by their husbands and hence consider themselves as unmarried. And few did not want to respond on the marital status. 30 per cent of them remain silent when they were asked about their marital status.

Gurubari aged 32, a Halwa tribal woman who works for the frontal organization of the party is active and trains basically women. She can walk more than 15 to 20 kms a day to reach the bordering villages of Koraput and Malkangiri. Her forefathers got displaced due to the big dams built in Malkangiri district, the then undivided Koraput district, as a result they were thrown out of the homes and hearths. She says that there will be nearly 50,000 to 60,000 people in various frontal organizations of the party and it is impossible on the part of the state to completely eliminate all of them.

As the conflicts of interests grow day-by-day the discontentment will grow and more people will become antagonistic towards the state, and more people will join. The migration is on rise, women are the most sufferers in this whole cycle of distress migration. She was the 1st women who raised voice against unequal wages paid to women. The contractors started harassing her, but no police helped her. The party stood beside her and since then she is working in the party. The party listens to the poor people's grievances and they are not like government officials. In an interior village of Mathili the landlord who was an outsider continued to harass tribals, he used to grab the tribal land, sexually harass tribal women and the same legacy was carried out by his son too. After the party threatened, he left the area and the women are safe now. The police and the administration did not take any step to stop the exploiter, but party did bring some change, so she started believing the party. She strongly shares that all women who join the party has a story of exploitation in some way or other in their personal life journey.

Educational Status of the Women Members

The educational status of both male and female cadres is low if we see in terms of the degrees they have received. In general, it was found that since there are no schools in their area or the teachers do not attend the schools, the tribals are not well educated. On the other hand, in general, it was also found that there is a sense of fear of getting sexually harassed in the school, the tribal girls do not go for high school studies. There are many unreported cases of sexual harassment in Rayagada and Koraput districts in tribal schools. This is one of the main reasons of the low educational profile of the female cadres.

Table 7.4: Educational status of Female Cadres

Sl. No.	*Communities*	*Educational status in (%)*				*Total*
		Illiterate	*Up to 5th std*	*6th to 10th std*	*Above 10th std*	
1.	ST	22.27	27.27	9.09	9.09	72.73
2.	SC	—	—	—	—	—
3.	Others	—	—	9.09	18.18	27.27
	Total	22.27	27.27	18.18	27.28	100

Table 7.4 shows the educational status of the female members in the movement. 22.27 per cent of the female members among tribal community are illiterate as the literacy rate of the study area among women is far less than the state average. The female literacy of Rayagada district is 24.31 per cent (Census, 2001) and for Gajapati it is 14.50 per cent in rural area. Many do not go to school for basic literacy, because the schools does not exist at all and even if they exist they do not function. 27.27 per cent of tribal women who attended schools and have completed up to 5th standard, are good indicators. As we see in the table the female members from other communities have a higher level of education which is 10th standard and above as compared to the tribal women. The women from other communities do identify with the same issues of tribal women and work for them. The party documents do say that, women feel that without this party the tribal women would have been in terrible state. The party has helped the women to raise their consciousness level and rise to the occasion. Women share that after joining the movement they live a dignified life, they are treated equally, even though they are illiterate the party makes all efforts to give them basic literacy along with political discourse. So, they appeal that all tribal women should join the movement for the real liberation.

Their Overall Contribution to the Movement Process

The overall achievement of the women in the movement has been tremendous as how they have transformed themselves into leaders, comrades and fighters. The journey of women in this movement is remarkable as they have hit at issues pertaining to their life like how they assess themselves, how long they have tolerated the violence against women, how they have restricted it, and how they have discussed for remedial measures in the village. So, the journey of women is long and it is never ending process. In the present scenario, a visible female participation is seen in the party including the armed cadre. When it was

Table 7.5: Self-Assessment by Females

Sl. No.	*Communities*	*Assessment on self (%)*				
		Covert	*Aggressive*	*Adjusting*	*Violent*	*Emotional*
1.	ST	11.76	17.65	11.76	23.63	5.80
2.	SC	—	—	—	—	—
3.	Others	5.88	—	5.88	11.76	5.88
	Total	17.64	17.65	17.64	35.39	11.68

asked in depth about their own self nearly 35 per cent rated themselves as violent, whereas 11.76 tribal cadres rated as covert. But the information inputs by the movement have made them certainly stronger.

As mentioned earlier each tribal village where there is an intervention by the party, has some link regarding their women. So, it was necessary to find out about their grievances related to women, whether they complained about it or not or did they discuss about the remedial measures. In one of the Gram Panchayats of Mathili block it was found that the people killed the landlord who was harassing the tribal women. Similar incidents were also found in the borders of Gajapati district and Narayanpatna block of Koraput district. The following three tables give details of the tolerance by women, their grievances mechanism and their measures to solve it.

Table 7.6: How long women have tolerated ill-treatment

Sl. No.	*Communities*	*Before independence*	*After independence*	*Both*
1.	ST	27.42	45.97	9.68
2.	SC	4.03	5.65	—
3.	Others	1.61	4.84	0.81
	Total	33.06	56.46	10.49

Table 7.7: How many times they Addressed the issue

Sl. No.	*Communities*	*How many times they have restricted*		
		Once	*Twice*	*More than twice*
1.	ST	23.19	14.49	42.03
2.	SC	—	—	10.14
3.	Others	3.66	—	4.88
	Total	26.85	14.49	57.05

Table 7.8: Discussion for Remedial measure

Sl. No.	*Communities*	*How many times they have discussed*			
		Once	*Twice*	*None*	*More than once with reasons*
1.	ST	20.35	21.24	—	38.94
2.	SC	—	5.31	—	6.19
3.	Others	2.65	3.54	—	1.77
	Total	23.00	30.09	—	46.90

The above three tables shows the face of violence against the tribal women, the issues have been taken at different levels for solution, discussed many times with government officials with sufficient reasons along with the village meeting. It is well indicated that nearly 45.97 per cent feel that after Independence 27.42 per cent of females strongly confirm that the violence on women in various forms have increased, but the tribal communities have brought out these issues (nearly 42.03%) at different levels for solution. Nearly 38.94 per cent of tribals have discussed at various levels with the State and also at their village council level to stop this. Like in Gajapati district mostly tribal women are used as kept forciably by the local landlords, whom the government does not accept and the women have now to prove it. The rich has more say in the system than poor tribal women. There are cases in Koraput district where the contractors repeatedly harass women. There are many such cases in Malkangiri district. In such situations they take the shelter of the revolutionary forces and hope for the change. 11.76 per cent of tribal women are covert, 11.76 per cent are adjustive and 23.53 per cent become violent and 17.65 per cent become aggressive. Every oppressed woman becomes a potential participant in the revolution.

When it was further probed about the remuneration paid to the female cadres, it was revealed that they do get some amount of money on a monthly basis. The party help them by providing red soaps, cloths, sanitary napkins, and medicines. The females are taken care if they are pregnant. The health problems related to gynaecology is much higher among females. Last year, one female cadre surrendered before the police of Koraput district as she had severe gynaecological problem. She negotiated with the party before she surrendered. Snake bites and malaria are the main causes of death. Some leaders do take care by advising the females to drink water after boiling and hygiene precautions. But nearly 45 per cent of the female cadres face health issues. Despite the media reports on harassment, the cadres share a healthy and cordial relation in the camps as observed.

References

1. Women Martyrs of Dandakarayan (a party document).
2. http:/southasianrev. wordpress.com / 2000

8
Causes of Tribal Support

"Honest differences are often a healthy sign of Progress."

—*Mahatma Gandhi*

Basic Reasons of Tribal Support

Naxalism has been the most remarkable underground movement since Independence or even before that in different forms in India. This political movement is always challenging the Indian State with changing phases, strategies, tactics, and operations in spite of various divisions. It started with one small district in Naxalbari and has spread over almost more than 160 districts in the country. In an interview given to the media on 24th April, 2007 where the questions sent to them by various newspapers (more than half of these questions were sent by BBC) the General Secretary CPI (Maoist) said after the completion of the congress.

Answering to a question on how much Indian Territory is under control, as Prime Minister said that it is 160 districts, he said the state has some statistics which is very thrilling, few researchers' reports reveal that it is increasing at the rate of two districts per week, may be even more than that.

The mass base is poor, oppressed, impoverished *Adivasis, Dalits*, women, the workers and the peasants. 82 per cent of the rural India deprived of basic needs[1]. And the movement focuses on the 82 per cent population and not the rest creamy layer. The increase of violent incidents, causalities, kidnapping of the security forces, government officials, political representatives has compelled the State to view it with intense unease. Their presence in the mineral rich regions were making the task of the companies a bit difficult as the respondents describe. The minerals are meant for big corporate industrial projects. The Rs. 13,000 crore Naxal Action Plan got a nod from Ministry of Home Affairs, and from the Prime Minister's office for Naxal affected districts which will be placed for approval in the Cabinet[2]. The Integrated Action Plan (IAP) is dedicated to the 60 districts in the states of Orissa, Chhattisgarh, Jharkhand, Madhya Pradesh, Bihar, Uttar Pradesh and West Bengal. Each district will get 25 crore for construction of schools, roads, and Anganwadi centres. The criteria to get these funds are:

- 25 per cent tribal population of the district,
- 50 per cent poverty ratio,
- 30 per cent forest coverage,
- Security related concerns, and
- Covered under backward region grant fund.

Any district having fulfilled the four conditions out of these 5 will receive funds. So, it is established that Naxalism is growing in those places where tribal concentration is more and the issues are more. Looking at the scenario of the study area, one of the person working in the government opined that:

> "All the democratic movements are repressed by the state by linking it with Naxal Movement, in fact forcing it to choose a path of Naxalism, all the tribals wanted to become in future Naxalites. And in a way their place is reserved in jail. All jails are becoming the knowledge centres of revolution. Every jail is loaded with tribals. The state is modernizing the police, but it has to construct, more jails for tribals. The state is not willing to solve the problem in real sense as it contradicts their interests. The discontent will grow through various democratic movements and each will be forced to turn into Naxal."

The root causes of this support by the tribals to Naxalism is basically seen from three aspects as mentioned in theories used in this research:

- Structural violence,
- The contexts of tribal living,
- Direct living, and
- And cultural violence.

The real causes of tribals support to the Naxalism are deeply connected to the agriculture and the prevailing social structure. Their life is designed with these two the agriculture is so very guided by land holding, access to land, food security, assets holding and social relations based on these factors. The hegemonic caste structure of the Indian society has played a role in alienating tribals from their lands when the higher caste outsiders did settle in tribal areas. The developmental projects of the state further alienated the tribals from their homes. The two structures of the society, one through the cultural hegemony, and the other through the structures of the state, have deprived them of the basic needs. Structural violence and cultural violence embedded in the social, economic and political structures of our society have forced the tribals to support the Naxals as a last resort.

Table 8.1: The Life Journey of the Activists

Sl. No.	*Communities*	*Life incidents from childhood (%)*				*Total*
		In relation to education	*Family*	*Traditions*	*Any other*	
1.	SC	4.76	—	4.76	4.76	14.29
2.	ST	19.05	16.67	9.52	33.33	78.57
3.	OC	2.38	0.79	0.79	3.17	7.14
	Total	26.19	17.46	15.07	41.26	100

The tribal Naxal activist describe that how their life journey has been a memory of different incidents relating to the social institutions such as school, family, with peer group and with the others in the village. 19.5 per cent of tribals do have some experience in schools, where they do not get proper space and justice in the sense to express their feelings. There are very less number of teachers who actually see all the children with equal eye. These children always feel neglected and feel shy to go to school. At the family level they have seen their parents working through out the year doing all sorts of work to survive and secure food. Despite all these efforts, they do not get sufficient amount to survive. With their traditions everyone is happy and owns it. But they do confess that few people consume more liquor in a group. The incidents have been always been bitter, be it the shopkeeper in the village, the moneylender at the Gram Panchayat, any official in the Government or anybody from outside their experience has always left a major scar in their hearts. They strongly feel that the outsiders including the government only preach and propogate the tradition of tribals but they do not do any solid work for them. In a state of despair and confusion the tribals are just sticking to their traditions to keep up some identity even though it is not cost effective while looking at their economic conditions. But everyone is so glamorous by this traditions that it has become the only to save them. Yes there are different kinds of fundamental forces which are pulling and pushing them since the last two decades. And few lose their identity and get attracted by these forces. But all these forces claim and do the same kind of activity like spreading the message of hating other religions. The tribals are aware about these facts but they have no choice. The values of collectiveness has been somewhere forcefully diluted by others.

Gradual Development of the Tribal Participation

The study area had witnessed many tribal revolts, in the past during British period, and also after Independence, the *Bhoo-satyagraha* in Koraput region had some impact in the minds of the tribals. Along with the history of revolts the displacement factor, poverty condition triggered the Naxalism to grow slowly in the study area. The backdrop information before the tribals entered into this brutal armed path. Two case stories give an interesting perspective of the gradual increase:

Gisu from village Gudaguda, (his village is a bordering of Malkangiri and Koraput) says angrily, "*the contractor has been killed in Govindapalli by the Naxals, the government will never go in a fair means to find out the root cause of the killings rather it will deploy one company of CRPF or any other such force who will harass poor villagers like us on a routine basis, all the government structures will be renovated and repaired here in the area... but what about people like us....? Will the state think about us and why this Naxal movement is propagating in a macro way. The state only thinks that it can solve this problem with law and order and with minimum developmental initiatives. But it is not true... it should first accept that a major percentage of people live with less than Rs. 12 per day even after 60 years of Independence. Is it justice that we are talking? Certainly not, the so called democracy has not reached the people for which the movement is quite appealing for us. Rather, we do not have any choice before us than to rebel. Will the state accept all this facts that the poor, the major chunk of people are unhappy, they are harassed and everyday they are marginalized in all aspects of life. They are frustrated with the eyewash activities of the government. When will the government reflect on its own system and its behaviour?*

Today, whoever fights for his rights is branded as Naxalite. If we raise our voice, we are killed in encounters, if we question we have to face illegal detention and in the coming years we will be languishing in jails for years waiting for bails. If we protest against dams, or any developmental projects we are called Naxalites. So, the state has a complete nexus to prove that it is right by all means and we have to face the consequences if at all we stand to the occasion. So, what can we do than to embrace Naxals against our wishes."

Sona, a Soura tribal person of Gajapati district says very happily that "*their way of talking (referring to the Naxals) is so touching; no government person has ever talked to me like the way they approach. It gives us confidence, knowledge and information. It gives to understand our own condition and it gives to go deep to understand and analyse why we are poor. The government has not taken such measures as Naxals to. It was found that during natural calamities in the cut off area, of Malkangiri district the Naxals have distributed the food grains with all the difficulties. This way their wings are spread.*"

Table 8.2: Gradual Increase of Tribal Participation

Sl. No.	*Responses*	*Number and Percentage*
1.	No activities in the cities and towns	10 (10)
2.	surrounded by the city life and their strategy to capture villages first	1 (1.33)
3.	Meet with their *sangha* members and interacted	1 (1.33)
4.	The movement is active after 1990 and their action is visible now	1 (1.33)
5.	Movement is not so open as it was in the past	1 (1.33)
6.	Witnessed the Koraput attack	1 (1.33)
7.	Hear from media and other sources	1 (1.33)
8.	They work with outfits, almost every week there is an incident	4 (5.33)
9.	Active in south Orissa	4 (5.33)
10.	Bandhs, raids is a regular activity	5 (6.67)
11.	Conduct meetings and kill the enemy	1 (1.33)
12.	All are not armed, some work for mass mobilization	5 (6.67)
13.	Observed many and they will increase	19 (25.3)
14.	They come and interact with is in the villages and we come to know about their plans	5 (6.67)
15.	Seen major activities 3 times in a year	1 (1.33)
16.	Since 5 years we see it every month	7 (9.33)
17.	This is a peoples movement leading to peoples resistance ultimately to resistance war	8 (10.67)

In the context of south Orissa, their activities are more and 19 per cent of the people have observed many of their actions and witnessed it.

And these activities are increasing within span of five years. The town areas, the villagers also do come to know as the naxals continuously keep in touch with them by any means. It is not hard for anyone who is staying in this patch of Orissa to meet any of their cadres, as they are present in many forms. The 5 per cent who are observed *bandh*, raids, and other actions do say that they don't harm the common people. They only keep an eye on the *sahukars* or the people who harass the poor. And wherever the Naxals have done bandhs and other activities, there is no problem but the communication affects and this causes a major concern of the people. 8 per cent of the people do feel that these actions which are done now, may be counted as events, but later it will lead to a poor people movement and then to a resistance war. As Table 8.2 shows that the presence and the incidents have increased after 1990s. Normally, the movement/conflict moves very tactfully. They open fronts at one place and remain silent at the other place. Sometimes, they open fronts at different places at the same to divert the attention of the security forces. They show their presence by major incidents like the Nayagarh operation, the land mine in Rayagada, the R-Udaygiri jail break. Sometimes, they don't arms as they did in Koraput. 25.3 per cent of the responding does feel that the activities are increasing. It is very difficult to keep track on them as they are very much with the people.

The following tables explains more in detail about their tribulations with other members of the society at large and this indeed making them to actively participate in the movement.

Table 8.3: Main turning Points in Respondent's lives for Participation

Sl. No.	*Communities*	*Turing points aspects (%)*				
		Related to family	*Relative to Education*	*Finance*	*Customs*	*Others*
1.	SC	4.96	—	4.28	3.55	3.55
2.	ST	16.31	7.80	21.99	4.26	29.08
3.	Others	6.71	—	0.71	—	2.84
	Total	26.98	7.80	26.98	7.81	35.47

Table 8.3 shows that 16.31 per cent of tribals have family related issues (poverty, death of parents, landless) and incidents like they have been facing a severe financial crisis, social insult by money lenders, for which they had to depart themselves from their education. 21.99 per cent had difficulty for money only for which they could not continue their

education. 29.08 per cent of them had problems with others like the problem of landlessness, migration. These are the turning points of their lives where they had to bury their feelings, emotions and their existence was a question. As mentioned earlier the human development indices of the universe show a very poor data where every year people die out of diarrhoea, cholera and malaria. The deaths occur due to malnutrition. These are real issues which are not on priority which in turn seems to help the movement to grow.

Table 8.4: Respondent's good experiences in Life

Sl. No.	*Communities*	*Good experience in life and with whom (%)*			
		In personal	*Family*	*Village*	*Others*
1.	SC	—	4.27	5.51	0.79
2.	ST	13.39	21.26	25.98	23.62
3.	Others	1.57	0.79	1.57	0.79
	Total	14.96	26.32	33.06	25.20

The above Table 8.4 gives a picture when the respondents were happy in their personal life. 21.26 per cent of tribals do have good family memories 25.98 per cent of tribals have good time in their villages with their clan members during festivals, marriages, and other occasions. The unity and we feeling of tribals gives them a sense of security. The others here referred as to the fellow tribes, other tribes and relatives of them in the neighbouring villages. When they exchange gifts, have community feast to show their solidarity and brotherhood. Like in a recent case where 9 adolescent boys were falsely taken for migration work from Koraput and Rayagada districts all belonging to Kondh community were charged for a murder and spent almost more than 6 months in juvenile justice home of Pune, Maharashtra, but they finally released by the court. They

Table 8.5: Respondent's worst experiences in Life

Sl. No.	*Communities*	*Worst experiences in life (%)*			
		In family	*In village*	*With govt. officials*	*Others*
1.	SC	3.91	3.91	4.69	4.69
2.	ST	9.38	14.06	36.72	17.97
3.	Others	0.78	—	2.34	1.56
	Total	14.07	17.97	43.75	24.22

went back to the villages, and in an interaction with them they said that for a tribal the village is very important, the land and the people. They are not like other communities who can go anywhere for work. The tribals of south Orissa are not prepared to face the outside world. Other tribal's communities in other part of the state are advanced, but not the tribals of Koraput region.

Table 8.5 indicates the worst experiences as shown, 3.38 per cent of tribals do have experiences at family when they are forces to marry at a tender age by shadowing all their dreams, and aspirations. 36.72 per cent of them have experiences with government officials like police, forest officials, revenue officials, advocates and block officials. They have very bad experience with revenue till now as these officials demand whatever the tribals have their poultry, their millets etc. why its till now happening and there is no change in the system. In an interior GP of Nandapur block last year two of the forest officials took more than 50 kgs of their millet produce with a say that they will help the tribals to get their rights over forest land. Whereas the government has given the right to the tribals over the forest land through an act. So, this is the existing system. 17.97 per cent have worst experiences people who give them money and food at time of need like the *sahukars*. The respondents share how frustrating it to stand in front of the *sahukar* and hear all his verbal insult. Though the tribals know that the money lenders exploit them but just to survive them with no choice they always stand in front of his door.

Table 8.6: Respondent's Good friends

Sl. No.	*Communities*	*Best friends (%)*		
		Siblings	*Villagers*	*Others*
1.	SC	7	5	5
2.	ST	20	40	16
3.	Others	—	6	1
	Total	27	51	22

Table 8.6 shows that 20 per cent of the tribals do like their siblings and 40 per cent of them like their clan's members, and 16 per cent include others who belong to their relatives in other village, very few mentioned that few organizations working in the village are linked by them. But none mentioned the state actors. As they have worst experiences with government officials. The overall causes of tribal support, has to be seen through the angle of structural violence as they have faced from

displacement, eviction from land, the direct violence as they are arrested time and again, they are sandwiched. But does identity with Naxals as Naxals take their agenda forward, help them to eliminate their immediate exploiter. The annihilation can be a human rights violation, but for the tribals take it as positive as the system is not answering them. Though they know this is a temporary solution, but still they hold on them as its some relief. The cultural violence, the structures of deprivation occurred do not contradictions of interests is a major cause of the support.

Extension of Activities

The economy of the country is going through a crucial phase, though we have elections at certain intervals, but it seems nothing is working for the people. In Orissa there are strong resistances democratic movements witnessed everyday. The democratic movements are the victims of structural violence, direct violence gradually becoming the part of the armed naxal conflict. The movement started in a small patch of the universe in late 1990s, by a tribal youth and spread to four nearby districts. Youths who were engaged in the open movement, most of them are now underground and part of the guerrilla force. When it was asked, why this change in them, 65 per cent of them says since our honest voices were not heard so we became a part of the conflict.

The Planned Way

The Kui Lavanaga Sangha was formed in between 1995 and 1996, under the leadership of Sunil who now works for Odisha Maobadi party a faction from the CPI Maoist. He started living near Gajapati district and had several interactions with the villagers. Late Dasuram Maleka was very active along with other members of the villages in Rayagada and Gajapati district. Dasuram was primarily a Kui person who had tremendous creativity to write poems and sing songs in the Kui language and used to create awareness on the corruption at various levels, and how the tribals can raise voice against it. He was caught and tortured in custody and later released from the jail. After coming from the jail he was frustrated with the system and went underground, died due to the lack of medicine in September 2007 when the areas was affected by cholera. Few of the tribal youth who came forward to form this organization died in encounter killing and few are in jail. The main objective of the this *sangha* was to

- To take up issues affecting the Kuis,
- To organize Kuis,
- To address the issues of Kui farmers and other poor farmers,
- To establish the separate Kui identity, and
- To get a recognition in the outside world that tribals are not always submissive and they can also become activists and can assert their rights.

First they too up issues of forest produce, where the traders were not giving good price, the first resistance was against these people and the *sangha* could able to rise the prices of tamarind, and other forest produce. Then they took the issue of raising the wages for the work taken by the contractors and equal wages for men and women. The wage rate was very low for the bamboo cutters and they had to take up this issue with the paper mills to raise the wages. It took five years for them to really organize the tribals into a strong organization and when an incident occurred in their areas, where a Anganwadi worker was sexually assaulted by a pastor, the *sangha* organized a big rally, but could not get actual justice for their demands.

But the pastor was transferred to another place. The tribal land was taken by panos, and the *sangha* requested many times to them to free their lands, but they didn't listen. So, the *sangha* tried to occupy the lands forcefully and started cultivating and harvested the crops. This way alone in Mandimera GP of Gajapati block the *sangha* could restore 70 to 80 acres of land. The *sangha* did a campaign against liquor. With all these activities the *sangha* still had the trust on the present system and they gave a candidate for *sarpanch*. But the *Sarpanch* did not do anything after he won the elections. So, they lost the faith in the system as whoever will enter into this he or she will be lost in that and will act as others want.

The tribals lost the belief. The land movement by the *sangha* (popularly known as Mandravaju Zami Andolan) was completely democratic and initially they requested the Panos to free the tribal lands. But the police started harassing the tribals and 9 people were killed during a demonstration. The police had camps near the tribal villages and used to harass the tribals by stealing their goats along with the Pano members. The women were then became the victims of eve teasing by the police and the nexus of Panos. When the tribals went to ask for compensation to the police station the police fired and 9 were killed. When they came out of the jail joined with the Naxals and in a way the actions taken by the government is acting in a negative manner. The Naxals are showing the tribals the right path to fight against injustice so the government is angry on them.

The quotes of the Respondents who direct the extensions of the organization.

> *The old man was beaten very rudely and he asks since 3 years I'm in jail and not been produced before the court, government pays to the police man who is killed and his family get money, now since many years we are all there in jail, so will the government give money for our loss of time and other resources. And all tribals are not produced before the court which is again a violation of rights. So, he is frustrated seating ideal in a jail. He is sad as he gets some food in the jail and worries about his family who are at the village. He worries that his family might be having only one meal and saving meal's money to meet him in a month.*
>
> *Kiran who works as a driver and had a loan from the government and somehow used to manage his family. But the police arrested him and forced him to sign a paper. So, the vehicle which he bought in loan is lying without use, and he cannot repay the loan also as he is inside the jail with no work. So, he thinks that on one hand the government with the help of the District Magistrate gave the loan and on the other hand it took everything. So, who is responsible for his condition? He was earning Rs. 1000 nearly for one day and thought a good future for his children. The security forces don't catch the real Naxals and always harass innocent people.*
>
> *Raju, a Dalit boy was not allowed to enter the school, but he has good qualities like he can play flute very well. The incident shocked him when he saw that he is not allowed into a school. And he was almost accepted that torture was their fate and they have to face it unless they attended a meeting of the party in their village.*
>
> *Sita's father works in the field and mother works in the frontal organization and she was educated mostly in the Bal Sangham run by the party in the village. The area of the tribals are lush green but they go empty stomach half of the year and that's the irony which the government do not understand and talks of only industrialization and why don't it provides schemes which will benefit the tribals. The government education system is failed*

and no schools function and bal sanghams are running effectively by the party. So, the party is imparting education on role of state, revolutionary politics and structures of deprivation.

James decided to join the party after he saw that no results in the democratic way which is slow and not tribal oriented. His village landlord had three wives and harasses other women also. He has the habit of going to the forests alone to collect food. So, one day he met the party people and then later convinced that this is way to get back his resources. He is preparing the tribal youth. After the party was active in their village the Zamindar left the area and the tribals got back their land. So, he believes in the violent way now as a last resort.

Gita questions why they are so poor, even though the country is independent? She wanted to have a cycle, but her parents could not afford it. So, she feels all poor should be united now to fight for their rights and improve their condition irrespective of their caste, religion and gender.

Graces father works in the Dandakaranya region as a medical worker for the party. Her mother works with the frontal organization and she is working in the south Orissa now as a local guerrilla squad member. Her sibling got education with the help of the party. She remembers the miseries they had when she was young. She feels that tribals don't speak much maybe that's the reason other people take advantage of them. So, the party is helping to analyze and reflect on their situation. The land movement helped them in getting some land from the encroachers. So, many tribal families where all the members are dedicated for the party. She is always on the forefront of the party during important raids and operations. It takes them more than 2 months to reach from one state to another state. She came to Orissa for the Nayagarh operation. But she gets news from her family from Mad area in Chhattisgarh. She is working here since one year. She is learning Oriya to build a strong rapport with the local villagers.

It is found that the tribal organization which was working for a land movement in Rayagada and Gajapati districts got derailed to be a part of the armed conflict. The opportunity favoured the CPI (Maoist) party to take control of the situation and create antagonism among the tribal mass against the system. But nearly 55 per cent of the youth wants to come back or fight without violence.

Psychology of the Active and Passive Tribal Members

The members of the CPI (Maoist) who have turned the movement into a violent conflict to have a major population of tribals in their party. They are good at educating the tribals, as they utilized their psychology making their life histories as a base.

- 50.57 per cent of respondents did have miserable experience, but they are very much attracted to their family members, love their family members.
- 16.09 per cent do love their village clan members.
- 11.49 per cent love their friends.

The experiences are related to the poverty, unmet needs, and there is also a communal content in the sense members of the same community. All these factors communal content, unmet needs, poor governance and the pressure on the state from the big power parties. These our factors are well understood by the tribals. The psychology is seen from their disliking, their distress conditions, their parent's aspirations, their needs to understand the holistic picture of their mind.

Table 8.7: Whom Respondents Dislike

Sl. No.	*Communities*	*Whom the respondents disliked (%)*			
		Dishonest people	*Traditions*	*Rich people*	*Others*
1.	SC	4.55	4.55	5.45	0.91
2.	ST	25.45	4.55	13.64	34.55
3.	Others	2.73	—	0.91	2.73
	Total	32.73	9.10	20	38.19

The respondents dislike the dishonest people who exploit the tribals, and loot their resources, 13.64 per cent of them dislike rich class as these class use their services but still harass them by all means. 34.55 dislike the government officials as they don't respect tribals. The CPI (Maoist) is using all these resources like the tribal youth, their frustrations which are true as they are unable to do anything and gradually ending up in armed conflict:

- 32.38 per cent of respondents wanted that they should get settled in life with good job, food and life.

- 10.48 per cent of the parents wanted their children should become financially well of and should not suffer they did.
- 29.95 per cent of them wanted they should have good land and livelihood.

But all these dreams were not fulfilled due to the structures of deprivation, the embedded violence of the society, and the direct violence by the state is paving ways for planned way for the armed conflict.

Table 8.8: Respondents' View on Socio-economic Conditions of Tribals

Sl. No.	*Communities*	*The condition (%)*			
		Satisfactory		*To some extent*	*Other reasons*
		Yes	*No*		
1.	ST	—	67.07	3.66	3.66
2.	SC	—	10.98	—	7.32
3.	Others	—	3.66	1.22	2.44
	Total		81.71	4.88	13.42

Table 8.8 shows that, more than 70 per cent of respondents feel that the socio-economic condition is not good of the tribals. As they are deprived of the basic needs.

Table 8.9: The Reasons for Distress

Sl. No	*Communities*	*Reasons (%)*			
		Govt. officials	*Customs*	*Geographical location*	*Others*
1.	ST	46.08	2.94	6.88	23.53
2.	SC	6.88	—	—	5.88
3.	OC	3.92	0.98	.98	1.96
	Total	56.88	3.92	7.86	31.37

46.08 per cent of tribals held the government to be responsible for their distress condition, from which 35.21 per cent say that exclusively government officials. 2.94 per cent of tribals do feel customs are responsible from which 7.75 per cent of them feel that customs like early marriage, ignorance on education have been the obstacles for distress. 23.53 per cent of them do feel that the exploiter classes along with the government have been the major responsible for their condition. So, these factors help the party to spread out. The voices from the field also do tell the story of pain.

> *A 45 year old Kandha tribal person feels that the tribals are very well lured by consumerism and the various market theories, but in fact losing their own identity and culture. It is hard to keep them away from all these when they see other people doing the same. But they the tribal group have to understand this and come out of this glorified world which is making many people poor, homeless and landless. When some media is highlighting the tribal issue he is happy.*
>
> *Kamu, 40 year old Halwa joined the frontal organization after he was disappointed working with NGOs, as he feels NGOs cannot go to raise the voice as they are legally bonded and have lot of limitations. So, he conducts meetings and helps to educate the tribal youth to assert their rights. Basically, he thrusts on 5 principles, those are no corruption and no bribe at all, no liquor consumption, no liars in the system. No harassment to women, good and systematic education for tribals and equality for all. These are the principles that he imparts on everyone. The meetings conducted by him are all self-sponsored by people. His songs are anti-company and revolutionary oriented. He feels that though the country has been independent, but still tribals are not able to get enough food, cloth and shelter. There is so much of land and if any tribal built a house then illegal. The tribals being the citizens of the country are criminals in their own land. The development has been done in south Orissa through dams, and industries, but the tribals are working as maids who owned once the resource. So, they are marginalized more now than before. He greets others with Lal Salaam and gives slogans of "Inquilab zindabad". They have their own panchayats and local courts where they decide about their tasks, fixes responsibility and plans to accomplish the work. Many people go there with their grievances to these meetings/courts where all the complaints are well recorded and necessary actions are taken. He focuses on the political understanding among the tribes, so that they understand what is exploitation, how they understand corruption, repression and injustice. He explains the whole nexus of state and the corporate and how the tribals*

are being resourceless in this context. There is a huge contradiction among the tribals and state. There is a major mismatch of interests among the tribals and the state. He appeals to the people to always move with their traditional weapon as it's a sign of tribal pride. If the police can move with the gun and why can't the tribals as their tradition. He believes that one day will come where the tribals have to fight with their traditional weapons.

Table 8.10: Aim of the life of the Respondents as Aspired by their Parents

Sl. No.	*Communities*	*Aim in life (%)*				
		To do better for society	*To get govt. job*	*To get married*	*To have enough good life*	*Others*
1.	SC	6.19	—	—	—	6.19
2.	ST	19.59	8.25	4.12	13.40	34.02
3.	Others	2.06	1.03	—	—	5.15
	Total	27.84	9.28	4.12	13.40	45.36

The movement increased after 1990, as the duration of post 1990 saw a major developmental where tribals had to face lot of problems. As the table shows 19.59 per cent wanted only to do something good for their own people. Rest 8.25 per cent wanted government secured job which they could not get. 4.12 per cent wanted a happy life. 13.40 per cent wanted to have good quality land which will fetch them good harvest, and 34.02 per cent of tribals wanted to be other professions like to join business, join politics, teaching or any other white collar jobs. So, their aspirations are not fulfilled. And they see the party as their saviors and join them gradually, so, slowly the movement is having a strong hold in the study area. The operation green hunt which is a step taken by the state to tackle the naxal menace is also making the tribals life miserable. So, they prefer to join with the party now.

Table 8.11 shows the attitude of tribals towards the party members. As all total 25.05 per cent of them feel that they are better than money lenders and others. As they come and interact with the villages closely ask their problem, and encourage them for the pollution. This way creates an interest among the masses to join them. Few quotes from the primary data:

Table 8.11: Is Naxalism a better alternative?

Sl. No.	Communities	Better than whom (%)			
		Money lenders	Traders	Government officials	Others
1.	SC	20.66	20.66	20.66	20.3
2.	ST	2.58	2.58	2.58	2.58
3.	Others	1.85	1.85	1.85	1.85
	Total	25.09	25.09	25.09	24.73

Kesab decided to join the party after he saw that no results. His village landlord had three wives and harasses other women also. He has the habit of going to the forests alone to collect food. So, one day he met the party people and then later convinced that this is the way to get back his resources. He is preparing the tribal youth. After the party was active in their village the zamindar left the area and the tribals got back their land. So, he believes in the violent way now as a last resort.

Krishna was very much motivated by Dasuram Malekaa teachings and songs. And he almost in tears when he remembers that he is no more with others. But still wants to take forward his teachings and ideals. The Kui songs trigger within him the identity of a tribe and he gets elevated. He had very bad experiences with forest officials as they harass tribal women. He feels that tribals are innocent and likes to mingle with each and everyone and easily believes everyone. But the other sections of the society have utilized us, they have not accepted our good qualities like community feeling, rather made use of our limitations like drinking and have always discouraged us from going to education. His father had brought a loan from a sahukar and the sahukar always used to compel his father not to send him to school and used to explain what will he do by studying after all he has to work to repay the interest. Few of the traditions among tribals are also not good in these changing tribal societies. Like the early marriages among the tribals whether it's a boy or girl. The tribals have lost their identity as they have lost their hills, forest and water resources. Only thing they preserve is in terms of customs and traditions. Many of them have de-tribalized themselves to Oriya culture. But these customs have become very costly to perform them. All these thought invoked something to do different so I joined the party. He joined in the cultural team who only used to create awareness for social revolution and awakening. But many of them got arrested under the Naxal profile, so, he joined the party as a guerrilla squad. He also works as a courier, he has to scope to read and write in the party apart from his work.

Table 8.12: Respondent's Self-Assessment (both Male and Female)

Sl. No.	Communities	Self-assessment (%)						
		Cool minded	Overt	Covert	Aggressive	Adjustive	Violent	Emotional
1.	SC	3.55	0.71	0.71	3.55	—	3.55	0.71
2.	ST	9.22	9.22	17.73	16.31	6.38	11.35	10.64
3.	Others	1.42	1.42	0.71	0.71	0.71	0.71	0.71
	Total	14.19	11.35	19.15	20.57	7.09	15.61	12.06

Table 8.12 shows that 17.73 per cent of tribals are covert and speak less unless they like the other person. 16.31 per cent become aggressive to there women are harassed and if some clan members are with them. 11.35 per cent can become violent if the discontent becomes very high.

The passive members of the movement do feel that, 1.3 per cent of the respondents does feel that it adding to the experience of class struggle, 23 per cent feel that its empowering the tribals, 14 per cent feel that it checks corruption at a milder level, 46 per cent feel this is the only option for tribals, 20 per cent feel that it is teaching the tribals to distinguish between right and wrong, 30 per cent of tribals do feel that the party do impose lot of restrictions on the tribals and in return they cannot questions the party.

But there has been a series of small, medium and large conflicts with the state in the study area with the state for their rights on resource which included the past, recent past and the one which are continuing now.

Uprisings in the Universe in the Past

This area has witnessed several uprisings in the colonial period and also in the independent India. It is described here to understand the background of the area in depth, to see the past that the psychology of the tribals is resist if the exploitation is too high.

- Sabara revolt (1856-57).
- Ghumsur revolt 1835.
- In 1961 there was a violent movement by tribals against the exploiter landlord Hari Misra in the village of Balikhamar near Therubali in Rayagada subdivision. Hari Misra was the *Deewan* of Kashipur Raja, from the coastal area, and all the tribal lands were under his possession. Tribals appealed with folded hands to him many times to return their land, without success. The matter went to the Court from 1952 to 1960, but without any result. In 1961 tribals forcefully occupied their land and when Hari Misra opposed it, the tribals killed him on the spot.
- Koya revolt 1922.
- *Bhoo-satyagraha* by *adivasis* 1951.
- Chtirakonda Trade union movement 1967.
- JK Paper mill workers movement 1968.
- Gunupur Movement in 1964 to 1968.
- Kui Lavanaga Sangha and Chasi mulia Sangha in 2000.
- Gudari Land Struggle 1999.
- Mandravaju Land Struggle 1998.
- Rights over Cashew Land by tribals in Koraput 2004 to 2008.
- Land struggle in Narayanpatna of Koraput from 2004 ongoing.
- Struggle for Good governance in Cut off area of Malkangiri 2009, 2010 and on going.

All these struggles were independent democratic movements by this region where the people have demanded their rights over resources. As mentioned in the theories to understand the participation of tribals in the armed movement certain theories are adopted and they were applied here to the study areas to see their validity as follows.

(i) Communal Content

From what the research has gathered it is evident that the primary groups in this movement are the tribals of south Orissa and the State. It is sensible to argue that the tribal being dominated by the others in political, social, cultural and in economic contexts, and for which the state is seeing the frustrations of that domination in all above mentioned facts. When the tribals are projecting their discontent meant against the state and also the settlers who have occupied their land. The tribals have been discriminated by others and for their activities they have been labelled as Naxalites by the state. So, this shows a communal content directed to one particular section of the society.

(ii) Needs

Malinovski's Theory on needs says that needs are not negotiable and they are universal, everyone is born with some needs. Human beings are not aggressive by nature. Conflict is generated when their basic needs are denied or are perceived as being under threat. Needs can be also categorized as divided into security needs, development needs, political access needs and identity needs. The needs of the tribals are not satisfied as seen from different factors.

The attack on the alleged Naxalites have increased the intensity of the conflict as tribals have been subject to harsh treatment like fake encounters, executions without due legal procedures, and disappearances of tribal people or whoever has raised their voices against injustice. It is very pertinent to say that whether the operations by the deployed force have affected the real Naxalites… or everyone as innocent civilians can easily be perceived as naxalites in a fiery situation. In addition, the constant presence of armed forces in this region has a frightening effect on the people by constant raids and search operations. This process has created an unsatisfied security need among the tribals.

They also have unsatisfied developmental needs, as they have not been benefited from the developmental projects undertaken by the state in the name of public purpose and national interest, and also they won't get anything from the upcoming projects. The investments in the region have undoubtedly improved infrastructure like hotels, colleges, insurance companies, business, other educational institutions, universities, cell phones network, new shopping centres, but this is not necessarily valuable for the poor tribals in the region.

On the other hand, the tribals have a difficulty to find a job in the companies as they don't have the necessary educational eligibility. Nor do they have the money to afford to go to these affluent colleges. So, the jobs are occupied by the outsiders, and ultimately the tribals are becoming more deprived and continue to work as daily wagers without any option. The legacy of exclusion and deprivation has become more intense as they are losing their resources and they are not equipped to take the challenge with others at the job market and as a resultant factor the embedded problems continues to remain as such. The state has interest in this region for its mineral wealth but the economy has not given importance to the needs of the tribals. So in this process, they have unsatisfied political access, availability and affordability needs.

On the one hand state is driving out tribals from their land to hand over the resources to the companies and on the other hand the tribals and their culture have been engraved in big cities. The tribals are confused about their identity. The tribals are forced to stay in camps living their forests where it cannot be called as assimilation, this way there is deprivation from their identity needs.

(iii) Governance

Our government is democratic in nature and the decision is taken also in a decentralized manner incepting from the grassroots level/Panchayati Raj to the all other levels. But the basic problem with the democratic system is the interpretation of democracy is in such a way that the voices of the poor are unheard. It has well found out by this research that after six decades of the democratic system the poor villagers are yet to have the information on the schemes that are available to them by the welfare state. The tribals areas have been neglected, development did not reach them until it was necessary to set up mines and industries in the region. So, they did not had the political access, neither took part in the decision making process, the system has curtailed their rights to some extent. The tribal leaders those went to the electoral process could not put forth their demands well and as we the government has clear priorities for the industrial development in this region, rather than the felt and expressed needs of the tribals. This way the outside migration in to these areas are increasing and the tribal population including the primitive tribals, in a dwindling state?

The Government has good solutions for the migrating population to these areas, but it does not have the solution for the tribals who are migrating in a distress condition to other State. The governance system has squeezed the space of tribals in all ways and it is going worse day by day. The research argues that political priorities of the Orissa state ruled by dominant groups who seems to lack skill, aptitude, and innovativeness to deal with the issues that arise when tribals complain, and they do not believe what the tribals say.

(iv) International Linkages

There is some international force on the Government of Orissa directed at human rights issues in the region. One of the persons who died in an encounter falsely did have compensation after 2 years. It is also found that many times this does not happen, due to policy of sovereignty. This issue of Naxalism is an internal issue, and other international organizations should not interfere in it. Since, it has been mentioned as an internal security issue, it implies that the state does not want to indulge itself to solve this. On the other hand there is an urge to modernize the security forces. The war on naxals has got a good political support also to allege the tribals as Naxals. The tribal region is rich in minerals and resources, so, all the multinational companies have an eye to exploit these, and the Naxals are the biggest eyesores for them as they oppose big developmental projects. On the other hand in a state of despair the Naxals do take money from the companies. This situation becomes very peculiar, when the companies are hiring their own private military or muscle power to overthrow the movements along with the help of the state sponsored forces. This exhibits that there are many actors involved, who do not push the tribal agenda rather than their own agenda.

According to Galtung, 'all kinds of violence can be seen as a relationship between contradiction, attitudes and behaviours'.

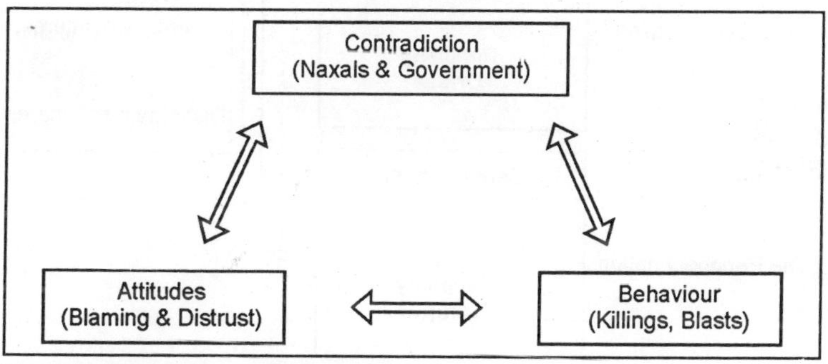

Note: Designed upon empirical study
Source: *Contemporary Conflict Resolution*, Ramsbotham, p. 9.
Fig. 8.1: Application of Galtungs model of violence

Contradictions have led to more violence in case of naxal. However, it would be relevant to take out the attitudes of the state, what are their perceptions and misperceptions on this conflict?

It is seems that there is no solution with state on the issue as it is not going in the favour of it and its harmful for the interests of the major actors who are involved in it. The other priority is industrial development, which is according to the state will bring employment and other opportunities for the tribals. But, how far the tribals can access and avail these opportunities is very doubtful, as the past witness. The problem of Naxals is seen as a law and order problem and it is seen as to bring stability in the region. But, how far stability can be brought by these projects evicting them forcefully is not the best option right now.

Based on Azar's model, violence is not the response for the unmet needs of the tribals. The new projects will not alleviate poverty and meet tribal needs but it will definitely increase the legitimacy of the state. The present condition has failed to produce results and further escalated violence. 70 per cent of population in this region is very poor. The research claims that it is a question of political willingness, to take initiative to solve this problem.

Galtung argues that the world consists of centre and periphery nations, and that both of these in turn have their own centres and peripheries. The theory of structural imperialism aims to explain the difference between these factions, especially between the centre of the centre and the periphery of the periphery.

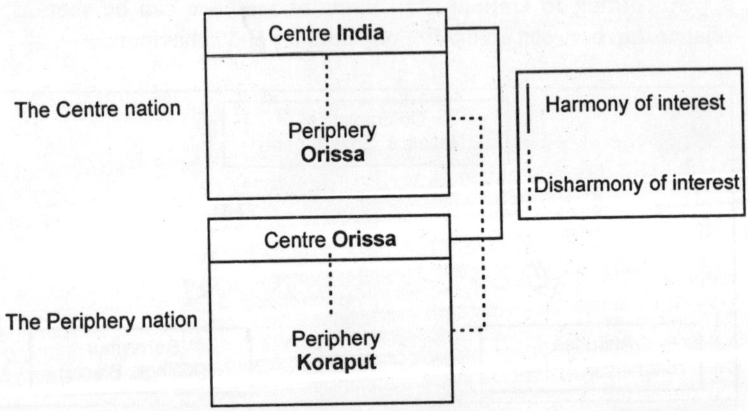

Fig. 8.2: Application of Structural Imperialism

As illustrated in the figure above, imperialism is a relation between a centre and a periphery nation with the following characteristics[3]:

- There is a harmony of interest between the centre in the centre nation and the centre in the periphery nation.
- There is more disharmony of interest within the periphery nation than within the central nation.

- There is disharmony of interest between the periphery in the central nation and the periphery in the periphery nation.

Here, in case of Naxal violence where the tribals are participating for their rights, the relation between the state of India and the south Orissa Tribal region said to have the same characteristics. Firstly, the governing elite in India be it Congress, BJD or BJP or any ruling party shares interests with the elite in the south Orissa tribal region, namely interests revolving around economic development, for mines and minerals, for water and regional stability. Secondly, we cannot rule out the existence of economic injustice and discrimination in other areas of Orissa which are not tribal dominated but there are poor sections with the same characteristic. The argument is that, the tribals are subject to several kinds of discrimination based on their ethnicity compared to others. As most displaced people constitute tribals. Thus, there is a larger disharmony of interest within south Orissa tribal region than within the rest of Orissa. Finally, tribals have unmet needs, and fulfilling these could affect the goals of the rest of the Orissa and as a whole Indian society. For instance, a higher degree of autonomy for the south Orissa tribals could affect the stability or economic development, which would undoubtedly affect the lower-class population or middle class population all over Orissa or India. It cannot be claimed that these interests are conflicting, but it can be certainly well said that the ruling party or class is likely to prioritize the interests of the others over the tribal interests and needs. This is in fact related to the ruling party legitimacy is more dependent on the approval of the other than the south Orissa tribals.

To infer it can be stated open ended that there is a structure of group interests in Orissa as well as in Indian society that suppresses the tribals and for the satisfaction of their needs. While the lack of transparency in higher political circles makes it difficult to verify, the reason being that by meeting the tribal needs and demands will go against their interests. And the basic perception is that if the state fulfils the need it is definitely going to affect their position. Here the research feels that the basic needs of the tribals are human needs and they are non-negotiable and must be addressed in order to address the Naxal violence.

Or to stop the conflict from becoming more violent one. As an escalation of the conflict is definitely not in the interest of the rest of the groups in the country and the ruling party or the state's failure to meet the tribal needs in the long term could pose a serious threat to the country's stability and there could be heavy losses on the economic scenario.

After seeing the validity of the theories in the study area condition and the reasons for participation of tribals, the data has derived into the following model why the tribals are entering into this; why a tribal is joining this risky movement, after the democratic movements like Chasi Mulia Adivasi Sangha and other movements which have undergone several repression by the state, the research shows the following model:

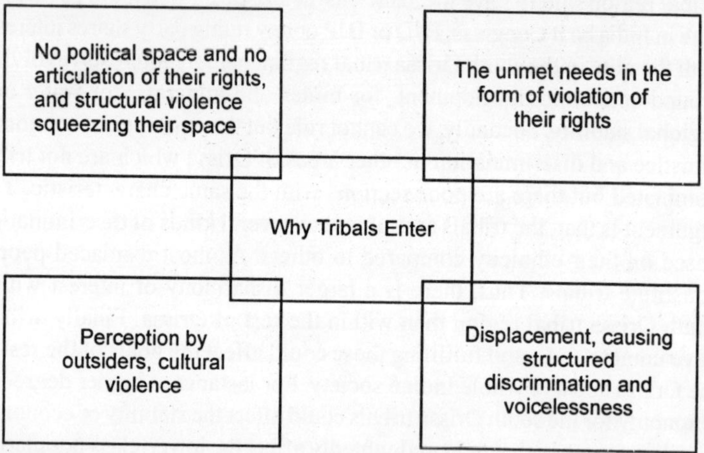

Note: Designed upon the Present empirical study

Fig. 8.3: Four Point Risk Model of Tribal Participation

The above model explains the risk factors, which invoke a desire within a tribal to get into Naxalism. Though they know very well that this will not give any concrete solution, they hope that it will at least act as a constant pressure on the government. This is the last resort, since with other ways there is no justice. History of struggles has witnessed and evidenced that whenever they have agitated they have made as a threat to law, so by going to this stage also they are branded as the same. So in both cases they lose. Their political space is squeezed and they have been victims of many developmental experiments, so all this has put them into a trap of Naxalism.

From the Edward Azars theory of protracted social conflict one can see the following model of the study area and how it will lead to a more destructive conflict; as the conflict in south Orissa can be categorized as a PSC, the research has attempted to show how the strategy of the Government is probably to influence conflict based on Miall's adaptation of Azar's PSC theory.

It is clear that the contextual background for the conflict is historical, ethnicity and legacy of colonial exploitation in south Orissa. The mass scale of MoUs with big multinational companies and the policies of the government have led to a difficult situation for the tribals. It is clear that they have discontentment, several unmet needs, particularly relating to political access, security, cultural identity, economic well-being and freedom of expression. However, it can't be said that the government is either incapable or unwilling to meet these needs. This leads to an increase in violence from the tribal Naxals, which is met by a strong military presence. The government also becomes increasingly suppressive, possibly implementing more limitations on the freedom of expression of thought, association, and belief and by detaining them as alleged Naxals, which is fact increasingly more towards the movement. The presence of the force and the nature of the conflict growing in these region is more likely to become destructive as shown in Figure 8.4.

The research shows that interpreting the data on the conflict in south Orissa through Miall's adaptation of Azar's theory of PSCs, it is found that the current strategy of the government only serves to escalate the conflict, unless the Government becomes sensitive.

The Conflict and the Human Rights Question

As stated in the theory, every human being is borne with needs. These needs when viewed from legal point of view it becomes as rights. The human rights principles are very well grounded with human needs, which can be claimed by any human being, the human rights are:

- Fundamental,
- In-alienable,
- Indivisible,
- Interdependent, and
- Universal.

The principles state that it is a gift from god and no one can be denied of it. The evolution of human kind has seen many developmental processes from time immemorial. The best thing it has given to the society is the vision of equality to all. It has observed resistance movements, celebrated the success, experienced wars and also witnessing growing conflicts in the society. Human beings are not aggressive by nature and no conflict takes place unless there is an absolute violation of their needs

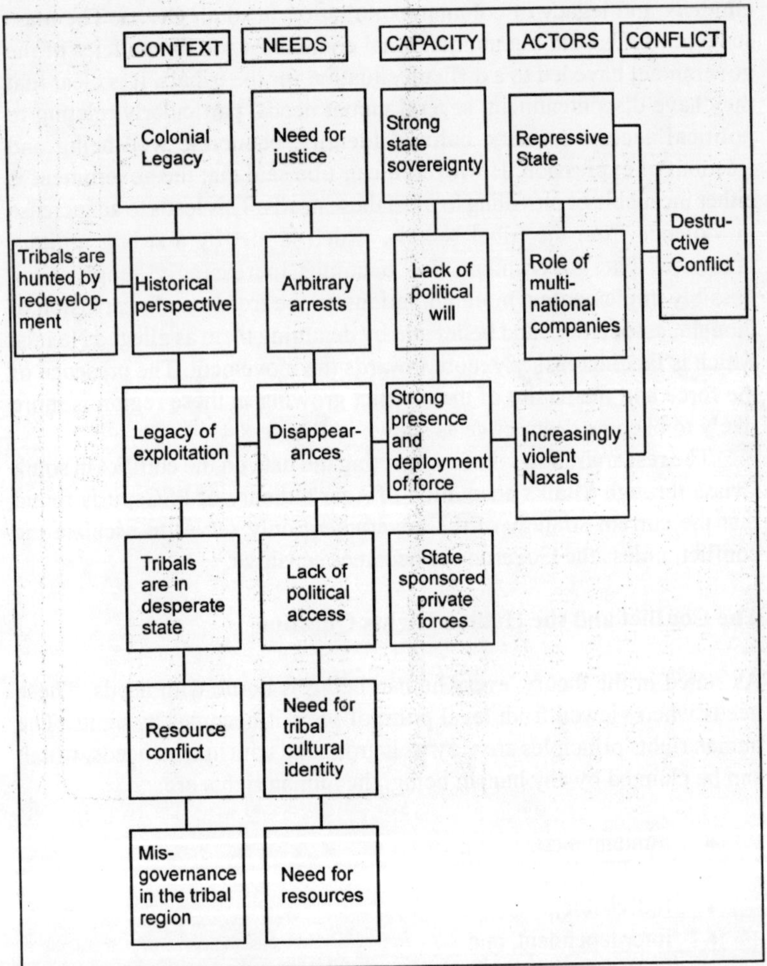

Fig. 8.4: Azar Model, Adaptation to Naxal Conflict (Designed upon the Present empirical study)

and rights. And south Orissa is among one such region where the majority of tribal population is deprived of basic rights and is in the condition of utter poverty. These Tibals are in a vicious cycle of torture by various forces and facing gross violations of rights under the banner of Naxalism. Both the parties the government and this region are in conflict with each other where both the parties face human rights violations, which include all kinds of violence. But in the whole state of affairs the human virtue is absent. This chapter is an exploration of the issue and cases of human rights, the south Orissa experience on violations, its timeline, and it gives the obvious picture of the present human rights scenario in the region.

Human rights are the basic *rights* and *freedom* that all people are entitled to despite of nationality, gender, age, national or ethnic origin, race, religion, language, or any other status. Human rights are common, universal and equal where all people have equal rights by virtue of a human being.

These rights may exist as *natural rights* or as *legal rights*, in both national and *international law*. The doctrine of human rights in international practice, within international law, global and regional institutions, in the policies of *states* and the activities of non-governmental organizations has been a cornerstone of *public policy* around the world. It has been said that: "if the public discourse of peacetime global society can be said to have a common moral language, it is that of human rights.[4] The basic of idea that was vibrant as an outcome of the Second World War and adoption of the *Universal Declaration of Human Rights* in Paris by the United Nations General Assembly in 1948. Human rights are rights intrinsic to all human beings and they are non-negotiable like needs. Every human being has some basic needs well explained by different schools of thoughts needs of material and non-material, whatever and wherever the human beings stay, these needs transcend all cultures. Similarly, the needs in the form of legal entity are the rights which are also equal and no one can be discriminated on the basis of any factors. These rights are all universal, inalienable, interrelated, interdependent and indivisible.

Universal human rights are often expressed and guaranteed by law, in the forms of various United Nationals instruments such as treaties, customary international law, general principles and other sources of international laws. These rights protect the citizens from all social abuses. Human beings have gone through a long evolution process where there has been a visible change and transformation in their political, social, economic and in cultural contexts and has been a significant change in their values systems. Where the focus on been on justice other than development. We have witnessed a number of uprisings, resistances in the pre-independent India and also in the post-independent India whenever the human population has been felt that their needs are not been met. Few of these took the shape of a movement and in some places it was prolonged conflict. So, it is well understood that human beings are not aggressive by nature. As they do have values, well expressed in the universal declaration of human rights, but conflict is generated when their basic needs are denied or are perceived as being under threat. But, the needs in the form of rights have the highest value for any individual and it has to be protected by all means.

The South Orissa Situation

The south Orissa the famous Koraput region for all mistaken reasons starting from the poverty, the renowned Koraput-Bolangir-Kalahandi (KBK) regional planning, the diarrhoea deaths, growth of migration among tribals and now the growing tentacles of Naxalism in remote tribal areas. The very unique positive aspects still it attracts the social scientists and anthropologists, the abundance of mineral resources, the perennial streams, the ethnic population, the forest coverage, the rich culture do attract not only the social scientists, but now the companies when they stress to harness the mineral and natural resources of the region. The region is like a laboratory where the government has poured all its resources in the form of different schemes which has not resulted in the development of the people of this region. The plan documents of the five years have remained a distant dream, as the glaring facts of the region reflects that the poverty ratios in the districts are Koraput is 83.81 per cent, Malkangiri is 81.88 per cent, Rayagada is 72.03 per cent respectively.[5] Economic Survey 2007-08, Government of Orissa[6], indicated the incidence of poverty to be 83.61 per cent and 88.86 per cent in Koraput and Malkangiri. Poverty among Scheduled Tribes in the southern region has been estimated at 82.80 per cent[7]. So, these figures tell us the plight of the people where the whole region is undergoing a phase of transition where they have no options rather to embrace conflict with the government. The development process in our country (1947 modern India) did constructed many secular temples in this region but the prayers of the people in this region could not be heard. Their devotion could not be valued. And this development process crated a major chunk of people left out to suffer, and their basic needs don't reach them.

It is assumed that, when needs are not met there is a growing discontent among human beings and the same has been occurring in the different Tribal sections of the south Orissa which is very bright as conflict now. The timeline of the conflict in India can be traced back from the pre-independence period when the country was under the colonial British where there were struggles against the British imperialism in violent and non-violent ways. The south Orissa also saw many uprisings when the people of this area felt that their resources are being looted. These struggles had a definite pattern, background, demographic, religious, socio-ethnic, political or economic structure which led to such kind of resistance and struggle. But all these resistance were misunderstood as law and order problem which can be tackled or sorted out by police action. The Britishers were brutal to people of this region and they suppressed the movements. All these movements had one very pertinent feature, i.e. "which seeking for justice and don't violate our rights". The movements halted for some time, but the anger desperation remained un-ventilated. It flourished whenever it saw an outlet in any form, be it the land *satyagraha* (when a Gandhian Late Sri Biswanath Pattnaik initiated a *Bhoo-satyagraha* for tribal land rights in Gunupur area of Koraput region), the Communist movement in the early 1960s, the collective democratic land movements in the 1990s, or be the present violent form of Naxalism. So, the whole range of conflicts has to be viewed from a different lens to get a myopic and broadminded view to understand it when the need remained unmet, rights are violated human population conflict takes place.

In the whole conflict map, the human element is missing as there are various issues of direct violence (when the people are encountered, killed), cases of structural violence (where people are detained arbitrarily and illegally, women are raped and molested in the affected region) there are cases of cultural violence (where a particular section the tribals are labelled as Naxalites, the research says that 80 per cent of the tribals are believed to be Naxals by the security forces. A particular profiling is done to label the tribals as Naxals, and whoever fits in that framework will be a targeted by the state irrespective of his or her involvement in the naxal activities). It is not that there are no cases of violations by the Naxals, there are also cases where there is gross violations as killing of the security forces, abducting them, taking the ration meant for the security forces, killing the people in the name of police informers, killing innocents in mistaken identity; so, these are done in the name of retaliation to answer the state and as a symbol of showing the power and presence. This sign of retaliation and counter-retaliation are undergoing an inhuman circle where there is no end to violence. In this circle of violence one thing is very evident that there are serious cases of unpleasant and brutal human rights violations. The violations are of different form, and different nature; there are violations when the democratic voices are repressed in the name of Naxals, banning the organizations that are raising the voices for rights, killing the people who are fighting against the companies. There is another kind of violation which is faced by the security forces who are deployed in extreme conditions, who are always in a low psychological states (65% of the forces believe that the tribal are undergoing an identity crisis and there is no political will to fight for their cause), who are killed almost every month.

The South Orissa: The Seed of Naxalism, Timeline and the Violation of Rights: An Overview

In the wake of the globalized country the new economic policies made tribals very poor where the land demand was more not only for dams, industries, railways, but for diverse usage like shopping malls, linear projects, and many more. Today every good tribal is either displaced tribal or going to be displaced. The land movement started in Gunupur region which comprises the Rayagada district and Gajapati district in 1995, under the banner of Chasi Mulia Samiti. They started mobilizing the people in Gudari block and by the end of 1998 they built a base in the area. By the end of 2000 the organization took a decision to work on the ceiling land which is still acquired by the *zamindars* and other people illegally. The organization took out all the names of the *zamindars*, the area acquired and the place of the land. Most of the *zamindars* are located in Padmapur, Naira and Gudari.[8]

The same procedure was adopted as it was in 1951 during the land-*Satyagraha*, but with a change of mode. During the 2nd spark of the land struggle in early 2000, first they selected 5 villages to forcefully acquire land, and the decision took place on November 2nd, 2001 in a village level meeting. The *zamindars* not only taken the lands of the tribals, but also they use the tribal women as their keeps. This is a sheer human rights issue where the tribal women are always used. The 5 villages which were selected for the forceful harvesting, other 12 villages joined hand with them as the Chasi Mulia Sangathan had a strong hold in the area. They were successful in harvesting the crops, then slowly it spread over 32 villages. As a result of which each village people organized themselves into revolutionary Chasi Mulia Sangathan. Then it spread over 100 villages in the area. In every village more than 400 people participated in harvesting. Government of Orissa deployed 25 platoons of police in the area, and all the total 72 persons were arrested including 23 women were sent to jail from 10 villages. People tried to resist the police, but they were badly injured. The same scenario in Narayanpatna block of Koraput district was, the tribals struggling for their land, and till date nearly 200 tribals are behind the bars for raising their voice, and few have been banned as Naxalites. The same situation prevails in 2009. So, the government didn't create the scope for the tribals to address their issues of rights and always used it as a case of law and order to save the interests of the powerful folk. This attempt by the administration though diverts the people from raising the voice from 1999 till in 2011, but it didn't have any concrete solutions. These conflicts though could not take the possession of the land but they organized themselves into a strong open conflict with the government. It is seen as a Naxalism but later made deliberately to join hands with the naxals as a last weapon. If we see the time line of human rights violations, the Mandravaju Land Struggle (Gajapati District) where 8 people were killed in land struggle.

The conflicts had some temporary outcome where few *zamindars* left the places, and few surrendered before the people. But Tribals could not get any permanent result from this struggle, as government set-up commissions and committees, but till now the report is not made public.[9] Jagadesh and Sahu—both non-tribal Brahmin landlords—belong to Gotlabadra panchayat area in Gunupur block of Rayagada district in Orissa. These landlords forcibly occupied 60-acres of land of the innocent *Adivasis* 30 years ago. During these 30 years, these lands were given on rent to the *Adivasis* by the landlords. The *Adivasis* not only lost their land, but also their labour power for these 30 years. The everyday violations of rights are not calculated unless they are opting for some strong step. The Tribals whose labour is used, whose land is taken away, and whose wages are not paid and all these life cycle tortures are leading towards Naxalism.

The killing of 8 tribals in Mandravaju Land Struggle in 1999:

- The banning of the organizations, on 9 June, 2006, Orissa Government banned the Communist Party of India (Maoist) and seven of its frontal affiliated organisations, namely Daman Pratirodh Manch, Revolutionary Democratic Front, Chasi Mulia Samiti, Kui Labang Sangh, Jananatya Mandali, Krantikari Kisan Samiti and Bal Sangram.[10]
- On the night of 7 July, 2006, Central Reserve Police Force (CRPF) personnel shot dead Siri Majhi, a landless tribal daily wage earner, in Rayagada when he went to defalcate. Next morning police informed Mali Palekka, the wife of the deceased that her husband was injured in an encounter with the security forces and was arrested on the charges of being a Naxalite. But later the state Human Rights Commission ordered for compensation, but one life was lost.[11]

- Tribals were harassed by security forces in the name of containing Maoist violence. In October 2006, in a complaint to the Orissa Human Rights Commission, tribals from at least 12 villages under R. Udaygiri and Adaba Police Stations of Gajapati district in south Orissa stated that the security forces have been committing excesses on them in the name of containing Maoist violence, this is a regular feature by the security forces.
- In two "encounter" incidents, one on 24-4-2011 at Tentulipadar village in Nakamamudi panchayat of Kudumulugumma block, Chitrakonda tehsil in Malkangiri district and the other on 9-1-2011 at Basangamali village in Kashipur bock of Rayagada district. While one woman Maoist was killed in Tentulipadar, 9 Maoists, including 5 women (at least three of them minors) were shot dead at Basangamali (independent fact finding report).
- Two adolescent girls were picked up by the police and presented to the media as Naxal women who had been arrested by the police during an encounter with a Maoist squad in the forests of Sangmui in K. Singhpur block of Rayagada district, Orissa. The two girls were later presented in court and remanded to juvenile home at Berhampur by court. Subsequently, their bail application was rejected by Juvenile Justice Board, Rayagada, consisting of SDJM as one of the members (independent fact finding report).
- Gajapati district has been subject to combing operations as the area is supposed to be having hectic Maoist activities. The arrest and rape of this woman has largely gone unreported and therefore, there was a need to investigate. An all-India women's fact finding team of four members went to Gajapati district in Orissa on September 30th–October 1st to investigate into the alleged rape[12].
- Gangula Tadingi (41 years) of Bagam village under Kumbhari Panchayat died of tuberculosis on 12th April, 2010 at the Koraput District Headquarter Hospital. He had been undergoing treatment for TB at Koraput District Headquarter Hospital for 20 days before his death. Another truth about Gangula is that he was an under trial prisoner at Koraput District Jail and had been lodged there from 17th December, 2009. Gangual was accused of "attacking Narayanpatna Police Station as part of a violent mob (*sic*!) of 200 tribals on 20th November, 2009" in which two of Gangula's comrades Singanna and Andru were shot to death by

police. Gangula was a member of Chasi Mulia Adivasi Sangh (CMAS) and also a leader of Bagam village. Gangula and three others, Kasu, Rajayya and Kantayya, of Bagam have been booked for the 20th November incident[13].

- Apart from the killings in the cases of naxals, there have been 30 tribals who have been shot dead from 1999 to 2011 in fighting against the companies from Maikanch in Rayagada (against Utkal alumina) till the land struggles in Narayanpatna of Koraput district (Table 8.13).

There are human rights violations in a conflicting situation like in the study area. The movement has turned into a lower intensity conflict. There are violations when two major parties are completely contradicted with each other. There are few violations when tribals falsely killed and implicated in cases and later were released and got compensation. The 6 tribals arrested in Gillkuta village in 2006 were released in 2008 who were just watching a hindi film called Lal Salaam. But after their jail sentence they wrote a small book called "Sehi Kala Ratrira Katha" the story of the night when they were arrested and tortured by the police (the court order of the case given in Annexture-4). One tribal person who was killed in Rayagada while attending a nature's call, his wife filed a petition and later the State Human Rights Commission offered her compensation. Her husband was killed in a false encounter. After the NALCO raid in 2009 where Katru Huika was killed falsely, her wife still waiting for justice (Head line of the below paper cutting is—"My husband was not a Naxal").

The media highlights show the other side of the human rights violations. There are violations from both the sides, question is not that who is doing more and who is doing less, the issue is that there are violations taking place. The killing in Kalinganagar, the killings in Kashipur, in Mandravaju, Gudari, Chandrapur, Malkangiri, most of them is false encounters. As the Naxal activists say that if it is an encounter then why the security force does not die and only Naxals die. There are different opinions regarding the question of human rights.

State of Children (When the Father or Both Parents are Involved in the Process)

There were very few cases found when both the parents are involved in the process. The study has almost 70 per cent of Naxal cadres from *Dandakaranya* region who are from Chhattisgarh state. They very well

ଯବାନଙ୍କ ଗୁଳିରେ ମୃତ କାଟ୍ରୁ ହୁଇକାଙ୍କ ପତ୍ନୀ ଜିଲ୍ଲାପାଳଙ୍କ ଠାରେ ଫେରାଦ

ମୋ ସ୍ୱାମୀ ନକ୍ସଲ ନଥିଲେ...

Source: Sambad, 22nd April, 2009.

DAMANJODI NAXAL ATTACK

Tribals come together to protest 'police excesses'

Express News Service
Jeypore, April 26

TRIBAL and Left party leaders of Koraput, Boipariguda, Laxmipur and Pottangi areas have joined hands to protest 'police excesses against gullible tribals in the aftermath of the Damanjodi Naxal attack'.

They have alleged that police have detained four innocent tribals and killed one in an encounter suspecting them to be Naxalites whereas none of them has past record in any Naxal-related incidents in the region.

They have alleged that police have detained four tribals and killed one suspecting them to be Naxals

"Police who are under tremendous pressure after the Damanjodi attack are arresting local tribals and terming them as hardcore Naxals," they alleged, adding, they would resort to a widespread agitation against the police administration if the latter did not stop harassing tribals.

Sources said over 300 hardcore Naxals, most of them women cadres of Orissa and outside, took part in the Damanjodi attack and local tribals were forced to carry their flags, posters and bags.

Table 8.13: List of people killed in the recent encounters

Date of encounter	*Place*	*No. of people killed*	*Name of Victims*	*Male/Female*	*Social group*	*Remarks*
27.12.10	Borasambar forest area in Paikmal Block	2	1. Madhab Singh Thakur 2. Ramesh Sahu	Male		
29.12.10		2		Female	*Adivasis*	
1.1.11	Tomka area in Jajpur district	5	Bobby, Savitri, Sujata, Jonga Dhiren	4 females including one minor girl and 1 male	*Adivasis*	None of the bodies has been claimed by family members. Police claimed one body had been identified by villagers.
9.1.11	Kashipur	9		5 females 4 males	*Adivasis* + others	Four bodies unclaimed
12.1.11	Keonjhar	2		Both males	*Adivasis*	
8.2.11	Sundargarh	2	1. Sameer Xalxo 2. Ahama Kerketta	Both Males	*Adivasi*	
11.2.11	Sundargarh	3	1. Md. Muslim 2. Nepal Bhumij 3. Susant Mahato	Males		
Total		25				

Source: Pramodini Pradhan, prepared on 19.2.11 of PUCL Orissa.

mingle with the tribals of south Orissa due to their class affinities. They all are educated in the *bal sangham* run by the party in Chhattisgarh. There are no recognized *bal sanghams* in the study area, recognized in the sense that it is not regular like in other state. But very soon they are going to start some *bal sanghams*. If both the parents are involved in the party, and they have a child the party well taken care of their education and upbringing of the child. Few moves along with the parents do have their names in the school and attend formal schools. The sympathizers who go from outside, their children are also well taken care by the cadres. The rights of the children are respected but they are educated in revolutionary thoughts. The male members well taken care if there are infants in the party during the camps.

Tribals as a Separate Cadre in the Movement Process

The struggle of Indian Maoism which is Naxalism has incepted through tribal peasants, revisited through them, it ongoing through them and blossoming through them. Tribals are the basic emphasizers in the process now. The opinion of the State committee head is given here to understand why tribals are a separate cadre, the basic force of the movement is tribals.

Why tribals as a Separate cadre as the spokesperson of the Orissa State Committee opines.... "The Communist Party in India had its own errors and weaknesses in the past, and before Naxalbari it has never paid any such effort to correct this gaps, which gradually widened among the party members and few turned to be opportunists, few can be called as revisionists and few kept on changing their stands as per the direction of the wind. At the time of Anti British struggle the Communist Party could not form appropriate strategies and tactics for Indian revolution. They tail behind the comprador capitalistic party congress.

The revisionist leaders of Communist Party withdraw Telengana armed struggle to participate in fake parliament. This was the said story in the history of Communist Party. If we see the history of revolutions in the world then we can significantly point on one thing that is wherever the revolution has shown its vigour and played a vital role in radically transforming the society may be the capitalistic revolution in French or England; or this socialist revolution of USSR, now democratic revolution of China and so on, but there the working class, the intellectual, the educated, the middles class came out their niche and contributed fully to the movement, in organizing the people.

As they thought that it is their prime duty and responsibility. The same symptoms were also seen in our country during the Naxalbari phase when thousands workers, poor peasants along with and thousands of students, doctors and elite people joined the movement living their life styles and aristocracy. The basic thrust of the movement was tribals showing resistance.

But the movement had a major setback, and it was retarded like anything for various tactical reasons. But after the grate hindrance that the movement faced again new attempts should have been made to facilitate the process to march ahead. But this didn't happen and it is a big stark reality of the undivided Communist Party in India. The party could not appraised the process during Telengana struggle, it could not learn much from it, and there were still major fragmentations like, the Naxalbari path is not correct; the Charu Mazumdar's way is not applicable, let us leave this path and go in the parliamentary way.

The Ideological Differences

But the fundamental question of Indian revolution was not answered and solved as the movement was not seen as a milestone of the episodic struggles of the undivided Communist Party of our country rather it was just digested as an event. So, Communist Party did not do much about how to keep the struggle in our country, how the revolution will occur here, so many questions were brushed under the carpet. There was no open confrontation, and constructive arguments on this. This question remained as a question. The party always foresighted the movement rather viewed it from an international perspective..., i.e. whether it is catching the fire in Russia or in China. It is good to learn from other solidarity countries but looking at our domestic situation, conditions; how the movement will be carried further no body was alert on such specialties. This is the area where the party lacked in the past. It is not the issue of pro-Russia or pro-China, but how it will be well suited to Indian conditions, that specific circumstances were overlooked or ignored. Rather the party assumed so many things that the ruling class parties will play a role in uprooting the hegemony which was in various forms of capitalism, imperialism, and feudalism. The attack of fascism on Soviet Union and the attack of imperialism on our country, both are most dangerous elements for us, both are to be counter attacked, but the role was limited in this kind of endeavours.

In 1947 Britishers transfer the power to their agent Indian capitalist and land lord classes. The same system continued and the situation prevail the same, colonial India had changed to semi-colony, only the actors on the upper hand changed their appearance. Before it was the whites and later the Indian neo and new born capitalists, those who always wanted to protect the interests of imperialism along with themselves. Here the party could not resonate the struggle. Rather CPI changed its earlier slogan "Ye Ajadi Jhuta Hai" and joined the fake parliament. CPI and after both CPI and CPM had become revisionists. Naxalbari struggle was the first break through in this process. It established the Indian revolutionary path—the protracted people's war. Break the revisionist party and formed the revolutionary party CPI (ML),

- the party of armed struggle, and
- the party of revolution.

The Orissa Scenario in the Past

Though there were struggles for land by tribals, in Gunupur area under the initiative of Biswanath Pattanaik, a Gandhian, but the Congress Party could not en-cash such uprisings. There were many problems which obstructed the struggles in Gunupur area; main reason was the nature of the ruling class during those days. As the same feudal, the elites, the rich constituted the Congress Party and after the independence they captured the power and followed the same path as the Britishers did. And Communist Party could not understood the strategies and tactics, rather was immature do grasp the character of such people.

The movement by Biswanath Pattanaik could not lead anywhere due to

- lack self-commitment and correct ideology, i.e. revolutionary ideology.
- indecisiveness in political thinking and confusion.
- only carried out by emotions which not only necessary, but also dedication and is political guidance essential.
- betrayal to the movement by his Congress Party.

So, the situation remained the same, for the tribals and if you see the whole nation the situation is the same. The poor saw a new face of the exploitation, one set went another few sets emerged. As per the Communist Party assumption that the rulers will take a new role after democratic revolution didn't happen in our country. It did not happen as all the rich had made their strong alliances skilfully to take maximum advantage for their own. Indian democratic revolution is not completed in reality, but the CPI they went to such an extent that in Orissa they took part in the dominion of the Government and 3 MLAs were elected in Orissa. So, the movement has been in a dwindling position. The Telengana movement was suppressed by state repression, and the party did not learn much from it and instead of reviving it, the party was silent and didn't take any action towards any change.

Why did the people revolted in different forms, be it Telengana, be it Gunupur *bhoo-satyagraha*, or be it Srikakulum... as they were in distress; but during those conditions what the party did; it took a completely different role. The state started reforms like *Bhoodan*. The instability of CPI was mainly due to the lack of effective leadership. The people who were leading the movement in those days hadn't the preparedness for such sacrifice for the cause. May be they were intelligent, voracious readers, few were wisdom pools like B.T. Randive, but they were incapable to address the basic question of the people ad revolution. Like which way is to be adopted for revolution in our country was unnoticed.

The Recent Past and Present

Till date the revolution wherever occurred in Capitalistic Countries with some democratic values has shown one in-depth model as insurrection. The rebellion was secret; with few demonstrations, and open platforms, but at the time when the enemy will be in crisis it strikes, at the central place of the enemy and acquire the power, and then spread its wings to countryside.

But how far it applicable to our semi feudal and semi colonial country where there is regional disparity, discrepancy in democratic values, where still people are in the clutches of the landlords with their regional powers centres, where there is rampant corruption in the villages. Where the forest guard and revenue officials everyday torture the common people, where is the democracy that we are dreaming of. Democracy is limited to cities and it is there for the rich people, and not for the poor peasants, *dalits* and tribals. There might be some scope to the small shops that took a demonstration against the reliance outlet, but if they start taking law into their hands, then the state will repeat the same as it did in Kalinganagar and in Maikanch. The scope of democracy has different dimensions and differs from villages and cities.

> *A landlord in the border of Gajapati and Kandhamal district, who had occupied 40 acres of land within a span of two to three decades of his arrival to the village, and he has the power and without his words nothing was possible in the village. After the movement flowed into the village, out of fear he has left the place, but the state is acting as a protector for his property. After he left the police force came to the village and harassed the people like anything, beating them, harassing the women etc. this is not the only incident there are many such incidents of such kind. So, it takes time to prepare the people again to occupy their lands and cultivate. In the initial days he didn't had any land, but later he occupied all the lands by all means. Moreover, the survey systems created a havoc and land and forest became the state property.*

So, what is the role that the state playing, repressing, torturing, with the force of a gun. So, people can't do much before a powerful organized power like state, if they do anything they will face bullets, and will be killed, and they will lose their battle before a gun. As they have witnessed the British smashed the tribals whenever they revolted. So, tribals might not have gone through the literature of Marx and Lenin, but they understood the crux of it out of their experience, so as alternative tribals have to fight and to fight these people also need arms. But also without any preparation also there are uprising today as in POSCO, Singur, in Nandigram, and in Kalinganagar. People are resisting and in front of the state they are also retreating and withdrawing. As the state is having the power of gun.

So, when the people don't have lands, don't have food to eat, there if we preach them to go on rallies and do demonstration peacefully it will definitely not fill their empty stomachs. Even though they fight as per their law, there is no guarantee that they will win, as they will be exploited by the lawyers. So, the present country and whatever is happening now ... here the common poor person can't face the state and there is no possibility to do so.

So, if the common poor think that he will not believe the system, then there should be an alternative before him. Then, if he builds it, then for this system to sustain there is need of arms, as the state is having it. As the power starts from the gun, as the DM and MLAs need guns to protect themselves and their exploitative system, if they don't need those then there would not have been any problem for the poor. They always want to have the security force around them, so, similarly people also need to build a strong army of their own.

When we started the alternative system we started with traditional weapons, but during the process we have acquired so much, and successful in Nayagarh operations. We have increased our area and today the outside world is aware of the DK, few areas those were in DK previously, but now in AOB. Today we have Orissa State committee formed since last 4 years. So, all these happened as people are in everyday struggle. Orissa has the three zones as per the geographical feasibility is OSC, AOB and BOJ. And the part is focusing more expansion to make them as liberated zone.

The Alternative System

When we start working in any area we sow seed which takes it form in the name of Biplabi Chasi Mulia Samiti or Krantikari Kisan Committee. There are so many villages in Orissa where we are working. The alternative system is, the villagers will organize the committee, they take all the decisions relating to the village in the *sabha*, they will derive their livelihood on the resources that are available near them. They will not take any Government assistance neither they will be a part of it. They boycott elections. They will try to resolve all conflicts in the committee. They will protect their natural resources. The development of health, education and various other things will be looked by the committee. But it will take time to liberate all the villages.

- Our village alternative—our village teachers and doctors are the local tribal/*Dalit* youth with a little education. They are not paid, but voluntarily give service to people. We are giving study materials, lamps, medicines etc. People also collect some funds to strengthen this process. Alternate education policy is not sufficiently developed so, they only continuing the general education along with some progressive ideas. Doctors are looking after health and cleanliness of the village, drinking water etc. Fruit cultivation is done along with the villagers. We distribute seeds and plants to villagers. We have initiated cooperatives also developed the agriculture.

The Opportunity Levels in the Villages of Orissa

We have the villages are in different phases of the movement:

- the primary stage where the Kisan committee can be formed and struggles can be initiated, formation of village defence squad,
- then making it an alternative system with the formation of revolutionary people's committee,
- then making it a stable, with army power,
- then making it a base are is another level, and
- then having a base are a and creating more base areas around it at another level.

➢ As per our protracted peoples war first we have to capture the rural backward areas with favourable terrain, and build their the base areas. So far this, we need suitable terrain no matter what ever states or regions to it belong. So, in the interests of such revolutionary process we are forming states/special zones to conduct our activities. In this respect AOB, DK and BJO the three units are working. But after revolution these is no need to form states in this way. If our strategic zones match to nationality areas, then it may happen. Hence, there is no doubt or contradiction for AOB, OSC etc.

➢ Tribals lost their traditional rights on their land, forest and on traditional livelihood since the British rule. In the present semi-colony—semi-feudal rule the condition continues. They are in lack of food, cloths, shelter, medicine, education due to this exploitation. They are in need of revolution for their lost rights and so to save their culture-language-identity. So, they are participating in revolution. At present displacement also hasten this process.

➢ Government reforms satisfy the poor people for a short time. You may satisfy a begger by giving one coin, but the poverty will not disappear. Government reforms are patching the powerless to be our rotten system.

➢ All workers, poor and landless peasants along with middle peasants, middle class such as teachers, students should be our supporters. Tribals, women and *dalits* are our natural ally. Some of this section is misguided by government and ruling class false fabricated propaganda. But all of them will support as the revolution will go ahead.

➢ Our poor strength in Urban, particularly in workers in movement is a great problem. This resulted in shortage in efficient cadre, leaders and logistical supply for protracted people was as well as in weak mass struggles and urban in support of protracted people's war.

- In South Orissa the erstwhile CPI (ML)—People's War DK committee send a batch of cadres to Malkangiri in 1980 and then after the movement developed there. Gradually, this force covered parts of Koraput and Rayagada. Another ML group started working in Rayagada and Gajapati districts in 1995 independently, which later joined with people's war in 1998. Thus, the Basdhara movement (in Rayagada and Gajapati districts) developed as a mass movement and also later started armed struggle. This movement further extended to Phulbai, Ganjam districts which touched up to Nayagarh. At present there is no such liberated zone in Orissa.
- We recruit party cadres from our mass organization and mass movements and also from militia organization and as tirbals are a separate cadre here in the party as they suit all the conditions to become a prospective cadre.

References

1. http:/www,hindustantimes.com, November 22nd, 2010.
2. www.economictimes.com, 17th November, 2010.
3. Galtung, 1971, p. 43.
4. http://cn.wikipedia.org/wiki/Human_rights
5. Panchayti Raj Department, Government of Odisha.
6. *Economic Survey* 2007-08, Government of Odisha.
7. Food Security Atlas of Rural Odisha, p. 15.
8. Party Document of People's War.
9. A case study from, Volume 2, No. 1, January 2001, Peoples March.
10. http://www.achrweb.org/reports/india/AR07/orissa.htm
11. http://www.achrweb.org/reports/india/AR07/orissa.htm)
12. Independent fact finding report by team of individuals during 2000, 2009, 2011.
13. *Ibid.*

9
Psychology of the Tribals in the Process of Involvement

"Science is nothing but Perception." —*Plato*

Tribal Mind, Sentiment and Perception

The earlier chapters have dealt with various issues of support, the reasons of support and other issues. The whole issues of Naxalism have seen different phases of uprising, strong resistance, ideological movement and now a lowering to middle intensity conflict. Sometimes it takes the form of movement through its various outfits and frontal organizations, but again it turns into a conflict contradicting to the present system.

- 65 per cent of the common tribals in the study area and 72 per cent of the passive supports at large cutting across the various sections of the society feel that it only restricts to few patches. In other places they don't indulge in any real work; rather threaten the business class people, and others to give money without any action against the exploiters. This view is quite prevalent and visible among the tribal people in the villages too, along with the towns.
- 47 per cent of the tribals feel that, the political being of tribal is so much in question as their feelings, emotions, attitudes, perceptions are not seen as their expression of outrage, but it is seen as a violent activity. Though the Naxalism has helped them to express their political space, but the overall behaviour is seen as violence. More than 80 per cent of security forces that all tribals in the study area are Naxals, but 20 per cent still feel that Tribals have to awaken themselves for their rights.

Perception generally defined as the way we look at people, accept things, events, and others. This perception helps in building our own self-concept which sometimes becomes a reality which acts as blockage to self-growth. In this way, the perception is connected with reality, beautiful things may be perceived as ugly and *vice versa* basing on the experiences. The experience is again depends on the observation related to the facts that one observes around her or him. In relation to tribals, the observation about the tribulations and facts surrounding them since generations portray their social, economic, political being on the society, their existence their real experiences and how they perceive. This perception event by the tirbals and perceiving the outsiders has evolved a stronger feeling among them. 80 per cent of the tribals feel that the outsiders are exploiters. This perception in turn creating a specific pattern of behaviour reflecting either through silence or through violence, and later by participating in the Naxalite process to assert their rights.

The perception inbuilt that they are voiceless so far has been a collective behaviour. Not only Naxalism, other spontaneous democratic movements are growing in the universe. The Mahendragiri Adivasi Movement in Mohana block of Gajapati district, the Chasi Mulia Adivasi Sangha in Narayanpatna, the guerrilla vahini in the border of Ganjam and Gajapati are of various forms of the visible perceptions.

- Over 70 per cent of the tribals in the study area strongly perceive that the Naxal cadres are only doing some work for the tribals, even though they are totally against the violent means.
- 57 per cent of tribals opine that whatever they have accumulated in their perceptions has taken them into and a stage that, where they have a vacuum and confusion. There are questions in the mind that if they join with the collective acting will it benefit them or not. So, revenge, warfare, taking acting through weapon is different notion of mind.
- It is obvious that many go to the movement and do come back leaving that. 20 per cent of the tribal youth cadre have returned to their original lives. One case was found who is in jail in the study area has surrendered as he didn't like the way. He didn't like the approach of Naxals as they want to treat all members of the village equally in terms of wealth. They don't acknowledge a person who has wealth and has genuinely accumulated it. They feel that all rich people who have money might have adopted illegal means which is not necessarily all the time true.

The mind is a result of many actions and reactions. It is the main section, on the basis of which the human behaviours which teaches the ways of survival, to preserve himself or herself and its own species too. More than 61 per cent of tribals feel that today their identity is at stake as their interests are not protected; their political space is squeezed by tagging them with a label of Naxalite. Their culture is lost by displacement from their own lands; all these factors have created certain images on the system. Though they know this will not give answer immediately but feel that this is the only option. The mimetic desire (sharing other's image) of holding a gun to show power and being powerful is another major behavioural change. They have always been scared for gun, so, when they hold a gun, along with their perceptions there is a sudden reaction to take revenge.

The perception was further explored on the various behaviours that they carrying with them as a mental baggage. The respondents were asked about their likings, and whom they see as their main blockage. The following table explains the disliking and their reason to revenge on them.

Table 9.1: Respondents disliking on the exploiting groups

Sl. No.	*Communities*	*To whom he or she dislikes (%)*		
		Moneylenders	*Government officials*	*Others*
1.	ST	27.36	22.64	26.42
2.	SC	4.72	5.66	6.60
3.	Others	0.94	4.72	0.94
	Total	33.02	33.02	33.96

27.36 per cent of tribals do not like moneylenders, government officials because they criticize tribal culture, exploit them do not help them. This process of hatredness continues in their generations some through direct experience and some through indirect experience. So, even though there is some good character persons from these sections still he or she is viewed with the previous experiences where genuinely is lost. The main reasons behind is bribe and exploitation for land.

> *The conflict as seen by one of the respondent in a remote village of Malkangiri is the state has built dams, and utilized power and didn't bother about the tribals at all, it is our goodness that we didn't react so many days. We observed the state and its*

> *officials to come and at least listen to our grievances and believe them. But the nature of the state towards the tribals is always apathetic. Every tribal is a Naxalite. Now, the tribals are only kept in the streets of the city like Bhubaneswar and in the museums. As they won't be any more in the forests. The companies will take the forests, rest who will remain be branded as Naxalites, and rest who survive has to work as labourers in the upcoming cities. And a major chunk that will be the agents of the state and be appointed as special police officers will kill their own clan members. The whole tactics of the state to displace forcefully alienate the tribals from their own land and forest. So, that it can be catered to the needs of the corporate world. The land can be given to the multinationals at wholesale price. This struggle is not the CPI (Maoist) party's, but it's the conflict for our resources, for our land, and for our identity. We are not like animals that will be always sacrificed for the sake of development of others.*

In 1960s, Johan Galtung proposed a model of conflict that consists of both symmetric and asymmetric relations, as shown in diagram below, that conflict can be seen as a triangle where C (contradiction), A (attitude) and B (behaviour). The C (contradiction) here means the fundamental or the basic conflict situation, and includes the actual and the perceived incompatibility of goals between the two conflicting parties.[1] In case of the Naxalite movement the two parties are the state on one hand and the Naxalite on the other. This can be shown in the following diagram in the study area:

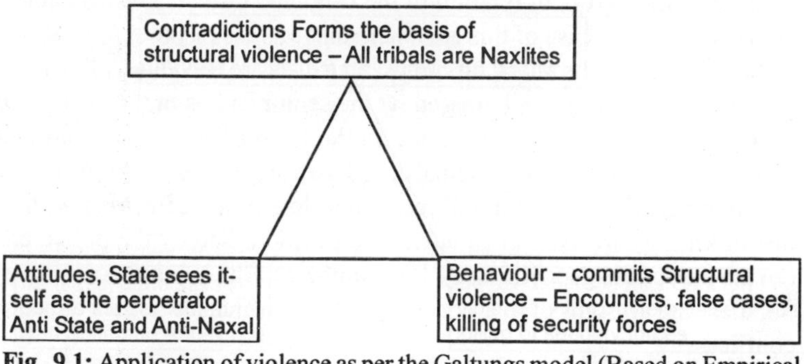

Fig. 9.1: Application of violence as per the Galtungs model (Based on Empirical data)

Attitudes include the way of accepting each other, between the two parties, the perceptions, or one can say the impression on each other, the misperceptions on each other. After they develop these impressions they incline or likely develop a stereotype or labelling on each other. These attitudes are influenced by fear, anger, or hate redness. Each party has their own set of attitudes towards the other. One has to analyse these aspects to understand the sources of conflict. This becomes very significant when the conflict is the violent one. In Naxal conflict the two parties have their own set understanding on each other, and they label each other in the same way. So, as per the state certain people holding certain kind of traits can be labeled as Naxalites as per their profile, and for the Naxalites certain people who confront with them with a gun, are organs of the state that has to be annihilated. "Prof. Hargopal who has been mediated in case of emergency abduction by the Naxals since 1993 has of opinion that the government is changes its interest as per their requirement. In this conflicting situation it is difficult on both sides to completely eliminate each other. Though the security forces will create a war like situation and may suppress the movement for some time, but it won't be able to answer the questions raised by the naxals."[2]

The bahaviour can be cooperative and can also be non-cooperative. In any conflict where violence is included it can start from threats to coercion, attacks, on each other. ABC constantly influences each other and they also change over period of time. As this triangle is very dynamic the conflict is seen in their manifestations, the clash of interests is seen more visibly and they develop a particular kind of behaviour. The parties do organize around this interests and the conflict starts to grow and spreads its magnitude. In this process of conflict growing, there are some secondary conflicts which grow in relation to the original conflict. The secondary conflict as seen in case of this Naxalism that there are a pattern of stories that one hears like the attack on camps, all tribals are Naxalites, all women who are surrendering are harassed by the senior cadres in the camp. So, these are certain patterns which are in the form of secondary conflicts which will only intense the original one. There are also few patterns which are shown by the direct and indirect supporters of the CPI (Maoist) that the all killings are false encounters, the people killed by the police are not the part of the guerrilla army, but members of the cultural committee. So, these are all signs of the secondary conflict which intensifies the core conflict.

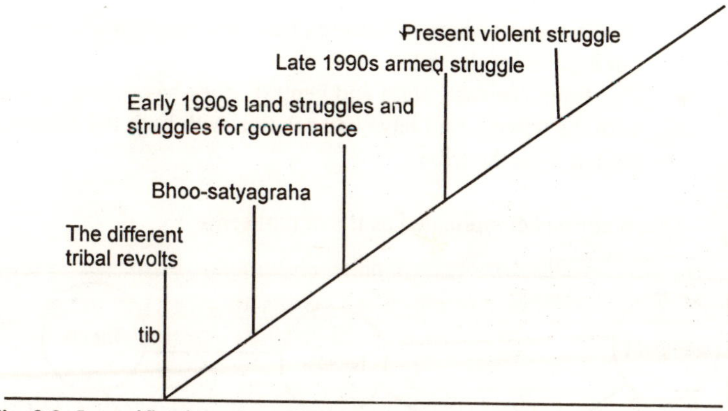

Fig. 9.2: Intensification of conflict in the universe of study

The diagram (Fig. 9.2) showing the different stages of the conflict of the Naxal movement and conflict in the study area: how the conflict increased unless there are some genuine attempts by the government and the Naxalites, then it is not going to decrease. Other theories do articulate that there has been different styles between the two parties,

(a) (where there is a high concern for self and low concern for others).
(b) Balancing between the two which is compromising.
(c) A problem solving mode where there is high regard for both.

From this above three styles till date it has always followed the 1st, if we see the different actors in while mapping this conflict, then we can see the following picture emerging out of it, where two same lines indicate strong bonding, the bigger the size the more the power it has, the spiral notion includes the relationship not so strong and not so weak. The line with a break-up mark shows that they don't have good relation. Now as per the picture, the conflict mapping can be shown as follows in the study area:

- We can see the government with more power with a big circle, and the Naxals with lesser power and the relationship is not good.
- Whereas the relationship between the Naxals and tribals are well bonded though they know it will not give them any answer.

- Media is somewhere in between has some relation with anyone but is far from the tribals.
- The force (private, state and central) does have good relation with the tribals. And have bad relation with both the Naxals as well as with the tribals.

This picture is complicated as it's in real sense.

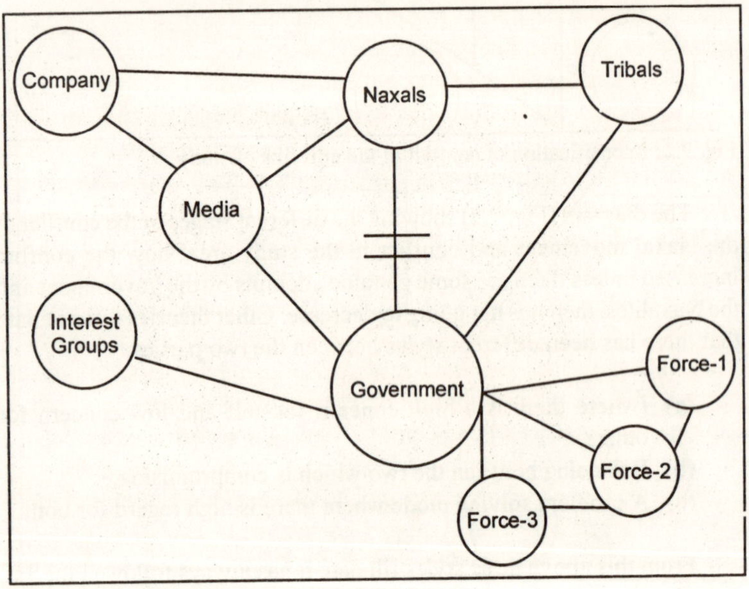

Fig. 9.3: Naxalite movement—mapping of actors

So, this is the situation that is persisting in south Orissa, where though the development has happened, but it has kept a major chunk of people in dark. The stage from *Bhoo-satyagraha* to this stage of conflict it has travelled a long path. The tribals do know that this is not the answer and if there is anything then the time has not come. But there are opportunities for peace building which is tricky, but achievable. There can be many more parties here which are associated with the Naxalism directly or indirectly, but the main parties are shown in the study area.

Non-participant Support from Outside

The Naxalite movement does get a lot of support from outside. The people who share the same psychology with the Naxals, who have been in the movement in the past, or who face the same issues like them. These are the three categories that help them. These support come as part time support mostly. As per the constitution of the CPI (Maoist) there are some part-time members in the party. In fact there are many who support by being non-participant. Such as from media, from legal side, from various informed organizations at the state and national level; right based organizations working at the national level, individuals with recognition and with certain stature in the society who the system can not easily put behind bars. There are many sympathizers sections and it is difficult to ascertain any statistics on them. Few sympathizers are also with the present government system, but sympathize a lot with Naxalism. It is difficult to find out their exact location, number and their occupation. But majority are there from coastal Orissa, eastern part of India, even few are from South Asia and UK based. When the respondents asked about their non-participant support, there was a clean answer that

- 10 per cent of them would give straight support in terms of various support systems.
- 20 per cent create solidarity support for the party.
- 19 per cent support them with cash and kind.
- 23 per cent defend them in various alternative media.
- 40 per cent of them simple know that the naxals are for a cause and hot a terrorist organizations.
- They have a large support from all other Maoist-Lenin (ML) groups working with trade unions, peasants, farmers, in the urban slums, and various other organizations. But as far as its sharing is concerned they are very secretive. They say that there are lot of people who support them from cities like Bhubaneswar and Puri etc. But they do not know them. But one thing is very clear that these are quite influential people whom the state will not have the doubt on them.

Financial Commitments and Benefits

Our honourable Prime Minister is restating always that the left wing extremisms in the form of Naxalism and Maoism is increasing every year. A notable media report considers the budget of CPI Maoist to be Rs. 2500 crore per year. There were many official assessments regarding the amount of the Maoist funds in 2009, including that of the Home Secretary Mr. G.K.

Pillai, who speculated it to be around Rs. 1,400 crore. The Chhattisgarh DGP, Mr. Vishwaranjan states that the Maoist funds may be a minimum of Rs. 2,000 crore, where extortion being the major source.[3]

Addressing a big public meeting in Orissa one of the tribal activists has openly said that the CPI (Maoist) has taken 50 lakh rupees from the mines around the Orissa and Jharkhand borders and very soon they will also demand money in the Koraput region mines. Though they have started it from few companies in Malkangiri. Many of the arrested central committee members do opine that they get huge money from levies, taxes and extortion. It can't be calculated in the study area, as no one shares how much they give to the naxal movement. The Panchayati Raj institution (PRI) do give in the form of kind like materials for tea making, the solar lights, rice which can obtained in the name of fake cards. But one of the *sarpanch* said with fear that the areas which are under their control or indirectly they influence all the *Gram Panchayat* elected members do give Rs. 2000 monthly. Apart from this, the shops and other business class people do give money quarterly. The big shop owners, hotels, bus owners do give money to the party. Rest of the sympathizers collect money from the cities like Bhubaneswar, Cuttack, Puri and in other places. There is as such no commitment, but there is a benefit attached to it. It is found that nearly 30 per cent of the tribals as they get some benefit in terms of money.

The CPI Maoist party always to collect money from all sources including NGOs off late. They recruit the grassroots cadre and give them a salary of Rs. 3000 monthly. This is another way to get employment by joining the movement. It is also true that the 15 to 20 per cent of the money collected by the party cadres don't reach the central committee people. During March to May the couples who surrendered before the Rayagada police took Rs. 25000 which was the part of the collection. In return the female complained about the sexual harassment in the camp.

- While interviewing the respondents almost 85 per cent of them didn't say anything when asked about the financial gain.
- 65 per cent did say that they receive rice and other grain from the villagers on yearly basis which will be around 25 kg per village.
- Almost all more than 90 per cent of the respondents receive salary, minimum for their legal cases if they are behind jails.
- The old members and who have worked for more years do get some benefit like medical care in case of emergency to their family members.

Ultimate Gain by Participation/Moral Support

The gain from this movement is unknown to most of the respondents. This movement has given some sporadic success, but nothing concrete as aspired by the tribals. But this is a way to put pressure on the government that is very clear. The following Table 9.2 has explained their way to achieve through this movement.

Table 9.2: The Respondents' Aspirations

Sl. No.	Communities	Their aspiration (%)			
		Change system	Make people aware	Plan and prepare for the future	Others
1.	ST	31.91	22.13	18.03	10.66
2.	SC	5.74	2.46	0.82	0.82
3.	Others	2.46	3.28	—	1.64
	Total	40.11	27.87	18.85	13.12

Table 9.2 shows that though violence is not the end but so far it has been a means for all the contradictions for conflict of interests which has occurred. These contradictions have created certain attitudes which has channelized in certain patterns of behaviour. As 31.91 per cent feel that this will change the system ultimately, 22.13 per cent tribals this is a way to make the people aware for mass mobilization of tribals including the oppressed the mass. 18.03 per cent feel that it is a platform to plan and prepare the mass for future revolution. As revolution does not occur overnight. 10.66 per cent of tribals feel that this is a way of expression of the discontent. The resistance is shown by the tribal as captured by the media is given on page 275.

Thought the ultimate gain is nothing so strongly visible by the respondents, but they are joining as a last resort, to get some benefit, to get justice, as an alternative, as a means to raise voice, under compulsion and fear. So, there are multiple aspects involved in the gain side. There are movements without the Naxal support which have come well in the universe.

If we see why the tribals enter into such violent Naxalism knowingly that these way will not be going to give them full justice rather a temporary relief. The two incidents where the directions of the people and the state are completely different and whoever has hoisted their voice against the injustice have ended up joining Naxalism.

ଆରଏସ୍‌ବି ଜନଶୁଣାଣିରେ ହଙ୍ଗାମା

ପ୍ରକଳ୍ପକୁ ତୀବ୍ର ବିରୋଧ, ଉତ୍ତ୍ୟକ୍ତ ଗ୍ରାମବାସୀ ଟେଣ୍ଟ ଭାଂଗିଦେଲେ

Public Hearing Held by RSB Company where agitated tribals damaged the tent
Source: Dharitree, 27th Oct., 2007.

ବିଶାଳ ସମାବେଶରେ ଯୋଗଦେଲେ ନାଚିକା

ଜେଲରେ ଥିବା ଆଦିବାସୀଙ୍କୁ ତୁରନ୍ତ ଖଲାସ କର

The tribal leader of Koraput district Nachika Linga joined public gathering
Source: Sambad 29th April, 2012.

The bright example is Nachika Linga (as shown in the media cuttings above) and the present conflict between the RSB Company and the tribals of Serigumma in Rayagada. These Serigumma village people will also follow the path of the once open leader Nachika Linga now a forced Naxal. He appears only during the mass meetings and he has done 3 to 4 times since November 2009. He is the most wanted for the state and has taken the shelter of Naxalism. He is well aware that if he is going to be over ground he will be killed without arrest. This is the main research perspective. So, how do we break such patterns of perception on both the sides is a debatable.

Tribal and Non-tribal Psychological Perception—A Comparison

The perception of the tribals and non-tribals is a very tricky thing to explore. The Naxalism has created different waves in different minds. Be it a villager in a tribal village or be it a tribal political leader or tribal participating in Naxalism. Similarly, the way the non-tribals have accepted differs from the background of the respondent. The main striking difference between the tribals and non-tribals is

- Non-tribals do not face the situation directly and their perceptions are often created by media as shown in table down....

Table 9.3: Perceptions of Non-tribals

Sl. No.	*Responses*	*%age*
1.	Media gives a glance	2.6
2.	Not much as they are basically organs of Indian bourgeoisie and give a distorted picture	5.2
3.	Different papers give different versions	3.9
4.	Media coverage is not much on the movement	15.6
5.	It gives many events, but how far its true can't be ascertained	5.2
6.	From interactions with media personnel and also with the villagers	1.3
7.	It gives instances	14.3
8.	Media is doing a good job in highlighting the issues	9.1
9.	No comments	14.3
10.	No idea about media as no access to newspapers and other sources	10.3
11.	Media's role is not so effective	10.3
12.	Media blames the forces and but it should understand their condition also	2.05

Twelve per cent of the people do feel that there is not much coverage by the media and they only highlight the events and nothing else. The events do tell them that this ism is violent and they do everything for money and there is no ideology. 78 per cent of non-tribals feel that there is no ideology with them. But this 78 per cent does strongly feel that they should target the high profile business men and political leaders instead of the people at the grassroots who are killed in the name of police informers. Two contractors were killed in Malkangiri and Koraput during 2009 and 2010. These two were rich and the nearby non-tribals also expressed some silent satisfaction over their killing. The contractor in Malkangiri was harassing the tribal's girls and was involved in more corruption of money. So, it is a mixed reaction from the non-tribals depending on the facts and events what is happening. The tribals (as they feel and seen) are basically organs of the bourgeoisie Indian socio-political system and they cannot pen down what they want. They do give distorted pictures of the whole issue. But 7 per cent on the contrary do say that media is doing a good job highlighting the issues of the Naxals, and due to this the government is vigilant in taking some actions and trying to reach the remote areas which previously they were not doing at all. So, it has helped the people to get some relief and their entitlements. Interestingly 11 per cent of the people do not want to comment at all on the Media's role, as they fear that it would have a negative impact on them. The people do not have an access to the newpapers, of course, does not have any idea what media does to their issues and how they link their issues to the Naxal movement.

When asked about their thinking whether this is the right path or not their responses were also mixed as shown in Table 9.4.

Twenty four per cent of the respondents do feel that this is required for our country and rest 30 per cent of the people in some or the other do show their support for the movement and affinity. They feel that this is the best strategy for the present time. And hope that this will increase, but on the whole the opinion is very strong that there is a necessity of some kind of revolution which should be ultimatum. 18 per cent of the people also feel that this is not the right path. Few also opine that the tribals are arrested in the name of being Naxal activists without sufficient evidence, for example, 18 tribal people who were arrested during February 2004 at Malkangiri while they were returning after attending an open convention in Bhubaneswar (called Janagarjan Samabesa). Later, they were released in groups of 5 and 7 after more than couple of months. In one such incident in Malkangiri two tribals were arrested (one female and male) and later

Table 9.4: Opinion on the Naxal Path

Sl. No.	*Responses*	*Number and Percentage*
1.	Due to the LPG the gap between the rich and poor is more, so unless there is a revolution nothing is going to change	1 (1.4)
2.	Violence is an effective weapon for radical changes	1 (1.4)
3.	Revolution but without arms	1 (1.4)
4.	Violence is not the way	2 (2.7)
5.	It is time for triblas to stand and be counted	1 (1.4)
6.	It is not, but they have met the aspirations of the tribals to some extent	1 (1.4)
7.	To some extent tribals get moral encouragement	3 (4.1)
8.	Yes	24 (32.4)
9.	No	18 (24.3)
10.	To some extent, it is the right path as this is a social problem	7 (9.5)
11.	No idea	3 (4.1)
12.	That is the ultimatum	6 (8.1)
13.	Right or wrong it suits the condition	3 (4.1)
14.	Revolution is necessary may be or may not through Naxalism	2 (2.7)
15.	It is good as an opposition	1 (1.4)
16.	There should be class annihilation and not person annihilation	1 (1.4)

they were released due to lack on evidence. So, it is in the air with the non-tribal people that the Naxals cannot be found guilty and accused. As no one will give the evidence. They have to be killed or else released after few years in jail.

When it was asked to understand a deeper perspective from the non-tribals on the rate of success by this path the reactions were as given in Table 9.5.

Eleven per cent of the respondents feel that there will be no success at all through this kind of endeavours as most of the time they are engaging in a fight or war with the state and doing very little to sustain their peoples base. Their mass mobilization aspect is completely lost fighting a war with the state. And 7 per cent do not want to comment on the said issue and 3 per cent could not say anything on the issue. But nearly 40 per cent of the people feel that, there is success in this way may be sporadic, late and very little, but that is the only option as it adds to the experience of the class struggle, very logical and it is going to become a science one day in the form of action and reaction. The movement is empowering the people and giving an option to them to raise their issues. But they have their conflict with the police because of many reasons as shown in Table 9.5.

Table 9.5: Opinion on Rate of Success

Sl. No.	Responses	%age
1.	Can not say	3.9
2.	It adds to the experience of class struggle	1.3
3.	May sporadic success	1.3
4.	Movement is certainly empowering the poor sections like tribals	1.3
5.	To some extent they are successful	13.2
6.	It checks the corruption	5.3
7.	To some extent but it's not possible for them to fight against the powerful state	1.3
8.	Yes	9.2
9.	No	14.5
10.	Late success	17.1
11.	Very little success	1.3
12.	There will be success	5.3
13.	Will be success provided they have good leadership	3.9
14.	This is the only option today for the poor	5.3
15.	Can't be determined	1.3
16.	The movement has been able to teach the tribals what's wrong and right	5.3
17.	No comments	9.2

The perception of the tribals over Naxalism is also very difficult to understand due to the following data from the study area:

- 90 per cent of the tribals have accepted that the Naxals do some good for the tribals.
- And more than 70 per cent of the tribals do have a heart for them as they take their agenda.
- 45 per cent of the tribals in the area where the Naxals are intervening do attend meetings, carry their load, supply the materials as agents and engaged in directly or indirectly against their wish.
- More than 60 per cent do not show any reaction in the affected villages, as they feel nothing is going to change their situation.
- 77 per cent of them do feel strongly that they are not taking up their issues and have nexus with them. As the villagers cannot question them in the meetings (as observed) and will have to be patient listeners and observers in the study area.
- Many tribal youth who are engaged in some developmental activity are forces by the Naxals to join the conflict (almost 40%). And these youth don't like due to their adopted ways does not suit them.

- The tribals do feel that the naxal activists (whether tribals or non-tribals) when arrested can't be proved their offence, so, the cases will be delayed as no one will give the witness. Either they will be killed or the police can holdup the case for several years. The incidents are true, the people participated in are also arrested but the link can't be established which is well-known to the tribal Naxal activists and also to the police force.

References

1. *Contemporary Conflict Resolution*, pp. 9-10. Party document of Chasi Mulia Adivasi Sangha.
2. *Jantantra*, Vol. 11, issue 2, July 1-15th, 2012.
3. http://www.vifindia.org/article/2011/january/14/Maoist-Funding-Dimensions-Sources-and-Implications

10
The Surrender Scenario

"Strength does not come from winning. Your struggles develop your strengths. When you go through hardships and decide not to surrender, that is strength." —*Arnold Schwarzenegger*

In this chapter, I have explained the surrender scenario, and few case studies. These facts basing one the newspapers and a very little data from the field is included here.

The Wikipedia defines surrender when soldiers stop fighting and eventually become the war prisoners, either as individuals or if they are ordered by the higher authorities. This surrender can be conditional (when the surrendering party agrees to do so, if the other party agrees to certain conditions and makes promises) and unconditional (when the victor party makes no promises other than which is allowed by the laws). So, it is understood any war or conflict is between two parties, where one becomes powerful and the other with less power. If apply the same definition to the naxalite situation, then the two most important parties are the government and the Naxalite. However, it is very tricky to highlight certain reflection here that:

- Does government views the situation as a war?
- Does this is the only question of internal security of something more than that?
- As its time and again stated that Naxalites are fighting for capture power starting from the peripheral areas and finally to the centre.
- As per the definition of the Wikipedia can it be considered the government to be the victor and the Naxalites as war (conflict) crimes?
- Is government agreeing to any conditions or promising before the Naxals surrender?

- The very premise (the introduction of the surrender policy) stand that the Naxalite violent situation has arisen out of age long neglect, deprivation and discontent toward the subjugated sections of our society, for which they are adopting violence. And the policy is aiming at offer them gainful employment and entrepreneurial opportunities, so that, they can join the mainstream. Having said this, the policy also advocates that this not only a policy for employment but evolved as a means of multipronged conflict resolution and management strategy. Is it the conveying the same meaning that the word conflict resolution has been described, discussed so far?
- Are Naxalites are going for violence only employment and entrepreneurial opportunities ? As the Naxals (the ground data indicates, more than 50 per cent who are underground) strongly feel that though they want to disown violence but the goals that they are fighting for is not manifested in the policy.

These are few questions that the research encountered in the study area. This question evolved as a part of the research.

The Surrender Policy

The Chief Minister of Odisha, Shri Naveen Pattnaik (during 2011) articulated in the state assembly answering to a question that 178 Naxal have surrendered before Police from the year 2001 to 2010. According to the surrender and settlement policy 2006 of the State government, action is being taken for their settlement. He also spoke that 145 Naxal related violence has occurred during the year 2010-11 up to the month of January and 260 incidents of violence occurred in past three years. Naxal activities noticed in 99 Police Stations in 19 districts of the state. Answering to a question of the Upper House (Rajya Sabha) the Minister of State in the Union Ministry of Home Affairs Shri Ajay Makan supplied the facts regarding the surrendering of Naxals in India. The basic objectives of these Guidelines for surrender-*cum*-rehabilitation of Naxalites in the Naxal affected States are by Government of India has the following imbibed:

(i) to wean away the misguided youth and hard-core Naxalites who have strayed into the fold of Naxal movement and now find themselves trapped into that net; and

(ii) to ensure that the Naxalites who surrender do not find it attractive to join the naxal movement again.

The eligibility criteria to surrender, anyone who surrenders with or without arms and it will be scrutinized by the Screening-*cum*-Rehabilitation Committee constituted by the concerned State Government, and if anyone is benefited earlier by the same policy will not be considered for further assistance. Government of India has approved guidelines which is revised, and says for an immediate grant of Rs. 1.5 lakh (kept in the bank in the name of the surrendered person and may be withdrawn after 3 years certified by an authorized authority) and Rs. 2000 (for a maximum of 36 months, if he or she gets a gainful employment then this will be discontinued) will be given to them for three years, along with that vocational training and incentives for surrender of weapons will be given too. The policy has clear specifications about the incentives of the weapons if anyone wants to surrender with arms. A Naxalite can surrender before any nodal officer (who is to identify and rehabilitate them) as designated by the State administration/Police administration, Central Para Military Force, ADG/IG or special branch officers. Screening of the surrender Naxal includes, that he or she is a hard core Naxal, (as over ground sympathizes and supporters are considered as exception cases), he or she is genuine Naxal, in the sense he or she should be make a clear confession about the incidents, financers, name of the organizations which will be verified. Serious crimes committed by the surrendered Naxals will continue in court and minor offences can be negotiated at the discretionary powers of the person assigned by the state authority.[1]

Table 10.1 shows the details of the surrender up to 25th November, 2010.

The List of Surrender in Orissa during last 2 Years

- Tukuna Badara *alias* Rakesh (20) and Sutuni Jamuda *alias* Maduri (15) of Baligotha village under Kalinga Nagar division surrendered.
- Three from Rayagada districts, Chandrapur division have surrendered. Trinath Shrambutika and Prakash Kimbaka.
- Savita Munda (20) Keonjhar who surrendered alleged that she was subjected to harassment.
- In March 16, 2010 Naxalites surrendered of Bansdhara divisional

Table 10.1: The State-wise details of Naxals surrendered in 2009 and 2010

State	Naxals Surrendered	
	2009	*2010 (up to 25 November)*
Andhra Pradesh	89	129
Bihar	16	13
Chhattisgarh	16	05
Jharkhand	8	20
Madhya Pradesh	1	02
Maharashtra	8	19
Orissa	10	46
Uttar Pradesh	01	00
West Bengal	0	06
Others	01	04
Total	150	244

Source: www. Satp.org.

committee Gajapati, Palekhmundi between 18 to 35 years of age.

- Jayob Majhi of Raigonda village under Adaba Police Station surrendered.
- Maoist couple from Kalinganar division surrendered during March 2010, namely Mamina Munda (18) and Mataram Munda (20).
- During February 2010 three in Kandhamal surrendered from Bansdhara division, namely Lodi Mondal, Binayak and Bishnu.
- On 23rd July, 2009, Dhasu (19) *alias* Surendra under Bissamcuttack Police Station and Rupi Pidikaka (18).
- Ghasiram Majhi and Jharana Majhi in July 2011.
- Akash during 2011 in Rayagada.
- Azad a top leader who worked for 15 years with the party surrendered last year.[2]

Why Surrender?

There are lot of speculations on the issue of surrender that is why the naxals even after being underground for more than 10 to 15 years they going for surrendering or giving away the arms. Recent media hype on surrender has brought much interest among the common people to know more about this.

Sabita Munda, a tribal girl from Orissa's Keonjhar district, was 16 when she surrendered before the district police. Sabita had been at several naxal camps and had taken part in many violent attacks on the Orissa police. She says she was exploited at the Naxal camps and that when she heard of the Orissa government's surrender policy she thought it was her chance of a better life. But more than a year since she surrendered, Sabita is still waiting for the promised benefits.

Sabita says, "We are put in this small room and are told to just eat and kill time. We are basically labourers. We want to earn a living. The house, livelihood and pension that was promised to us by the government while surrendering, has never reached us. We simply want to leave this place."[3]

The question why to surrender has many aspects and each case is different. One of the leader who was caught last year in Koraput district (Semeliguda block) his wife was facing some gynaecological problem and she negotiated with the Communist Party of India (Maoist) to go for giving up arms. It was difficult for her to work in the forests. This is one unique case where the CPI (Maoist) itself allowed its cadre to go for surrender showing sensitivity towards the female cadres.

If we see the ground data, nearly 30 per cent of the members go for surrender because they cannot survive in the hardest conditions of the forest.

Thirty per cent do want to extend their families and settle and they go opt for surrender.

Off late, a new trend has been seen in the CPI (Maoist) that many are entering to the party as stated in the earlier chapters where they only see that they can get some benefit for self from the party. As its open and many go with their self and ulterior motives. They do act as per their own interests (which do not match the ideology of the party) by not in coordination with their high commands. As it is seen in the killing of Swami Laxamanananda Saraswati. So, there is a lot of ego clash between the party itself. The party is going under a severe leadership crisis. 20 per cent of the Naxals who have been working with the party for a long time do surrender because of this leadership fights.

But 30 per cent who surrender as they feel that this path cannot give any justice though the ideology is good.

Many Naxals (at least 3 to 4 of them in the study area) have collected money and later flee from party to surrender.

Looking at the media reports and the ground data it can be said that there are various reasons that cadres to surrender. One of the girls Rani (name changed) who surrendered from Rayagada district, the media highlighted that she was sexually harassed by her seniors in the camp. When an independent fact finding team from different civil liberty groups met her and enquired she said, she is not aware of the facts what the media has so far shown. She also mentioned that she does not know the person who blamed to supply girls to different Naxal high cadres. But after she expressed her view to the fact finding team, on retaliation the police picked her brother for no reason. After this incident none of her family member wanted to speak.

It is true in one case in Jharkhand that a girl was raped with whom she was having an affair when she is used to work for the party, but when she left the party for personal reason, she was raped. One of the person who was killed in the Basangmali encounter in Rayagada district was not armed cadre but was a mobilizer. He was new to the party and worked for only for a year. In fact he wanted to come out of the party (as he was not satisfied with the behaviour of others), but he was killed unfortunately. There have been lot of allegations on sexual harassment to female cadres in the party as shown in the media, and after the female members have open a complaint was also filed with the State Women's Commission Orissa, to probe. So far the Women's Commission has not arrived on any concrete outcome. The research could not get any data on the issues of sexual harassment, but many do surrender after they want to engage in affair and other biological activities.

Different Voices on Surrender

The surrender policy for the naxals by different State Government and by the Government of India, Ministry of Home Affairs is a well thought approach to bring them back to track so that they can get an direction. But, how far it has acted in the real sense that cannot be measured as of now. It is too early to come for a conclusion as this policies are very new and not been matured to such an extent where it can get the attention of the underground cadres. But many people have different opinions on the same issue.

Shri Dandapani Mohanty (Convener of Jan Manch, who was the interlocutor during kidnapping the Malkangiri Collector in February 2011, he is also labelled as the over ground Naxalite and a sympathizer of Maoists) condemned the media reporting on sexual harassments. He said the police is forcing the female cadres to say so before the media on gun point. If they will not say then their families will be tortured. This is all done by the media in nexus with the security forces of the government. Having said that he also expressed that let the Women's Commission probe into the matter, as we all respect the Commission. But, he did vouch on some of the factors that the research has found out on surrender.

"Police sources say that there are several cadres in the Naxal camp especially women who are allegedly exploited and are willing to surrender. But, if the fate of the Naxals who have already surrendered is not very encouraging the rest might hardly find any motivation to do the same."[4]

The Naxal leaders active in the region have rejected the government's Surrender Policy outright, calling it a complete sham. According to Suresh, a senior Naxal commander who operates in the forests in North Gadchiroli, bordering Chhattisgarh, the government's offer has no substance. Speaking to *Tehelka*, he described the surrendered Naxals as "fringe elements". Suresh describes himself as the "in-charge of the Kobhra Mendha squad, Uttar Gadchiroli, Regional Gondia Division." "The government says that 90 Maoists have surrendered. However, they are not the hardcore Naxals. They are mostly porters or innocent villagers who sympathise with us. Only a couple of real Naxals have surrendered, that too because they could not bear the hardships of forest life. The police have been unable to make the top commanders surrender," he says, "While the government is spending millions of rupees to quell the uprising, the (police) forces are unable to locate us. Rather, they are committing atrocities on innocent cattle grazers, labelling them Naxals. Recently, three women were kidnapped in Tipagarh forests in Dhanora taluka in Gadchiroli. They were later raped and shot at. While two died on the spot, one was seriously injured," Suresh says, "We are Maoists, fighting for the right of these oppressed people. It is the politicians who are the real terrorists. Not us. We are revolutionaries. In the name of globalisation and development, companies are on a land-grabbing spree, leaving the poor farmers helpless. When they rightfully demand their rights, they are either lathicharged or shot at"[5].

Seven surrendered young Naxals have been forced to live in the police quarter for the last one year. 24-year old Suresh Sundhi was a hardcore Naxal. After surrendering, Suresh shared vital intelligence with the police which led to the arrest of several naxals. Now, Suresh is in the hit list of the Naxals. Suresh feels betrayed as he can neither return to his village because of the threat to his life nor has he got any of the benefits of the surrender policy. Suresh says, "I know that there are many Naxals like me who are in the camp and want to surrender. But when they see that we are treated like this and the promises are not kept, I do not think they would think of that option anymore."[6] On the same issue the Superintendent of Police of Keonjhar SP, Ashish Kumar Singh says, "We have to verify their criminal record which is a time taking process."

The different opinion on surrender has catched the attention of many stakeholders who are involved directly or indirectly in the Naxalite situation (conflict) as shown in the conflict mapping in the earlier chapter. But this is a one step towards peace making.

References

1. www.mha_nic.in
2. naxalblogsopt.com and other primary sources.
3. www. Ibnlive.com/news/Orissa, posted by Jajati Karan, January 4th, 2011.
4. www. Ibnlive.com/news/Orissa, post by Jajati Karan, 4th January, 2011.
5. *www.tehelka.com*, 21 January 2012, *State vs. naxals*, revolution interrupted.
6. www. Ibnlive.com/news/Orissa, posted by Jajati Karan, 4th January, 2011)

11
The Solution
Possible and Not Possible

"A perfection of means, and confusion of aims, seems to be our main problem." —*Albert Einstein*

Gaps between Initial Ideology and Present State of Affairs

The solution of Naxal Movement is based here on respondents from the field data basing on their fear, their expectations and on their future prospects. The empirical data from the field as depicted in the previous chapters clearly show certain trend as follows:

- Despite the blasts, ambush, killing by the Naxals the pace of the movement in not the same in all the places as variations witnessed in the study area.
- In many areas it is found that few of the activists are withdrawing from the underground fold due to many factors. One of the important factors remains the ideology dilution by the leaders.
- It is also witnessed in the recent past that the revolutionary party is undergoing a tremendous tussle for their own actions.
- Time and again the Secretary of Orissa State Committee has raised the issues over killings of innocents, killing of religious leaders, and killing of security forces. "He is been questioning that their main ideology is been thinned down when the party is killing the force without any reason." There are several inner party debates going on in many issues starting from killing, use of finance, treatment of the females, on the issue of religion, use of alcohol. It was found that many of the ground level cadres do enjoy alcohol and try to intimidate villagers and outsiders for money.

- But it is also found that there is a strong amount of respect by the tribals for the movement where they see a good leader who mobilizes them and work for them.

Apart from all these factors it is found that there is a strong sense of desperation from the party to hold constituencies for which they are ready to opt for any means and methods, in this process the party is going to kill their own members as it happened in the past with MCCI. Certain feud is going to take place. But one pattern which clearly emerges out of this is the differences observed in the initial and the present ideology. The tribals have felt that there is erosion of ideology.

Directions of the Movement and Deviations

It is very difficult to predict any direction of the movement though it has slightly deviated from its main ideology. Conflict research could assume that the whole scenario of conflict is always directed towards the interests of the opposites, where two parties are involved, the other parties who directly or indirectly involved in the conflict apart from the main parties do make it more complex and tricky to solve it. The main parties who are antagonistic to each other take a back seat, and others take advantage from the conflict. The two main parties could be two communities, between the two powerful parties or between two opposites who are not in the same power and position. The Naxalite conflict is between the state and the proletarian who are the common poor people with an ideology or without it only holding the anger to ventilate. There are situations where people don't have the conducive atmosphere for everything; there is distrust, suspicions and dominance of one group on the other, like the tribals have been dominated by many actors since age old.

Conflicts are a part of life in any community as seen in the study area. Conflicts can come out into the open through anger, words, hurtful actions, ideologies and through movements as seen in many uprisings in the study area. They can create a climate of fear, intimidation, despair and desperation. Conflicts generally have several layers to them the immediate conflict is often a dispute about some issue or event. That dispute is intensified by an underlying conflict, which involve a history of clashes in values, interests, needs and emotions. As seen in Narayanpatna block of Koraput districts the struggle for land by the tribals have shown violence. Conflict describes a situation in which two or more actors pursue incompatible yet from their individual perspectives entirely just, goals. Here the perception of the state and the perception of the Naxalites are entirely different and they have their own mind-sets on each other and as a result of this there is always an atmosphere of distrust, violence. The resultant factor is always seen as the structural violence by the state in various forms.

The analysis of this conflict, and the analysis based on the people's perspective and the states perspective, taking into account the ground realities, how to see this and go for its prevention, its directions, and resolution of the same. At this juncture the state and the naxalites are just two parallel lines aiming to overthrow each other with their capacities. To look at this conflict, one needs to look at the conflicting behaviour or how to handle the whole process in a non-violent, innovative and rational way which will be accepted by all parties. If we see the directions of the movement that it has come to a situation of conflict with the government and in few cases it has positively deviated to a movement and in few cases it has negatively deviated by creating a situation of killing.

First of all let us assume that are we taking this discontentment of the poor as conflict or not? The history of conflict in India can be traced back from the pre-independence period when the country was under the colonial British where there were struggles against the British imperialism in violent and non-violent ways. All that struggles which took place had a definite pattern, background, demographic, religious, socio-ethnic, political or economic structure which led to such kind of resistance and struggle. The conflicts are always seen and misunderstood as law and order problem which can be tackled or sorted out by police action. And at times they are taken with such intensity that they turn into conventional wars where there are few operations and use of weapons. The history shows the pattern that the movement, conflict, and war do follow one after another.

But it has to be also kept in mind that the conflicts are always people-centred and can has the potential to convert an idea into an revolution. So mere reliance upon arms under operations will only favour the situation towards revolution by people. And it will not yield any effective results, as it has not shown any positive results in case of Naxal movement. There are several conflicts in our country where one can see how the idea or the ideology has changed the people and have shook up the conflict in case of Kashmir, Nagaland, Manipur, Darjeeling, and also in case of Naxalites where the idea has germinated in several states. The whole scenario has to be viewed from a different lens to understand the Naxalite conflict if the state wishes for solution, and for peace keeping.

The definite pattern of conflict as earlier mentioned is always limited to a certain geographical boundary where there is the main thrust and the secondary derivatives and offshoots might exist in other places, but the main geographical area is the focus where tactics and strategies are made from. As in case of the Naxal conflict the study area remained as the thrust area.

Today our country as well as the state of Orissa is undergoing lot of changes and transformations. The globalization has shaped our cultures in a ways that the whole society is going through economic, social and political transformation where the role of the police is very visible. The society is becoming a volatile or unstable mixture of tribes, races, religion, where violence is playing a key role. Be it the communal riots, struggle for state boundaries or the people's conflict over resources.

The Naxalite conflict has been social, political and economic struggle and it has various underlying issues of ideology, identity, and neglect by the state and it has various untouched dimensions of state where it has totally failed to listen to the discontent of the people. Where it has listened to the discontent it has acted violently and labelled them as Naxalites and put them behind the bars. But the basic issue of mis-governance in the interior tribal pockets of the south Orissa has remained a far dream to achieve. And the tribals have completely lost faith and they feel that it is the state who wanted to maintain its dominance and wants to crush people by all means. There are other factors which also determine the path of the movement in the future. The market economy, the diverse use of land, the role of the government in creating equal space for the tribals, to access their rights as opined by many of the respondents.

The increase of private sector has squeezed the state's role. At this juncture where most of the tribals population is backward, so, the gap between rich and poor is widening; as the there is a huge difference between the economic levels of the educated urban and have not section. The justice system is not working effectively as the cases are not solved in whole life time, these all aspects tend towards the rise of social tensions. The populist measures given to the voters are not acting in the proper ways rather the words are becoming like slow poison to the people. When the society is not stable how can we expect productive and equal growth for all? The 1950s Balwant Rai Mehta Committee report to opt for multi-layered Panchatyati Raj systems and the historic achievement of the 73rd and 75th Constitutional Amendments could not reach up to the expectations of the people, it acted as inimical to the people. The

Nehruvian vision and principles are yet to materialise, but the many conflicts have moved ahead with different halting.

Social tensions occur when there is a huge gap between the haves and the have-nots and it is synonymous to social conflict. The manifestations of tension could be many. Social tension often characterizes, or leads to conflict which has a bearing on the social relations, social position or the very endurance of some social groups. Now, it is pertinent to say that how do we decrease this space between the rich and the poor so as to decrease of transform the social conflict in order to check the naxal movement.

The movement can be explained in Figure 11.1. The left side of the graph shows from the explolitation to the raising voice and the stage of violence. The present stage is a violence one as per the movement is considered. Well it is not necessary that it will go through a stage of war

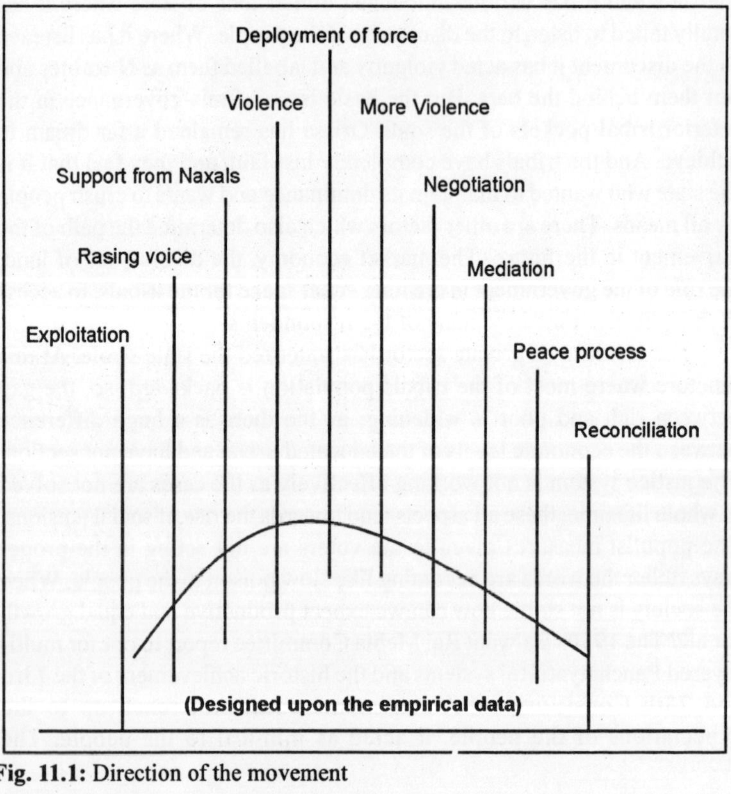

Fig. 11.1: Direction of the movement

or more violent stage, but it can go to a stage of ceasefire followed by a negotiation if both the parties show a strong sense of affinity towards each other or else it could go to a more violent or to a stage of war. This is in a very crucial stage.

Deviations of the Movement

Figure 11.2 shows that there can be 5 types of approaches to a conflict between the two parties.

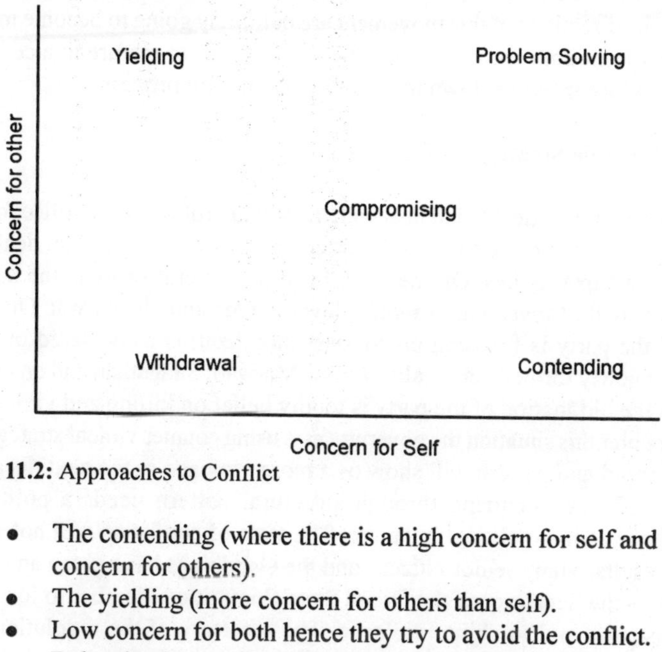

Fig. 11.2: Approaches to Conflict

- The contending (where there is a high concern for self and low concern for others).
- The yielding (more concern for others than self).
- Low concern for both hence they try to avoid the conflict.
- Balancing between the two which is compromising.
- A problem solving mode where there is high regard for both.

In the context of the Naxalite movement, the yielding style is very much prevalent where both the parties are concerned about their aims, priorities. It has been witnessed that in the last two years in Orissa, the parties have traversed through a stage from yielding to balancing between the two which is compromising stage. During the crisis situations like kidnapping of the collector and the member of the Legislative Assembly (February 2011 and March 2012) there have been some attempts made for a temporary arrangement without any concrete future action. This indicates that in a way two parties are going towards the stage of avoiding the conflict, which is a sort of deviance, though does not yield any permanent solution, but not harmful for both the parties.

The inner Maoist party debates were high during these abductions, that the Maoist only demanded the AP cadres and not the Oriya cadres which show a sharp division within the party. So, the parties are trying to avoid conflict for self-interests as per the data reveals.

In case of Naxal conflict it can be said that we are either in approach (a) or (c), but the appropriate would be (e).

The directions of this movement are definitely going to become more violent from both the parties and the violence has to mature to a certain level before it settles down to a conflict resolution process.

The Possible Strategy of Coming Back

The government decided to deal with the Naxal problem with police force along with the development as decided in many conferences on dealing with the Naxal issues. On the other hand the several splits in the naxal party take the movement to another level of feud and bloody war. On one hand the party is focusing on an mass mobilization as declared by the recent newly formed party called Orissa Maovadi Sangathan and on other hand the old faction of the party is totally belief on killing and violence. To counter this situation the government is using counter violent strategies. This trend and pattern will show us a more violence in the next decade. The violence occurring through structural pattern needs a political response as it is political in nature. The state of confusion will not give any results. Many senior citizens and the Gandhians have given an open letter to the Secretary of the Orissa State Committee Member to join the mainstream and to abjure violence. The secretary of the revolutionary party has also welcomed such an initiative, but also has appealed the citizens to start a dialogue process.

This way seems to be a better option for the revolutionary party, but again it has to be seen that whether the parties move for a compromising situations or a problem seeking solution. As of now, there will be no sign of problem solving stage.

Triabls and Non-Tribals Expectation from the Movement

The Naxals need to fight with true ideology what they had in the 1960s, and this has been well agreed to a degree of 30 per cent by the Naxals itself. Few of the interviews with the old leaders were conducted, 35 per cent of the leaders who were in the armed revolution in 1960s don't agree to the present form of ideology and they strongly say that they are only Naxals for the name sake and don't follow the idcology. The present Naxals are engaged in extortion, looting which was not the right way. Having said that if the looting and extortion has anything to good for the tribals then they can engagc. But it is very difficult to ascertain who is right and who is not. The old leaders and the present both justify their own ways. Few of the contradicting views from the leaders are stated below who include tribals and non-tribals:

- "The Koraput District has very unique features. As this region which can go as contiguous patch up to the Gajapati have different stages of the society. The region has inhabited by tribals who are at the hunter gatherer stage, pre agricultural stage, and also agricultural stage. This region also has the primitive tribes who are isolated from the mainstream. They are a different cultural stage. The tribal instincts are there in this region. That is to punish the criminal rather to correct him or her. This region is the most suitable for such guerrilla warfare which the CPI (Maoist) is adopting now. So, when there does such a disparity exist and the tribals are unable to reach the cultural changes of the present governance system and the system is not pro-tribals, at such a juncture the movement is to take a strong stand. Before the state goes for any kind of dialoguing it should take time to make radical and practical changes which are suitable to tribals."
- During the early 1970s the movement had a large scale mass mobilization, but could not go further as the leaders became selfish. But the present leadership in south Orissa seems to be good. Some of the people from the society need to be eliminated as they exploit people and the state will protect them by any means. *"If I perceive the present movement the people life comrade Sabyasachi Panda are very rure but this will be intense unless the government is going to implement and enforce proper laws. The system has to change; the movements will remains as a part of the evolution of mankind till there is class difference. The tribals also are well aware of the fact that the system is not going to help them in any way, so they feel that this is the best way to eliminate their immediate enemy. The system needs to*

be revamped and unless the government can't go for any dialogue process. The tribals join the movement today because that is the last resort for them, as there is no land, no identity and nothing is left for them. They don't trust the system at all. As the tribals are not able to occupy themselves in productive work their minds are ideal with no identity. This is the best stage to distract themselves so there are almost more than 10,000 people who support the movement in south Odisha. The movement will sustain in the coming days."

- An old leader who was involved in the movement during 1967-1972, later he left the movement, now he is an active member of the Communist Party of India Marxist-Leninist Liberation. The village Gurandi was the hotspot of the movement during the 1960s under the influence of the Srikakulam movement and also with the Koraput movement. He was involved in the first revolutionary phase in the Indian Communist history for the first time after independence. The struggles before the independence were also fought bit due to the failure of the left government in India the movement took place becomes much significant for the History of Communists.

His version: "*When we felt the right when for an armed stage of revolution we did it in Naxalbari. The party witnessed various splits in 1964, 1969, and later in 1972 and so on so forth. The Communist Party also did experimented in few places, in organizing the tribals, taking the small areas the making it as units, liberating them and finally covering the urban areas. This has been the thought of Mao. But looking at the Indian conditions the party could not succeed as the stage of revolution was different. But we are under a process of a total revolution. But after losing our cadres due to police repression we changed the style and thought that gun is not the only means, legal struggle is much more important for which arms are required, armed squad is not the way. Armed struggle, but it has to be through an agrarian revolution by exposing the inequalities of the system should come as a peoples resistance movement. But I don't accept the present CPI Maoist style of people's mobilization as they are far away from the masses. As the tribals are recruited without any political sharpness and there is no movement as such among the tribals. But without understanding the issues of the tribals the government says that the tribals are Naxalites. There is need to a great deal to prepare mentally and psychologically. I feel that the success through the present movement is very less and we have to prepare the masses by bringing them to the mainstream and we need to review our constitution also and focus more on the mobilization of the peasants and emphasis on the agrarian problems. As I feel that two aspects are directly proportional to each, i.e. the more the problems are unsolved the more will be the preparation by the people.*"

He also feels that minimum 20 to 30 years to reach that stage of people's mobilization. Though, we also adopted the line of annihilation for some time, but that will not solve the problem as attacks and counter attacks will follow and the very idea of struggle will be diluted. He does not support the path of negotiation and I feel that Naxalism is a theory and it will be proved along with the time. It is not a law and order situation, by making some roads, and giving support to tribals will not solve the issue, there has to be changes in the system. It was also found that almost 60 per cent of the passive supporters carried a view that the poor tribals did not have any other way, so, they are compelled to protest. To protest there is no other platform available so, this is the only base that exists in the tribal area which is a way gives solutions to their problems so they are obtaining without widening their knowledge on the ideology and theories."

- The Naxalite movement in Koraput district started under the influence of the Srikakulam movement. But the foundation can be traced from the background of Chitrakonda Power Project Trade Union Movement. The Trade Union Movement started with the leaders who had connections with the leaders of Naxalbari, but till 1968, Koraput region did not had any violent incidents. But many people like Intellectuals, advocates etc. participated in the underground movement for a short phase among them the famous leaders were D. Bhuvan Mohan Pattnaik, Naga Bhusan Pattnaik, Gananath Patra, Purusottam Palli. Comrade Palli and other were already a part of the Communist Party. But the Naxalbari call made their actions very visible and the spark was very lightening all over the areas.

The Chitrakonda Dam project had different rules for the labourers. They had a system of retrenchment where they had systems like 8 month of work and 4 months of off, where the workers did not receive any benefit. So, the trade union had a demand charter... they organized a rally and demanded for same facilities to the contractual staff as for the regular staff, go home allowancc, retrenchment allowances, unhealthy allowances. So, all the Communist leaders came to organize the trade union movement in Chitrakonda. But during the strike many of us got arrested and also arrested. But after the strike we are succeeding in getting few demands. So, we got faith in the leaders and the workers movement was the first significant achievement by the Communist party of Koraput in 1966, but as workers we did not knew the line of struggle and the politics, we fought for our rights. The new leaders gave us strength and belief to trust the mass mobilization. When the arrests were more the leaders went underground, but we had a tremendous support from outside intellectuals and they used to keep contact with us and inform us how to proceed further. The other members escaped from the police, we the workers always helped the leaders to escape. I used to give shelter to the leaders and supply them food and medicine, but when we were in jail we had regular classes on Communism. We had two sections in jail, communists and non-communists. Purusottam Palli was one of the most active tribal leaders and he had the whole map of Koraput district on his finger tips and he was like a wisdom pool. When we went for a strike, after the strike was called off we took the salaries of 10 days as a prestigious issue out of 25 days.

There were regular demonstrations till 1970s, the slogans created an environment for action. Many students also joined the movement and supported, and since the Naxalbari movement was on its peak, so we the workers told the leaders that we cannot support them directly, but we will be their sympathizers. The police was torturing the people like anything. I feel the people who were harassed by the police in those days are now completely active in the movement. The main emphasis of the movement was mass mobilization. There were differences among the leaders, few wanted to boycott the court and few wanted that they should use court to expose the laws to the public, as the people will hear the court arguments and will know the exact face of the laws and the system.

"During my jail stay we went on strike to get radio, and to get the status of political prisoners, and the Chief Minister visited us and granted a radio for us. Police also used to harass the people and many died and became mad with that harassment. The harassment was to such an extent that the juvenlles were kept along with the adults and not separately. I was there in the jail for 5 years and released in 1974, after my release I used to take part in the rallies and demonstrations and was threatened by police and started working in the dam project again.

I saw there were lots of fractions in the party and few started believing in parliament path and I don't believe in the path but I believe in mass mobilization path. I also, don't believe in the violence way, as how many we can kill, the police also belong to the class struggle and they should also come and unite with the movement. There is brutal torture in the democratic system. Still feudalism exists and the exploitation continues. If the line of naxalbari is wrong then why the people still adopting it. Today there is no education, no facilities for the people and there is discontentment within the people. Till now we have done opposition (*pratirodha*). I feel the messes are not ready to take up arms and if they are ready then there should not be any problem. Why the people are joining in such a large numbers from the cut off area in Malkangiri because they have faced ages of police torture and they are taking revenge.

Government can't do anything to stop the movement. Can it go for pro-tribal development, can it distribute land, so I also don't believe in the system. The nature of the system should change and the revolution will take different shapes and for that a class war is needed which has already started and it's not visible so much. But as the water is stable if we see from the top but there are under currents and may explode anytime."

- "I entered as communist revolutionary with *adivasis* in 1967… I was going to the villages to organize them, how to protect the *adivasis* from forest, chowkidars, forest guards, from exploiters Even till now it continues…. Then I felt my job was an obstacle to my work…. so left the job…. I went to Malkangiri subdivision to work. We were organizing the masses, so that, they will become vocal, protest against exploitation. The *adivasis* were doped in many false cases by the police officials and by the forest department. We were forming village-wise organizations. And the movement faced severe repression. As Government was a vigilant at that time, anything organized by communist revolutionaries the Government was eager to suppress the efforts, by arresting the people and the leaders."

But for a movement open leadership was also necessary and it was really tough. The forces joined the movement from different sectors of the society, but certain sections believed in, that the election way is not the path, but to boycott it everywhere for all times to come or to participate in a limited way which will help the movement; was the discourse going on. Naxalbari type of movement, and to coordinate the effort based on the Marxims-Leninism and Maos thought through guerrilla warfare, is our path… this debate continued. But the role of the mass movement was to accelerate, and a squad was formed everywhere to protect the movement, this theory was postulated. I will call it as a communist revolutionary movement than Naxalite movement or a peasant movement led by the tribals. Tribals are or tribe is a stage of development in the human society. Tribal movements are everywhere, I am involved in the movements, why do we call it as Naxalite movement, it should be called a communist revolution or revolutionary movement. There are several divisions of MLS (Marxists and Leninists), now also there is a some movements going in Koraput, in Narayanpatna and Bandhugaon blocks, where the *sahukars* are evicted and the land is recovered from them.

I am a communist revolutionary and I follow the Naxalbari line, with Marxism, Leninism, and Mao's thought. Though in some cases the Maoists are taking the advantage of the mass movements by arming the people. And the people are immature enough now to take up arms, but now, the time has not come. They are definitely patriots, but they are also mad, it should be a combined struggle. Mass line should be the way. Urgency to understand the ideology of Marx by the *Adivasis*, the time has not come to take up arms.

The above views do portray that there are different stages of development among south Orissa and all the tribals are not in a same state where they can take up arms and it is not the right time either that every tribal group will opt for violence. It is also clear that the south Orissa acts a link between the Andhra Pradesh and undivided Madhya Pradesh and it suits to shelter the Naxals. There is discontent among tribals, and it is a good place for shelter, and it is also a place where the big companies want to mine the minerals, and want to stop the tribal protests by all means, with the backdrop of exploitation that the areas has, all these conditions are a positive factor for the Naxals to spread their tactics and support base. In any conflict and movement it has been observed that few live the movement and take a different line. In case of Naxal movement many left the movement in 1960s and many new faces joined. The present state is to fight with the government and to counter the violence. And to suffice this important need they are collecting money. They fix money or kind per month from almost all kinds of stakeholders, such as hotels, from bus owners, nearby factories, corrupt non-governmental organizations, other business complexes, Panchayati Raj members, engineers, political leaders and also from the government officers. It is a very tricky situation as well as complex that all give money but they deny.

The Naxals do get into areas where there is something wrong going one, like cheating by landlords, or by officials they step in and call for a Praja court. Yes tribals do take advantage of this sometimes. As they are harassed by all and the party is there to hear them. So, it is both way sometimes complementing to each other. In the study area of Koraput, Malkangiri, Rayagada and Gajapati (the areas bordering to Andhra Pradesh in this districts) where the major tribals groups as Kandha, Soura, Jatapu, Bhumia, Paraja, Koya, more than 10,000 tribals do support Naxals directly or indirectly. To counter all the governments tactics the Naxals have developed networks, so that, they get information about the security forces who they call as their enemy. It is not that the Naxals came only within the past five years to South Odisha, they were very much present in Rayagada and Malkangiri district from the 1980s. According a indicators MPI, multiple poverty index developed by UNDP eight states in India include Orissa, Bihar and West Bengal are in abject poverty. and these states along with five other state account for more people than in 26 poorest South African nations combined.[1] Poverty is the main reason and when a tribals undergoes all the ill treatment he has no choice and he cannot think about the larger cause and he finds acceptable the present way of violence. So, the Naxals who were just using the south Orissa as a hideout place, has expanded their work.

The movement has given many aspirations for the tribal and non-tribals to benefit from them intellectually and to get a recognition. This means the movement has created many tribal leaders and non-tribal leaders from the first phase of the movement. It has been seen that there are three kinds of expectations from the movement from the non-tribals:

- To get famous and extract money;
- To get be labelled as a Maoist sympathizer to get attention;
- To get associated genuinely;
- On the part of tribals the expectations are as follows:
  - To get associated for solutions of their issues,
  - To get some benefit,
  - As a choice and alternative, and
  - As a compulsion.

Conflict and Cooperation of Tribal and Non-Tribal Ideology in the Process

The jointly agreed Press Statement[2] given on 20th February, 2011 when the Collector, Malkangiri, was abducted; the interlocutors assured that no harm will be caused to the collector, and the Junior Engineer. And they agreed that no combing operation will be done in the area by the state, and also the Naxals should not cause any incident that will vitiate the negotiation. This was among the interlocutors Prof. G. Hargopal former professor Kakatiya University, Late Prof. R. Someswar Rao (former Professor Sambalpur University) and Sri Dandapani Mohanty. The 2nd day discussion was on the basis of the letters and demands which came from the Naxals through the media persons and reached the mediators and they agreed that:

- Declare Naukadora as scheduled tribal communities; on this issue the State government responded very firmly and told that, they had recommended to the Ministry of tribal affairs, the same has been submitted by SCSTRTI with a detailed report, and the matter will be placed in the next tribal advisory council meeting for consideration.
- Stop Polavaram project which will submerge the Odisha villages and parts of Telengana. On these issues, it was explained that the State government of Odisha has been opposing project and a case has been filed in the high court against Andhra Pradesh Central Water Commission that the present height of the dam will cause severe damage to the villages of Malkangiri district.
- Issue of record of rights/*patta* to the tribals in Koraput, Malkangiri, Narayanpatna whose lands have been illegally possessed by others. On this issue it was discussed that, a Senior Officer in the rank of Additional/Joint Secretary with statutory powers will be posted in Koraput and Malkangiri to expedite the cases of tribal land. Along with this, a high level committee under the chairmanship of a senior officer will also be constituted who will make recommendations on the effective measures for tribal land rights.
- Construct a canal from Kotapalli to Maneguda to provide irrigation facilities to Kalimela farmers, on this demand, the funds have been earmarked by the government and the work will start soon by Minor Irrigation Department.
- Torture by the Koraput jail authorities and health care to the jailed naxal supporters, the response to this demand by the government was both the supporter died in hospital while they were shifted for treatment, and their families have filed writ

petitions and the government also filed and both the parties are waiting for the order by the High Court.

- Release of central committee women members Shila and Padma who are suffering from health problems, they government responded that since the matter has been brought into notice now so the steps will be taken.
- Stop mining lease in tribals areas. In response to this the government explained that, all the laws like PESA, forest rights act, and forest conservation act should be followed in its true spirit and the displacement of tribals should be minimized and they should be adequately compensated and rehabilitated.

During 3rd day there was a joint press statement on 22nd February, 2011,

- A person Sittana was taken away from the Police in Narayanpatna village and what has condition, as per the information with the government no complaint was filed by his family members, and he was not arrested, he is staying outside his village.
- Pay compensation to the farmers of Balimela reservoir as there is a chance of displacing again, government responded that no complaint has been raised so far and government will take actions within its guidelines if there are any such complaints.
- Provide justice to the NALCO displaces, government responded that the grievances must be reduced to the district collector.
- Stop operation green hunt, government responded that there will be no coercive action by the security force as long as there is no unlawful activity by the Naxals.
- Release the members of Chalsi Mulis Adivasi Sangha who are behind the bars of Koraput and Malkangiri jails. In response to this demand, government is taking *sou motu* action to with draw cases against the tribals. And 9103 cases have been dropped which were minor, and within a period of three months all the cases will be reviewed and also land disputes of Narayanpatna and this process will start within 15 days. The mediators suggested that Prof. Radhamohan and Shri Sudhakar Pattaniak will pursue this matter with the government.
- Release the central committee members, Ganti Prasadam, Sirisha, Eswari and others who are in jail, government responded that, government will take steps to withdraw cases against Ganti

Prasadam, Kandula Sirisha, Anfaluri Eswari, Roja Mandangi and Gokul Kildipia following the due process of law[3].

After the discussion for 3 days and the visit by the interlocutors to the Koraput district and appeal to the Naxals was quite appreciated, Prof. Hargopal stated that, "we the mediators express our satisfaction with the outcome of the mediation. We express our appreciation of the concerns of Naxals for the tribals. The release of tribals was utmost concern for the Naxals, and the cases will be taken by the government on top priority, the government of Odisha has closed a large number of cases against the tribals and this tradition makes us believe their due attention. We also appreciate that the cases against the Naxals will also be taken up in the review of Odisha government."

From the above discussion the aftermath which followed was not appreciated by the Naxals, as their top leader is still behind the bars. The cases have not been withdrawn, as alleged by the Naxals though the few cases are withdrawn, but the tribals are again booked under different cases. It was also questioned by the party later this year that only the non tribals were asked to release and not the tribal members. The abduction became a pattern in 2011 and 2012 for release of their non-tribal members and the tribals issues took a back seat.

The tribal members of Chasi Mulia Adivasi Sangha are still languishing in jails, but its remarkable to say that the central committee member comrade Ganti Prasadam has been released in June 2nd week. But no move has been made under as per their other demands and governments discussion. There were no such repeated demands on the tribal issues nor about their release, but the violence continued. Media, both electronic and print have said it very clearly that its war situation, where few areas of South Orissa (including the study area) has been put on sanctions where no outsider is allowed, there is continuous deployment of force and there are human rights violations by both the parties involved in the conflict. According to Websters Third New International Dictionary the term 'war' ultimately derived from the old high English noun Werra, meaning confusion. This term might have come from an ancient Greek verb meaning to go to ruin. The modern English noun war, and according the Webster's these two words, confusing and/or ruinous conditions. In both the cases the conditions are hostile and antagonism prevails in both the situations. So, in a process to release their non-tribal leaders the situation has become a war like. It shows that there is some kind of dispute between the two. These questions were raised in the inner party debate about where the party is heading, whether it is working for the tribal agenda or it is only using the tribals as their sub ordinates. On the other hand 76 per cent of the tirbals do feel that they are sandwiched and this situation will continue, but they have their own learning. They will support the leader if he or she works for their empowerment.

But more than 80 per cent of the tribals feel that their areas have been militarized in this process where the violations have not been accounted by the government. But they know they have to undergo this phase as there is no alternative. The Global Militarization Index (GMI) is a comparison of country's military expenditure and its health expenditure. A contrast between the number of military and paramilitary forces in a place or country with the number of physicians present there.[4] It can be well said that in the study area, each block has more than 100 number of force which include state force and other, if we go by this definition. So, whether this is a situation of War or not it is very difficult to ascertain.

Johan Galtung argues that the absence of war is a state of negative peace, its absence of violence. And positive peace is the presence of social justice and ecological justice, transforming the situations with dynamic mediation processes.

With the above road map that Odisha government had in 2004 and 2011, and the non-stated, but declared a war in the Naxal infected districts, in this juncture is an agreeable solution possible is a real big challenge for not only the government of Odisha, but also for the Naxals who are fighting with the force, their pressure from the government is mounting, they have less time for mass mobilizations, their ideologies have diluted, the demands and needs of the oppressed classes are changing. On the other hand, the conflict interest of the powerful people in the government and lack of political will, apathy of the majority of the government officers towards tribals and in tribal areas, have pushed the tribals back to a position where there is absolute poverty, and they have no faith in the government. So, it is a fluid state where a possible solution has to be sought out.

Ultimate Tribal Responses and Reactions to the Movement

During August 2004, when the celebration of the 37th year of Naxal Movement was on full swing, many people from tribal dominated district participated in the event and later they submitted a memorandum to the State government mentioning the following key points:

- Judiciary enquiry to the killings of tribals in the south Orissa-Andhra Pradesh bordering districts in the name of encounter.
- Withdrawal of Central para-military force from Orissa-Andhra Pradesh bordering districts.
- Release of innocent tribals of Rayagada, Gajapati, and Malkangiri districts who are behind bars.
- Conversion of fifth scheduled areas into sixth scheduled areas, confiscating all land owned by non-tribals.
- Employing all unemployed bamboo cutters.[5] (The version of Shri Dandapani Mohanty, Convenor, Jan Adhikar Manch.)

After submission of this charter of proposals the frontal leaders demanded publicly that the state government should take immediate steps for land reforms. On the same year in September a meeting was held in Bhubaneswar which was convened by Daman Pratirodha Manch (now banned and the case is pending for final hearing). Daman Pratirodha Manch (DPM) is an organization whose main goal is to bring all the voices of dissent into one platform and put pressure on the government. DPM strongly opines that Naxalite problems are a socio-economic problem. DPM places its demands before the Honourable Chief Minister, Government of Odisha and the demands were:

- Withdrawal of central para military force from the southern Odisha districts.
- Release the person behind the bars who are arrested under the purview of labelled Naxalites.
- Stop the entry of Andhra Pradesh Police into the Odisha districts.
- Judicial enquiry of all encounter killings.
- Withdraw of ban on public meetings by Naxals.
- Detailed plan to end natural calamities, stop distress sale of agricultural produce and take necessary steps to stop middle agents business in tribal areas.
- Give employment to bamboo cutters and restore their livelihoods.
- Ban on holding land by non-tribals and redistribute it among tribals.
- End the industrial projects like Vedanta, Utkal Alumina.
- Health care in tribal areas.

It is very pertinent to note here that these demands placed by DPM were in response to the willingness of peace talks by the Honourable Chief Minister, Government of Orissa.

The whole meeting on 14th September, 2004 was properly designed and well conducted with a good gathering and this was popularly known as Jangarjan Samavesh. In fact, the Chief Minister gave a positive note that the government will discuss on the proposals submitted to them. The significant people who were present in the meeting, Mr. Dandapani Mohanty (convener of Daman Pratirodh Manch, and later interlocutor during the abduction of Vineel Krishna), Kui poet Late Dasu Ram Maleka, revolutionary poet Varvar Rao. But when the Jangarjan Samavesh was over and the tribal were returning to their homes, Odisha Police arrested 18 from Kalimela and Motu areas of Malkangiri district claiming them they were most wanted criminals. This was a confusion created by the whole context in 2004. Though government introduced some pro-tribal measures, but it did not satisfy the belief of tribal-Naxals.

On 4th October, 2004 Home Secretary, Government of Odisha, informed the press that State government is prepared for unconditional talks, any condition will act as an obstacle, the Naxalites should stop from violence and return the arms. But the State of Orissa as well as the Naxals could not utilize this space.[6]

The Naxals in return disapproved this and opined that the violence is a form of expression by the people because of Governments apathy and negligence towards them. When the Government wants to displace the tribals due to big industrial projects which will bring no benefit to the tribals, so unless there is an end to the existing violence by the government in different ways, peace process cannot be started. Emphasizing again that the 12 *gram panchayats* of Kudumulugumma, Kalimela blocks of Malkangiri where more than 150 villages are cut off from the main land due to the big dams, have no access to health care and educational facilities. This state of confusion as a whole diluted the whole process of peace talks and it died even before it started in real.

When a teacher was abducted in western Odisha by Maoists but later freed, reacted that the Maoists have heart, but the police didn't even have that. Not only the teacher many of who got abducted by the Naxals say that they were treated well. From 2004 to till now, if we see the physiognomy of violence then both the conflicting parties have tremendously increased their violent activities. The encounter killings and the blasts by Maoists were always started occurring on a regular pattern to settle scores among each other. The government starting blaming the Naxals as terrorist organization whereas the naxals started blaming that the government has no interest to do anything for the tribals, its showing all its tribal areas to get more fund under the security issues. Two trends with conflict of interests can be seen in the last eight years. The tribal responses are clear in the sense that this movement though helps them to raise voices, but have not been yielded results to them. Again when it was questioned about the results there is a certain blueprint in the naxalite movement in the study area. Where the leadership is good, mass mobilization is good tribals see this as an alternative in case of Gajapati and parts of Rayagada districts. Where the tribals are targeted by the state they do join the Naxalite movement as there is no way, as seen in parts of Rayagada and Koraput district. And in the other hand, where there is an age long negligence by the government they join the Naxals as a last choice which shows the tribals reactions.

To understand the tribal situation a background of the study area is given below to critically analyse the tribal situation.

The tribals who were once the owners of land have now become the labourers in their own niche. In this country, according to the census of 2001, India, constitute 8 per cent tribals and in Orissa it is 22 per cent, after undivided Madhya Pradesh, Odisha stand as the second largest tribals populated state in India. The tribals of Odisha once living in their own territory with the traditional rights over natural resources, i.e. over land, water and forest and forest produce. Their rights are governed by community ownership, where there was a sense of equity, equality and respect. They had a collective feeling in all their distribution of resources. They had absolutely no contact with the mainstream society or what we call as outside world. They worshipped nature, nurtured it and were totally dependent on it for their lives, livelihood and sustenance. They used to practice *podu* cultivation which later took a different form of cultivation, the forest lands are called *Jungul chasa*. It is said so that many tribal areas were remained virgin unless they were discovered by the reach of the British. They were governed by their own customary laws which helped in organizing of the societies.

They did had ways of arbitration and conflict resolution systems to regulate their societies, as self-governance system. Later they did started cultivating the areas near the river side, but still their rights and dependency on the *podu* land were untouched. The tribals faced the days of misfortune, with the advent of outsiders in their area, who were not tribals who created wide earthen roads to reach the interior parts of the tribal land. When the kings, and Mughals wanted include the tribal areas into their own empire. The cycle of exploitation was initiated. Each phase of rulers in the tribal areas changed their face of use and abuse towards the tribals. The dense forested areas, the disease, the temperature to face all this dangers of life by an outsider were not easy to sustain themselves and continue their misuse. So, the kings and other rulers, who wanted to control the tribals but could not reside in their geographical areas, started settling other non-tribals in the area, so that, they will act according to the whim and pleasure of the rulers.

It was also easy for the rulers to incept a process of tribal abuse by their own servants who have been settled at their mercy. Be it the Dombs, Sundhis in the Koraput region, the Panos in Gajapati district, later the Paikas, Rana, Goudas, Kampa, Kumuti and Brahmins all higher castes have slowly travelled to the tribal land. Many higher castes were asked by the King of Jeypore to settle for execution of the emperors work. It is said that the Belmas of Kotapd were settled by the King of Jeypore who were fighters. The kings who could not believe the tribals ability and their execution power, and other communities were made settled in the tribal areas for administration and defence activities. In this process, people from the other areas slowly started settling in the tribal zone.

Then in the later half people from Andhra Pradesh, Madhya Pradesh came in due to the advancement of communication facilities to the area. They did help the kings too. All outsiders started dominating the tribals and their resources. In a way they became the owners of the resources over a period of time. In the early nineteenth century, many who did not had any occupation in their own place, went to Koraput region in search of work. Few from the poor sections could get well knitted with them in the cycle of exploitation and others still lead a life of poor. If we see the major hotels, garment shops or any major commercial establishment in the study area all have travelled from coastal Odisha, Andhra Pradesh or from undivided Madhya Pradesh.

When the competition was going on between the non-tribals and other weaker sections, but all had no pity for tribals and showed the same kind of behaviour towards them. Those who became reluctant at first instance about settling in these areas, but after seeing the easy way of making wealth and the innocence of the tribals they have been always used. As mentioned several times about the intrusion to the tribal areas,

- Castes settled by kings for administration.
- Castes settled by kings for defence.
- Castes came to Koraput region in search of work.
- Also refugees who were victims of internal displacement in wars

among states. The east Bengali refugees settled since four decades in Koraput region. Others in the later stage who came here were the victims of the 1960s uprising of the Srikakulum and a major chunk of people from Andhra Pradesh came and settled permanently in Koraput, Rayagada, Gajapati and Malkangiri districts.

- Many rich people who wanted to invest in cash crops like coffee, tobacco acquired lands playing games with the officials.

In many areas the tribal population in the state is dwindling, for example in Tripura the tribal population has reduced. In Odisha, the decrease in tribal population has very many socio-economic reasons where their resources are looted and acquired by others and they are made slaves in their own territory. The forest policy in 1865 by the British, curtailed the rights over land and forest of tribals. Introducing excise policy they regulated the preparation of the country liquor by tribals which was their tradition. In 1793, the land related laws were introduced for individual ownership; tribals had community ownership who used to cultivate collectively and who enjoyed the yield.

When the land survey was introduced, all the lands were recorded in the name of the Mukhia or chief, as he was the incharge to distribute land. If the Mukhia was good he still preserved the tradition of collectiveness, and where the Mukhia was not of good character he and his generations enjoyed the lands. Many of the Soaras are victims of this process where their Mukhias are enjoying the lands, but others are just landless labourers. The law created confusion which deliberately made few tribals as landlords and few others are marginalized. In this process many non-tirbals mis-used the law and owned lands. There are different stories that much higher caste used to make friendship with tribals to acquire their lands. Many areas in Koraput region, such as Bandhugoan, Narayanpatna, Gudari, Gunupur, Ramnaguda, Kashipur, Bissamcuttack where, other castes have abused tribals.

Looking at others there was a divide created among tribal societies who started exploiting their own tribals. The same stories have been explained by Late Shri Gopinath Mohnaty[7] in his book *Paraja* and how the forest and revenue officials have cheated the tribals. Late Shri Biswanath Pattnaik and Late Shri Gopinath Mohanty did not have any Communist bent of mind but could feel the anger of the tribals.

In south Odisha especially a regional plan has been approved for the districts called the KBK, but nothing reaches the tribals due to the siphoning of money by the middle agents be it the political leaders, government officials and other vested interest groups. This is another stark reality of the Koraput region that the development funds don't reach the people.

After 40 years when the tribals started reacting to this, there was a paradigm shift by the government where funds have been allocated for security from development. "55 per cent of the respondents have opined that, all the time media and others ask us that Naxals are not allowing roads, and other establishments; but it is wrong, we are not against roads, but why the government didn't construct roads till 60 years of independence? And why they are interested now, because they can take the resources of tribals whatever left. They are building roads so that the force can reach and other companies can reach. It is not for the tribals. It is very interestedly told that, every year the government conducts a tribal exhibition to portrays the tribals as members of a zoo, so that, others can see them and their life style. But indeed, the government doesn't want this as they are displacing tribals from their home and hearths."

The whole history of intrusion, exploitation, structures of deprivation in the society and how the whole cycle of development has pushed them from even catering to their immediate needs. The *Panchasheela* has failed, and even the laws extended to scheduled areas have not done miracles due to the faulty way of implementation and there is a demand to change the system, but this ventilated with violence. A tribal person who is entering into the Naxalite situation does not understand the theory and they feel he or she needs not to understand either, as they have been seeing it since their childhood and experienced. So, the familiarity of exploitation by tribals has been a shield to the Naxals and their party. This will escalate till their political space is squeezed and it will go towards a destructive path.

Future of the Tribals in the Movement Process

The Naxalite movement will mature through the tribals participation and it will show some positive way. Having said this it is also necessary to say that the tribals will be matured through the Naxalite movement. The violations taking place in tribal areas will transform them to take leadership in the movement in a much more non-violent way. As clearly said in above point that the tribals political space and their identity is at stake and this situation is lucrative for the revolutionary party for spreading the activities. Tirbals will mature through this movement as 45 per cent of the respondents strongly feel that. This movement has given them confidence to resist against the injustice. Since, there are variations in the tribal participation in the study area, but in the coming two decades the tribals will consolidate their experiences to build a strong movement.

Can a solution be possible as the respondent's opinion?

- If government machinery comes nearer to the Naxals for an open dialogue and show their concern in actions.
- If anti-corruption measures be taken to a high satisfaction.
- If kin members especially the leader try to motivate the tribals for a better movement without violence.
- If few committed social workers and researchers mediate. In this case the government has to go for multi-track diplomacy (which means it included stakeholders from all sectors).
- If the development activities expedited as per suggested in the Planning Commission Report (2008) by the experts.
- If the government sets up a special ministry for peace (along with the Ministry of Social Justice existing now) and appoint few experts to solve this issue. The Government of Orissa can pioneer in this regard and become a model for others.
- If every State government undertakes a study on the Naxal affected areas with the help of the STSCTRTI to throw more light on the issue.

References

1. www. theviewspaper.net
2. Interview with one of the interlocutor.
3. Press statements and conditions agreed during the abduction of District Collector, Malkangiri, Orissa. (in an interview with the mediator Dandapani Mohanty).
4. www. bicc.de
5. Interview with a sympathizer.
6. *Naxal Movement and State Power,* Das, Satyaprakash, Swarup & Sons, 2006.
7. Interview with Dandapani Mohanty only on his role in the process of releasing the District Collector.

12
Conclusion and Findings of the Study

"All progress is precarious, and the solution of one problem brings us face to face with another problem."

— *Martin Luther King, Jr.*

Testing of the Hypotheses and Findings

Naxal Movement, of whether extent or type, it is primarily a social, process where almost all responsible factors are causally related and correlated. The socio-economic backwardness and sufferings are most basic to all the manifested activities. People wait for solution for a considerably long time from the authority but when all expectations go in vain, the situation took a revolutionary trend. Till the expression or peoples reaction, though every activity follows a principle based on the socio-cultural norms, beyond it, the socio-cultural background losses its importance. Further course of action proceeds arbitrarily. The movement, the situation, turns violent-vested interests of the leaders as well as the participants become more exclusive and ultimately a movement takes birth.

With the attempt to study such a type movement systematically, I have formulated a number of working hypotheses in order to explore the nature and extent of such a movement like that one Naxal one with the sole purpose to find the right solution. I have tried to the best of my ability with the help of several working hypotheses for a solution based objective. They are rightly tested and included in this concluding part of justify the purpose of my research.

The working hypotheses which were made have been tested and explained as follows:

No. 1: Naxal movement, like any other movement never had sudden rise from the people's grievances and sufferings to the battle.field of movement. It takes up all the basic steps in a long run basis like people's

sufferings due to exploitation, crossing the limit of their tolerance, the long term awaiting for the justice and solutions, the extent of exploitation by the outsiders (mostly officials) and then motivation by the activist leaders and finally leading to the enforcement for joining the Naxal force.

It is seen that the economically backward tribals are the victims of development and this created the disillusionment among them to move towards a new phase opting the Naxalite movement. It is true that the tribals opted for a Gandhian path in 1951 to get their rights over land in the universe but the path of *Satyagraha* labelled them as trouble creators. Later they came in contact with the first spark of communism in 1960s, but still they wanted that the government should come forward for their help. But it didn't result them anything. The levels of the exploiters, starting from the king, then the outside settlers, the planned development models of the government and now, the big companies all want the resources, but no one wants to hear their plea. In a desperate situation when there is no one to hear their grievances, their unheard voices are felt by the Naxalites and they are motivated to join them. As stated in chapter 3, the tribals did opt for a *satyagraha* for land in 1951 under the leadership of a veteran Gandhian Late Shri Biswanath Pattnaik but failed and their *stayagraha* was seen as a law and order problem. Later through *Bhoodan* Movement Vinoba Bhave also did not yield much results for the tribals of the study area as mentioned in Chapter 3. And their sufferings got increased from the time of independence in India where they were displaced, and this dispossession led them to join the movement in the end of 1990s as mentioned in Chapter 3. It is also implied from other factors that it is not a sudden rise as there were many gaps in their movement till it went to a violent naxal movement. The tribals went through many phases from the pre-formation stage, formation stage, constructive stage, post constructive stage, and now the development stage. Theses stages as described in Chapter 3. The movement also witnessed several setbacks, but got motivated mainly from the exploitation of the government officials as mentioned in Chapter 4. The tables in Chapter 4 do indicate that the circumstances which pushed the tribals to the movement were mainly social which were attributed towards their education, poverty which is more than 45 per cent among tribals.

No. 2: Even though the tribals are illiterate or pre-literate, in the

face of suffering, exploitation and prolonged economic backwardness, they are compelled to accept the naxal ideology with immediate effect.

The research has investigated the various issues and problems of tribal that they are associated with conflict which is a daily phenomena that tribals encounter. These are of different types—intra-, and inter-conflicts. The conflict has much to do with behaviour of the human being/tribals which is guided by the environment. The human being/tribals are surrounded by socio-psyhco-cultural environment which helps her or he to meet the needs if the needs are not met then the conflict escalates. The needs are seen from the legal angle as rights. When rights are violated or needs are not met, than it is assumed that, there is a growing discontent among the different sections of human beings. The process of human evolution has created many conflicts and it is inevitable. If we see the timeline of conflicts in India, the history can be traced back from the pre-independence period when the country was under the colonial British when there were struggles against the British imperialism in violent and non-violent ways. All that struggles took place had a definite pattern, background, demographic, religious, socio-ethnic, political or economic structure which led to such kind of resistance and struggle. But it has to be also kept in mind that the conflicts are always people centred and can have the potential to convert, an idea into a revolution. To meet the needs the environment is a very important factor as many stakeholders desire many things form the same environment. This is the situation where the goals clash and few of the weaker sections are left out and their needs are not met.

The tribals of the universe are facing the same situation where their needs are not met and they join the movement with urgent effect. The age long exploitation process has left the tribals with no choice. Table 5.1 do indicate that the universe of the study shows an increase in the Naxal activities in all the blocks from presence to their spread. It is also mentioned in Chapter 4 diagram in the four steps how they tribals opt for arms in the naxal movement. This participation included more than 50 per cent of the tribal youth.

It is also critical to understand that the factors which promote the participation of the tribals is the unmet needs as explained in Chapter 5, i.e. 67 per cent of the tribals do have unmet needs, from which 68 per cent of them feel that they are targeted as naxalites. 87 per cent of them feel that violence is last resort as explained in the same chapter.

The main factors behind the joining into this movement is justified as this is the only way to get their needs meet as explained in 5.2 where it has shown the various factors why the tribals get into the movement with immediate effect. The same factors explained by various case examples of the study area where the respondents have shared their stories.

No. 3: Tribals as per their cultural standards accept readily and comfortably the matters which are served at their door step. Whereas government officials hardly reach the tribal people face to face, naxal leaders reach people at their door step and able to convince them comfortably to join naxalite movement.

It is found that many tribal groups in the universe entering into the movement with choice, by force or as an alternative and very few get into the movement to get some benefit. Many of the tribals did not receive any justice from the existing system so, they got into the movement. And all most of the tribals believe that this movement will bring change in their lives. More than 90 per cent of the respondents in the universe believe that the government officials have not reached them on the other hand the Naxalites have gone to their door step, heard their stories, believed them and showed them a new way to revolt, as explained in Chapters 4 and 5. The study showed that tribals accept any new person in their villages. In this way they do accept Naxals and offer them food as part of hospitality and sometimes on demand. The Naxals spend time with the tribals. The field data shows that more than 50 per cent of the tribal youth in Lamtaput, Nandapur, and Boipariguda blocks of Koraput district; 30 per cent of tribal youth in Rayagada district are in a state of vacuum as no one believes them as explained in Chapter 4. In this way the tribals and Naxals do share some sort of ideas and a place for each other. And two, very distinct patterns that emerge from the field regarding the motivational aspect are given below:

- those tribals who believe that this is the only way.
- 2nd group of tribals who believe that as there is no option this is the last resort.

No. 4: The exploitation of moneylenders, landlords and other opportunist migrant population (in addition to government officials) are most often taken as clue and supportive cause for motivating the tribals to join naxalite movement.

It is found in the studied universe that the tribals were first exploited by the kings by putting heavy land revenues and extracting free and bonded labour from tribals. There are stories, as the respondents have poured, their ancestors have travelled more than 100 km by walk to offer free service to the king of Jeypore as explained in Chapter 3. The British started the land systems but the core issues about the relations of land and tribals were never answered. The governance initiatives never took into consideration of the tribal dilemmas. More than 60 per cent of the tribal believe that the socio-economic conditions are poor because the government always heard the rich and the powerful as explained in Chapter 5. The land holding of the respondents in Chapter 5 shows that the tribals have very little land which are rain-fed. The small and marginal farmers are poor and in a way are in distress condition. The life journey of tribals as explained in Chapter 8 has many contours which does not move as per their convenience but has to follow the rules of many outsiders who rule their lives. The incidents do live a mark in their memories which are related to the village, traditions, in schools, as more than 26 per cent of tribals have some kind of bad experience in their schools with the teachers as explained in Chapter 8. 41 per cent of the tribals have some kind of negative experiences with the money lender, government officials directly or indirectly which always lives a bitter experience to their memory. They were displaced; the outsiders who came here and settled always came to exploit the tribals. In each of these districts a large chunk of migrant population found settled and who controls the economy. They are mainly from the neighbouring districts of Andhra Pradesh, coastal Orissa and the undivided Madhya Pradesh. Exploited, poverty, all the circumstances form clues to join the movement. Many case examples show that the tribals have long agony for the exploiters as given in Chapters 5, 6, and 8.

No. 5: Primary and subsequent observations in the tribal area confirm that most of the tribals after joining the movement, are so much so red-marked that they fear to come back to normal life even if they realise their breaching of law and order of the state. In case of extreme torture only, they take a drastic decision to come back and surrender.

The tribals do join the movement with a lot of aspirations, with an aim to have a better economic condition. The tribals do feel strongly that there are no tribals leaders who can take their cause to the proper platform.

But it is also observed that they do fail in their own way and want to come back to the normal life. When they see that the ideology of the Naxalites is different, there are cases where the tribals have resisted taking money from the political leaders (as a form of extortion) and questioned their community mobilization strategy. But they are so much profiled as red by the system that they fear to come to the main stream. There are many reasons of coming back to main stream, few cannot take the hardships of the underground life, as they are not given leave to visit their family, personal reasons, ego clashes for leadership is another major front. There are some cases of torture which are quite ambiguous, in the sense that the few of the respondents say (out of fear of the police) that they were sexually harassed and few say that they really wanted to go for family. So, it is difficult to infer anything and by saying these critical issues one can only trivialize the matter. There are cases pending with the State Women's Commission and in due course things will be clear. But it is untrue that there are few cases where the few female cadres are used by the leaders. When situations go to acute in any personal and professional sense or due to health grounds they do come out and submit themselves before the government. Few voices on surrender issue have been explained in Chapter 10, but it is not so very clear on their coming back to the main stream. More than 30 per cent of the tribals do feel that the actions do not match their ideology and they want come back. But there are other cases found that when tribals want to do some good work they are targeted as Naxals and kept in jail. When they are released they are joining the armed action. So, both the cases do exist.

No. 6: Even though Naxalite movement proceeds on a single track basing on a single ideology it has not been able to maintain consistency and uniformity because of variable strategic operations of the government and variations in the local cultures (Economic as well as Cultural backwardness). Like Naxal ideology, the participation of people especially the tribals never accept the movement in a similar manner, variations emerge as a result of their economic backwardness and cultural variations.

The Naxalite Movement goes on a single ideology variously termed as Marxism, Leninism or Mao's thought. Their ideology is very clear to over throw the state to bring an alternative system through armed struggle. Their presence was noticed in Gajapati district in the late 1990s and early 2000 through two frontal organizations named the Chasi Mulia Sangha and Kui Lavanga Sangha. These two organizations only believed in mass mobilization and taking up issues that affect the tribals, like land, liquor and stopping harassment of women by the local landlords as explained in Chapter 3. Though they had support from the, the then people's war groups of Andhra Pradesh but never opted for gun culture. Their land movement in few Gram Panchayats of Gajapati and Rayagada districts was quite successful in amplifying the voices of the tribals and highlighting the issues. But the movement was crushed by using police force and everyone in a ways was forced to join the Naxalite movement. As the Naxalite movement had gained the impetus in the States of Andhra Pradesh and Chhattisgarh in bringing up laws in favour of tribals, but in Odisha they could not go ahead with the same agenda. By the time the movement picked up in Odisha, the Naxalites merged their parties and went for peace talks in Andhra Pradesh. Till date there is a huge inner party debate going on within them, that whether it was right time to go for peace talks? It was a major setback for the party where many of the caders were killed and talks failed. The discussion on Odisha also halted. So, in Odisha the pressure was never built up the way it acted in other neighbouring states. The party claims that in Odisha the intellectual support is less compared to other states. Employment of force acted a major obstacle for them, as most of their time is consumed in targeting the force than in mass enlistment. This has been explained in Chapters 3 and 4, where there is again split in the party.

No. 7: As regards, the inclusion of the tribals in the movement process, it is verified that tribals everywhere in south Odisha are more or less from similar or uniform cultural bases. In some districts, tribals accept and support the movement in some districts in order to take revenge on the exploiting population come forward to join, in some districts they join the movement without any choice, and in some districts they see it as an alternative way to ventilate their anger. It is also true that in some areas where government activities are satisfactory, people hesitate to join the movement.

The four districts in the universe are not at the same step in the ladder, variations are seen in their operation, leadership, style of recruitment, mobilization strategy and in other aspects. The universe has three committees working as per their party's structure is concerned the Odisha state committee which works in Gajapati, and parts of Rayagada district, the Andhra-Odisha border Special Zonal Committees which works in

Rayagada and Koraput districts, and the Dandkaranya Special Committee which majorly operates in Malkangiri district. Apart from these major administrative units there are other district, divisional, inter-district, area and special divisions do function in carrying out their activities as explained in Chapter 6. Gajapati district has a good base of support and people do believe in them. Parts of Rayagada district also have a popular support. Few of the areas in Koraput district the tribals hesitate to join them as the government is very active there. But these areas are a good shelter place for them so they rule those areas creating fear among the tribals. Malkangiri is an exceptional and unique case where the tribals have mingled with them and join them without any choice. The tribal feels that even though they don't join the police will arrest them. Many tribals in Kalimela and Podia blocks have repeatedly gone to jail without committing any crime. So, they are sandwiched between the Naxals and the police force. Few join the movement to take revenge on the exploiters, as it happened in Gajapati, Malkangiri and Koraput district. The tribals are harassed so much that they ultimately end up in taking action. It was found in Malkangiri district where a landlord who was from coastal area was harassing the tribal women so much that he was killed. So, the situations are different in the universe and it won't be wise to say that all the areas are naxal infested. Instead of taking the district as a unit, may few regions can be taken as affected. And there are again different variables exist in these regions with regard to their presence.

No. 8: Besides the cultural and other local variations, the participation in the movement always takes a bi-fold path, firstly some people because of the surrounding problems remain as active participant and others who are not very much affected, only ideologically remain as passive participant of the movement.

It is found that the movement is able to thrust on the incidents faced by the tribals in their life and channelizing it into action very effectively. Few of the participants who have had some bad experiences in their life normally come forward in the meeting and share their problems in the Praja court. Normally in a Praja court many issues are placed, with a planning followed by actions. This is conducted at emergency conditions or on a regular basis. So, the active participants who join the movement normally lead the others, yes there are variations too among these participations, as some are villager leaders, some are just fence sitters, some are contributors, some just participate because they reside there, and very less who oppose them. Oppositions are never welcomed and they are eliminated. This is explained in Chapters 4 and 6.

No. 9: From ideological point of view, the Naxal movement had attracted the attentions of the economically backward tribals, but as observed from different incidences (as published in the media), the ideology is noticed to be diluted due to the incorporation of personnel vested interests of some leading Naxal ideologues and their activists.

It is found from the primary data that majority of the leaders are either engaged in facing the security forces or engaged in collection of funds. The tribals who are not participating in the movement have started asking questions especially in Koraput district when they see the party leaders engaged in manipulating funds. Many leaders who have worked in the party are very arrogant and adopt all incorrect measures for their own interests which are not good for the party. Very few leaders who are left with pure ideology and not sufficient for them as there is massive police who want to kill and destroy their camps. A respondent who surrendered before the Koraput police had problems with leadership with the Odisha state committee, so, the party is facing severe stumbling blocks as far as the ideology is concerned. But in a long movement like the Naxalite, these temporary setbacks are quite usual phenomena, as it had many times hindrances in the past. This has been explained in Chapters 3, 4, 7, 8 and 10.

No. 10: As known at the international, national and at the state levels, the sovereign governments most often follow the incidences of movement, whereas the movement makers always take a strategically superior stand by following an offensive role in the whole process.

The government is following the incidents of the Naxalites on regular basis thorough meetings, thorough force and through technology. The Naxals in Odisha have opted a new strategy of kidnapping since 2006 from Gajapati district. But it was not as serious as they wanted to show their strength. Since last year they have gone one step ahead in kidnapping members of legislative assembly, foreign tourists and the district magistrate. This has created troubles for the government and its showing some kind of compromising attitude without any results. The press statement given by Dr. B.D. Sharma and Shri Dandapani Mohanty during April 7th, 2012, who were negotiating between the Naxalites and the government had four Promising gestures of Mutual Trust; Finalisation of the frame for release of prisoners; Discussion about basic issues such as command over resources and their use; and Aspects of Governance in Scheduled Areas. But, no step taken by Government till today. This is explained in Chapter 11. The government is not taking any prior action and taking always a defensive role to protect itself. In this situation, the activists are on a high hand.

No. 11: As observed anthropologically, the solutions to such an undesired movement process, seem to be far reaching mainly because, there is no absolute solution—seeking dialogues, compromises and compromising attitudes between the two parties involved, so far.

As shown from the primary responses and the theories the parties have incompatible goals. Structural violence and cultural violence is playing an important role in justifying the actions of brutality. Many of the activists are abandoning the movement for personal and professional reasons. There is no atmosphere for third party mediation or peace diplomacy. Conflicting attitudes are only allowing the tribals to enter into the risky model rather giving them any solutions. State repression will call for more resistance than mainstreaming of the tribal Naxalites. There will be episodes of surrender under pressure from various forces, but this strategy will not work as new problems replace the older ones. Violence is the way only, but it is not the solution as many of the actors are not involved in it. This is explained in Chapter 9 with diagrams.

No. 12: The conflicting and confronting attitudes of both sides are ought to create bloody fights and loss of human lives. In fact, the two parties involved in the conflict (leading to movement) are at fault, which they never realise. Therefore, unless both the parties sincerely desire for a solution, no solution would be possible.

The complications of such a movement are very diverse and any easy and straightforward solution do not seem to be possible at this juncture. It is reverted from the data that both the conflicting parties want to maintain the present *status quo* to fulfil their own motives. Preventing situation from violence, preventing from escalating violence and preventing further violence after ceasefire, i.e. after the negotiations three major issues seen in the movement. As demanded by the naxalites that the government should show some positive gestures in action. Also there was one important suggestion that a holistic peace talks model is necessary involving multiple stakeholders in the process. And this process should take place in all the Naxal affected states parallelly. But the stage of realisation has not reached. As the data shows that violence has to reach to its peak where both parties will come to a common platform as explained in Chapter 9.

Conclusion

India is a democratic country and all the citizens of the India has accepted the Constitution as the highest doctrine to guide its citizens, and gives track to all the pillars of the society to govern, make policies to ensure justice and development for all the citizens irrespective of any attribute where the element of humanity is present in all senses. The market with its new economic policy stand firm and resource grab by the powerful seems inevitable. Though civil society acts as a neutral force between the state and the market but it doesn't help the masses to reach to a logical end. In this confusing state the radical forces wants to overthrow the existing system and wants an alternative. It is found that working with this framework for more than sixty five years, the country has come across many uprisings, revolts, sectarian movements, social movements and conflict which the country has felt to be the biggest security challenges of the present India. It is found that there are various kinds of political thoughts exist in the country, the right wing forces and the left wing forces, the democratic forces and the radical forces like the Naxalites. The Naxalbari started in one village and today it is capturing more than 25 per cent districts of the Indian subcontinent. They have many divisions and shown a trend that they exist with their largest network and both over ground and underground networks they continue to strive to keep their struggle with the masses.

Their history in India is a little more than four decades old. Their stronghold on tribals though had variations on different states in yielding results but the tribals movement is maturing through the process of Naxaltie movement. The movement started with mass mobilization, annihilation and now has opted violence, though it is advocated by the Naxalities that it is for self-defence, but it is violent in nature.

There are differences seen in the party and also in the universe of the study. Why the violence is growing and getting a suitable ground in majority of the places because it is seen that the government has not been able to reach to a larger tribal areas where they exploited since ages in the name of land administration, in the name of development and now in the name of growth where the resources are on demand. Its time and again questioned and debated by the Naxalites that whether this democratic system has any justice for the masses, the Naxalites who believe in Communist ideology fought elections in 1957 and failed to cater to the needs of the many.

And there were three major divide noticed among them, those who believed in armed struggle started their journey from Naxalbari, and after huge modifications have come to a point here they have formed Communist Party of India. The Indian form known as Naxalites whose base is mainly the tribal regions. It is found that in the universe of the research many blocks are infested with Naxalism in four districts and many more nearby districts are coming into their fold.

Though the ideology and their theories have taken back seat and distorted over the period of time, there is also an ideological confusion among their leaders where there is no mass mobilization. It is found that in few of the areas of they have also given a *diktat* to rule people in the universe. A huge number of cadres want to come out of the party and surrender as they found this way is not practically possible. One of the respondent of the universe who joined the party with enthusiasm, but he wanted to come out of the party, as their ideologies and actions were not the same. But he was killed in an encounter in January 2011 in Rayagada. Few of the areas of the universe it is found that they have taken mass mobilization as a major step. In district of Gajapati and parts of Rayagada there is lot of mass mobilization among the tribals and they see the ideology working on ground. Few areas of Koraput, they operate on command basis, and desperate to join with the democratic movements of tribals. Malkangiri was their initial shelter base and tribals do join them for three main motives, as lack of any choice, lack of governance, and out of fear. So, variations have emerges and the same pattern is found almost everywhere.

In few of the areas, due to the heavy deployment force by the government it is a war like situation, where there are human rights violations from both sides involved. In some areas it is in a situation of lower intensity conflict where they are antagonistic to the government. The present circumstances are crucial and an open debate is necessary on the same topic in all the forums where an honest answer can be evolved through consultations. The recent kidnapping by the Naxalites have given a chance to the government to opt for a temporary comprising stage but this will not yield any good result in the long run. The mediators though come to a common table in the crisis situation to rescue the persons and in a way to support the Naxalites indirectly as they are aware that the Government will not take any urgent action on issue of land, on displacement, on pending land cases in Koraput region and on many issues affecting tribals. The presence of force is not the solution as far witnessed in the universe. As violence in another form to respond to the violence.

The report given to the Planning Commission is a detailed document which has covered all the aspects of tribals and other backward castes issues and needs to be implemented. There are non-government organizations working, the government should use them effectively instead labeling them along with the Naxalites. As it is seen that a Gandhian working in Chhattisgarh whose office was demolished putting him in false charges. Government has to create that space so that the neutral people can go for peace diplomacy those are working at the ground level. The Naxalites can create aspirations among tribals to fight as they always stay among them. Whatever their diluted ideology, violence, differences in the party, sexual exploitation to the female cadres despite all these they have been able to hold the tribals. Sometimes, it is also found that the security forces use mis-propaganda to defame the leaders by saying sexual harassment to the females. As one of the respondents when asked didn't know anything and opined that she said out of fear of the police. So, there are cases of different types and the situation is very complicated. The security forces only can worsen the situation as whatever democracy the tribals are able to access will completely lost. The data shows that it is going towards destructive nature and violence will increase.

The peace talks in Andhra Pradesh did pave some ways which the government could not be able to encash. At the same time the discussion held in Odisha, but there was no one to follow it up. Peace talks, mediation, negotiation are not time event, it should be a process which will take many years. There should be a shift from law and order towards a socio-political-economic approach where there is a need of political response from the government. It is the need of the hour of the government to show its feelings to the tribals to restore peace. It is important to say that the government should access information from the research, and still more research is needed in the area of conflict and naxalite movement.

It is the time to rethink on the role of research for such of conflicts and violent movement to throw light on different perspectives. Research will help in framing the political response of the government to such an issue.

The role of peace making could be initiated and as it is a cumbersome process and it will take minimum five years to reach at a stage where both the confronting parties to come to a platform. This is again debatable whether government is going to invest so much of resources in peace keeping process for such a long period. The peace making stage will lead to peace keeping and ultimately to peace building. But constant and continuous negotiation with multi-track diplomacy should be a process and not as one time event. Many models are available for peace making which can be adopted or a group of experts can come up with a model. This model could be adopted by all the Naxalite affected zones to get a uniform outcome. The peace process should be taken parallel in all the states for a firm outcome.

Setting up a peace and conflict resolutions commission at the state level would definitely gear up the process. And if this is done in all the states which are affected by the Naxalite conflict which may bring some concrete results.

Whether it is right time for the government to initiate a peace process is the question. The route of Naxalite movement at the movement is on a violent path, and this will grow more violent as the research shows. Any further step from the government may enhance their hold. Since, the merger of their parties in 2004, they are also facing many challenges, and its right time for both the parties to show positive gestures for peace and justice as a first step to halt violence from both the sides. The need of the hour is to go for understanding each other and leaving behind the violent attitude, both of them should have peaceful dialogue to meet each other's need. Otherwise, there would be no end to the movement process; rather it will go beyond the socio-economic struggle to a complex path of war by joining hands with the neighbouring countries and with other extremist groups. We have to start the dialogue process immediately; otherwise, there may not be any right or auspicious time possible in future.

PHOTOGRAPHS

Photo 1: Shri Dandapani Mohanty interlocutor with other senior Members of the Party in Public Meeting

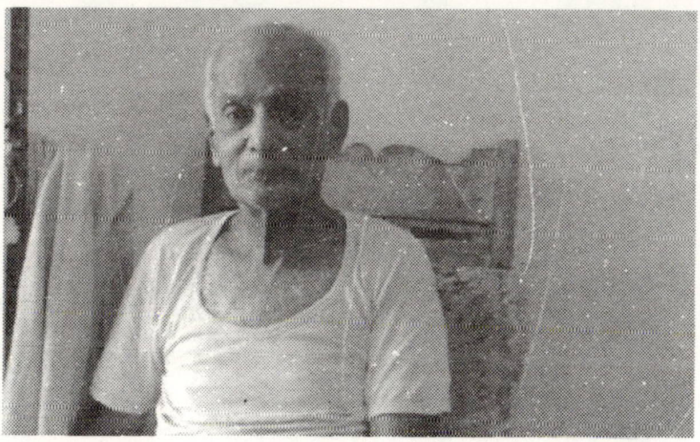

Photo 2: Late, D. Bhuvan Mohan Pattnaik, Communist leader of 1960s in South Orissa

Photo 3: Late Shri Biswanath Pattnaik with his team popular as Gandhi of Koraput

Photo 4: Jailed in 2006 from village Gillakuta of Gajapati, for watching a film called Lal Salam, they were released in 2008 and later talking about their plight in a public meeting

Photo 5: Malkangiri Collector in a Praja court

Photo 6: Martyrs Remembrance sign by the party

Photo 7: The alternative voices in an open meeting

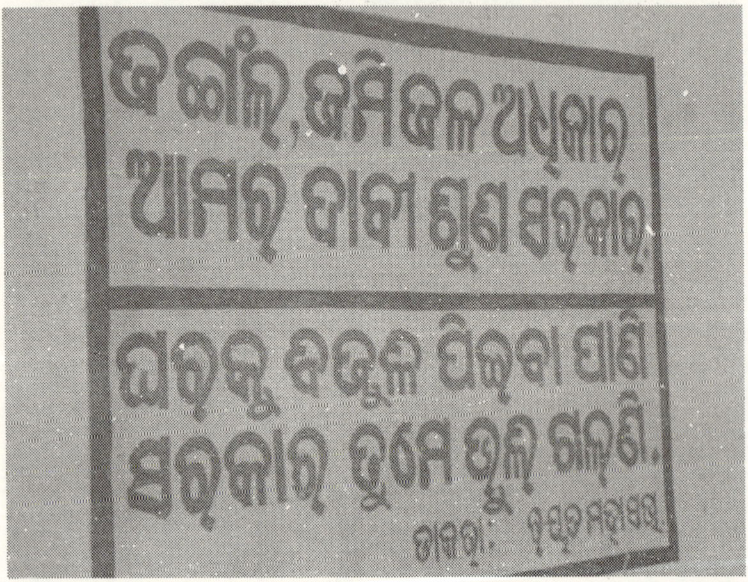

Photo 8: Other voices of dissent

Photo 9: Sahid stamba in a village bordering Koraput and Ma!kangiri.

Photo 10: BSNL tower blast by the Naxals

Annexures

Annexure-1

Case Study Points

(TO BE USED FOR ACADEMIC PURPOSE)

For Active Supporters: Koraput, Gajapati, Malkangiri, and Rayagada

1st Phase of Schedule and Questionnaires

Background

1. Age
2. Sex
3. Profession
4. Land holding
5. Type of land
6. Other assets
7. Family history (age, sex, marital status, educational status, relationship with the head of the household, their occupational details)
8. House pattern (size of the house, type of house)
9. Life Incidents from childhood days (social, cultural background)
10. His hobbies (since childhood days)
11. Aim in life (what he or she wanted to be in life)
12. What he dislikes the most
13. Turning points in life (since childhood days)

14. The good experiences in life (in family, village, what all situations elevate you)
15. Worst experiences in life (in family, village, with government officials)
16. Who are your best friends (since childhood, mention by name)?
17. What was his desire of his father and mother for his future/about his future?
18. What all of his friends are doing now?
19. Whom he trusts the most (in the family and in the village)
20. If married, the type of marriage (love, arranged, or any other, this is to understand the psychological perception of the person)
21. How he assess himself (cool minded, overt, covert, adjustive, aggressive, violent, emotional)
22. How he is attracted to his mother and father, brother, sister, friends, (to whom he likes the most).

2nd Phase of Schedule and Questionnaires

1. In his viewpoint, the present economic condition of tribes is satisfactory or not?
2. If tribes are in distress, what are the reasons responsible for such sufferings ?
3. Who have created such distress (government officials, money-lenders, traders, or other)?
4. To him what would be the possible remedies for it?
5. What role he can play personally for the prevention and remedy?
6. How long he and his tribesmen have tolerated such toruture?
7. When he became conscious about such situations?
8. Does he faced himself or listened from others?
9. How many times they have restricted the government officials, moneylenders and other torturing people?
10. Does their women have been tortured, molested, or raped by any outsiders?
11. How many times they have discussed the matter in the village council or at the village level meeting?
12. How many times they have requested the government officers for the remedy?

3rd Phase of Schedule and Questionnaires

1. Under what circumstances he or she was compelled to join movement?
2. Who motivated him or her first?
3. What was the justification in favour of the motivating factor ?
4. Does he or she finds them righteous, honest, truthful and disciplined persons or he or she was simply motivated because of his personal experiences (as tortures)?
5. Does he find them better than the moneylenders, traders, the government officials and other people ?
6. How he became the member of the troupe?
7. What was his first experience in the group?
8. What are the principles they believe in and follow in practice?
9. The daily life in the camp and in various operations?
10. Does he or she believe that such movements will reward justice to them?
11. Wherefrom they get money for their sustenance?
12. Difficulties they have to tolerate and overcome during the camp life, the type of training, type of punishment in case of any deviation?
13. How the male and female relationship is regulated in the camp life? Or do they have illicit relation whenever the opportunity comes?
14. Is there any religion practice or celebration in the camp days?
15. Various cadres in the organization and their power, roles?
16. How the Naxal members maintain relationship with their family or children and any difficulty faced in this regard?
17. What was the code language or ways of communication used in camps?
18. During illness how they manage in the camp?
19. How do they move (mobility)?
20. What type of weapons they use and mention cadre specific weapons?
21. How they are trained ?
22. Whom they target most?
23. Do they believe in change through violence/armed struggle? If yes why can not they feel for their family members whom they killed?
24. Why, they become so brutal and violent?

25. Can not they go for any other alternative to achieve their goal? (collect their ethics, principles, constitution)

4th Phase of Schedule and Questionnaires

1. Historical background of Naxal movement in Korpaut region?
2. Who initiated first? And what were the principles in the beginning?
3. Historical changes in subsequent periods along with the principles and constitution?
4. Why the present change to brutal action have been made?
5. Justify with reasons?
6. What is the future action they intend to and if through negotiation and discussion they are advised to achieve their goal ... will they accept?
7. Do you feel that naxal movement is commercialized its goal? now it is used as a source of income?
8. So far, how they have helped the poor sections of the society and struggled against re-chained torturing people?
9. Who are the direct supporters of naxal movement inside the tribal community and outside?
10. Those who are not supporting, are they doing any harm to them? What are the reasons for their non-support?
11. Anything they would like to share? Do they he or she wants to suggest any framework for change to the government?

Annexure-2

Questionnaire for Passive Supporters

(TO BE USED FOR ACADEMIC PURPOSE)

Topic—Role and Participation of Tribals in Naxal Movement—A Situational Analysis of South Orissa. Focus area—4 districts, Koraput, Malkangiri, Rayagada and Gajapati of Orissa.

1. How much do you know yourself about the movement?
2. How much you have observed such activities in your surroundings?
3. How much you get to now from media.
4. What does the pamphlets and posters of Naxals say, if you have seen any of them?
5. What do you think is it the right path to establish equity and equality in the society?
6. Do you feel that is there any kind of success in these kinds of endeavours?
7. Do you accept them, personally? What do you feel about the class structure of our society? Is it providing a ground for them?
8. Do they do any good to the people or tribal communities?
9. Why government and especially police is having conflict with them?
10. Why they are against the system?
11. Why they do not believe the government machinery?
12. In the present scenario which is the best option. .... The existing government or the system that is they dream (Naxals)?
13. If you have any framework in mind for dialoguing with Naxals please suggest?
14. If you find an occasion how do you extend your support to them?.. to Naxals, to the movement?
15. Do you believe, in spite of democratic government which is for

the people, by the people and of the people, how Naxal revolution will help the common people better?

16. How this conflict can be resolved, do you have suggestions on the peace framework to the Government?

Annexure-3

Leaflet of Koraput District Communist Party—Fight Against Exploitation by Money Lenders and for Land Rights (Year 1964-65)

ରୟତ ଭାଇଙ୍କୁ କମ୍ୟୁନିଷ୍ଟ ପାର୍ଟିର ଡାକରା ।

ଭୂମି ବଣ୍ଟା ଆଇନପାଇଁ -ବନ୍ଧାଭୂମି ମୁକୁଳିବାପାଇଁ, -ଭୂମିସତ୍ତ୍ୱ କାଟିବାପାଇଁ, -ପଡିଆ ଭୂମିର ଏଟାପାଇଁ -ପୋଡୁ କେଶ ରଦ୍ଦ କରିବାପାଇଁ -ଏକ୍ୟୁଟ [illegible]

ସରକାର-ସାହୁକାର ମେଣ୍ଟ ହଟାଅ ।

[illegible]

[illegible]

[illegible]

[illegible]

(୨)

[illegible]

[illegible]

[illegible]

[illegible]

[illegible]

। ଇତି ।

ଶ୍ରୀ [illegible]

ସମ୍ପାଦକ

କୋରାପୁଟ ଜିଲ୍ଲା କମ୍ୟୁନିଷ୍ଟ ପାର୍ଟି

"ଭାରତ ଜନତାର—ଜୟହେଉ ।"

"କମ୍ୟୁନିଷ୍ଟ ପାର୍ଟିର—ଜୟହେଉ ।"

୧ ଶ୍ରୀ [illegible]—କୋଟପାଡ଼

୨ ଶ୍ରୀ ଭଗବାନ [illegible] ନାୟକ—[illegible]

୩ ଶ୍ରୀ [illegible]—ନବରଙ୍ଗପୁର

୪ ଶ୍ରୀ [illegible]—[illegible]

୫ ଶ୍ରୀ [illegible]—[illegible]

୬ ଶ୍ରୀ [illegible] ପଟ୍ଟନାୟକ—[illegible]

୭ ଶ୍ରୀ [illegible]—କୋଟପାଡ଼

୮ ଶ୍ରୀ [illegible]—[illegible]

୯ ଶ୍ରୀ [illegible]—[illegible]

୧୦ ଶ୍ରୀ [illegible]—[illegible]

୧୧ ଶ୍ରୀ [illegible]—[illegible]

୧୨ ଶ୍ରୀ [illegible] ମାଝି—ନବରଙ୍ଗପୁର

୧୩ ଶ୍ରୀ [illegible]—[illegible]

୧୪ ଶ୍ରୀ [illegible]—[illegible]

୧୫ ଶ୍ରୀ [illegible]—[illegible]

୧୬ ଶ୍ରୀ [illegible]—[illegible]

୧୭ ଶ୍ରୀ [illegible]—[illegible]

୧୮ ଶ୍ରୀ [illegible] ନାୟକ—[illegible]

୧୯ ଶ୍ରୀ [illegible]—[illegible]

୨୦ ଶ୍ରୀ [illegible]—[illegible]

Annexure-4

Judgement Copy of Additional Sessions Court, Gajapati on acquittal of six tribals of R.Udaygiri case (Dated. 15.05.2008)

In the Court of the Additional Sessions Judge,
Gajapati, Parlakhemundi, Orissa.

Present: Shri A.K. Acharya, M.A., LL.B.,
Additional Sessions Judge,
Gajapati, Parlakhemundi.
Session Case No. 22/07,
Date of argument: 08.05.08
Date of Judgement: 15.05.08

(Committed by the J.M.F.C., R.Udayagiri in G.R. case No. 174/06 arising out of Adava P. S. case No. 41/06 u/s. 124-A/506/384 I.P.C. and Sec.17(2) Crl.L.A. Act)

State. ... Complainant.

Vrs.

1. Anita Majhi, *vs.* Biar Mayee Majhi, D/o. Patasingh Majhi, *vs* Patra Majhi, aged about 20 years by occupation cultivation, Mauza Mandarabaju, P.S. Adava, Dist.Gajapati.
2. Anatha Mudrika *vs.* Prasanti *vs.* Susanta, d/o. late Mohan Mudrika, aged about 21 years, by occupation labour, Mauza Ratnaguda, P.S. Muniguda, Dist. Rayagada,
3. Kalidah Majhi *vs.* Manoj Majhi, s/o. late Denga Majhi, aged about 21 years, by occupation cultivation, Mauza Andarlina, P.S. Gudari, Dist, Rayagada.
4. Rameswar Ulaka *vs.* Narendra Dengamaka, s/o. Ghasiman Ullaka, aged about 25 years, by occupation cultivation, Mauza Ratnaguda, P.S. Muniguda, Dist. Rayagada.
5. Agata *vs.* Sunita Majhi, D/o Senu Majhi, aged about 26 years, by occupation cultivation, Mauza Mandrabaju, P.S. Adava, Dist. Gajapati.
6. Maheswar Brendela *vs* Muluku Majhi, s/o. late Sukru Brendela, aged about 21 years, by occupation cultivation, Mauza, Ratnaguda, P.S. Munigada, Dist. Rayadada.

... Accd. Persons.

Offence u/s. 124-A/506/384/34 IPC. and Sec. 17 of Crl. L.A. Act.

Counsel for the Prosecution : Sri Padmanabh Mund, P.P.
Counsel for the Defences : Sri U.P. Nayak, Advocate.

JUDGEMENT

The above named six accused persons stand trial u/s. 124-A/506/384 read with section 34 I.P.C. and u/s.17 of the Criminal Law Amendment Act.

2. The prosecution case as revealed from the FIR, in brief, is that on 22.9.06 at about 11.30 p.m. night the C.I. of police of R. Udayagiri received a reliable information that a group of Maoists along with their supporters were camping at village Gillakuta. It is alleged that the C.I. of police then proceeded to the said village along with his other staff and force during that night and surrounded the village from all sides. It is alleged that he saw that a group of males and females were performing some cultural programmes by dancing and singing songs in the village street, that he found the present accused persons there conducting the said cultural programme under the leadership of the accused Dasuram Majhi and that he came to know that in order to preach Maoist ideology in the village the accused persons have compelled the villagers not only to prepare food for them, but to witness the programme from beginning to end. It is alleged that in the course of such cultural programme the accused persons performed different dances, sang different songs and also showed different books and hand notes written in support of the Maoists which was banned by the Government of Orissa. It is alleged that the accused persons were intentionally conducting the cultural programme including the video show of films like Lalsalam, Kranti and songs of Charu Majumdar besides distributing booklets containing Kalinganagar issue with a view to bringing about a sense of hatred and disobedience towards the Government and its administrative machinery besides propagating the Maoist ideology among the villagers. It is alleged that upon raid though the present accused persons were caught red-handed on the spot their leader, i.e. the co-accused Dasuram Majhi fled away and that during the night itself the C.I. of police himself drew up the present F.I.R. and got it lodged before the O.I.C. of Adava P.S. on the next day. On this basis, this case was registered and after investigation, the police charge sheeted the present accused persons and the said

Dasuram Majhi showing him as an absconder under the above offences punishable u/s. 124-A/506/384/34 I.P.C. and u/s. 17 of Crl. Law Amendment Act where-under the present accused persons stood subsequently committed to the Court of Session except the said Dasuram Majhi the case against whom stood split up before commitment. The accused persons also stood subsequently charged under the said offences to which they pleaded not guilty and hence this trial.

3. The defence plea is one of denial.

4. The points for determination are:

Whether during the night of 22-9-06 in between 10-30 p.m. and 11.30 p.m. at village Gillakuta the above named accused persons along with the said Dasuram Majhi (split up) in furtherance of their common intention:

1. brought/attempted to bring hatred/contempt and excited/ attempted to cause disaffection towards the Government established by law by dancing, singing and showing different books and hand notes in an organised cultural programme/ meeting in support of Maoist activities;
2. criminally intimidated the audience of the said cultural programme/meeting by threatening them with injury to their persons intending to cause alarm to them;
3. committed extortion by intentionally putting the said audience in fear of dire consequence/injury to them in order to get them joined with their organisation; and
4. being a member of an unlawful association, i.e. the Maoist, organisation they took part in the meeting, assisted and promoted the said meeting in support of Maoist activities?

5. To above the case, the prosecution examined nine witnesses in all. P.W. 1 is the informant, being the then C.I. of police, R. Udayagiri and P.W.9 is the then O.I.C. of R. Udayagiri P.S. P.Ws. 2 to 7 are stated to be the eye witnesses to the occurrence/seizures and P.W.8 is the I.O. concerned of this case. On the other hand, the accused persons did not examine any witness in their defence.

6. The informant, i.e. the then C.I. of police of R.Udayagiri (P.W. 1) stated that on 22-9-2006 in the evening he received reliable information and that accordingly he along with the then O.I.C. of R.Udayagiri P.S. alongwith other police staff of that P.S. immediately proceeded to village

Gillakuta situated within the jurisdiction of Adava P.S. According to him, they reached the village at about 10-30 p.m., surrounded that village from all sides by deployment of force and upon search he found that a cultural programme was being held in the village. According to him, the accused persons being outsiders were present there and they were conducting the cultural programme by dancing, singing and exhibiting video shows. According to him, the accused persons also forced the villagers not only to prepare food for them, but to sit and see the programme. According to him, he came to know that the accused persons were the supporters of Maoists and by conducting the cultural programme they were preaching the Maoist ideology by speaches, video shows and distribution of various pamplets containing slogans against the Government and the administration. According to him, he also found other printed and hand written materials containing the biography of Charu Majumdar and his literary works, besides the recent Kalinganagar issue from their bags. According to him, the accused persons also admitted themselves to be the Maoist supporters besides admitting that they have come to that village to preach Maoist ideology. According to him the leader of the accused persons, i.e. one Dasuram Majhi fled away from the spot. According to him, the Maoist activities were completely banned by the Government and hence he prepared the FIR., *vide* Ext.1 on the spot and handed over the same to the O.I.C. of Adava P.S. for further action. The then O.I.C. of R. Udayagiri P.S. stated that after the informant received information on 22-9-2006 that some naxal people had gathered in village Gillakuta under Adava P.S. he (P.W.9) accompanied the informant to the spot alongwith other police staff. According to him, upon reaching the village he found the accused persons there and of them one male and one female were singing songs in the village road. According to him, since the said songs were in Kui language (Adibasi language) he came to know from the villagers that through the said songs the accused persons were attracting the villagers to involve themselves in Maoist activities. According to him, there was a BPL T.V. and three C.Ds., of Lalsalam and Kranti pictures, a number of dancing equipments and some literatures containing topics against the Government and in support of the Maoist organisation. According to him, there was a Newspaper cutting also showing that the banning of the naxal organisation was challenged in the High Court. According to him, the informant then drew up the plain paper F.I.R. on the spot. According to him, the leader, i.e. Dasuram Majhi fled away from the spot seeing the police. The other witnesses (P.Ws.2, 3, 4, 5, 6 and 7) did not support the prosecution case at all by deposing that they did not know either, the informant or the accused persons or anything about this case and that they are not examined by the police. P.Ws. 2 and 3, however, further added, that they gave their signatures vide Exits. 2 series and 3 series on four papers as the police told them.

7. The I.O. (P.W.8) stated that in the evening of 22-9-2006 he received a telephone call from the informant (P.W. 1) about the gathering of naxal people at Gillakuta village and that hence he along with his other police staff of Adava P.S. proceeded to that village. According to him, on reaching the village he found, the accused persons there including the two women accused persons. According to him, he then seized the cultural instruments *vide* M.O. V to IX, three C.Ds., namely Lalsalam, Kranti and Lalsalam video M.O. I to III and some other papers including torch light, umbrella etc. from the possession of the accused Narendra as per seizure list *vide* Ext. 3/4. He examined the seizure witnesses, seized one TV, one V.C.D. player, one cot and a sound box, from one Siman Raita as per seizure list *vide* Ext. 2/8, examined the witnesses, visited the spot and arrested all the six accused persons. On the next evening he returned back to Adava P.S. along with the accused persons and the seized articles, registered this case as per F.I.R. vide Ext.1 which he had received from the informant on the spot and took up investigation. He forwarded the accused persons to the court, verified the addresses of the accused persons, prepared the spot map *vide* Ext. 6 and examine the accused persons after bringing them to police custody. On 26-11-2006 he released the video equipments except the C.Ds. in zima of Siman Raita as per zimanana *vide* Ext. 4/1 and also prayed to the S.P. Gajapati to obtain the sanction of the Government for prosecution u/s. 124-A I.P.C. and after completion of investigation, he submitted the present charge sheet against the accused persons.

8. The chargesheet has been placed against as many as seven accused persons including the present six and as discussed above, the case against the remaining co-accused, i.e. Dasuram Majhi was split up. The charge has been framed u/s. 124-A/506/384/34 I.P.C. and u/s. 17 of the Crl.Law Amendment Act, 1908. It can be noticed that in respect of the charge punishable u/s.124-A I.P.C. the sanction of the Government has admittedly not been obtained and the net result in view of the conspicuous omission would be that this charge has to fail completely.

9. As the evidence of the I.P. (P.W.8) goes, he seized a number of articles from the spot as per seizure lists *vide* Ext. 3/4 and 2/8 in the presence of witnesses. Not a single such witness supported the fact of seizure and the prosecution case and though they (P.Ws. 2 to 7) were

declared hostile and were cross-examined by the prosecution with reference to their earlier statements before police and as per the seizure lists nothing material was elicited from them in support of the prosecution and the seizures. Though the video equipments were seized from the possession of one Siman Raita (P.W.4) and though those articles were also left in his zima he (P.W.4) never supported that fact and made it clear that he did not see the police in the village in the night of 22-9-2006. Similarly, the version of the I.O. that he seized the objectionable articles from the possession of accused Narendra Dengama does not find any corroboration from both the police officers, i.e. the informant (P.W.1) and P.W.9 who never stated that fact in their evidence.

10. Now, coming to the charges punishable u/s. 506/ 384 I.P.C. and u/s.17 of Crl. Act it can be noticed that there is absolutely nothing in the evidence of all the three police officers (P.Ws.1, 8 and 9) in specific terms that the accused persons issued threats to any body of that village. The villagers, i.e. P.Ws. 2 to 7, as already discussed, did not whisper a single word on the point and the version of the informant (P.W.1) that the accused persons also made the villagers sit and see the programme under compulsion, as it appears, has also not been supported in specific terms by the other two police officers, i.e. P.Ws. 8 and 9. The then I.I.C. of R. Udayagiri P.S. (P.W.9) who was there stated that the accused persons were talking in Kui language and that the Ward member, namely Pitar Majhi and the villagers, namely Joseph and Danial told him that the accused persons through Kui language were giving speeches against the Government besides attracting the villagers to involve themselves in the Maoist activities. There is nothing of the sort in the evidence of the other two police officers, i.e. P.Ws.1 and 8 and the fact also remains that the said Pitar Majhi (P.W.6), Joseph (P.W.2) and Danial (P.W.5) did not whisper a single word to corroborate the version of P.W.9. Anyway, the aforesaid is apparently the basis for the police officers to know the contents of the talks and songs of the accused persons in Kui language and it is, therefore, further apparent that had the said three persons (P.Ws. 2, 5 and 6) not explained the Kui versions of the accused persons in Oriya to the police officers, i.e. P.Ws. 1, 8 and 9 who were on the spot then the matter would have been different. As this court finds, the aforesaid basis is not proved for the simple reason that there is not only no corroboration to that effect in the evidence of both police officers (P.Ws. 1 and 8), but no support also from, the so called translators (P.Ws. 2, 5 and 6). The versions of the police officers (P.Ws. 1, 8 and 9) that the accused persons compelled the villagers to prepare food for them and to witness the cultural programme from beginning to end do not get any support from

any of the villagers being apparently the victims and the fact also remains that while the informant (P.W.1) stated that he could not name the singers and the dancers whom he saw from a distance and that he did not remember the exact dialogues which the accused persons were uttering to influence the villagers P.W. 9 stated that he could not name the owner of the house in front of which the programme was going on nor he could name the person from whose house the electricity was obtained for the video show which was already complete by the time of their arrival, and P.W. 8 stated that he could not name the language in which the accused persons were singing songs, that he did not engage any person knowing Kui language to translate the versions of the accused persons for recording their statements in Oriya and that he did not site all police officers/constables as witnesses in this case. Thus, the quality of the evidence as adduced by the police officers themselves (P.Ws.1, 3 and 9) is as above and the fact also remains that the version of the informant (P.W.1) that the accused persons themselves admitted to be the Maoist supporters besides admitting that they have come to the village to preach Maoist ideology does not find any support from the evidence of other two police officers, i.e. P.Ws. 8 and 9. Anyway, even if it is accepted for the sake of argument that the accused persons admitted so before the informant being a police officer the same cannot at all be used against them being clearly inadmissible. Admittedly, the seized articles were not submitted to the court along with the chargesheet and it was suggested to the I.O. that being instructed by the Administration he falsely implicated the present accused persons being innocent Adibasis and it was suggested to the informant, i.e. the then C.I. of police that instead of apprehending the real Maoist culprits he falsely involved these accused persons to save his skin. Be that as it may. The evidence, as the court finds, is too discrepant to be safely relied upon beyond reasonable doubt.

11. In view of the discussions of the entire matter from all angles this court is of the considered opinion that the charge punishable u/s.124-A I.P.C. not only cannot succeed for want of required Government Sanction, but the charges punishable under remaining sections, i.e. 506/384 I.P.C. and u/s.17 of the Criminal Amendment Act read with section 34 I.P.C. have also to fail completely for the simple reason that the alleged occurrence and the involvement of the accused persons therein has not at all been proved by evidence on record beyond reasonable doubt. In the facts and the circumstances, the accused persons are entitled to get the benefit of doubt and hence the prosecution has thus utterly failed in this case. In the result, therefore, it is ordered that:

1. All the six accused persons are hereby found not guilty and are acquitted of the offences punishable u/s. 124-A/506/384/34 I.P.C. and u/s. 17 of the Crl. Law Amendment Act, 1908 under the provisions of section 235(I) Cr.P.C. All of them be set at liberty forthwith.
2. The bail bonds of both female accused persons shall stand cancelled.
3. The order relating to the seized articles will be passed at the time of the disposal of the pending split up case against accused Dasuram Majhi.

Typed to my dictation, corrected by me and pronounce in the open court on this the 15th day of May, 2008 under my hand and seal of this court.

sd/- A.K. Acharya, 15-5-2008,
Additional Sessions Judge,
Parlakhemundi.

Witnesses examined for the prosecution:

P.W.1	Asok Kumar Sahoo
P.W.2	Joseph Majhi
P.W.3	Mikhail Majhi
P.W.4	Siman Raita
P.W.5	Danial Majhi
P.W.6	Pitara Majhi
P.W.7	Lasmi Majhi
P.W.8	Raisan Murmun
P.W.9	Trilochan Swain

Witness examined for the defence:—None.

Exhibits marked for the prosecution:

Ext. 1	Plain paper F.I.R.
Ext.1/1	Signature of P.W.1
Ext. 2	Signature of P.W.2
Ext. 2/1	Signature of P.W.2
Ext. 3	Signature of P.W.2
Ext. 3/1	Signature of P.W.2
Ext. 2/2	Signature of P.W.3

Ext. 2/3 Signature of P.W.3
Ext. 3/2 Signature of P.W.3
Ext. 3/3 Signature of P.W.3
Ext. 2/4 Signature of P.W.4
Ext. 2/5 Signature of P.W.4
Ext. 4 Signature of P.W.4
Ext. 3/4 Seizure list
Ext. 3/5 Signature of P.W.8
Ext. 3/6 Signature of P.W.8
Ext. 2/6 Seizure list
Ext. 2/7 Signature of P.W.8.
Ext. 2/8 Signature of P.W.8.
Exit.5 Formal F.I.R.
Exit. 1/2 Endorsement of P.W.8 on Exit.1.
Ext. 6 Spot map.
Exts. 7 to 14 Police requisitions.
Ext. 4/1 Zimanama.
Ext. 4/2 Signature of P.W.8.

Exhibits marked for the defence:- Nil.

M.Os. marked for the prosecution:

M.O. I Lalsalam C.D.
M.O. II Lalsalam C.D.
M.O. III Kranti C.D.
M.O. IV KUI, Bina, Bambugadi.
M.O. V Kalinganagargadi.
M.O. VI Charu Majumbdargadi.
M.O. VII Telephone index.
M.O. VIII Nine pairs of gungurus
M.O. IX One pair of daskatia.
M.O. X Paper cutting

M.Os. marked for the defence: Nil.

sd/- A.K. Acharya, 15-5-2008,
Additional Sessions Judge,
Parlakhemundi.

Typed by:
Read by:
Com. by:

T. ws. 3460

T. es. [illegible]

Examined and found to be a ture Copy Folios correctly assessed. Stamps properly paid.

[illegible] 7/6/08

Head Comparing Clerk.

Certified to be a ture copy.

[illegible]

Sheristedar

Bibliography

Books, Articles and Journals

Abraham, Itty and Nayaka, Sumie. (2007) Uncertainty, Knowledge and Violence in Southern Thailand: *EPW*, Vol. No, XLII, No. 24.

Aiya, S.P. (1979). *Political Violence in India*, Ajmer: Sachin Publications.

Anatomy of a Confrontation. The Babri Masjid-Ram Janambhumi Issue.

Baipai, Kanti (2001): Managing a Strategic Triangle: India, China and Pakistan," in Sahadevan, P. (2001) *Conflict and Peacemaking in South Asia*, New Delhi, Lancers Books, pp. 81-105 (24 pp.).

Balgopal, K. (2005), Naxalites in Andhra Pradesh: *EPW*, Vol. XL, No. 13.

Ball, Nicole, (2001): The Challenge of Rebuilding War-torn Societies in Crocker, Chester, A. Fen Osler Hampson and Pamela Aall (eds), *Turbulent Peace: The Challenges of Managing International Conflict*, Washington DC: United States Institute of Peace. Ch. 42, pp. 719-736, (17 pp.).

Banerjee, Parthasarathi (2006) Land Acquisition and Peasant Resistance at Singur, *EPW*, Vol. KLI, No. 46.

Banerjee, Sikata (1996): "The feminization of violence in Bombay: Women in the politics of the Shiv Sena", in *Asian Survey*, Vol. 36, No. 12 (December 1996), pp. 1213, 1225.

Banerjee, Sumanta (2005). All quest on the Maoism Front, *EPW*, Vol. XL, No. 6.

Banerjee, Sumanta (2005). Hobson's Choice for Indian Communist, *EPW*, Vol. XL, No 19.

Banerjee, Sumanta (2006), Peasant Haves and Capitalists Hounds of Singur. *EPW*, Vol. SLI, No. 52.

Banerjee, Sumanta (2006). Beyond Naxalbari: *EPW*, XLI, No. 29.

Barash, D.P. and C. Webel (2009) (2nd ed), *Peace and Conflict Studies*. Thousand Oaks (also New Delhi, India): Sage Publications. Chap. 1,4,5,6,7,8,9.10,13,14,15,16,17,18,19,20,21 (364 pp.).

Barash, D.P., Webel, C.P. (2009), *Peace and Conflict Studies*. Los Angeles: Sage Publications.

Basu, Pradip (2000). *Towards Naxalbari, An Account of Inner Party Struggles*, Calcutta: Progressive Publishers.

Behuria, N.N. Madras Act of 1 of 1917, *Final report on the major settlement operations in Koraput district, 1938-64,* p. 253.

Bera, Gautam (2nd) (2008). *The Unrest Axle, Ethno-social Movements in Eastern India*, New Delhi: Mittal Publications.

Bhadra, R.K. and Bhadra, Mita (ed.) (2007). *Ethnicity, Movement and Social Structure Contested Cultural Identity*, New Delhi: Rawat Publications.

Bhatia, Bela (2005) Naxalism in Central Bihar: *EPW*, Vol. Xl, No. 15.

Bhattacharya, Dipankar, (2006). Trial Blazed by Naxalbari Uprising (discussion). *EPW*, Vol. XLI, No. 50.

Bose, Anima (1981): "A Gandhian Perspective on Peace", in *Journal of Peace Research*, Vol. 18, No. 2, pp. 159-164 (5 pp.).

Bose, Sugata and Ayesha Jalal (1998): *Modern South Asia, History, Culture, Political Economy*, New Delhi: Oxford University Press, pp. 165-189 (24 pp.).

Bouffard, Sonia and David Carment (2006): The Sri Lank Peace Process: A Critical Reviews, in *Journal of South Asian Development*, Vols. 1, 2, pp. 151-177 (26 pp.)

Casets, Remi (2003), *The Uighurs in Xinjiang: The Malaise Grows*, China Perspectives No. 49.

Chandke, Neera, (2005). Seeing the State in India, *EPW*, Vol. XL, No. 11.

Choudhury, Rajiv (2006) Fourth World: Marxism, Gandhian, *EPW*, Vol. XI, No. 42.

D.T. (2007) Uighur Culture Faced with Endless Campaigns, China Rights Forums, No. 4.

Das, Ratan (2004). *Gandhi and Mao*, New Delhi: Sarup & Sons.

Das, Ratan (2004): *Encountering (Cultural) Nationalism, Islam and Gender in the Body Politic of India, in Social Identities*, 10:3 London: Routledge, pp. 369-398 (20 pp.).

Dash, S.N., *A Study of the problems of land alienation in tribal areas with special reference to the district of Koraput, 2001.*

Dash, Satyaprakash, (2006), Towards a knowledge based society: *EPW*, Vol. XLI, No. 37.

Development Challenges of Extremists Affected Areas, Report of an Expert Group of Planning Commission, Government of India, 2006-2008.

Diliya, Kanak Muri (2005) Perspectives on Nepal Absolute Monarchy to Obscure Democracy: *EPW*, Vol. Xl, No. 15.

District Gazetteer Koraput, 1918, Francis.

District Gazetteer Koraput, 1945, Bell, RCS.

District Gazetteer Koraput, 1966, Senapati.

Doudet, Veroniue, (2008): Non-violent Resistance and conflict transformation in power asymmetries, in Fisher, Martina, Hans J. Giefsmann and Beatrix Schmelzle (eds.) (2008): *Berghof Handbook for conflict transformation*, Berlin: Berghof Research Center for Constructive Conflict Management.

Dubey, Amaresh and Haan De Arhan (2005) Development of Underdevelopment in Orissa, Poverty Disparities, *EPW*, Vol. XL, Nos. 22 and 23.

Economic Survey 2011-2012, Planning Commission, Government of India.

Economics, in *Journal of Peace Research*, Vol. 36, No. 3 (1999), pp. 349-361 (13 pp.)

Editorial *EPW* (Sept. 10-16) 2005: *Deadly cycle of violence*. Vol. XI, No. 37.

Engineer, Asghar Ali (2003): *On Developing Theology of Peace in Islam*, New Delhi, Sterling Publishers Private Limited, pp. 26-37 (11 pp).

EPW Commentary 2005: Royal Gamble in Nepal. Vol. XL, No. 8.

EPW, Vol. XX, No. 1.

Esteva, Gustavo (2001): Development in Sachs, Wolfgang (ed.) (2001): *The Development Dictionary, A Guide to Knowledge as Power*, London: Zed Books Ltd., pp. 6-24 (19 pp).

Farriingtor, John, and Other (2006). Tribal land Alienaton in Andhra Pradesh *EPW*, Vol. XLI, No. 52.

Fernandes, Sujata (2006): Way Forward for Left in Latin America, *EPW*, Vol. XII, No. 31.

Fernandes, Sujata (2006): With or Without Fledl: Future of the Cuban Revolution: *EPW*, Vol. XLI, No. 38.

Food Security Atlas of Orissa, (2008): Foundation for Ecological Society, Orissa.

Francis, Diana (2004): "Culture, Power Asymmetries and Gender in Conflict Transformation" in Fischer, Martina, Hans J. Giefsmann and Beatrix Schmelzle (eds.) (2004): *Berghof Handbook for Conflict Transformation*, Berlin: Berghof Research Center for constructive conflict management.

Functioning of the Fifth Schedule of the Constitution in the State of Orissa, NCDS 2001.

Functioning of Welfare Schemes for the Scheduled Castes and Scheduled Tribes: A Report on Orissa, NCDS, 2001.

G. Pdhy, Subhash (2008). *Social Movement in Orissa (1936-76)*. Kolkata, MPR Printers.

Gail, Omvedt (1992): Hinduism, Social Inequality and the State, in Allen, Douglas (eds.) (1992): *Religion and Political Conflict in South Asia, India, Pakistan and Sri Lanka*, West Port Connecticut, Greenwood Press, pp. 17-36 (19 pps).

Galtung, Johan (1990): Cultural violence, in *Journal of Peace Research*, Vol. 27, No. 3, pp. 291-305 (14 pp).

Galtung, Johan, (1971), A structural theory of imperialism, In David P. Barash (ed.), *A Reader in Peace Studies (2000)*, New York, Oxford University Press.

Gellener, David, *EPW* (May 1902) 2007, *Nepal: Towards a Democratic Republican*, Vol. XLII, No. 20.

Gluckman, Max. (1971), *Politics Law and Ritual in Tribal Society*, London: Basil Blackwell Oxford.

Goodhand, Jonathan (2002): Aiding Violence or Building Peace? The role of International Aid in Afghanistan. *Third World Quarterly*, Vol. 23, No. 5, pp. 837-859 (22 pp).

Government of India, Planning Commission, *Report on Development of Tribal Areas*, National Committee on the Development of Backward Areas.

Government of Orissa, *Report on the Annual Administration of Scheduled Areas of in Orissa for 1991-92*, Public Welfare Department, Bhubaneswar, p. 1.

Government of Orissa, *Evaluation Report of ITDA*, Malkangiri, Operation Research Group, Bhubaneswar, pp. 292-294.

Government of Orissa, *Report on the Annual Administration of Schedule Areas of Orissa for 1992-93*, Public Welfare Department, p. 1.

Government of Orissa, *Tribal Sub-Plan for Eighth Plan 1990-95 and Annual Plan, 1991-92*. Orissa, Draft, Harijan and Tribal Welfare Department, November 1990.

Guha, Ramachandra (2007): Advasis, Naxalities and Indian Democracy. In *Economic and Political Weekly*, August 2007, pp. 3305-3312 (8 pp).

Gupta, D. Tilak (2006): Maoists Movement in India: *EPW*, Vol. XLI, No. 29.

Gusterson, Hugh (1999): Nuclear Weapons and the other in the Western Imagination, in *Cultural Anthropology*, Vol. 14, No. 1, pp. 111-143 (33pp).

Hansen, Wibke; Oliver Ramsbotham and Tom Woodhouse, (2004): Hawks and Doves: Peacekeeping and Conflict Resolution in Alex Austin, Martine Fisher and Norbert Ropers (eds.) *Transforming Ethnopolitical Conflict: The Berghof Handbook*, Wiesbaden: VS Verlag for Sozialwissenschaften/ GWV Fachverlage GmbH, pp. 296-319 (23pp).

Hardiman, David (2003): *Gandhi in His Time and Ours*, Delhi, Permanent Black, pp. 198-237 (39 pp).

Hardiman, David (2003): *Gandhi in His Time and Ours*, Delhi, Permanent Black, Chap 3, pp. 39-65 (28 pp).

Harshe, Rajen (2006). Culture Identity and International Relations: *EPW*, Vol. XLI, No. 37.

Hebbar, Ritambhara (2006), Forest Bill 2005 and Tribal Areas of Jharkhand, *EPW*, Vol. XII, No. 48.

http://cmdata.iucn.org

http://en.wikipedia.org/wiki/global peace index.retrived global index, 2010, Results and Findings, Institute of Economixs

http://en.wikipedia.org/wiki/Human.rights

http://mikeely.wordpress.com

http://naxalrevolution;blogspot.com/search/lebel.links

http://rdf-2005.blogspot.com

http://recpkarnataka.blogspot.com

http://resistanceindia.blogspot.com

http://rpkeral.blogspot.com

http://southasisnrev.wordpress.com.2000

http://tamilporali.blogspot.com

http://web.archieve.org/wed/*/http://www.geocities.com/cpimlpwg

http://webarchieve.org/wed/20030823153035/http://peoplesmarch.com

http://www,berghof-handbook.net/uploads/download/duduet_handbook.pdf, retrieved on 6.04.2009 (27 pps)

http://www.achrweb.org/reports/india/AR07/orissa.htm

http://www.bannedthought.net/india

http://www.berghof-handbook.net/uploads/download/francis_handbook.pdf. retrieved 2.4.2009 (16 pp)

http://www.geocities.com/cpimlpwg

http://www.hrichina.org/public/PDFs?CRF.4.2007/CRF-2007-4.uyghur.pdf

http://www.rediff.com/news.slide-show/slide-show-1-kashmiri-freedom-movement-has-been-derailied/20100906.htm

http://www.shvoong.com.social-sciences

http://www.vcn.bc.ca/citizens-handbook August 2001

http://www.vedamsbooks.in/no48384/peace-diplomacy-amalendu-guha

http://www.vifindia.org/article/2011/January/14/Maosit-funding-dimensions-sources-and –implications

http://www.visionofhumanity.org/gpi-data

http://www.worldliveevenet.com/naxalite-movement-in-india

http://yojana.gov.in

Huges, Kristy (2005). Crisis coming to a lead: *EPW*, XL, No. 37.

Human Development Report, 2004. Orissa.

Hunger Amidst Plenty (editorial). *EPW*, Vol. XLI, No. 40.

Integrated Tribal Development Agency, Koraput, Orissa, Project Report 1983-85.

International Crisis Group (2004): Myanmar, Sanctions, Engagement or Another Way Forward? Yangon/Brussels, *ICG Asia Report*, N. & 8, pp. 12-24 (12 pp).

Jacobsen D.I. (2003), (Spl. edition), *Understanding Conflict and Violence, Theoretical and Interdisciplinary Approaches*, N.W. Routledge.

Jain, Madhu (2005), Draft Scheduled Tribe Nill – a comment, *EPW,* Vol. XL, No. 21.

Jja, Praveen (2005), State Education: Withering Commitments and Weakening Provisions: *EPW*, Vol. XL, No. 31.

Johannesen, A. Tufte, P.A., Kristoffersen, L. (2007), *Introduksjon till samfunnsvitenkapelig metode*, Abstrackt forlag AS.

Johansen, Robert C. (1997): "Radical Islan and Non-violence: A Case Study of Religious Empowerment and Constraint among Pashtuns", in *Journal of Peace Research*. Vol. 34, No. 1, pp. 53-71 (18pp).

Joshi, Barbara R. (1992): "Untouchables, Religion, and Politics: The Changing Face of Struggle", in Allen, Douglas (ed.) (1992): *Religion and Political Conflict in South Asia, India, Pakistan and Sri Lanka*, Westport conecticut, Greenwood Press, pp. 37-54 (17 pp).

Jungle Bhitaraku Rasta, Abhay Mohapatra (an old book which didnt had its publishers name on it).

Kaldor, Mary (1998): *Old Wars in New and Old Wars. Organized Violence in a Global Era*, New Delhi: Natraj Publishers, pp. 13-30 (18 pps).

Kaldor, Mary (1998): "The Politics of New Wars", in *New and Old Ward. Organized Violence in Global Era*, New Delhi: Natraj Publishers, pp. 69-89 (20 pp).

Kannibiran, Kalpana and Kannirbiena Vasantha and Others (2005), Reflections on Peace Process in Andhra Pradesh. *EPW*, Vol. XL, No. 7.

KBKroundtable@googlegroup.com

Khan, Irene (2004): "Protectiing the Rights and Refugees", in Sammaddar, Ranabir (ed.) (2004): *Peace Studies. An Introduction to the Concept, Scope, and Themes*, New Delhi, Sage, pp. 190-205 (15 pp).

Khattak, Saba Gul (2005): "In: Security Afghan Women Refugees", In Faizal, *Farah and Swarna Rajagopalan* (eds.) (2005): *Women, Security, South Asia, A Clearing in the Thicket*, New Delhi, Sage Publications, pp. 112-133 (21 pp).

Khora, Sthabir, (2005), Low Literacy in Orissa, *EPW*, Vol. XL, No. 10.

Kikon, Dolly (2005), Engaging Naga Nationalism, *EPW*, Vol. XL, No. 26.

Korn, Richard, R. and Mocorkie, W. Lloyd, (1960), *Criminology and Penology*, New York, Holt, Rinehart, and Winston Inc.

Koshy, Ninan (2002): *The War on Terror, Reordering the World*, New Delhi, Leftword.

Koshy, Ninan, (2002): *The War on Terror, Reordering the World*, New Delhi, Left word, pp. 31-42 (11 pp).

Kujur, Rajat, and Chakraborty, Bidyut (2009): *Maoslim in India*

Reincarnation of Ultra Left Wing Extremism in the Twenty First Century, New Delhi, Manohar Publications.

Kumar, Airn, (2006): Culture, Development and the Control Capitalists of France, *EPW*, Vol. XLI, No. 40.

Ladur, Vinay (2005), When the Violence, find voice, *EPW*, Vol. XLI, No. 27.

Lawer, Peter (2008): "Peaces Studies" in Paul D. Williams (ed.) (2008): *Security Studies: An Introduction*, U.K. Routledge, pp. 73-88 (16 pp).

Lel, Sharrachchandra, (2007) Forest: A Defining Moment, *EPW*, Vol. XLII, No. 25.

Levien, Mike (2006): Narmada and Myth of Rehabilitation, *EPW*, Vol. XII, No. 33.

MacGinty, Roger (2006): "*Conflict in No War, No Peace*. The Rejuvenation of Stalled Peace Processes and Peace Accords", New York, Palgrave MacMillan, Chap. 3 (23 pp.).

MacGinty, Roger (2007): "Liberal Democratic Peace" in No War, No Peace, The Rejuvenation of Stalled Peace Processes and Peace Accords,' New York, Palgrave MacMillan, Chapter 2 (25 pps).

Madsen, Stig Toft (2002): "Indo-Pakistani Ward and Wat Scares". *NIAS Nytt* 3, September, pp. 26-27, 30 (3 pp.s).

Malinowski, Bronilsaw (1926), *Crime and Custom in Savage Society*, London, Routledge and Kegan Paul Ltd.

Manchanda, Rite (2001): "Where are the Women in South Asian Conflicts ?" In Manchanda, Rita (ed.) (2001): *Women, War and Peace in South Asia*, Beyond Victimhood to Agency, India, Sage Publications, pp. 9-41 (32 pp.).

Martindal, Don (1961): *The Nature and Type of Sociological Theories*, London: Routledge and Kegan Paul.

Mehdi, Syed Sikandar (2007): "Pakistan, Conflict, Migration and Peace", in Asteriskos (2007) 3/4 pp. 55-84 (30 pp).

Menekamap, Manique and Others (eds) (2003): *Searching for Peace in Central and South Asia*, London, Lynne Rienner Publishers.

Menon, Ajit (2007) Engaging with the Law on Adivasi Rights. *EPW*, Vol. XLII, No. 24.

Miall, Hugh (2004) "Conflict Transformation: A Multi Dimensional Task", in Alex Austin, Marlina Fisher and Norbert Ropers (eds) *Transforming Ethnopolitical Conflict*, The Berghof Handbook, pp. 67-89 (23pp).

Mishra, B. and Mohapatra, P.C. Evaluation Report of Malkangiri Integrated Tribal Development Project, Koraput District, Orissa. Department of Analytical and Applied Economics, Utkal University, Bbsr, 1980.

Misra, Amalendu (1998): "Review on South Asian States and the State of the Nations in South Asia" in *Third World Quarterly*, Vol. 19, No. 5, pp. 963-969 (6 pp).

Mitchell, Cristopher (2003): "Mediation and the Ending of Conflicts" in Darby, John and Roger macginty (eds.) (2003) *Contemporary Peacemaking, Conflict, Violence and Peace Processes*, Great Britain: Palgrave, pp. 77-85 (8 pp).

Mohanta, Nanigopal (2005) *Assam: Politics of Making Peace.*

Mohanty, Biswaranjan (2005): Displacement and Rehabilitation of Tribals, *EPW*, Vol. XL, No. 13.

Mohanty, Manoranjan (2006): Challenges of Revolutionary Violence, *EPW*, Vol. XLI, No. 29.

Mohanty, Manoranjan, (1977): *Revolutionary Violence, Maoists Movements in India*, New Delhi: Sterling Publications.

Moolakkattu, John Stephen (2005): "Peace Facilitation by Small States Norway in Sri Lanka", in *Cooperation and Conflict*, 2005, Vol. 40 (18 pp).

Morton, Stephen (2003): "Third World" Women and Western Feminist Thoughts, in Morton, Stephen (2003), *Gayatri Chakravorty Spivak*, London, Routledge Chap. 4, pp. 71-90. (20 pp).

Mukherjee, Aditya (1991): "Colonialism and Communalism", in Gopal (eds.) 1991. *Anatomy of Confrontaton: Ayodhya and the rise of Communcal Politics in India*, Zed Books, London.

Nair, K.R.G. (2005): Kerala's Development Experience, *EPW*, Vol. XL, No. 30.

Narula, Smita, and Macwan Martin (2001): *"Untouchability": The Economic Exclusion of the Dalits in* India, Geneva. International Council on Human Rights Policy, pp. 1-12 (12 pp.).

Nigel Young: "Peace Movements in History", Elise Boulding. Buidling Utopias in History, Richard Falk, "on Humane Governance Selections from Barbara Tuchman. The Gund of August, Selections From Irving Janis, Victims of Groupthink, Micheal Howard: The Causes of War, Johan Galtunf: A Structural Theory of Imeperialism, Micheal Kalare: Redefining Security: The New Global Schisms, Selections from Alva Myrdal: The Game of Disarmament, Jonathan Scheel: The Gift of Time, Lloyf Dumas: The Role of Economic Conversation in Shaping the 21st century, Henry David Thoreau, Civil Disobedience, Leo Tolstoy "Letter to Ernest Howard Crossby", Edna St. Vincent Millay:Conscientious Objector, Albert Camus, Neither Victims nor Executioners, Mohandas Gandhi, Ahimsa or the Way of Non-Violence, Gene Sharp: Civilian Resistance as a National Defense and Chapter 4 (non-violence) in Barash, D.D.P. (2000) *Approaches to Peace*, New York and Oxford (also New Delhi, India Oxford University Press (100 pp).

Ojha, R.K. (April 21-27(2007: Poverty Dynamics in Rural Uttar Pradesh, *EPW,* Vol. XLII, No. 16.

Oomen, T.K. (1990): *Protests and Changes, Studies in Social Movement*, New Delhi, Sage Publications.

Orjuela, Camilla (2003): Building Peace in Sri Lanka, A Role for Civil Society, in *Journal of Peace Research*, Vol. 40, No. 2, pp. 195-212 (17 pp).

Pankhurst, Donna (2003): The Sex War and Other Wars. Towards a Feminist Approach to Peace Building, in *Development in Practice*, Vol. 13, No. 23 (May) pp. 1540-63 (23 pp).

Parik, Ashok, Popil and others (2005) Migration and Development, *EPW*, Recent Poverty Estimates Myth artefact on real, Vol. Xl, No. 43.

Party Documents of Communist Party of India (Maoist).

Pattnaik, Niranjan and Pradhan, Chakrapani (1991): *The Oriya Movement (being a demand for a united Orissa)* (Cuttack), Bharat Bharati Publications.

Pattnaik, Prabhat, (2007): in the Aftermath of Nandigram, *EPW*, Vol. XLII, No. 21.

Peoples Bulletin (e-bulletin).

Pospisil, Leoplad, (1971): *Anthropology of Law, A Comparative Theory*, London, Harper & Row Publishers.

Prasad, Jitendra, (2005): *Tribal Movement in India*, New Delhi, Kilaso Books.

Ramanv, P.V. (ed.) (2008): The Naxal Challenges Causes, Linkages, and Policy Options, New Delhi, Pearson Longman.

Ramsbotham, Oliver, Tom Woodhouse and Hugh Miall, (2005): *Contemporary, Conflict Resolution*, Cambridge UK, Polity Press, Chapters 1,2,9,10, 12,13,15 (115 pp).

Rao, M.S.A. (ed.) (2000): *Social Movements in India* (Studies in Peasant, Backward Classes, Sectarian, Tribal and Womens Movements), Manohar Publications.

Rao, Nitya, (2005): Gender Equality, Land Rights and Household Food Secutiry, *EPW*, Vol XL, No. 25.

Ray, Kaushik. 2007. Historians and Historiography: situating 1857, Remembering 1857, *EPW* (May 12-18), Vol. XIII, No. 19.

Reardon, Betty (2000): "Sexism and the War System" in Barash, D.P. (2000). *Approaches to Peace*, Oxford University Press, pp. 250-257 (8 pp.).

Reddy, Sanjay (2006): World Development Response, *EPW*, Vol. XL, No. 42.

Reimannn, Cordula, (2004): Assessing the state of the art in conflict transformation, in Alext Audtin, Martina Fisher and Norbert Ropers (eds.) *Transforming Ethnopolitical conflict, The Berghof Handbook, Wiesbaden:* V.S. Verlag Fur sozialwissenschaften/GWVFachverlage GBH, pp. 42-66 (24 pp).

Report of the Commissioner for Scheduled Caste and Scheduled Tribe, Twenty Seventh Report (Part-1) 1979-81, pp. 141-144 and pp. 326-327.

Roy, Dayabati, Banerjee, Sarathi (2007) Behind the Peasant Unrest, *EPW,* Vol. XLII, No. 22.

Roy, Burman, B.K. (2006) Creating Consternation Draft National Tribal Policy, *EPW,* Vol. XLII, No. 34.

Rudra, Ashok (2006) (XXIV-2) Intelligentsia as a Ruling Class Critical Question, New Delhi: *Indian Economic Review*.

Rush, B. Gary and Serge, R. (1971) *Social and Political Movement Appleton – Century Crofts*, N.C. : Educational Division, Meredith Corporation.

Sachs, Wolfgang, (2001): "One World", In Sachs, Wolfgang (ed.) (1992): *The Development Dictionary, A Guide to Knowledge as Power*, London/ New York, Zed Book & Ltd., pp. 102-115 (13 pp).

Sahadevan, P. (2006): Negotiating Peace in Ethnic Wars, in *International Studies*, Vol. 3, No. 3 (2006), pp. 239-266 (27 pp).

Saigoal, Rubina (2006): "The State and the Limits of Counter Terrorism-I: The Experience of Pakistans and Sri Lanka", in Ahmed, Imtiaz (ed) (2006): *Understanding Terrorism in South Asia, Beyond Statist Discourses*, New Delhi: Foundation Books, pp. 93-102 (10pp).

Samal, J.K. (2000): *Economy of Colonial Orissa* (1866-1947), Munshiram Manoharlal Publishers.

Sarangi, Debraj, and Mohanty Saroj (2005) State Repression in Kashipore, *EPW,* Vol. XL, No. 13.

Sen, Arnab and Lalthrietper, Esther (2006): Scheduled Tribes Bill: A View from Anthology and Call for Dialogue, *EPW,* Vol. XLII, No. 39.

Sengupta, Roshini (2005) Communal Violence in India, *EPW,* Vol. XI, No. 20.

Sharma, B.D. (2010): Unbroken History of Broken Promises, Indian State and the Tribal People, New Delhi, Sahayog Pustak Kutir and Freedom Press, the Publication Division of Peoples Academy for Social Change and Development.

Shiva, Vandana (2001): "Resources", in Sachs, Wolfgang (ed.) (2001): *The Development Dictionary. A Guide to Knowledge as Power*, London: Zed Books Ltd., pp. 206-218 (12 pp).

Siddique, Ayesha (2006): "Terrorism in South Asia", in Muni, S.D. (2006): *Responding to Terrorism in South Asia*, Colombo: Manohar, pp. 335-359 (24 pp).

Singh, K.S. (ed), *Tribal Movements in India* (Vols. 1 and 2) New Delhi, Manohar Publications.

Singh, Sashi Bhusan (2005): Naxalism and Caste Relations in a South Bihar Village, *EPW,* Vol. XL, No. 29.

Singh, Ujjwal Kumar (2009): Human Rights and Peace: An Introduction, In

Singh, Ujjwal Kumar (ed.) (2009): *Human Rights and Peace, Ideas, Laws, Institutions and Movements*, New Delhi: Sage Publicatons, (7 pps).

Singharoy, K. Debal (2004) *Peasant Movements in Post-Colonial India*, Carlifornia, Sage Publications.

Skjelsbaek, Inger (2001): "Is Femininity Inherently Peaceful? The Construction of Femininity in the War", In Skjelsbaek Inger and Dan Smith (eds.) (2001): *Gender, Peace and Conflict*, London: Sage Publications, pp. 47-47 (20 pp).

Subramaniam, K.S. (2007): *Political Violence and the Police in India*, New Delhi, Sage Publications.

Suhrke, Adtri *et al.* (2002): "After Bonn: Conflictual Peace Building", In *Third World Quarterly*, Vol. 23, No. 5, pp. 875-891 (16 pp).

Sundar, Nandini (2005) Custom and Democracy in Jharkhand, *EPW*, Vol. XLA, No. 41.

Survey and Settlement Report of Koraput. N.C. Behuria.

Talbot, Ian (2005): Understanding Religious Violence in Contemporary Pakistan, Themes and Theories, in Kaur, Ravindar (ed.) (2005): *Religion, Violence and Political Mobilisation in South Asia*, New Delhi, Sage Publications, pp. 145-164 (19 pp).

Thapa, Ganga Bahadur (2008): "From Authoritarianism to Democracy" in Behera Chadha, Navnita (ed.) (2008): *International Relations in South Asia, Search for an Alternative Paradigm*, New Delhi, Sage Publications, pp. 152-176 (25 pp).

The Indian Journal of Public Administration, Vols. XI, XII, July to September 2002.

Theissen, Gunnar (2004): "Supporting Justice, Co-existence and Reconciliation after Armed Conflict: Strategies for Dealing with the Past", in Austin, Alex *et al.*, (eds.) (2004): *Transforming Ethnopolitical Conflict, The Berghof Handbook*, Berlin, Verlag Fur sozialwissenschaften, pp. 222-440 (18 pp).

Touval, Saadia and I. William Zartman (2001): "International Mediation in the Post Cold War Era", in Crocker, Chester, A: Fen Osler Hampson and Pamela Aall (eds.) *Turbulent Peace: The Challenges of Managing International Conflict, Washington DC*, United State Institute of Peace, Ch. 26, pp. 427-443 (16 pp.).

Upadhyaya Carol, (2005) Community Rights in Land, *EPW*, Vol. XL, No. 41.

Uyangoda, Jayadeva (2005): "Negotiation in Intrastate Conflicts", in *Conflict, Conflict Resolution and Peace Building*, University of Colombo, GTZ, Sri Lanka, pp. 48-75 (27 pp).

Uyangoda, Jayadeva (2005): "Civil War Ending and Peace Building", in Uyangoda, Jayadeva (ed.) (2005): *Conflict Resolution and Peace Building*, University of Colombo, GTZ, Sri Lanka, pp. 96-119 (25 pp).

Varshney, Ashutosh (1992): "Three Compromised Nationalism: why Kashmir has been a Problem", in Thomas, Raju G.C. (ed.) (1992): *Perspectives on Kashmir, The Roots of Conflict in South Asia*, US, Westview, pp. 191-234 (44 pp).

Varshney, Ashutosh (2008): "Is India becoming More Democratic?", In Banerjee-Debe, Ishita (ed.) (2008): *Caste in History*, New Delhi, Oxford University Press, pp. 215-231.

Vayrynen, R. (1991): "To Settle or to Transform? Perspectives on the Resolution of National and International Conflicts", in *New Directions in Conflict Theory, International Social Science Council*, London, Sage Publications, pp. 1-23 (23 pp).

Ved, Prakas (col) (2008), *Terrorism in Indias North East. A Gathering Strom* (in three volumes), New Delhi, Kalpaz Publications.

Vinayak, Abhijit, Basu, Kaushik and Others. *EPW* (April 28 to May 4) 2007, Beyond Nandigram: Industrilization in West Bengal: Vol. XLII, No. 17.

Wallensteen, Peter (2007): "The United Nations in Conflict Resolution" in Wallensten, Peter (2007): *Understanding Conflict Resolution, War, Peace and the Global System*, London/New Delhi: Sage Publications, Chap. 9, pp. 220-250 (31 pp).

Weber, Thomas (1999): *Gandhi, Deep Ecology, Peace Research and Buddhist*.

Weber, Thomas (2004): "Johan Galtung-Peace Research moved Beyond War", in *Gandhi as Disciple and Mentor*, Cambridge: University Press, Chap. 10, pp. 203-17 (15 pp).

Wenden, Anita L. (1995): "Defining Peace: Perspectives from Peace Research" in Schaffner Christina and Anita L. Wender (eds.) (1995) *Language and Peace*, Amsterdem: Harwood Academic Publishers, Chap. 1, (13 pp).

www. Writetokill.com

www.buzzle.com/article.socialwork

www.economictimes.com. Retrieved on Nov. 27th, 2010.

www.egyankosh.ac.in.bitstrea/123456789/34911/1/unit4.pdf

www.http://en.wikipedia.org

www.ifad.org

www.IPCS.org.retrieved

www.oxforddictionaries.com

www.smwnews.com

www.tehelka.com

XaXa, Virginia, (2005): Politics of Language, Religion and Identity Tribal in India, *EPW*, Vol. XL, No. 13.

Yadav, Bhupendra (2006): Wither the Social Sciences, *EPW*, Vol. XII, No. 36.

Index

Activism, 67
Adam Ferguson's Conflict Theory, 49
Adam Smith's Theory, 50
Adaptation to Naxal Conflict, 246
Aggressive activities, 43
Agricultural activities, 20
Agricultural Cooperative Society, 194
Agricultural development, 152
Alternative development model, 152
Andhra Pradesh Central Water Commission, 302
Anganwadi centres, 221
Anger desperation, 249
Antagonism, 231, 304
Anti-party activities, 200
Anti-war activist, 18
Armed action, 141, 318
Auxiliary activities, 173
Azar's Theory, 51, 57–58, 244–45

Backward Caste Movements, 45
Biological activities, 285
British imperialism, 52, 119, 248, 290, 315
Buddhism, 99, 101
Bureaucracy reconciliation, 73
Bureaucratic authoritarianism, 119

Camps, 25–26, 77, 100–101, 131, 161, 168, 195–96, 219, 229, 240, 256, 268, 272, 285–86, 321
  displaces, 131
  permanent, 195
  special, 195
Cannibalism, 37, 70
Capitalism, 32, 140, 257
Caste-discrimination, 198
Causal factors, 63
Ceiling land, 111
Census analysis, 93
Central Reserve Police Force (CRPF), 131, 150, 223, 251
Chasi Mulia Adivasi Sangh (CMAS), 170, 253
Chitrakonda police station looting case, 125
Cholera, 8, 178, 226, 228
Coercive action, 303
Colonialism, 56, 120
Combing operations, 252, 302
Communism, 32, 115, 120, 144–45, 152, 182, 185, 298, 314
Communist Party of India (CPI), 3–5, 33–34, 76–77, 116–18, 120–21, 123–25, 140–45, 151–52, 182–83, 198, 211, 231–32, 258–59, 267–68, 284
Conflict
  armed, 231–33
  asymmetric, 60
  class, 24
  core, 268
  de-escalation, 54
  definite pattern, 52, 291
  destructive, 244
  escalation, 54
  history of, 52, 290
  ideology, 174
  influence, 244
  intensification of, 269
  of interests, 60, 197, 273, 308
  intrastate, 51
  lower intensity, 253, 324
  management, 21, 73

map, 249
mapping, 18, 269, 287
middle intensity, 264
prevention, 18, 21
research, 51, 289
resolution, 19, 21, 194, 281, 326
rooted, 51
situation, 18
social, 17–18, 42, 292
societal, 22
stage of, 5, 270
studies, 18
theories, 51, 62
transformation, 21
transforming, 73
violent, 18, 53, 232
Conflict Theory
Bodin, 48
Hobbe's, 49
Ibn Khaldunte, 47
Machiavelli's, 48
Polybius, 46
Social Work, 61
Constituted Principles of Action, 197
Consumerism, 234
Contemporary Conflict Resolution, 241
Cooperative behaviour, 68
Core Naxalite zones, 30
Cottage industries, 98
Cultural practices, 99

Daman Pratirodha Manch (DPM), 306
David Hume's Theory, 49
Deep-rooted factors, 53
Desperate situation, 314
Development/Developmental
activities, 152–53, 278
indicators, 210
model, 30
processes, 87, 245
stage, 133, 145–46, 148, 151, 154, 300, 314
temples, 210
theories, 62
Didayis, 90, 94
Displacement factor, 223
DP camp, 168
Drift of Literacy, 109

Economic
activities, 96–97
association, 97
development, 23, 63, 243
equality, 134
institutions, 42, 58
justice, 17–18, 28
policies, 12, 198
policy, 261
Educational institutions, 239
Edward Azar's Theory, 51, 56, 244
Egocentric acts, 65
Electoral politics, 28, 118–20, 125
Empowerment theory, 62
Environmental factors, 77
Ethnic Movement and Insurgencies, 22
Ethnicity, 20, 23, 243, 245
Exploitative
landlords, 116
practices, 19
Eyewash activities, 132, 223

Factors communal content, 232
Female
activists, 211
cadres, 214–16, 219, 284–85, 325
literacy, 217
Feminist Social Work Theory, 62
Feudalism, 119–21, 140, 144, 186, 257, 299
Feudalism-capitalism, 120
Forest
coverage, 248
dense forested areas, 309
dwellers, 88
expanse, 151
guards, 259, 299
map, 167
minor, 146, 194
reservation policies, 2
rights, 45
semi-forest areas, 153
thick, 152
Forest Act, 127
Forest Protection Committee, 194
Forestry, 98
Full-fledged development, 3

Galtung's Theory, 59, 65, 175
Gandhian Development, 65
Gandhian Theory of Development, 64
Global Militarization Index (GMI), 305
Globalized era, 16
Gudaguda, 131, 223
Guerrilla Zone (GZ), 145, 152–54

Hegemonic caste structures, 222
Hill dwellers, 88
Hill tribes, 19
Hilly areas, 146–47
  forested, 146
  interior, 125
Hilly terrains, 8, 91, 133
Hilly tracts, 19
Hinduism, 99, 101
Human development index, 64, 128, 129, 226
Human Development Theory, 64
Human right activists, 176
Humanism, 64
Hyderabad Nizams, 121

Imperialism, 7, 66, 118, 140, 144, 199, 242, 257–58
Industrial civilizations, 127
Industrial development, 240–41
Industrial projects, 14, 306
Industrial revolution, 127
Industrial townships, 127
Industrialism, 194
Industrialization, 41, 127, 214, 230
Institutional factors, 41
Institutionalisation, 73
Integrated Action Plan (IAP), 105, 221
International Women's Day, 187, 212
Intra-tribal institutions, 75
Irrational factors, 10
Irrigation facilities, 104, 188, 302
ism, 98, 135, 176, 276

Jainism, 99, 101
Jhoom, 127
Journalism, 152
Juvenile Justice Board, 252

Kashmir Freedom Movement (KFM), 21
Knowledge centres, 221
Koraput-Bolangir-Kalahandi (KBK), 7, 98, 129, 167, 248, 310

Land distribution rules, 115
Land reforms act, 148
Land struggle, 238
Legal institutions, 40
Liberal peace, 74
Liberalization, 176
Liberated guerrilla zones, 152
Liberation guerrilla army, 173, 182
Liberation Tigers of Tamil Eelam, 132
Linguistic factors, 41
Literacy programmes, 194
Livestock development programmes, 194

Malinovski's Theory, 239
Mao Zedong theory, 5
Maoism, 29, 207, 256
Maoist Communist Centre of India (MCCI), 3, 26, 125–26, 141–45, 198–99, 289
Maoist-Lenin (ML), 33–34, 116–18, 121, 123, 125, 141–45, 152, 183, 198, 211, 258, 263, 271
Marginal farmers, 102, 317
Marxism, 25, 63, 120, 198, 300, 318
Materialism, 49, 65
Military commission, 200
Millennium Development Goals, 106
Mineral
  extraction of, 129, 197
  industrial, 127
  map, 167
  resources, 8, 248
  wealth, 2, 129, 239
Minimum Developmental Initiatives, 131, 223
Minor Irrigation Department, 302
Modernization theory, 63
  anthropological, 63
Motivational factors, 111, 158–60, 162
Mutual contact, 47
Mutual cooperation, 155

National liberation struggles, 117
National ST Commission, 178

Naxal
  blog, 34
  cadres, 191, 203, 205, 253, 265
  camp, 284, 286
  commander, 286
  conflict, 110, 158, 165, 172, 246, 268, 291, 294
  constituency, 164
  forces, 181
  hideouts, 155
  ideology, 28, 79–80, 82, 315, 321
  menace, 235
  movement-conflict, 197
  path, 277
  profile, 237
  sympathizer, 2, 81
  violence, 3, 243
Naxalbari, 3, 5–6, 26, 29–30, 115–16, 119, 121, 127, 139–40, 181, 183, 186, 220, 256, 323–24
Naxaliam, 184
Naxalite(s)
  conflict, 162, 168, 172, 289–91, 326
  hard-core, 281
  ideology, 129
  influence, 129
  intervention, 197
  jailed, 76–77
  revolt, 26
  sympathizer, 132
  tribal, 322
Nayagarh operations, 225, 231, 261
Nehruian vision of socialism, 139
Neo-liberal policies, 2
New economics activities, 98
Non-Governmental Organizations (NGOs), 95, 165, 174, 206, 208, 234, 247, 272
Non-migrating cultures interact, 50
Non-state actors, 18
Non-tribal rules, 126

Official declaration, 27
Oppressed caste, 26
Organizational effectiveness, 68
Organizational practice, 69
Oriya tract, 13

Panchayati Raj Department, 102
Panchayati Raj Institution (PRI), 272
Parliamentary fractions, 118
Peace building activities, 18
Peasant convention, 139
Peasantry liberation struggles, 183
People's Guerrilla Army (PGA), 145, 204, 208
People's Liberation Army (PLA), 145
People's Liberation Guerrilla Army (PLGA), 145, 200, 204, 206, 208, 213
Permanent development, 130
Planning Commission, 6, 98, 105, 312, 325
Podu cultivation, 308
Police
  camps, 122
  custody, 123, 141
  torture, 186, 299
Political
  economy, 24
  violence, 17
Poor tribals, 104, 148, 177, 188, 193, 239, 297
Post-colonial era, 2
Post-Development Theory, 63
Potential factors, 77
Praja Court, 301, 320
Pre-independence governments, 30
Proletarian, 25, 45, 181, 289
Pro-Maoist, 33, 36
Protracted Social Conflicts (PSC), 51, 56–58, 244–45
Pro-tribal
  development, 299
  measures, 307
Psychological theories, 66–68
PWG, 7, 125, 144, 146, 151, 154, 198–99

Radical communism, 29
Rain Fall and Census Analysis, 93
Religious
  institutions, 193, 196
  practices, 101
Resettlement camp, 168
Revenue Board, 138
Revisionism, 119

Revolutionary idealism, 119
Revolutionary Internationalist Movement (RIM), 143, 164
Risk factors, 244
RSB Company, 274–75
Rural caste communities, 89
Rural families, 102

Satyagraha, 6, 15, 137–39, 314
Search operations, 239
Sectarianism, 144
Self-criticism, 142, 144
Self-expression, 68
Self-sufficiency, 65, 129
Semi-feudal country, 3
Semi-Liberated zones, 1, 207
Sexual harassment, 213
Shifting cultivation, 95
Sikhism, 99
Situational analysis, 77–78
Social activities, 20
Social analysis, 187
Social cognitive theory, 61
Social Constructivist Theory, 62
Social institutions, 42, 222
Social movement, 67
Social problems, 61–62, 67
Socialism, 3, 139, 144–45, 152
Socialist theory, 62
Special Economic Zones (SEZs), 4, 127
State actors, 227
State Human Rights Commission, 251, 253
State Military Commissions, 204
State Women's Commission, 285, 318
Structural imperialism, 65–66, 242
Suppressive actions, 33
Systematic education, 234

Tactical operations, 71
Tenancy act, 148
Terrorism, 31
Theory of Protracted Social Conflict, 51, 56
Theory of Structured Imperialism, 65–66
Theory of Violence, 59–60
Thomas Malthus' Theory, 50
Traditional weapons, 235, 261
Tribal
  activists, 272
  economy, 37
  exploitation, 23
  factors, 81
  families, 231
  farmers, 130
  pride, 235
  protest, 300
  woman, 130, 211, 215
  zones, 309
Tribalism, 101
Tribe-caste continuum, 23
Turgot's Conflict Theory, 49

Ultimate Tribal Responses and Reactions, 305
UN General Assembly, 72
United Liberation front of Assam, 164
United Nations General Assembly, 247
Universal Declaration of Human Rights in Paris, 247

Vendetta, 19, 40
Village development committees, 154
Village level governance system, 192
Village Sangha, 193
Violence
  absence of, 56, 72, 305
  counter, 105
  cultural, 17, 74, 221–22, 228, 249, 322
  direct, 17, 73, 178, 228, 233, 249
  embedded, 158, 233
  escalating, 58, 322
  interpersonal, 59

Wage work, 105
War practices, 39
Wing extremisms, 271
Women cadres, 212, 215
Women's Commission, 285–86
Workers' Movements, 45
World Bank, 130

Zamindari State Abolition Act, 148
Zamindars, 38, 133, 147–51, 193, 231, 236, 250